# EU COMPETITION LAW IN CONTEXT: ESSAYS IN HONOUR OF VIRPI TIILI

Competition law belongs to the traditional core of Community internal market law and continues to play an important part in EU law and the case-law of the Court of First Instance and the Court of Justice of the European Communities.

Competition law does not form a static and hermetic domain but should, perhaps now more than ever before, be seen in a broader context and as a dynamic area of law.

The topics in this book include pure competition law issues, such as who should be held accountable and responsible for competition law infringements, when is a price so high that it becomes abusive, or the object or effect test under Article 82 EC. Moreover, they include competition law issues in a broader context, such as the influence of competition law on free movement rules, the application of competition law to international maritime transport, consumer interests in the application of competition law, unfair competition law and trade marks, confidentiality issues, the interplay between administrative law and competition law, or the principle of fiscal neutrality, not forgetting State aid issues.

This book draws together contributions from well-known experts in EU law and competition law in particular, being either current or former members or *référendaires* at one of the Community Courts. It is a tribute to Judge *Virpi Tiili*, who, when leaving the Court of First Instance in autumn 2009, will be remembered for her long and outstanding contribution to the Court's case-law, notably in areas such as competition law and intellectual property law.

Judge Virpi Tiili

# EU Competition Law in Context: Essays in Honour of Virpi Tiili

Edited by
Heikki Kanninen, Nina Korjus and Allan Rosas

HART
PUBLISHING

OXFORD AND PORTLAND, OREGON
2009

Published in North America (US and Canada) by
Hart Publishing
c/o International Specialized Book Services
920 NE 58th Avenue, Suite 300
Portland, OR 97213-3786
USA
Tel: +1 503 287 3093 or toll-free: (1) 800 944 6190
Fax: +1 503 280 8832
E-mail: orders@isbs.com
Website: http://www.isbs.com



Hart Publishing Ltd, 16C Worcester Place, Oxford, OX1 2JW
Telephone: +44 (0)1865 517530 Fax: +44 (0)1865 510710
E-mail: mail@hartpub.co.uk
Website: http://www.hartpub.co.uk

British Library Cataloguing in Publication Data
Data Available

ISBN: 978-1-84946-034-7

Typeset by Tatiana Galarza
Printed and bound in Great Britain by
Lightning Source UK Ltd

# PREFACE

The scope of EU law is not what it used to be. Today, there are few areas which are left completely untouched by the expanding body of EU primary and secondary law.

Competition law, on the other hand, belongs to the traditional core areas of Community internal market law. Despite the broadened agenda of the European integration project, competition law, including State aid law, continues to play an important part of EU law and the case-law of the Court of First Instance and the Court of Justice of the European Communities.

This said, competition law does not form a static and hermetic domain but should, perhaps now more than ever before, be seen in a broader context and as a dynamic area of law. This is one of the motives for this book, which draws together contributions from well-known experts in EU law and competition law in particular, being either current or former members or *référendaires* at one of the Community Courts.

At the same time, the authors have wanted to pay tribute to Judge *Virpi Tiili*, who, when leaving the Court of First Instance in autumn 2009, will be remembered for her long and outstanding contribution to this Court's case-law. After a highly successful career at the University of Helsinki, the Finnish Central Chamber of Commerce and as Director-General of the Finnish Office for Consumer Protection, Judge Tiili joined the Court of First Instance in 1995 to become its first Finnish judge.

While thanking wholeheartedly the authors for their participation and Ms Anne Koenig for much appreciated technical assistance, the editors, all compatriots of Judge Tiili, would like to express their conviction that this book will constitute a timely and essential contribution to EU competition law, seen in its broader context. It should also be a respectful salute to Judge Tiili and her impressive work for the clarification and development of EU law, notably in such areas as competition law and intellectual property law. Last but not least, we would like to express our sincere thanks to Hart Publishing for having accepted the book for publication and above all for the rapid and professional treatment that they have accorded to the project.

Luxembourg, 8 July 2009.

Allan Rosas
Judge at the Court of Justice of the European Communities

Heikki Kanninen
Judge at the EU Civil Service Tribunal

Nina Korjus
*Référendaire* at the Cabinet of Judge Tiili
Court of First Instance of the European Communities

# TABLE OF CONTENTS

# LIST OF CONTRIBUTORS

Azizi, Josef: Judge at the Court of First Instance since 1995.

Barennes, Marc: *Référendaire* to Judge Küllike Jürimäe at the Court of First Instance. Formerly *référendaire* to Judge Virpi Tiili at the Court of First Instance (2006–2009).

Baumé, Tristan: *Référendaire* to Judge Arjen Meij at the Court of First Instance since 2005.

Bohler, Arnaud: Head of the Cabinet to President Marc Jaeger at the Court of First Instance. Formerly *référendaire* to Judge Virpi Tiili at the Court of First Instance (2004–2006).

Czúcz, Ottó: Judge at the Court of First Instance since 2004.

Haukka, Sari: Registrar of the Board of Appeal of the European Chemicals Agency. Formerly *référendaire* to Judge Virpi Tiili at the Court of First Instance (1998–2007).

Jaeger, Marc: President of the Court of First Instance since 2007. Judge at the Court of First Instance since 1996.

Kanninen, Heikki: Judge at the Court of First Instance since 2009. Formerly Judge at the EU Civil Service Tribunal (2005–2009).

Korjus, Nina: *Référendaire* to Judge Heikki Kanninen at the Court of First Instance. Formerly *référendaire* to Judge Virpi Tiili at the Court of First Instance (2002–2009).

Laurila, Maija: Deputy Head of Unit of Product and Service Safety at the Health and Consumers Directorate General of the European Commission. Formerly *référendaire* to Judge Virpi Tiili at the Court of First Instance (1995–1998).

Lenaerts, Koen: Judge at the Court of Justice. Formerly Judge at the Court of First Instance (1989–2003).

Lindh, Pernilla: Judge at the Court of Justice. Formerly Judge at the Court of First Instance (1995–2006).

Meij, Arjen W.H.: Judge at the Court of First Instance since 1998.

Mengozzi, Paolo: Advocate General at the Court of Justice. Formerly Judge at the Court of First Instance (1998–2006).

Montesa Lloreda, Aitor: *Référendaire* to Judge Heikki Kanninen at the Court of First Instance. Formerly *référendaire* to Judge Virpi Tiili at the Court of First Instance (2007–2009).

Papasavvas, Savvas S.: Judge at the Court of First Instance since 2004.

Pelikánová, Irena: Judge at the Court of First Instance since 2004.

Rosas, Allan: Judge at the Court of Justice since 2002.

Vanhamme, Jan: *Référendaire* to Judge Marko Ilešič at the Court of Justice. Formerly *référendaire* to Judge Virpi Tiili at the Court of First Instance (1995–2002).

Vesterdorf, Bo: President of the Court of First Instance since 1998 until 2007. Judge at the Court of First Instance (1989–2007).

Wahl, Nils: Judge at the Court of First Instance since 2006.

## TABLE OF CASES

### Court of Justice of the European Communities

**Court of First Instance of the European Communities**

**European Court of Human Rights**

**International Court of Justice**



**International Tribunal for the Law of the Sea**



**France**



**United Kingdom**



**United States of America**

# 1

# *The Court of First Instance and the Management of Competition Law Litigation*

MARC JAEGER

## PERSONAL REMARKS

Judge *Virpi Tiili* has greatly contributed to the establishment of the Court of First Instance of the European Communities (hereinafter CFI) as a pragmatic, problem-solving jurisdiction, especially in the field of competition litigation, thanks to her hard work throughout her fourteen years of service.

She has done so with her style, delighted to engage in theoretical intellectual discussions, yet always very pragmatic when it comes to applying theory to the specific facts of the file at stake and finding a solution to the issues at hand with great impartiality and independence of mind. A style which is indeed crucial for an institution such as the CFI, which is called upon, on a daily basis, to apply often blurred, on occasion even contradictory, principles to very concrete circumstances of immense importance to the parties before it and capable of having a great impact on Europe and its citizens at large.

This approach is pivotal, especially during times of difficulty, such as the recent past, the present and unfortunately the immediate future. These are times when ideology risks interfering with the taking necessary, pragmatic, measures. In the words of an economist 'the only important structural obstacles to world prosperity are the obsolete doctrines that clutter the minds of men'.[1]

A style, I repeat, in which Judge Tiili has been an example for us all. A style which I have had the honour and the pleasure to appreciate on a daily basis over the years during which we have worked side by side, as colleagues and friends.

[1] A Krugman, *The Return of Depression Economics and the Crisis of 2008* (London, Penguin, 2008) 191.

## INTRODUCTION

The CFI has been created with a view to maintaining a high quality and effectiveness of judicial review in the Community legal order. The first objective was to enable the Court of Justice of the European Communities (hereinafter ECJ) to concentrate its activities on its core task of ensuring uniform interpretation of Community law, and the second objective was to establish a two-tier jurisdiction system, with a first instance jurisdiction dealing with actions requiring close examination of complex facts, and the consequential improvement of the level of judicial protection granted to individuals.

It cannot be denied that the first objective has been attained. At first, the transfer of jurisdiction from the ECJ to the CFI was limited to actions brought by civil servants of the European Communities (staff cases), and by natural or legal persons relating to the enforcement of the competition rules contained in the EC Treaty and the Coal and Steel Treaty quota system.[2] In the light of the CFI's success in these areas, reflected in the quality of its decisions, and in the light of the increase of the stock of cases pending before the ECJ, competences attributed to the CFI have been progressively extended, so that, today, the CFI is the common judge for all direct actions brought by individuals.[3]

Thus, as far as the alleviation of the workload of the ECJ is concerned, even if the ECJ is still at the limit of its capacity, the establishment of the CFI has had a very positive impact and it has succeeded in avoiding the total congestion of the ECJ. Indeed, in total, between its setting up in 1989 and the end of 2008, almost eight thousand cases were brought before the CFI, while during the same period, almost nine thousand cases were filed before the ECJ. Overall, as of 31 December 2008, just over 25 % of CFI appealable decisions were actually appealed. The establishment of the CFI has, thus, significantly reduced the number of cases to be dealt with by the ECJ. Today, more cases are brought before the CFI than before the ECJ (in 2008, 629 cases were filed before the CFI against 592 at the ECJ).

In addition, the establishment of the CFI has undoubtedly contributed to the improvement of the quality and effectiveness of judicial review thanks to the possibility of a continuous dialogue between the two jurisdictions.[4] This

[2] Now expired.

[3] Extension of competences of the CFI: Council Decision 93/350 of 8 June 1993 amending Council Decision 88/591/ECSC, EEC, Euratom of 24 October 1988 establishing a Court of First Instance of the European Communities [1993] OJ L/144/21, extending the competences of the CFI extending to all actions for annulment, actions for failure to act, actions for damages or action based on an arbitration clause, brought by natural or legal persons, with the exceptions of actions relating to anti-dumping measures, which were transferred a year later by Council Decision 94/149 of 7 March 1994 [1994] OJ L/66/29; Council Regulation (EC) No 40/94 of 20 December 1993 on the Community trade mark [1994] OJ L/11/1 and Council Regulation (EC) No 2100/94 of 27 July 1994 on Community plant variety rights [1994] OJ L/227/1 attributing competence to the CFI to rule on cases in this field; the Treaty of Nice; Decision 2004/407/CE, Euratom of 26 April 2004 amending Articles 51 and 54 of the Protocol on the Statute of the Court of Justice [2004] OJ L/132/5.

[4] On this point, see K Lenaerts, 'Le Tribunal de première instance des Communautés européennes : regard sur une décennie d'activités et sur l'apport du double degré d'instance au droit communautaire', (2000) 3-4 *Cahiers de droit européen* 323.

dialogue has taken place, and continues to take place, primarily within the appeal mechanism. The development of the case-law relating to access to file is a perfect example of how this type of interaction between the CFI and the ECJ can produce a significant increase in the level of judicial protection of the individual.[5]

Furthermore, faced with actions requiring close examination of a great number of complex facts, it is generally recognised that the CFI has succeeded in improving the judicial protection of individuals' interests, in particular, through scrupulous control of the facts of the case at hand, detailed analysis of all arguments put forward by the parties, thorough hearings, and fully reasoned decisions.

In carrying out its role, entrusted together with the ECJ with the interpretation and application of European law under Article 220 EC, the CFI has regularly dealt with new questions of law. This is particularly the case in the field of competition law. Thus, throughout the years, the CFI has greatly contributed to the development of competition law as part of its role as jurisdiction of judicial review, both in relation to the interpretation and application of the substantive rules applicable to undertakings, and the procedural rights to be respected by the Commission whilst carrying out its role as enforcer of competition law.

It is important to note from the outset that, while the gradual increase in the areas of competence of the CFI has somewhat diluted the dominance of competition law litigation in terms of the raw number of cases in its portfolio in this area (although, even so, competition and State aid litigation represented in 2008 approximately one third of cases filed before the CFI), competition litigation still represents, in terms of complexity, relevance to public interest, impact on the wider business community, but also time devoted by the institution, the CFI's most significant area of activity.

In terms of the importance of competition cases in the context of the mandate of the CFI to interpret and apply Community law, it should be pointed out that the importance of competition law in the EC legal order is apparent from the wording of the EC Treaty itself. In particular, Article 3 EC, which lists the main activities of the Community, provides at paragraph (g) that the Community shall further 'a system ensuring that competition in the internal market is not distorted' in order to fulfil the tasks of the EC, set out in Article 2 EC, and in particular to promote 'a high degree or competitiveness and convergence of economic performance'.[6]

Thus, one can easily see from all the foregoing why, by and large, the rules of procedure at the CFI are tailored to address the needs of competition law litigation and, to the extent that they were not originally fit for purpose, were later amended with this aim. One clear example of this is the introduction of

[5] See, eg the 'dialogue' resulting from the following sequence of cases: Case T-84/03 *Turco v Council* [2004] ECR II-4061; Joined Cases C-39/05 P and C-52/05 P *Sweden and Turco v Council*, judgment of 1 July 2008 nyr, and Case T-403/05 *MyTravel v Commission*, judgment of 9 September 2009 nyr.

[6] Although Art 3(g) EC might disappear, if the Treaty of Lisbon is ratified, it is, in my personal view, unlikely that this will have any impact on the importance of competition law in the EC legal order.

the expedited procedure, which, in competition litigation, is currently applied primarily in cases in which parties require a definitive solution to their dispute as a matter of urgency, such as in the area of concentrations.

To the extent that other types of litigation, not requiring the same procedure as administrative review in competition law litigation are assigned to the CFI, it should be recognised and accepted that such other areas must be dealt with differently.

This was the case for example with respect to civil service matters, in relation to which it was recognised that the specific nature of this category of litigation justified the creation of a specific judicial panel under the provisions of the Treaty of Nice (with the CFI hearing appeals on points of law to ensure consistency).[7]

It is also the case in relation to trademark litigation. The different features of this type of litigation recently prompted the CFI to adopt some reforms to its rules of procedure (such as the introduction of a possibility to do without the hearing stage).[8] More reforms may be considered necessary to tailor the applicable procedure before the CFI to this specific type of litigation. For example, it should be considered whether a single judge formation can be envisaged for this category of cases or, whether the creation of specialist trademark chambers within the CFI, or indeed the creation of a separate judicial panel similar to that which was set up for civil service cases, is now opportune.

These measures ensure that the procedure which is of general application at the CFI, and which was developed to deal best with fact-intensive judicial review cases requiring detailed economic analysis, such as, precisely, competition law litigation, could be effectively applied without causing unnecessary delays.

## THE MANAGEMENT OF LITIGATION

In essence, management of litigation is one of the main tasks of a jurisdiction entrusted with the interpretation and application of law. Neither Article 220 EC nor any other provision of the EC Treaty contains, however, any indication on the manner in which the Community Courts should perform these tasks. This, after all, makes sense, as it is precisely these jurisdictions which are better placed than anyone else to identify the objectives they need to achieve and the means they need in order to be in a position to achieve them. Yet, unfortunately, this principle is not entirely reflected in the current EC institutional architecture. In particular, the fact that the Community Courts' rules of procedure have to be approved by the Council, and that the Community Courts are not, alone, the masters of their own rules of procedure remains a true obstacle to the achievement of an efficient administration of justice.[9]

[7] Council Decision 2004/752/EC, Euratom of 2 November 2004 establishing the European Union Civil Service Tribunal [2004] OJ L/333/7.

[8] Art 135a of the Rules of Procedure of the CFI.

[9] In this regard I regret to note that, although specifically requested by the Community Courts in their contribution to the Nice IGC, the possibility for the Community Courts to adopt and amend independently their own rules of procedure was not eventually granted.

It is self-evident, in any event, that the management of litigation by a jurisdiction like the CFI involves the processing of a file, from the moment an application is lodged by an applicant with the Registrar to the moment a decision is issued, in a way that furthers the objectives of (i) providing a just result (through a just process), (ii) providing a meaningful solution to the parties, (iii) ensuring a timely outcome to the dispute, and (iv) ensuring legal certainty.

It is clear that these objectives may, from time to time, come in conflict with one another. Thus, good management of litigation, which furthers an efficient administration of justice, is management which achieves the best equilibrium between the different objectives mentioned above, in any given case. After all, what is the value of the best quality judgment if it is delivered so late that it becomes meaningless or of no application? Conversely, what is the value of a decision which is very quickly adopted but which is not the result of a thorough analysis of the underlying facts, or one which is based on a poor analysis of the parties' arguments, or which does not clearly set out the reasons on which it is based? The weight which should be given to each of these objectives in any particular case and at any particular time varies significantly according to the type of litigation involved. One of the peculiarities of competition litigation is that, amongst the areas of competence of the CFI, it is perhaps the type of litigation in which the tension between the objectives mentioned above is the most acute.

Firstly, a 'just result' is a universal objective in the administration of justice. This, for our purposes, means that, irrespective of the strength with which any other objective might pull in other directions, in an action for judicial review of a Commission decision enforcing competition law, the CFI will have to ensure that all evidence before it is carefully reviewed and analysed, that the law is correctly applied to the facts, that the parties appreciate that this process has taken place, that their right of appeal has been respected, and that, in particular, a detailed motivation of the CFI ruling is provided. Also, of crucial importance for the purposes of this objective is that, at all stages of the procedure before the CFI, the rights of the parties to judicial proceedings, and in particular the right to a fair trial, are respected. This means, for example, that it must be open to the parties to bring proceedings in any of the official languages of the EU, that parties have an opportunity to meaningfully put forward their case, by, for example, being allowed to submit observations in response to any new point raised by the other party, and that the court hearing the case carries out an independent and impartial review of the facts of the case at hand. This, inevitably, and rightly, requires time.

Secondly, Article 2 EC states that one of the tasks assigned to the European institutions is to '… promote throughout the Community a harmonious, balanced, and sustainable development of economic activities'. The Community Courts, as European institutions, can further this task by ensuring that pragmatic solutions, within the boundaries of law, are available to economic players facing business disputes. Such an approach will, in turn, lead to a business-friendly environment based on the rule of law. Accordingly, providing meaningful solutions to legal disputes is equally an important part of litigation management.

Thirdly, it should not be forgotten that the right of the parties to a decision within a reasonable time is a fundamental part of the right to a fair trial which the Community Courts must respect. Timing is often critical for many of the litigants, especially, before the CFI. For example, litigants are often undertakings that have business plans that either cannot wait for the outcome of litigation or that might be based on this outcome. It follows that this objective is strictly connected to another objective just discussed, namely that of providing useful solutions. As mentioned above, for dispute settlement to make sense to the parties, the result must be delivered within a useful time frame. However, we should not forget that the reverse is also true, and this is, therefore, one of the most significant tensions between objectives in litigation management, particularly in competition cases.

Fourthly, and finally, ensuring overall legal certainty, that is, allowing the public to predict how the law will be applied in future similar circumstances, is, unquestionably, an important objective. This is particularly so in the application of competition law, an area in which litigation is often seen as the option of last resort, due to the tension between the time frame required by judicial review and the 'real-time' time frame of most twenty-first century business decisions. The importance of this objective is reflected in the European Commission's extensive use of guidelines consolidating the Community Courts' case-law in a number of important areas of competition law enforcement.

In recent years, the importance of the time factor in competition cases, the third of the objectives listed above (of course not in order of importance), has been repeatedly and insistently stressed by representatives of the corporate world, lawyers, academics, and politicians. This is rightly so. A quick look at the raw data relating to the duration of proceedings at the CFI demonstrates that the average duration of the category of cases which includes competition proceedings[10] in 2007 was approximately 29.5 months. 2008 figures show a slight improvement, with decisions being rendered within 26 months of the application being lodged. This is the first – small – sign that a series of internal measures adopted during the course of last year are starting to bear fruit. Even if it can be expected that the impact of the recently adopted internal reforms (discussed in more detail below) will become more significant as more cases benefit from their snowball effect, it is clear that more, and more radical, reforms will be required to reduce more significantly (to the extent that this is compatible with the judicial review nature of the litigation before the CFI) the duration of proceedings. Such action is rendered particularly urgent by the constant and steep increase in the overall number of cases introduced before the CFI which has taken place in recent years and which we expect to be even more significant in the near future. In considering ways to reduce the time frame for delivering a

[10] All cases excluding trade mark related litigation and appeals on decisions by the Civil Service Tribunal.

judgment, however, it is imperative that we do not get carried away, and that any action taken to achieve this goal does not have an adverse impact on the other objectives.

Considering that, as discussed, since the establishment of the CFI, competition cases have been the cornerstone of the Court's activity, I find this a good opportunity to take a step back and look at what are, in my personal view, the most important principles which inspire the management of such cases, in the context of what remains, in any event, a generalist judicial review jurisdiction. It is a good opportunity, also, to analyse how the CFI has, to the extent that this was necessary, adapted its working practices based on how such principles apply to the specificities of competition litigation. Finally, in the development of these considerations, I will try to identify further adaptations which might be necessary to address any remaining shortcomings and to best prepare the CFI for an anticipated escalation in the number of cases introduced.

As a starting point it should be stressed that, of the four objectives identified above, the most important ones are 'delivering just results', and 'ensuring a timely outcome to the dispute'. Whilst the two remaining objectives are also important, one could argue that, firstly, the objective of ensuring 'legal certainty', on the one hand, falls under the broader concern of delivering 'just results', and that, on the other hand, in the greater scheme of things, it should be a more pressing concern for an appellate jurisdiction (in this case the ECJ), than for a jurisdiction of first instance, such as the CFI. Secondly, the objective of providing a 'meaningful solution to the parties' must be seen as a secondary concern in the light of the CFI's primary role as a judicial review jurisdiction of first instance entrusted with the review of the legality of administrative decisions of other EC institutions.

## What Type of Review?

To better appreciate the meaning of the objectives mentioned above in the context of competition litigation before the CFI, it is important, at the outset, to consider the role of the CFI, and the broader institutional context in which it operates.

In contrast with the United States system, the EC competition enforcement system is primarily one of judicial review of administrative acts of enforcement. Both in the field of antitrust enforcement and of the control of concentrations, the Commission enjoys extensive investigative, prosecutorial and administrative decision-making powers.

Many commentators have questioned whether this concentration of powers in the hands of the Commission is compatible with the right to a fair trial provided for in Article 6 of the European Convention for the Protection of Human Rights and Fundamental Freedoms (ECHR) signed at Rome on 4 November 1950.[11]

[11] See, eg D Waelbroeck and C Smiths, 'Le droit de la concurrence et les droits fondamentaux' in M Candela Soriano (ed), *Les droits de l'homme dans les politiques de l'Union européenne* (Brussels, Larcier, 2006) 135.

In essence, the European Court of Human Rights' answer to this question is provided in its *Öztürk* case.[12] On the basis of this ruling, Article 6(1) of the ECHR does not prohibit such a concentration of powers within an administrative body, even if, in itself it does not satisfy all the requirements and procedural guarantees that apply to courts of law, provided that the right of access to an impartial tribunal which can review the decisions issued by such an administrative body is guaranteed. This principle was acknowledged in the Community legal order on a number of occasions, and more recently in the CFI's *Schneider* case.[13]

It follows that the concentration of the enforcement powers in the hands of the Commission described above is acceptable only if effective judicial control is exercised by an independent and impartial tribunal, in this case the CFI. Considering how far-reaching the Commission's powers can be, and the dramatic increase in the level of the fines imposed by the Commission in recent years, such a control by the CFI is all the more crucial.

According to Article 230 EC, the Community Courts have jurisdiction on grounds of lack of competence, infringement of an essential procedural requirement, infringement of the EC Treaty or of any rule of law relating to its application, or misuse of powers. Only with regard to fines does Article 229 EC provide that the Community Courts may be granted unlimited jurisdiction. This might, at first sight, appear to indicate that in non-fines-related litigation only a limited type of control applies. In reality, this is not entirely the case, and the CFI exercises, also in those cases, a very serious and in-depth review of the legality of the decisions of the Commission, with the aim, inter alia, of ensuring compliance with Article 6 of the ECHR.

The CFI enjoys full control over every question of law, subject to appeal before the ECJ. This is the core business of the CFI judge. It is for the CFI to determine which rules are applicable, to interpret them, and to verify whether the Commission correctly applied them in the case at hand. As mentioned above, most of the cases before the CFI raise new questions of law and the Court, although established to deal with cases requiring close examination of complex facts, has a very important role in this respect as well. It is generally recognised that the CFI has contributed significantly to the improvement of the judicial protection of individual interests in the field of EC competition law. In this context, one clear example is the development of the case-law relating to the rights of defence (for instance in the area of access to the Commission's file).

Competition cases before the CFI often raise more general administrative law questions, such as questions relating to the conditions and limits to a delegation of competence, distinction between preparatory measures and decisions giving rise to a right of appeal, admissibility *ratione materiae* or *ratione personae*. Litigation based on competition law may also raise questions relating to general legal principles, such as non-discrimination, the rights of defence, including access to the Commission's file, equality of arms, legitimate expectation,

[12] *Öztürk v Germany* Series A No. 73 (1984) EHRR.

[13] Case T-351/03 *Schneider Electric v Commission* [2007] ECR II-2237 para 183.

privilege against self incrimination, legal professional privilege, right to be heard, presumption of innocence, non bis in idem; or questions relating to judicial procedure, such as the right to intervene and status of the interveners, and confidentiality. Thus, due to the general nature of the questions raised by many competition cases, the fact that such cases are, at first instance, dealt with by a single jurisdiction of judicial review must be viewed as a positive feature of the European judicial system. Accordingly, the creation of a specialist judicial panel to deal with competition cases (or even certain categories of competition cases), often put forward as a possible solution to the current overload of cases pending before the CFI, would not be, in my view, a satisfactory solution. Indeed, not only would it, in fact, increase the possibility of delays due to the resulting addition of a possible 're-examination' procedure of CFI appeal decisions before the ECJ, but it would also lead to the unacceptable risk of loss of the cross-fertilisation advantage within the domain of EC administrative law, which is inherent in the current system.

Furthermore, the CFI exercises, at first and last instance, a full review of the assessment of facts on which a challenged decision is based. In this context, for example, the CFI establishes whether the evidence on which the Commission relied in a particular case is factually accurate, reliable and consistent. This is a crucial point in competition cases, which are often based on complex factual scenarios, and it was one of the main reasons for the creation of the CFI, since it was felt by a number of commentators that the ECJ, due to insufficient human and material resources and the need to concentrate itself on its core activity of ensuring a uniform interpretation of EC law, did not scrutinise sufficiently the facts established by the Commission and left the Commission with too wide a margin of appreciation.[14] As evoked in the recitals to the decision establishing the CFI, competition cases require close examination of complex facts.[15] They may involve delicate economic or technical questions and necessitate a thorough examination, particularly because the contested facts are rarely 'simple facts' but are the result of complex combinations of facts or sequences of events. Competition files may thus contain thousands of pages, and the thorough analysis which they require is often time-consuming.

The control exercised by the CFI is, however, less extensive with respect to appreciations made by the Commission on the basis of its recognised margin of discretion. The regulations applicable in the fields of antitrust and State aid enforcement, and merger control, confer on the Commission a wide discretion in appraising complex economic scenarios. Based on Article 230 EC and according to settled case-law,[16] the review by the Community Courts of assessments of complex facts requiring detailed economic analysis made by the Commission in the exercise of the discretion conferred upon it by the

[14] 'Perspectives de développement de la protection juridictionnelle dans la Communauté européenne' (Baden-Baden, Nomos Verlagsgesellschaft, 1987) 73.

[15] Council Decision 88/591/ECSC, EEC, Euratom of 24 October 1988 establishing a Court of First Instance of the European Communities [1988] OJ L/319/1).

[16] See Case T-201/04 *Microsoft v Commission* [2007] ECR II-3601 para 88 and the case-law cited.

relevant regulations must be limited to ensuring compliance with procedural requirements, and the requirement that a decision be adequately reasoned, as well as ensuring the accuracy of the facts, and the absence of manifest errors of assessment. The role of the Community judge, therefore, is not that of substituting its own appreciation to that of the Commission; it is instead that of sanctioning, if necessary, any manifest error of appreciation. This reflects the institutional partition of competences between the Commission, entrusted with the enforcement of Articles 81 EC and 82 EC, the control of concentrations, and the shaping of the EC competition policy, on the one hand, and the Community Courts in charge of reviewing the legality of the Commission decisions, on the other.

This, however, does not mean that the CFI will not exercise an effective control over Commission decisions in the competition field outside of fines-related litigation. On the contrary, even where an assessment within the Commission's margin of discretion is at stake, this

> does not mean that the Community Courts must refrain from reviewing the Commission's interpretation of information of an economic nature. Not only must the Community Courts, inter alia, establish whether the evidence relied on is factually accurate, reliable and consistent but also whether that evidence contains all the information which must be taken into account in order to assess a complex situation and whether it is capable of substantiating the conclusions drawn from it.[17]

The CFI must refrain from extending its action to a 'de novo assessment', and there is a very delicate balance to be found between rigorous control aimed at ensuring judicial protection, on the one hand, and the need to respect the margin of appreciation of the Commission based on the institutional repartition of competences, on the other.

## Delivering Just Results

Having discussed what results are expected of the CFI in the administration of justice in the competition area, based on an understanding of its role within the Community architecture, I can now turn to the first of the objectives, which, as mentioned above, the CFI strives to further, namely that of delivering just results.

Broadly, by 'delivering just results' I mean producing rulings that correctly identify and interpret the applicable law, correctly apply the law to the facts of the case through a procedure that fully respects the parties' rights of defence, and contain well-reasoned explanations of why the court has reached a particular outcome. To achieve this objective, in any given case, judges must fully engage with the facts of the case at hand so that they can correctly apply the relevant legislation and the applicable case-law.

In this respect, the safeguard of the parties' rights of defence is fundamental, not only because they are, in and of themselves, an indispensable part of a fair

[17] Case C-12/03 P *Commission v Tetra Laval* [2005] ECR I-987 para 39.

trial, but also because they serve as a crucial tool for the achievement of a just outcome to the dispute. It is only if the parties are given the possibility to put forward their views in respect of all questions raised by the case at hand that a judge can be in a position to adopt a fully informed and just decision.

In addition to the safeguard of the rights of defence, one pivotal element of a just result is that of a 'perception of justice'. The CFI aims to ensure that, in any given case, the parties are in a position to fully understand the legal reasoning behind the decision and accept that it produces a just result. The CFI invests significant resources to achieve this goal at each of the many different stages of procedure (for example through well prepared hearings, and in drafting thoroughly reasoned judgments), and this is one of the areas in relation to which the CFI has had to adapt the working methods inherited from the ECJ, to be in the best position to reach just decisions fulfilling its role as competition court of first instance.

These concerns are reflected in particular in the CFI's measures of organisation of the procedure, the very extensive preliminary report, and the report for the hearing. Measures of organisation of the procedure,[18] such as written questions to the parties, requests for information or documents, informal meetings etc., allow the chamber hearing the case to obtain all the necessary elements of fact and all the parties' arguments before the hearing stage, so that the hearing can truly be an opportunity to get to the bottom of the crucial issues at stake. This approach is particularly relevant for the cases before the CFI, and it represents one of the most notable differences between ECJ and CFI proceedings. On the basis of this pre-hearing information gathering exercise, the *juge rapporteur* prepares a preliminary report in which he or she summarises all the pleas and arguments of the parties, suggests questions for the hearing, and possible solutions to the main issues at stake, as well as any further measures of organisation of the procedure which he or she considers advisable. Before the hearing, the judges in the formation will meet to discuss the file and the preliminary report, and to agree on the next steps to be taken.

Considering the fact-intensive nature of competition cases, which generally require in-depth economic analysis, the measures of organisation of the procedure have been developed through the years to ensure that the preliminary report, and consequently the report for the hearing, is as detailed as possible so as to allow all of the judges in the chamber to master from the earliest stages of a procedure all of the facts at stake and the crucial legal issues that need answering, and, on that basis, to make the hearing as meaningful and informative as possible. This procedure requires significant resources, but, by ensuring that the parties are aware of the CFI's approach to the issues at stake, significantly contributes to the parties' acceptance of our final decisions as just.

[18] Following the introduction of the possibility to adopt measures of organisation of the procedure at the CFI, the rules of procedure of the ECJ were amended in 2000 to include, under Art 54a, the possibility for the *juge rapporteur* and the Advocate General to request from the parties all documents, information, or other elements that he or she deems necessary.

## The CFI and Competition Litigation: Dealing with Cases at Reasonable Speed while Ensuring a Fair Trial

The issue of time in the context of CFI proceedings is summarised in the following enlightening extract from Advocate General Geelhoed's Opinion in the *Sumitomo* case:[19]

> [F]rom 2000 to 2004 the [CFI]'s workload in terms of pending cases roughly doubled from 520 to 1012 cases. That increase shows that during that period the demand for decisions by the [CFI] manifestly exceeded the available capacity.
>
> As the workload of a judicial body grows, the average duration of the proceedings will increase. This also manifests itself in the statistics of the [CFI]. The average duration of the category of proceedings to which competition cases belong gradually increased from well over 30 months in 2001 to well over 35 months in 2005.
>
> This phenomenon whereby, in the case of a body whose workload exceeds its capacity, the average speed with which cases are dealt with decreases, arises from the 'waiting-room effects' which are seen mainly after the end of the written procedure and after the end of the oral procedure. At those times, the Court or Chamber hearing a case must first prepare the preceding cases for the hearing or, as the case may be, complete them with a judgment, before it can start dealing with the following cases. [...]
>
> Against that background, a period of four years and three months taken to deal with the present voluminous and complicated cases cannot be regarded as disproportionately long.

The time issue leads me to express a number of considerations.

Firstly, the current average duration of proceedings is compliant with the right to a fair trial under the ECHR. As discussed above, a quick look at the statistics concerning competition cases demonstrates that the average duration of proceedings before the CFI is much shorter than in a number of Member State jurisdictions, and that on the basis of the Court's *Baustahlgewebe* case-law[20] (which sets out the conditions under which a CFI judgment might be set aside if the proceedings in that case did not satisfy the requirements concerning completion within a reasonable time) the CFI's time frame is legally acceptable. Having said that, of course, for the purposes of this assessment, what really matters is not the overall average duration of proceedings, but the duration of proceedings in each specific case. Thus, the assessment must be carried out on a

[19] Opinion of Advocate General Geelhoed in Joined Cases C-403/04 P and C-405/04 P *Sumitomo Metal Industries and Nippon Steel v Commission* [2007] ECR I-729 points 162–165. The figures quoted in this extract from Advocate General Geelhoed's Opinion, updated as at the end of December 2008, would lead to the following adjustment: '[F]rom 2000 to 200[8] the [CFI]'s workload in terms of pending cases roughly doubled from 520 to 1[178] cases'. This indicates that, following its doubling in the four years between 2000 and 2004, the overall backlog has increased by only approximately 10 % in the last four years.

[20] Case C-185/95 P *Baustahlgewebe v Commission* [1998] ECR I-8417, applied in Joined Cases C-120/06 P and C-121/06 P *FIAMM and FIAMM Technologies v Council and Commission*, judgment of 9 September 2008 nyr.

case-by-case basis, and, although every effort is made to avoid delays, it cannot be excluded that, in the current situation of case overload and backlog, instances may occur in the future, in which the duration of proceedings is deemed to be excessive. This is why I consider that a significant structural reform of the institution is now urgent, to address the 'bottleneck' issue mentioned above.

Secondly, in any event, we cannot be satisfied with the current average duration of proceedings. This is so because of the very nature of competition litigation. Indeed, for many of the litigants before the CFI timing is frequently critical. Accordingly, since September 2007, the CFI has adopted a number of internal reforms to address what is considered a high priority issue. These reforms, which apply to all cases before the CFI and therefore also to competition cases, include: (i) switching from five to eight chambers (in addition to the appeals chamber); (ii) holding hearings five days per week (morning and afternoon); (iii) implementing a new system to monitor and manage the number and duration of proceedings per chamber and per *juge rapporteur*; (iv) rationalising the mechanism for attributing cases to the chambers through a wider interpretation of the possibility to derogate from the rotation system on the ground that cases are related or with a view to ensuring an even spread of the workload,[21] and (v) small but significant changes to the way in which the dossier is 'processed'. Significantly, each initiative that improves the efficiency of processing the dossier at a given stage will also improve efficiency at later stages; thus, each change can have a dramatic snow-ball effect on the same file and, consequently, on other files pending in the 'waiting room'. For example, if the CFI declines to address all grounds put forward by an applicant when one ground is accepted and on that basis the application is successful, time is saved in studying the dossier, researching the issues, drafting the judgment, correcting the judgment, checking and revising the judgment, and translating the final judgment.

The CFI could increase this snow-ball effect advantage further by promoting and adopting in the future measures to institutionalise and make more regular and systematic use of case management tools. Informal case management measures in competition cases have been used occasionally in the past, on an *ad hoc* basis, by the *juge rapporteur*. A particular obstacle to an increased use of these measures has been the difficulty for a *juge rapporteur* to deal with cases in real time, in the light of the – very significant – current backlog of cases. A reduction of the backlog would thus be a pre-condition for a wider use of case management measures. This possible development could involve case management meetings at an early stage between, on the one hand, the *juge rapporteur*, or a *référendaire* in his or her cabinet, or indeed a new person specifically designed for this task, namely a *rapporteur adjoint*, and, on the other hand, the parties to the dispute.

In the course of such case management meetings the CFI interlocutor could propose to the parties to focus on the legal grounds that are, according to

[21] Criteria for the assigning of cases to the Chambers [2008] OJ C/197/18.

him or her, the most serious and worthy of consideration, and to give up any redundant legal grounds, or legal grounds which, on the basis of settled case-law or common sense, can be considered unworthy of further consideration.

The parties, should they wish to follow the proposal of the CFI interlocutor, could withdraw of the relevant parts of their application, which would be formalised in a record held by the Registrar. Should the parties choose not to follow such indications it would, of course, remain open to them to stick to their original submissions and receive, in the main judgment, an – appealable – explanation of why a particular legal ground has been rejected.

The advantages brought by this development are clear. In particular, it would assist the parties in identifying the most important aspects of their case with the aim of reducing as much as possible the delay within which a judgment could be delivered by the CFI, and maximising the resources they invest in the litigation. In this context it is worth noting that, should the parties chose to follow the indications of the CFI interlocutor, the benefits in terms of time gained in the analysis of the dossier by the *juge rapporteur* and the *juges assesseurs* would be amplified during the later stages of the procedure. The efficiency gains produced through active case management would increase exponentially if parties elected to make use of this opportunity on a widespread basis. Once this development is fully operational, furthermore, it might allow a *juge rapporteur* to establish a more transparent timetable for the successive developments of the file. An additional element could be introduced in this context to encourage parties to take full advantage of the case management process and to deter them from strategic and vexatious litigation. One could envisage to impose costs on a party that has refused to withdraw a legal ground, despite recommendations from the CFI interlocutor, if this legal ground is later rejected and the costs can be attributed to such refusal, even if this party is otherwise successful in the action on the basis of other legal grounds.

New measures of this type would be very helpful. As demonstrated by the 2008 figures mentioned above, the measures adopted since September 2007 are now starting to bear fruit, and resulted in a 50 % increase in the number of cases decided in comparison with the previous year. Even so, there is no reason to lower the guard at the CFI. Indeed, such an increase in productivity has not brought about a reduction of the stock of cases pending, since it was met by a further increase in the number of cases introduced before the CFI. In particular, whilst, also thanks to the measures just discussed, the CFI was capable of closing in 2008 a record number of 605 cases, in the same year, a record number of 629 cases were introduced. This led to yet a further increase in the stock of cases pending, to a record number of 1178, thus increasing the 'waiting room' issue mentioned in Advocate General Geelhoed's Opinion mentioned above.

Thirdly, and in addition to the constant increase of the number of cases filed before the CFI (which, as seen above, cannot be tackled through simple internal reforms, even if these are significant), it can be anticipated that, in the coming years, the Community Courts will face a new series of challenges and, correspondingly, a further increase in the number of applications lodged. The factors contributing to the Community Courts' anticipated increase in their workload include: a) the full integration of the Member States that acceded in 2004 and 2007; b) increased trade mark litigation coming from the Office for Harmonisation in the Internal Market (trade marks and designs) (the OHIM) in Alicante (in 2007 the number of Boards of Appeals increased from four to five; in addition a reduction in registration fees took place on 1 May 2009 which is likely to attract more registration applications, and, consequently, more litigation); c) new litigation arising from challenges to decisions by the European Chemicals Agency in Helsinki (REACH litigation); d) if the Lisbon treaty enters into force, the ECJ would gain new competences, and, most significantly, the admissibility criteria under Article 230 EC would be loosened; e) the deepening of European integration, both in terms of an increase of EC competences and in terms of an increased exercise of such competences, which results in an intensification and diversification of legislative and executive activity; f) the increased workload for the ECJ that the entry into force of the Lisbon treaty would entail, as well as other pressures on the ECJ's resources caused by, for example, the new procedure for urgent preliminary rulings in the area of freedom, security and justice, could lead to increased competences being transferred to the CFI; g) an increasingly litigation prone society; and h) the growth of 'urgent' litigation (in the first full year of my Presidency, in 2008, I have had to rule on over 50 applications for interim measures).

Should the CFI not be fully prepared and equipped to face these challenges, the first to suffer would be the rule of law. This would cause great harm to the people and the undertakings which rely on the CFI for judicial protection, and the Member States and Community institutions which rely on the CFI as a pivotal part of the Community institutional balance. Ultimately, it would be the Union and the European economy at large that would suffer, and this is a risk that the Community cannot afford to incur, especially in the current economic climate.

In addition, in considering ways to maintain the current positive results in the face of an increased inflow of cases and to reduce the time frame for delivering a judgment, it is imperative that any action taken to achieve this goal does not have an adverse impact on the quality of our judgments or the rights of the parties to a fair trial. Thus, although a few steps can still be taken to tackle the problem of the duration of proceedings through internal reforms aimed at optimising resources (one clear example being more structured and proactive use of case management), this process cannot be stretched too far without the risk of compromising the access to justice and the quality of it.

Thus, although the reforms discussed above will certainly help the CFI process cases more quickly, there is a serious risk that these reforms constitute mere fire fighting, and that, alone, they are not sufficient to address the increasing workload. In these circumstances, the CFI cannot be left alone to tackle the backlog of cases pending.

Fourthly, and lastly, I would once again refer to the words of Advocate General Geelhoed in the *Sumitomo* case:

> For the sake of completeness, I would point out that, if the demand for decisions by a Community judicial body structurally exceeds that body's capacity and internal measures to increase productivity are no longer possible without affecting the quality requirements with which that body's decisions must continue to comply, it is the responsibility of the framers of the Treaty to maintain the conditions under which the Court of Justice as a Community institution can continue to fulfil the task assigned to it in Article 220 EC.
>
> Confirmation that the framers of the Treaty recognise that responsibility is to be found in the Treaty of Nice which, with regard to the [CFI], makes various provisions in order to keep its capacity in line with the demand for decisions. I think in particular of the possibility under Article 224 EC for more than one judge per Member State to be appointed to the [CFI] and of the power conferred on the Council by Article 225a EC to create judicial panels at first instance.[22]

Therefore, I believe that we should consider undertaking a more far-reaching review of the CFI's structure and resources to identify the more radical reforms that are required. These reforms will most likely require amendments to the Rules of Procedure and the Statute of the Court and a significant budget injection, and may include one or more of the following options: (i) the creation of a specialised panel for IP cases, (Article 225a EC); (ii) increasing the number of judges and possibly creating specialised chambers within the CFI; (iii) and the creation of *rapporteurs adjoints* to assist in the management and preparation of a greater number of files at the same time.

## CONCLUSION

It is thus clear that in ensuring a good management of competition law litigation, the CFI is faced with a daily challenge of balancing a number of, sometimes conflicting, objectives. Critics can easily focus on one such objective alone, such as delivering a judgment within a short time frame. However, by focussing on one objective alone such critics will ignore the other, equally important, objectives which the CFI must take into account when managing litigation, and especially competition litigation.

All in all, therefore, I wish to express my pride in the way in which the CFI has so far, also thanks to the contribution of Judge Tiili, tried to strike the best balance between the various objectives. I am also proud of the way in which the CFI has been alert to the issues, identified them clearly, adopted improvements to deal with them to the extent that this was within its powers and competences, and proposed possible solutions to the extent that such solutions are beyond its competence.

[22] See n 19 above, points 167 and 168.

# 2

# *The Influence of Competition Law on Free Movement Rules*

PERNILLA LINDH

## INTRODUCTION

It is a well-known secret that judges of the Court of First Instance of the European Communities (hereinafter CFI) devote a considerable amount of their time to competition cases. So much so, that after a few years, other areas of Community law such as the 'four freedoms' (goods, services, capital and people), rarely form part of their daily regimen. Yet, the law on free movement – in particular with respect to goods – seems ever present, discreetly looming in the background of competition judgments. When, after over a decade together with my friend *Virpi Tiili* at the CFI, I joined the Court of Justice of the European Communities (hereinafter ECJ), I was eager to observe from within how competition and internal market rules interact. This short chapter offers some personal reflections on the complex chemistry that binds these two areas together.

For a competition law practitioner, the starting point is of course the persistent and somewhat puzzling influence of free movement rules on competition law, in particular in the antitrust field. In hindsight, the reverse phenomenon – the influence of competition law on free movement rules – probably deserves more attention than it has received. The EC Treaty provisions on free movement share certain traits with their competition counterparts, in particular Article 81 EC and those governing State aids. Both are structured around a prohibition/exception dichotomy and, procedurally, were until recently enforced through a centralised system at the EC level. While useful in the formative years of the Community, this has led to a situation of legal and administrative over-stretch. With the scope of the prohibition extended beyond what appeared to be its natural width, the focus of the analysis shifted to the exception. The last decade or so has been characterised by a rebalancing of priorities and a renewed focus on the essential.

Seen through the prism of the new 'economic' approach, internal market and antitrust rules belong to two autonomous spheres and operate under different sets of rules and assumptions. While the EC Treaty antitrust and free movement provisions both seek to protect the market, they do so in different ways. Antitrust law is designed to protect the market from its own excesses, when it reaches its most accomplished form: monopoly. Free movement rules protect the market from excessive State intervention, a politically sensitive endeavour. Articles 81 EC and 82 EC prohibit certain business conducts, not State regulation. Conversely, free movement rules prohibit trade barriers resulting from State regulation, not business conduct. EC competition rules apply above a certain *de minimis* threshold: anticompetitive conducts which do not have an appreciable effect on the market do not come within the ambit of the EC competition rules. Competition rules can be applied with respect to conduct taking place outside the EC, provided that the effects of this conduct are felt within its territory, but there is no extraterritorial application of free movement rules.

On closer examination, these distinctions appear more elusive. Particularly telling is the example of the opposition between State and business conduct. Free movement rules have been applied directly to non-State actors[1] and competition rules have been applied to State entities.[2] State monopolies (for instance, Sweden's State monopoly on the distribution of alcoholic beverages) are simultaneously governed by the Treaty provisions on the free movement of goods (Article 31 EC) and competition (Article 86 EC). In addition, certain judgments tend to shield State entities from antitrust rules, both when the ECJ took into account overriding public policy considerations in order to 'disapply' Article 81(1) EC in *Wouters and Others*,[3] or when it held in *FENIN v Commission*[4] or in *Kattner Stahlbau*[5] that State entities providing health and social services are not undertakings subject to competition law if they do not perform an economic activity but rather operate under the principle of 'solidarity'. As a consequence, the distinction between free movement and antitrust rules has been obfuscated by the 'privatisation' of the former and the 'publicisation' of the latter.[6]

Furthermore, the law of free movement has not benefited from the same process of conceptual maturation that we have witnessed in antitrust with the 'economic approach' in the aftermath of the Antitrust Revolution of the 1970s. Lessons drawn from the antitrust field could help us is simplifying free

[1] See, eg Case C-415/93 *Bosman* [1995] ECR I-4921; Case C-341/05 *Laval un Partneri* [2007] ECR I-11767, and Case C-281/98 *Angonese* [2000] ECR I-4139. See contra Case 311/85 *van Vlaamse Reisbureaus* [1987] ECR 3801 para 30.

[2] Case C-265/95 *Commission v France* [1997] ECR I-6959.

[3] Case C-309/99 *Wouters and Others* [2002] ECR I-1577.

[4] Case C-205/03 P *FENIN v Commission* [2006] ECR I-6295.

[5] Case C-350/07 *Kattner Stahlbau*, judgment of 5 March 2009 nyr.

[6] M Waelbroek, 'Les rapports entre les règles sur la libre circulation des marchandises et les règles de concurrence applicables aux entreprises dans la CEE' in F Capotori *et al* (eds), *Du droit international au droit de l'intégration : Liber Amicorum Pierre Pescatore* (Baden-Baden, Nomos Verlagsgesellschaft, 1987) 781.

movement rules. It seems that, first and foremost, we need the equivalent of a theory of competitive harm. Small incremental changes could also be implemented in order to promote efficiency over efficacy in free movement law. I would like to address these two points by suggesting that (I) market access could provide us with the equivalent of a unified theory of competitive harm in the free movement realm and that (II) a *de minimis* rule applied to non-discriminatory barriers to trade could both contribute to reaching a satisfactory balance between economic integration, subsidiarity and the efficient administration of the law of free movement.

## MARKET ACCESS AS A THEORY OF COMPETITIVE HARM IN FREE MOVEMENT LAW

Antitrust law is now commonly understood as a tool designed to protect the dynamic process of free market economics: bringing more goods and services to consumers, at lower prices while promoting innovation and the efficient allocation of resources. Historically, this has not always been the case. The emergence of economic efficiency and consumer welfare as the main objectives of competition law is the direct result of a gradual development in law and economics thinking. While this evolution has been observed in many jurisdictions, the close relationship between competition law and the law governing the internal market remains a striking feature of the EC system.

Given their centrality to the European project, internal market considerations have permeated competition law, influenced by the suggestion that, for the internal market to succeed, firms cannot be allowed to fragment the continent along the very national boundaries that the four freedoms were meant to make redundant. The 'four freedoms' were intended both to promote the free movement of economic activity throughout the Community and to 'expose economic operators to the wind of competition from other countries'.[7] Indeed, economic integration is never a narrow exercise in free trade economics but always closely linked to a political process requiring some form of supra-national majoritarian rule. Economically, free trade would imply that, under perfect conditions and after adjustment for transaction and transport costs, the price of a given good should be the same in different locations. Price arbitrage between different geographic markets would bring about price convergence, which, in turns should lead to greater economic cohesion.

Early on, the ECJ recognised that the two sets of rules complement each other.[8] This has led the EC to view vertical agreements with great suspicion and explains why the EC has clung its focus on intra-brand competition,

[7] D Edward, 'Competition and National Rule-making' in A von Bogdandy *et al* (eds), *European Integration and International Co-ordination: Studies in Transnational Economic Law in Honour of Claus-Dieter Ehlermann* (The Hague, Kluwer, 2002) 129.

[8] Joined Cases 56/64 and 58/64 *Consten and Grundig v Commission* [1966] ECR 429.

a characteristic which has not been significantly altered over the years.[9] In addition to resale price maintenance, any restriction on the behaviour of firms which could be analysed as an attempt to partition the market along geographic lines or to hinder cross-border trade are considered to be illegal per se and, as a consequence, are unlikely – in practice but not in theory – to benefit from an exemption under Article 81(3) EC. In particular, agreements designed to hinder parallel trade (export bans; geographic price discrimination) are analysed as *per se* infringement of Article 81 EC,[10] without any regard for their actual economic impact. For example, price differentials between geographic markets are often interpreted, legally, as evidence of the sort of market partitioning that free movement rules seek to abolish despite economists' warnings that price discrimination is often a symptom of market power that can be explained by many other reasons than illicit collusion or abuse of dominance.

Internal market imperatives may therefore clash with the economic efficiency objectives of competition law. The influence of free movement rules on competition has been increasingly criticised for depriving firms from achieving efficiencies in the form of international distribution networks. According to this view, efficiency was sacrificed in the name of market integration, a confusion which in the long run could be detrimental to both.

As the Commission's thinking evolved and economic analysis began to gain centre stage in competition law and policy, new practices and instruments were put in place. A particularly noteworthy departure from past practice was the adoption of block exemption regulations where market power became key criteria in determining whether a given conduct could escape the prohibition of Article 81(1) EC and the issuance of a series of policy pronouncements in the form of administrative guidance notices from the Commission.

Equally important were a series of CFI rulings that clearly indicated that competition is subject to a specialised body of law where economic efficiency is of paramount importance. The most significant of these cases deal with pharmaceuticals, a category of products for which differences in regulatory schemes (marketing authorisation, pricing and reimbursement) at the Member State level have left the European market segmented along national lines. In a market where free movement rules did not deploy their full effect because of conflicting health and social requirements, the rationale for applying the existing case-law on restriction of parallel imports was repeatedly challenged.

In its *Bayer v Commission*[11] judgment, the CFI distinguished the existing case-law on free movement of pharmaceuticals, relating to Member State obstacles to

[9] BE Hawk, 'The American (Anti-trust) Revolution: Lessons for the EEC' (1988) 1 *European Competition Law Review* 53. Twenty years after this article, the core of the argument concerning the EC attachment to the promotion of internal market objectives through competition law remains current when it comes to vertical arrangements. From the same author, see also, 'System Failure: Vertical Restraints and EC Competition Law' (1995) 4 *Common Market Law Review* 973.

[10] Case 19/77 *Miller International Schallplatten v Commission* [1978] ECR 131; Case C-279/87 *Tipp-Ex v Commission* [1990] ECR I-261, and Case T-62/98 *Volkswagen v Commission* [2000] ECR II-2707.

[11] Case T-41/96 *Bayer v Commission* [2000] ECR II-3383.

trade, from the competition policy objectives of Article 81 EC. The CFI indicated that the law on free movement of pharmaceuticals 'does not in any way presume a general prohibition on preventing parallel exports applying not only to Member States but also, and in all cases, to undertakings (...)' It continued:

> [U]nder the system of the Treaty, it is not open to the Commission to attempt to achieve a result, such as the harmonisation of prices in the medicinal products market, by enlarging or straining the scope of Section of Chapter 1 of Title VI of the Treaty, especially since that Treaty gives the Commission specific means of seeking such harmonisation where it is undisputed that large disparities in the prices of medicinal products in the Member States are engendered by the differences existing between State mechanisms for fixing prices and the rules for reimbursement, as in the case here.[12]

In 2006, in *GlaxoSmithKline Services v Commission*,[13] the CFI overturned a finding of illegal restriction on parallel trade where the Commission had concluded, on the basis of the existing case-law, that export pricing schemes infringe Article 81 EC per se. The thrust of the CFI's reasoning was that the anti-competitive impact of such restrictions required an economic analysis; anti-competitive effects could no longer be presumed on the basis of earlier cases decided with respect to integrated markets which displayed none of the complexities of the market for medicinal products. In 2008, in an abuse of dominance case concerning parallel imports of drugs, the ECJ also gave some indications that the hard line against parallel imports should be adapted to the specific circumstances of the pharmaceutical market.[14]

The extent to which this gradual decoupling is likely to proceed is of course impossible to tell. If the United States jurisprudence were to be a harbinger of things to come, even the per se approach towards resale price maintenance could be subjected to the acid test of the 'economic approach'.[15] In any event, the momentum with which allocative efficiency has emerged as the underlying policy rationale of competition law contrasts with the difficulties in identifying a similar concept for the internal market, an area subject to oscillations between anti-protectionism and de-regulation.

With respect to trade in goods, the ECJ favoured a broad reading of Article 28 EC. It first followed a purely anti-protectionist bearing, pursuing measures which de jure or de facto discriminate, directly or indirectly, against imports (*Dassonville*[16]). Subsequently, the ECJ engaged Member States on a different terrain with *Cassis de Dijon*[17] where, faced with a situation where diverging – albeit non discriminatory – national rules, it considered that the imposition of a dual regulatory burden on an imported product could fall under Article 28

[12] *Ibid* paras 178–180.

[13] Case T-168/01 *GlaxoSmithKline Services v Commission* [2006] ECR II-2969. At the time of writing this chapter, the appeal against this judgment is still pending.

[14] Joined Cases C-468/06 to C-478/06 *Sot. Lélos kai Sia and Others*, judgment of 16 September 2008 nyr.

[15] *Leegin Creative Leather Products Inc. v PSKS, Inc.* 127 S. Ct. 2705 (20047).

[16] Case 8/74 *Dassonville* [1974] ECR 837.

[17] Case 120/78 *Rewe-Central (Cassis de Dijon)* [1979] ECR 649.

EC. After *Cassis de Dijon*, bringing suit under Article 28 EC was no longer the prerogative of foreign businesses that had been denied market access on equal terms with domestic producers. Nationals could challenge domestic regulations imposed indiscriminately on all market participants, in an attempt to be relieved of burdensome State measures, such as price regulations,[18] Sunday trading laws,[19] or limits on sales methods or advertising.[20] As State interference with free market economics became the target of Article 28 EC litigation, *Cassis de Dijon* paved the way for regulatory competition and 'home country' rule. In the words of a former ECJ judge, the philosophical underpinning of *Cassis* is liberalism, with an 'open, market economy' as its principle and State intervention, on grounds of public policy, as the exception.[21]

With *Keck and Mithouard*,[22] the ECJ applied the brakes, holding that 'national provisions restricting or prohibiting certain selling arrangements' would not fall within Article 28 EC, provided that they apply in a non discriminatory manner to (i) all traders and to (ii) imported and domestic goods alike. National rules such as a prohibition on sales at below-cost price or rules limiting the distribution of goods to certain outlets would no longer be treated as falling within the prohibition in Article 28 EC. Although *Keck and Mithouard* underscores 'market access' as its underlying rationale, this case rests on a purely legal criteria (the nature of the national rules) as opposed to an economic one (the existence of trade distortions).

Against this backdrop, could 'market access' supersede the distinction between rules affecting the physical characteristics of products (*Dassonville* and *Cassis de Dijon*) and those affecting their 'selling arrangements' (*Keck and Mithouard*). There should be little difficulty in recognising that market access is an interest protected by Community law. Focusing on the impact of the conduct or measure in question on the market would be lead to an 'effect-based approach' reminiscent of antitrust law. Following judgments such as *Alpine Investment*,[23] rendered with respect to the free provision of services, several recent cases from the ECJ have relied on market access as criteria for the identification of barriers to trade. In *Commission v Italy*,[24] the ECJ found that an Italian prohibition on the use of trailers by motorcycles amounted to a trade barrier, as it had the practical impact of reducing local demand for trailers specifically designed for motorcycle use but was nonetheless justified on account of road safety objectives. The ECJ specifically referred to the 'principle of ensuring free

[18] Case 229/83 *Leclerc* [1985] ECR 1.

[19] Case C-145/88 *B & Q* [1989] ECR 3851.

[20] Case C-362/88 *GB-INNO-BM* [1990] ECR I-667, and Case C-126/91 *Yves Rocher* [1993] ECR I-2361.

[21] P Pescatore, 'Variations sur la jurisprudence "Cassis de Dijon" ou la solidarité entre l'ordre public national et l'ordre public communautaire' in M Monti *et al* (eds), *Economic Law and Justice in Times of Globalization, Festschrift for Carl Baudenbacher* (Baden-Baden, Nomos Verlagsgesellschaft, 2007) 543, at 546.

[22] Joined Cases C-267/91 and C-268/91 *Keck and Mithouard* [1993] ECR I-6097.

[23] Case C-384/93 *Alpine Investment* [1995] ECR I-1141.

[24] Case C-110/05 *Commission v Italy*, judgment of 10 February 2009 nyr.

access of Community products to national markets',[25] after the Advocate General recommended a switch to a market access test as a mean to bring some order to the post-*Keck* world of Article 28 EC.[26] More recently, in *Mickelsson and Roos*,[27] the ECJ held that Sweden's limits on the use of certain motorcraft outside of designated waterways does constitute an obstacle to trade as it effectively dampens consumer demand for motorcraft but may nonetheless be justified on environmental or safety grounds. Similarly, with respect to services (Article 49 EC), market access is present in the ECJ's analysis of the Swedish unions' right to collective action against foreign firms in *Laval un Partneri*,[28] of a mandatory occupational health insurance scheme in *Kattner Stahlbau*[29] or, with respect to a registration requirement for certain financial services firms in *Fidium Finanz*.[30] Finally, 'market access' is also the reason put forward by the ECJ in *CaixaBank France*[31] with respect to freedom of establishment (Article 43 EC).

This is not the right place to speculate as to how an emphasis on market access could translate into a single or even a series of legal tests. Suffice it to say that, at least for goods, national measures which are, de jure or de facto, discriminatory should be summarily assessed and only subject to the limited grounds for exemption under Article 30 EC. All other national measures would have to be more carefully scrutinised as to their impact on market access and, their possible justification under Article 30 EC grounds or other mandatory requirements. A *de minimis* standard would be a natural corollary to market access.

## DE MINIMIS

It was in 1969 that the ECJ effectively added an additional requirement for the applicability of Article 81 EC, when it held that 'an agreement falls outside the prohibition in Article [81 EC] when it has only an insignificant effect on the market, taking into account the weak position which the persons concerned have on the market of the product in question'.[32] The absence of significant competitive harm does not warrant public intervention through Article 81 EC. Quantifying what is significant has been left mostly to the administrative practice of the Commission. According to the Commission's 'notice on agreements of minor importance which do not appreciably restrict competition under Article 81(1) [EC] (...)',[33] the *de minimis* rule does not apply to per se or 'hard-core' infringements such as cartels or resale price maintenance schemes.

[25] *Ibid* para 34.

[26] *Ibid* Opinion of Advocate General Bot points 109–138. For other recent examples of 'market access' cases, see: Case C-265/06 *Commission v Portugal* [2008] ECR I-2245 and, under Art 29 EC, Case C-205/07 *Gysbrechts and Santurel Inter*, judgment of 16 December 2008 nyr.

[27] Case C-142/05 *Mickelsson and Roos*, judgment of 4 June 2009 nyr.

[28] See n 1 above, para 99.

[29] Case C-350/07 *Kattner Stahlbau*, n 5 above.

[30] Case C-452/04 *Fidium Finanz* [2006] ECR I-9521 para 46.

[31] Case C-442/02 *CaixaBank France* [2004] ECR I-8961 para 12.

[32] Case 5/69 *Völk* [1969] ECR 295 para 7.

[33] [2001] OJ C/368/13.

With respect to the internal market, the problem faced by the ECJ was essentially the same: an overstretch of the legal prohibition had artificially inflated the number of measures or practices caught in the net of the Community law definition of obstacle to trade. Advocate General Jacobs argued in *Leclerc-Siplec*[34] that a *de minimis* standard would have been better suited than the test in *Keck and Mithouard* in order to limit the scope of Article 28 EC and avoid excessive interference with Member State regulatory powers. The Advocate General suggested that the *de minimis* rule should only apply to non-discriminatory measures, those that are not subject to the strictest standard. The ECJ did not openly follow this path.

Certain commentators have lauded the ECJ for refusing to establish a *de minimis* rule in Article 28 EC cases,[35] arguing a) that State conduct hindering trade is inherently more dangerous for the internal market than business conduct; b), as fundamental principles of the Community, the four freedoms cannot be subject to a *de minimis* standard and c) such a standard would give rise to considerable practical difficulties.

Nonetheless, the *de minimis* approach has not been flatly rejected by the ECJ. In 2005, in *Burmanjer and Others*,[36] the ECJ was asked to rule on the interpretation of Article 28 EC, with respect to a Belgian ban on itinerant sales. The ECJ examined this regulation as falling within the 'selling arrangements' category, under *Keck's* two-pronged test. The first part of the test was easily met, as the national ban applied indiscriminately to all economic operators, without any distinction based on their nationality or the origin of the goods in question. However, when turning to the second part of the test, the ECJ could not reach a positive determination. The information available to the ECJ did not enable it to establish with certainty whether the national rules on itinerant sales affect the marketing of products from Member States other than the Kingdom of Belgium to any greater degree than that of products from that State. The ECJ went on to add:

> Nevertheless, it seems to follow from the information in the file transmitted to the ECJ that, if those rules did have such an effect, it would be *too insignificant and uncertain* to be regarded as being such as to hinder or otherwise interfere with trade between Member States.[37] (emphasis added)

Although couched in evidentiary terms ('the information available to the Court did not enable it to establish…'), this formulation brings to the fore the very idea of a *de minimis* exception, as advocated by Advocate General Jacobs, at least in the narrow context of *Keck*.

A few months later, in *A-Punkt Schmuckhandel*[38] the ECJ followed the same line of reasoning. At issue was an Austrian restriction on 'doorstep' selling. The

[34] Opinion of Advocate General Jacobs in Case C-412/93 *Leclerc-Siplec* [1995] ECR I-179 point 42.

[35] PJ Oliver, *Free movement of goods in the European Community*, 4th edn (London, Sweet and Maxwell, 2003) 100.

[36] Case C-20/03 *Burmanjer and Others* [2005] ECR I-4133.

[37] *Ibid* para 31.

[38] Case C-441/04 *A-Punkt Schmuckhandel* [2006] ECR I-2093.

ECJ examined the national measures in light of Article 28 EC. Applying the second part of the *Keck* test, the ECJ found that the information available did not 'allow it to ascertain beyond doubt whether the prohibition on selling in private homes [...] affects the marketing of products from Member States other than Austria to a greater degree than it affects the marketing of products from that Member States', but left this point to be determined by the national court in its capacity as prime trier of fact.[39]

It is probably too soon to tell these two examples are part of a broader trend towards the recognition of a *de minimis* exception in Article 28 EC or are merely attempts at fine-tuning *Keck and Mithouard* where the impact on market access is too insignificant or uncertain to reach a final determination. For the purpose of this chapter, I would nonetheless argue that their significance lays in the fact that they seek to establish enforcement priorities on the basis of a quantitative analysis of the impact of the measure on the market. Whether a *de minimis* rule would give rise to unsurmountable difficulties is open to debate. Obtaining a rough estimate of market size does not necessarily require highly sophisticated scientific tools. The administrability of such a rule would have to be weighed against the current situation, rather than against a perfect rule which may only exists in the abstract. In other words, it may work in practice, but will the theory follow?

[39] *Ibid* paras 25 and 26.

# 3

# *The Role of Competition Law in the Evolution of Community Law*

IRENA PELIKÁNOVÁ*

## CONTEXT

European Community law is generally understood to be predominantly grounded in public law. The question of the dualism of public and private law does not appear to be of great interest, in particular to legal scholars. And yet, this issue is all the more important, given that private and public law co-exist even within the domain of EC law.

Community law is predominantly public, since it is a product of European integration efforts flowing from international public law. The progress of the integration process gave rise to a major supra-national social entity, which can no longer be described within the traditional concepts of international public law. However, at the same time, this entity does not possess all the elements of a federal State, and it appears that the Member States generally lack the will to take the necessary steps towards the implementation of this model.

As it has often been stated, EC case-law is evolving faster than political consensus. The principle of primacy of Community law has allowed for the progressive development of a new legal order which increasingly permeates the national legal systems of Member States, without formally denying their autonomy. Nevertheless, the autonomy of a legal order which is not clearly separate from EC law, but instead intertwined with it, is a most problematic concept.

The Community law system is marked by the circumstances and the limitations related to its creation. In particular, the Community legal order cannot overcome the fact that it is based on an international treaty. In fact, such a treaty is not a constitution, despite fulfilling a similar role, and therefore does not offer a basis for the development of a comprehensive legal order. Also, Community law is not

* The author wishes to thank Jan Převrátil for editing and translating the Czech text and Samuel Sadden for a linguistic revision of the translation.

based on codifications, and the gap between primary and secondary law, despite being attenuated to a certain extent by the case-law of the EC judiciary, is too broad to allow for a coherent normative system. This is all the more the case when Community legislators endeavour to tie their secondary legislation into national legal orders. Indeed, there remains significant variation between the national legal orders, both conceptually and terminologically.

Since their beginnings, European integration efforts were focused on economic integration. The protection of competition was their essential objective from the outset. Although competition law existed before in different European countries and European lawyers were familiar with US antitrust law, the birth of EC competition law brought a new dimension into this domain. Conversely, to a large extent, EC competition law has shaped Community law itself in that principles of EC competition law have played a significant role in the evolution of Community case-law and have led to the stabilisation of several essential notions. A certain number of these notions have been adopted in other domains of Community law, albeit with caution, and progressively penetrate even the national legal orders of the Member States.

Already before the Second World War, competition laws generally included both a private law element, that is, unfair competition law, and a public law element, represented by cartel law. In the context of the European Communities, only the latter element has been extensively developed, unfair competition law being until this day only marginally treated by secondary legislation in the form of the Directive on Misleading and Comparative Advertising.[1] However, the expansion of consumer protection in the Community context casts competition law in a new light and puts forth the question of the need for common unfair competition rules. Another aspect which should be borne in mind is the broad scope of EC competition law, which tends to include State aid, antidumping and public procurement. As a result, competition law, under its broad definition, presents many points of contact with the field of private law.

Although rules against the restriction of competition maintain their public law character, given in particular that they are applied by administrative decisions adopted by the Commission, new elements, often reminiscent of private law, appear even in this field. Thus, the emphasis put on, and the support expressed for, private enforcement of competition law, via claims for compensation of damage caused by illegal behaviour sanctioned by Commission's decisions, confirms the links existing between the different areas of EC law. Also, there are tentative plans to implement certain well known features of United States antitrust law, such as plea bargains under which the Commission would reduce the amount of fines imposed in exchange for the acknowledgment of a violation by its perpetrator. Reflections on the criminal nature of sanctions imposed in antitrust cases, although rejected by the Court of Justice of the European

[1] Council Directive 84/450/EEC of 10 September 1984 relating to the approximation of the laws, regulations and administrative provisions of the Member States concerning misleading advertising [1984] OJ L/250/17, as amended by Directive 97/55/EC of the European Parliament and of the Council of 6 October 1997 so as to include comparative advertising [1997] OJ L/290/18.

Communities (hereinafter ECJ) so far, cast yet another light on the nature of competition law.

These circumstances bring forth the question of the ways in which competition law exerts influence on the development of EC law in general and *vice versa*. The future evolution of this relationship of mutual influence represents another topic of interest.

It is submitted that an essential contribution of competition law is the progressive delimitation and refinement of certain fundamental Community law notions. As a result of the requirement for the coherence of the EC legal system as a whole, this gradual development, due essentially to case-law, influenced other areas of Community law. Concurrently, competition law absorbs elements from case-law rendered in other fields of Community law, the result being that in certain instances, the legal evolutionary process operates in both ways and is therefore even more complex. This general finding could be illustrated by a multitude of examples, only two of which will be presented here.

## THE UNDERTAKING

The most important contribution of competition law to the evolution of Community law is the articulation and progressive development of the notion of an 'undertaking'. Thanks to this development, the barrier of legal subjectivity can be overcome in the course of an investigation of anticompetitive acts, with the analysis returning to the level of legal entities at the moment of the application of sanctions. It is interesting to note that the first steps towards the articulation of the notion of an undertaking were made outside of the ambit of competition law in its narrow sense, in cases relating to the ferrous scrap equalisation scheme under the European Coal and Steel Community Treaty. At first, in *Snupat v High Authority*,[2] the ECJ stated in a clear and unequivocal manner that:

> [t]he concept of an undertaking for the purpose of the treaty may be identified with that of a natural or legal person, since the treaty uses this concept primarily to define persons with rights and obligations arising under community law.
>
> It could be accepted that several distinct companies may constitute a single undertaking [...] only if the treaty contained an express provision to that effect.
>
> In the absence of such a provision it cannot be presumed that two separate and distinct companies can constitute a single undertaking for the purposes of the Treaty, more particularly when they each have distinct legal personality in the eyes of their national law.[3]

The ECJ then mentioned several problems which would arise if the contrary argument were accepted.[4]

[2] Joined Cases 42/59 and 49/59 *Snupat v High Authority* [1961] ECR 101.
[3] *Ibid* para 80.
[4] *Ibid* paras 80 and 81.

However, in the following year, the ECJ began to soften the definition of an undertaking which it announced in *Snupat v High Authority*. Thus, in *Mannesmann v High Authority*,[5] the ECJ first presented the famous definition, employed ever since in competition case-law, in scholarly works and even in the legislation of Member States:[6]

> [a]n undertaking is constituted by a single organisation of personal, tangible and intangible elements, attached to an autonomous legal entity and pursuing a given long term economic aim.[7]

Nevertheless, in the following paragraphs of the judgment, the judges refused to abandon the link between the notion of undertaking and legal subjectivity, stating that:

> the creation of every legal entity [...] involves the establishment of a separate undertaking; a particular economic activity cannot be regarded as forming a single unit in law when the legal effects of that activity must be separately attributed to several distinct legal entities.[8]

The position of the ECJ further evolved in *Société des Aciéries du Temple v High Authority*,[9] where it admitted *a contrario* that the above link could be severed:

> [t]he concept of 'undertaking' within the meaning of Article 80 of the ECSC Treaty, a concept which distinguishes persons having rights and duties and which, unless the context otherwise provides, refers to an economic entity distinguished by a distinct legal personality.[10]

From there on, in the field of competition law, the Commission continued to articulate the concept as it is known today, applying the legal qualification of the behaviour of an undertaking as that of an economic unit comprising a group of companies, at first, to prohibited agreements and concerted practices, and later to the abuse of a dominant position. This evolution has been confirmed by a substantial amount of ECJ case-law.[11]

As a last step, the application of the concept of joint and several obligations brings forth the legal consequences of the unified economic-legal concept of the undertaking, since a sanction imposed jointly and severally on more than one legal subject is not explicitly and fully individualised. In this case, the final individualisation is left to interpretation.

The progressive development and refinement of the criteria of economic activity and organisational unity of personal, tangible and intangible elements led not only to the notion of an undertaking becoming independent of the legal

[5] Case 19/61 *Mannesmann v High Authority* [1962] ECR 675.
[6] See, eg Art 5 of the Czech Commercial Code, law no. 513/1991 of the Collection of laws.
[7] *Ibid* para 371.
[8] *Ibid.*
[9] Case 36/62 *Société des Aciéries du Temple v High Authority* [1963] ECR 583.
[10] *Ibid.*
[11] Starting with Case 22/71 *Béguelin Import* [1971] ECR 949. For details, see S Poillot-Peruzzetto and M Luby, *Le droit communautaire appliqué à l'entreprise* (Paris, Dalloz, 1998) 29.

form of the entity, but even to it overcoming the link between the organisational form of the entity and the nature of activities it performs. Gradually, the notion of an undertaking has come to be viewed as describing a field of activity defined by the exclusive conceptual criterion of provision of products and services on a market.[12] Therefore, the qualification is not dependent on whether the activity is performed to profitable ends, on its exclusive nature or on the manner in which financing is provided, and presence on the demand side of a market falls outside of the scope of the notion. As a result, an entity may constitute an undertaking with respect to certain aspects of its activity only.

The flexibility attained by ECJ case-law in this context is remarkable. In some instances, a highly pragmatic approach is adopted, such as the refusal to extend the notion of an undertaking to entities positioned on the demand side of a market which acquire the goods or services in question for noneconomic purposes; indeed, otherwise, the limits of the notion would be blurred up to the point of losing any degree of certainty.[13] More generally, the interpenetration of the private and public sectors represents a major issue in this respect, given that experience acquired in the field of competition law clearly demonstrates that actions of public sector entities may lead to substantial distortions of competition. A strict limitation of competition rules to the private sector could lead to such actions escaping any control. An avoidance of such a situation is, in the end, the rationale for incorporating State aid and public procurement into competition law in its broader sense.

Thus, competition law serves as a laboratory where the relationship and the intermingling of public and private aspects are examined from the point of view of their effect on competition.

The notion of an undertaking is used in many sectors of EC law. It is commonly used in State aid law, trade mark law, fiscal law and public procurement law. In consumer protection law, it is usually replaced by the terms 'seller or supplier' or by similar words such as 'trader', 'lender' and so on, without the connection to the concept of undertaking being mentioned.[14] However, a very close material link exists. In fact, competition law does not exclude self-employed natural persons from the scope of the concept of an undertaking,[15] and, conversely, the notion of 'seller or supplier' under consumer protection law is naturally not limited to such individuals. Indeed, in many cases, a 'seller or supplier' will be a major multinational group. It appears nevertheless that, even though future evolution may bring further convergence of competition law and consumer protection law, the limits of legal subjectivity will not be overcome in the latter

[12] See, eg Case C-41/90 *Höfner and Elser* [1991] ECR I-1979; Joined Cases C-159/91 and C-160/91 *Poucet and Pistre* [1993] ECR I-637, and Case C-364/92 *SAT Fluggesellschaft* [1994] ECR I-43.

[13] Case T-319/99 *FENIN v Commission* [2003] ECR II-357 para 37 in particular.

[14] However, the term 'undertaking' is occasionally used within the ambit of consumer protection law. See, eg Opinion of Advocate General Trstenjak of 21 October 2008 in Joined Cases C-261/07 and C-299/07 *VTB-VAB and Galatea* nyr.

[15] See J Faull and A Nikpay, *The EC Law of Competition*, 2nd edn (London, Oxford University Press, 2007) 189.

area for the time being. Indeed, currently the objective of consumer protection rules is essentially to impose legal obligations on the stronger contractual party and to define liabilities arising from their non-respect. Yet, a contractual party is a specific identified legal subject.

The Opinion of the Advocate General in *VTB-VAB and Galatea*[16] is noteworthy with respect to the concept of an undertaking under consumer protection law. The case concerns a reference for a preliminary ruling related to the compatibility of rules on combined offers set by the Belgian Law on trade practices and consumer information and protection[17] with the Unfair Commercial Practices Directive.[18] Belgian legislation is based on a concept opposite to that of the Directive – combined offers are prohibited in principle and are only admissible in exceptional cases specified in a limitative enumeration. Under the Directive, all the relevant practices are prohibited only as far as they are unfair. Therefore, the Advocate General concluded that the more restrictive Belgian rules were incompatible with the Directive.

The link with competition law and the notion of an undertaking lies not in the main issue of the case examined by the Advocate General, but in the wording of the national rules under review. According to Article 54 of the Law on trade practices and consumer information and protection:

> [a]ny combined offer to consumers which is made by a seller is hereby prohibited. Any combined offer to consumers which is made by *several sellers acting with a common purpose* is also hereby prohibited. (emphasis added)

Here, once again, the national legislator severs the link between illegal conduct and legal subjectivity of the trader, thus bordering on rules relating to prohibited agreements – a common purpose may well equate to anticompetitive collusion.

In her Opinion, the Advocate General also mentioned that the Unfair Commercial Practices Directive protects not only competitors, but also, indirectly, competing businesses. Hence, she touched upon an important issue evoked in the preamble to the Directive and implied by the amendments to the Directive on Misleading and Comparative Advertising. In fact, the Community legislator not only came to require full harmonisation, but even addressed unfair competition law as the missing link in the normative coverage of economic competition as a whole.[19]

In the context of consumer protection law, terms such as 'undertaking', 'enterprise', 'operator' or 'branch' are usually not defined and are treated as less precise, approximate equivalents to the notion of a company. A certain

[16] See n 14 above.

[17] Loi du 14 juillet 1991 sur les pratiques du commerce et sur l'information et la protection du consommateur (Moniteur belge, 29 August 1991, p 18712).

[18] Directive 2005/29/EC of the European Parliament and of the Council of 11 May 2005 concerning unfair business-to-consumer commercial practices in the internal market and amending Council Directive 84/450/EEC, Directives 97/7/EC, 98/27/EC and 2002/65/EC of the European Parliament and of the Council and Regulation (EC) No 2006/2004 of the European Parliament and of the Council [2005] OJ L/149/22.

[19] See n 14 above, points 71 and 72 and the 6th preamble to the Unfair Commercial Practices Directive. Also see amendments to the Directive on Misleading and Comparative Advertising resulting from the Unfair Commercial Practices Directive.

terminological blurring is understandable, given the variability of organisational forms under which businesses enter the market, depending on markedly different regimes defined by different national laws. Yet, this effort to cover a range of specific cases does not lead to a notion as extensive or as flexible as that of an undertaking under competition law, since the outermost limit is generally constituted by the category of a legal subject. It can therefore include natural and legal persons, the latter in the form of companies, cooperatives, partnerships and so on. The inclusion of associations and other entities pursuing non-profit objectives or associated to the public sector is less certain. However, if such entities act as sellers, suppliers or traders in consumer contracts, there is no reason for a negative answer. Even the issue of groups of companies can be important in relation to consumers, for instance, in liability matters with respect to the question of whether a consumer may present his claims to a subsidiary or a sister company of the supplier.

A very similar problem can be identified with respect to intellectual property law. Thus, trade mark registrations are generally being applied for or opposed by legal entities pursuing business objectives, without any restrictions as to their legal form. Yet, such will not necessarily always be the case.[20] Even if in this domain, the possible variants will again likely not be as broad as for the 'undertaking' according to competition law, the issue merits attention. Not the least because intellectual property law comes into close contact with competition law due to the concept of an abuse of a dominant position.

The heterogeneous situation existing in different parts of Community law described above may lead to a lack of coherence and a reverse impact on competition law, where the distinction between the notions of 'company' as a legal entity and 'undertaking' as an economic one is blurred in some instances, despite a need to rigorously respect the precise concept underlying the second notion at all times. The ensuing confusion can serve as another example of the mutual influence, this time undesirable, existing between competition law and other domains of Community law.

## ABUSE OF A DOMINANT POSITION AND ABUSE OF RIGHTS

EC competition case-law also plays a significant role in the development of the doctrine of abuse of rights.[21] Its scope is even broader than in the case of the notion of an undertaking, given that any right can be abused. Thus, the major particularity in relation to competition law is not the application of the doctrine in itself, but rather the direct legislative prohibition of abusive behaviour in primary law. Due to this explicit basis, the specific question of abuse of rights by a dominant undertaking became the object of case-law developments at both the EU and national levels.

[20] For an example of a trade mark registered by a charitable association, see Case C-442/07 *Verein Radetzky-Orden*, judgment of 9 December 2008 nyr.

[21] See, eg D Weber, 'Abuse of Law' (2004) *Legal Issues of Economic Integration* 43.

A further particularity is related to the fact that already in the older, 'pre-European Community' tradition of competition law in Europe, the link connecting the abuse to its subjective aspect was weakened. As an example, the law of unfair competition which evolved in Czechoslovakia before the Second World War[22] already admitted that liability could be recognised – and therefore, the relevant behaviour could be prohibited and a restoration of the original state could be ordered – regardless of fault, proof of which was only necessary in order for damages to be awarded. In this last case, the level of fault required was explicitly set to gross negligence only.[23] The legislation also provided that where a vexatious claim had been introduced, the ECJ could order the payment of damages – damages resulting in fact from the abuse of the unfair competition proceedings – and even allowed for the imposition of sanctions in this case.[24] Indeed, in its essence, the object of unfair competition law is nothing but a liability for an abuse of the right to participate in economic competition, a definition explicitly retained in the Czech commercial code.[25] EC competition law follows the same trend.

The difficulty of establishing the subjective element of liability for an abuse of a dominant position is the essential, pragmatic cause of the weakening of the subjective requirement. In fact, this circumstance could lead to a situation where it would be impossible in practice to prove any abuse. Within the ambit of competition law, similar considerations led to the adoption of a particularly flexible interpretation of the concepts of 'agreement' and 'concerted practice' in cartel law. A comparison with the notion of 'contract' under general private law clearly shows the opportunistic nature of such an interpretation. However, such an interpretation is inevitable if the concept of liability has to retain any sense at all in the domain of economic competition.

In an apparent contradiction with the inherent nature of the notion of 'abuse', the abuse of a dominant position under EC competition law is generally analysed without regard to fault, even if a certain level of fault is usually implicitly presumed. However, the relevant case-law has developed the doctrine of 'objective justification', the proof of which can exculpate the undertaking concerned.[26] This doctrine may be seen as an expression of the subjective element of the conduct prohibited by Article 82 EC.[27]

[22] Act No 111/1927 of the Collection of laws and regulations against unfair competition. According to s 1;

> [w]hoever acts, in economic relationships, against the good manners of competition through a conduct capable of prejudicing a competitor, may be sued so as to refrain from such conduct and repair the irregularities he has caused; if he knew or ought know that his conduct was capable of prejudicing a competitor, he may also be sued so as to repair the damage so caused.

[23] S 16, ss 1 of the Act.

[24] ss 19 and 20 of the Act.

[25] See s 42, ss 1, of Act No 513/1991 of the Collection of laws, the Commercial Code: 'Abuses of the participation in the economic competition consist of unfair competition conduct ... and prohibited restrictions of economic competition.'

[26] See, eg Case T-30/89 *Hilti v Commission* [1991] ECR II-1439 para 20.

[27] See, eg Case T-201/04 *Microsoft v Commission* [2007] ECR II-3601 para 1144 in particular.

The concept of objective and subjective abuse is occasionally addressed in scholarly works. Thus, in this area, F Lagondet[28] speaks of subjective and objective theory and distinguishes, on the basis of this categorisation, between an exercise of a right to the detriment of a third person (subjective abuse) and an exercise contrary to the social function of the relevant rule (objective abuse). However, this categorisation is not based on fault, since F Lagondet clearly considers both cases as culpable acts. He further distinguishes the exercise of a right where one of the conditioning elements is falsified or concealed. Such an approach corresponds to the nature of the French notion of *la faute*, which always includes both the element of illegality and the element of fault, thus complicating the analysis in instances where liability can arise without a culpable act. The case-law on non-contractual liability of the Communities defines three conditions – illegality, causal nexus and prejudice – and does not mention fault as a specific requirement, either in general or with respect to claims pertaining to abuse of rights; the concept of culpability is more often present in connection with the question of a sufficiently serious breach of EC law. However, the abundant case-law of the ECJ in matters pertaining to abuse of rights granted by Community law includes instances where a subjective element is explicitly required.

The first such case, related to export refunds on agricultural products, is *Emsland-Stärke*.[29] The ECJ unequivocally linked the concept of abuse of rights to a subjective element, stating that:

> it is clear from the case-law of the ECJ that the scope of Community regulations must in no case be extended to cover abuses on the part of a trader. [...] A finding of an abuse requires, first, a combination of objective circumstances in which, despite formal observance of the conditions laid down by the Community rules, the purpose of those rules has not been achieved. [...] It requires, second, a subjective element consisting in the intention to obtain an advantage from the Community rules by creating artificially the conditions laid down for obtaining it.[30]

The same rule has been applied by Advocates General in other areas of EC law, such as the free movement of persons,[31] fiscal law[32] or the free movement of capital.[33]

[28] F Lagondet, 'L'abus de droit dans la jurisprudence communautaire' (2003) 95 *Journal des tribunaux* 8.

[29] Case C-110/99 *Emsland-Stärke* [2000]ECR I-11569.

[30] *Ibid* paras 51–53 (citations omitted).

[31] Opinion of Advocate General Geelhoed in Case C-109/01 *Akrich* [2003] ECR I-9607 point 96. The Advocate General quoted the relevant wording of *Emsland-Stärke*, n 29 above.

[32] Opinion of Advocate General Ruiz-Jarabo Colomer in Joined Cases C-439/04 and C-440/04 *Kittel and Recolta Recycling* [2006] ECR I-6161 point 56:

> The second element relates to the purpose of the operation, which is none other than to create the right claimed, and obtain an undeserved profit. It appears to be essential that the person claiming the discount be both aware of the fraud and in agreement with the other participants, so that the contract, having no independent financial content, is simply a smokescreen for the profit (citations omitted).

[33] Opinion of Advocate General Stix-Hackl in Case C-452/04 *Fidium Finanz* [2006] ECR I-9521 point 97: 'Evidence of abuse [...] requires an objective and a subjective element' (citations omitted).

In the field of consumer protection, the notion of abuse is also present. In particular, in a global view, the Unfair Contract Terms Directive[34] and Unfair Commercial Practices Directive demonstrate the complementary nature of EC competition law and consumer protection law.[35] Efforts to maintain undistorted competition are primarily aimed at obtaining the most advantageous market position for the consumers, and consumer protection rules directly pursue the very same goal. In both cases, the method employed to reach the said objective consists in a limitation of the freedom of business entities. The close relationship between both branches can also be seen in EC case-law. The ECJ has stated that a national judge reviewing the validity of an arbitration award may decide *ex officio* on the invalidity of an unfair term in a consumer contract, even though the corresponding plea had not been invoked during the arbitration proceedings, but merely on judicial review.[36] Both the ECJ and the Advocate General stated that the rules on unfair terms are a matter of public policy, in the same way as Article 81 EC prohibiting agreements and concerted practices between undertakings.[37]

Finally, Community case-law has extensively developed the notion of misuse of powers and its variant, the misuse of procedure.[38] Once again, the behaviour is characterised by an abuse of rights, with the subjective element being presumed. The close relationship between the notion of misuse of powers and the more general concept of abuse of rights is confirmed by the fact that, in corporate law, the former is used in direct association with the latter, in particular with respect to the abuse of the voting rights of a shareholder.[39]

## CONCLUSION

The two examples of conceptual connections described above demonstrate that Community law is an interlinked normative system, the functional cohesion and efficient operation of which is dependent on the relevant actors considering not only the unique circumstances of a specific case, but also the general context. Neglecting the latter leads to the risk of constituting differing notions, often under the same designation, with the resulting adverse impact on the coherence of interpretation of EC law. Hence, when trying to answer a legal question relating to a particular area, it is also necessary to assess case-law from other

[34] Council Directive 93/13/EEC of 5 April 1993 on unfair terms in consumer contracts [1993] OJ L/95/29.

[35] The complementary character is touched upon, eg, in F Gómez Pomar, 'The Unfair Commercial Practices Directive: A Law and Economics Perspective' (2006) 1 *Indret* 25 (www.indret.com).

[36] Case C-168/05 *Mostaza Claro* [2006] ECR I-10421.

[37] *Ibid.* The relevant statement can be found in para 37 of the judgment and in points 54 and 60 of the Opinion of Advocate General Tizzano.

[38] See, eg S van Raepenbusch, *Le droit institutionnel de l'Union et des communautés européennes*, 3rd edn (Brussels, De Boeck Université, 2001) 509 and 510. In Case 148/87 *Frydendahl Pedersen v Commission* [1988] ECR 4993, the ECJ stated that the fact for the Commission to ask a Member State to withdraw a request and to re-submit it at a later date in order to prevent a failure by the Commission to respect a time limit in taking a decision constitutes a misuse of procedure.

[39] See, eg T Tilquin, *Traité des fusions et scissions* (Brussels, Kluwer, 1993) 417.

fields, all the while taking into account their specific details. The balancing act between maintaining conceptual coherence and respecting relevant divergences is one of the particularly difficult aspects of the decision-making process of the Community judiciary.

# 4

# *The Commission's Activity Upstream and Downstream Ascertaining and Sanctioning Antitrust Behaviours*

PAOLO MENGOZZI

## THE IMPORTANCE OF THE ACTIVITY THAT THE COMMISSION CARRIES OUT UPSTREAM AND DOWNSTREAM ASSESSING AND SANCTIONING VIOLATIONS OF ARTICLES 81 EC AND 82 EC

Judge *Virpi Tiili's* contribution to the formulation of the modalities to be followed by the European Commission in ascertaining and, as the case may be, sanctioning infringements of Community competition law has been remarkable. In paying tribute to her for the clarifications which, through her work within the Court of First Instance of the European Communities (hereinafter CFI), have been made to the regulation of such important functions of the Commission, it is worth remembering that she has always stressed that the Commission's activity deserves to be taken into consideration with reference to what it does both 'upstream' and 'downstream' in the exercise of such functions.

Consideration is to be given, on the one hand, to the activity carried out 'upstream', with reference to the Commission's decisions of whether or not to open investigations. This is because, in this phase, it constitutes the mechanism which enables the channelling and, at the same time, filtering the contributions that natural and legal persons, through complaints, can make in order to maintain fairness in the single market.

On the other hand, the activity that the Commission carries out 'downstream' in assessing violations of Articles 81 EC and 82 EC and imposing sanctions deserves to be considered and analysed because as the Commission has to rely on the help provided for by the administrations of the Member States for the concrete application of these sanctions, it is essential that the Commission takes measures in order to check that the objectives pursued are not thwarted. Otherwise one might run the risk that, due to a possible inadequacy of the contribution of a national administration, all its efforts would be devoid of practical effect.

## THE COMMUNITY INTEREST IN FILTERING COMPLAINTS MADE BY NATURAL AND LEGAL PERSONS AND THE CRITERIA FOR APPLYING IT

The technical notion which the Commission invokes in channelling and filtering complaints presented by natural and legal persons in order to consider whether or not to start an examination procedure is that of a 'Community interest'. It is on the basis of determining the existence or not of such an interest that the Commission establishes priorities for dealing with them.

The fact that the Commission establishes priorities and applies the criterion of Community interest is linked to the administrative, rather than judicial, character of its activity and to the fact that, as is observed in the Commission Notice on the handling of complaints by the Commission under Articles 81 and 82 of the EC Treaty,[1] 'while national courts are called upon to safeguard the rights of individuals and are thus bound to rule on cases brought before them, public enforcers cannot investigate all complaints'. The latter, in fact, must follow the criteria of effectiveness and promptness, which imply the rational utilisation of staff and available resources and, consequently, a remarkable degree of discretion; therefore the individuals' rights cannot prevail over the public objective that competition is not distorted in the single market; between those two interests, one can only reach for a reconciliation.[2]

This is confirmed in Regulation No 1/2003/EC on the implementation of the rules on competition laid down in Articles 81 and 82 of the Treaty[3] which, at recital 18, recalls the possibility allowed to the Commission of 'rejecting a complaint for lack of Community interest, as the case-law of the Court of Justice of the European Communities (hereinafter ECJ) has acknowledged it may do', stressing, at the second paragraph of Article 7, that 'those entitled to lodge a complaint [...] are natural or legal persons who can show a legitimate interest'.

Since the judgment of the CFI in *Automec v Commission* case,[4] Community judges have, however, deemed that, even in the determination of the existence or not of a Community interest, the Commission must respect some rules of law and have specified which these are and according to what criteria they must be applied. They have considered that what has to be taken into account, is first of all, a) the significance of the alleged infringement as regards the functioning

[1] [2004] OJ C/101/65, recital 8.

[2] See G Di Federico, *La riforma del procedimento comunitario antitrust e i diritti di difesa* (Naples, Editoriale Scientifica, 2008) 162.

[3] Council Regulation (EC) No 1/2003 of 16 December 2002 on the implementation of the rules on competition laid down in Articles 81 and 82 of the Treaty [2003] OJ L/1/1.

[4] Case T-24/90 *Automec v Commission* [1992] ECR II-2223. On this judgment see MC Baruffi, *La tutela dei singoli nei procedimenti amministrativi comunitar* (Milano, Giuffrè, 2001), 80 *ff* and the bibliography therein.

of the common market, b) the probability of establishing the existence of the infringement and c) the scope of the investigation required; and, secondly, a less specific criterion, constituted by all the circumstances of law and fact of each specific case.

## THE ATTENTION TO BE PAID TO THE CIRCUMSTANCES OF LAW AND FACT OF EACH SPECIFIC CASE AND THE RELEVANCE OF THE CESSATION OF THE VIOLATION

The application of this last criterion very soon gave rise to a dispute, in the *Ufex and Others v Commission* case, which led, first to a judgment of the CFI[5] and, later, to a judgment on appeal, of the ECJ.[6] This enabled the Courts to clarify the intensity of judicial control with respect to the application of this criterion.

Ufex had filed a complaint with the Commission concerning the logistic and commercial assistance which it claimed that the French postal administration, La Poste, had given to its subsidiary, the Société Française de Messageries Internationales (SFMI), operating in the international express mail sector. It affirmed that such an assistance constituted an abuse of dominant position within the meaning Article 82 EC. The Commission, in its answer to Ufex, explained it had decided to file the complaint because of lack of Community interest, as the alleged infringement had ceased. Furthermore, it pointed out that the infringement had ceased because of a decision in which the Commission had stated its non-opposition to the realisation of a concentration to which La Poste was a part and had imposed on the latter an obligation to offer any active operator in the international express mail sector ready to sign a contract with it, on the same conditions, the access facilities granted to SFMI.

The fact that the situation at issue had ceased because La Poste discontinued its preferential behaviour in favour of SFMI and accepted to expand its assistance to any other active operator in the sector was considered by the Commission as a relevant circumstance of fact in the case. It considered that there was no Community interest as the objective was to solve problems concerning the current and future competition in the field of international express mail and not that of intervening where the facts relate to the past.

The CFI rejected Ufex's action against the Commission's decision. In order to support the position of the Commission, it made reference to the nature of the interests which constitute a Community interest; it distinguished those which can be deemed as objective interests of the market – that is, that the market is competitive at present and in the future – from the subjective interests of the undertakings which introduce complaints – whose interests can concern also infringements of the past, as this can be useful for actions for compensation. It excluded, in general, a Community interest for the latter case as the 'essential

[5] Case T-77/95 *Ufex and Others v Commission* [1997] ECR II-1.

[6] Case C-119/97 P *Ufex and Others v Commission* [1999] ECR I-1341.

object' of pursuing such a case would be to make it easier for the complainants to prove liability in an action for damages in the national courts.

The Advocate General of the ECJ reacted strongly to the distinction made by the CFI between the objective interest of the market and the subjective interests of the complainants and the exclusion of a Community interest to pursue practices that have already ceased.[7] He contested that the interest of undertakings for the ascertainment of past infringement of competition law can be qualified as a distinct interest from the public interest to defend the competitive character of the market. According to the Advocate General the undertakings which complain perform a public function as they

> perform an activating function or, so to speak, act as catalysts for measures by the Commission involving two orders of interests – the interests of the undertakings themselves in averting commercial damage as a result of the unlawful practices of their competitors, and the general interest that the competition rules should be observed, an interest which is safeguarded by Community law and must be protected by the Commission. Where the latter interest exists (because the sector in question undoubtedly has a Community dimension and Community significance and it is relatively easy to detect the breach complained of in that sector, without the need for exceptional measures of investigation), it cannot be argued that the Commission's measures would only serve to produce evidence with a view to an action for damages in the national courts.[8]

The emphasis which the Advocate General placed on general interest that undertakings perform in introducing complaints and the fact that the ECJ took into account in the judgment in the case at issue as well as in subsequent cases had, indeed, some consequences. As I shall stress below, these two elements explain the rigidity with which the ECJ affirmed that the Commission, when denying the existence of a Community interest, must respect the right of the complainants to a detailed and reasoned answer.

## THE ACTIVATING FUNCTION TO BE RECOGNISED TO UNDERTAKINGS WHICH INTRODUCE COMPLAINTS

The opinion of the Advocate General in *Ufex and Others v Commission* had many repercussions. It led the ECJ to affirm that 'when deciding the order of priority for dealing with the complaints brought before it, the Commission may not regard as excluded in principle from its purview certain situations which come under the task entrusted to it by the Treaty';[9] and, with specific reference to the case at issue, it went on to specify that the Commission 'cannot rely solely on the fact that practices alleged to be contrary to the Treaty have ceased, without having ascertained that anti-competitive effects no longer continue and, if

[7] *Ibid* Opinion of Advocate General Ruiz-Jarabo Colomer.
[8] *Ibid* points 74 and 75.
[9] Case C-119/97 P *Ufex and Others v Commision*, n 6 above, para 92.

appropriate, that the seriousness of the alleged interferences with competition or the persistence of their consequences has not been such as to give the complaint a Community interest.'[10]

How, according to the Community Courts, should the Commission proceed in each specific case to determine the existence of a Community interest to launch the investigations required by a complaint? The basic conditions, as already seen, consist of the significance of the alleged infringement as regards the functioning of the common market, of the probability of establishing the existence of the infringement and of the scope of the investigation required. The CFI took into account these conditions in its recent judgment in *Scippacercola and Terezakis v Commission*,[11] where it affirmed:

> 1) the Commission is under an obligation to state reasons if it declines to continue with the examination of a complaint. Since the reasons stated must be sufficiently precise and detailed to enable the CFI effectively to review the Commission's use of its discretion to define priorities, the Commission must set out the facts justifying the decision and the legal considerations on the basis of which it was adopted[12] and
>
> 2) the judicial review of decisions to reject complaints must [...] focus[..] on whether or not the contested decision is based on materially incorrect facts, or is vitiated by an error of law, a manifest error of assessment or misuse of powers.[13]

As far as these conditions are concerned, it is particularly important that, in proceeding to the examination necessary to establish the existence of a Community interest, the Community judges do not confuse the analysis of the importance of an alleged violation of competition law for the functioning of the common market (or, in other words, of its incidence on the situation of competition in the Community) with the analysis of the presence of meaningful current or potential harm to Community trade. To the latter type of analysis Community judges might be called upon to proceed only where the Commission, once it has ascertained the existence of a Community interest in checking the conformity with Community law of a competitive practice, had really exercised such a check. The examination of the existence of a Community interest is carried out 'upstream' and implies an evaluation of quite a different type. It does not imply a verification of the existence of a concrete infringement of Articles 81 EC and 82 EC, but only requires the determination of whether the behaviour of an undertaking is detrimental to the functioning of the internal market.

[10] *Ibid* para 95.

[11] Case T-306/05 *Scippacercola and Terezakis v Commission*, judgment of 16 January 2008 unreported; confirmed on appeal by order of 25 March 2009 in Case C-159/08 P *Scippacercola and Terezakis v Commission* unreported.

[12] *Ibid* para 96.

[13] *Ibid* para 97.

THE EXECUTION OF ANTITRUST SANCTIONS BY MEMBER STATES' AUTHORITIES AND THE COMMISSION'S OBSERVATIONS BEFORE MEMBER STATES' COURTS

Turning to the activity that the Commission carries on 'downstream', that is, the concrete application of sanctions after the ascertainment of an infringement of Article 81 EC or 82 EC, the third sentence of Article 15(3) of Regulation No 1/2003 deserves special consideration. According to this provision, where the coherent application of Article 81 EC or 82 EC so requires, the Commission, acting on its own initiative, may submit written observations to courts of the Member States.

As regards the practical execution of sanctions in the internal legal orders of the Member States, it is worth considering whether the Commission may, *ex officio*, submit written observations to national courts when a problem of national law may arise before them. An example of this might be an individual company, part of a group which has been fined for violating competition law, which purports to deduct its share of the imposed fine from its taxable income. This question arises as some national courts have accepted such a deduction, considering that the fines essentially have the function of depriving the contravener of the profits obtained from the infringement of Articles 81 EC and 82 EC.[14]

Taking into account the risk that such case-law may have in limiting the dissuasive effect of fines in the Community law competition system,[15] can the Commission intervene under third sentence of Article 15(3) of Regulation No 1/2003?

One difficulty in admitting such an interpretation of the provision in question may result from the fact that it authorises the Commission to submit observations before national courts when 'the coherent application of Article 81 [EC] or 82 [EC]' requires while the fines are foreseen by acts – former Regulation No 17[16] and current Regulation No 1/2003 – which have been adopted by the Council on the basis of the competence attributed to it by Article 83 EC.

However, this difficulty must be considered in the light of a) the link which exists between Articles 81 EC and 82 EC, on the one hand, and Article 83 EC, on the other, and b) the differences between the notions of 'application' and 'interpretation' and the meaning which has to be given, on the whole, to the words 'application' and 'coherent'. The latter question also has to be considered in the light of other language versions of Regulation No 1/2003.

[14] In this respect, see Case C-429/07 *X* pending.

[15] On the main function of fines in repressing illicit behaviours and preventing repetition see Case 41/69 *ACF Chemiefarma v Commission* [1970] ECR I-661 para 173; Case C-308/04 P *SGL Carbon v Commission* [2006] ECR I-5977 para 37, and Case C-76/06 P *Britannia Alloys & Chemicals v Commission* [2007] ECR I-4405 para 22.

[16] Regulation No 17: First Regulation implementing Articles 85 and 86 of the Treaty [1962] OJ L/13/204.

## The Link which Exists between Articles 81 EC and 82 EC and Article 83 EC

As to point a) above, one cannot neglect the close link that exists between Articles 81 EC and 82 EC and Article 83 EC. In the Treaty system and in the concrete philosophy which inspires it Articles 81 EC and 82 EC cannot function and cannot be interpreted separately from Article 83 EC. A coherent application of Articles 81 EC and 82 EC requires that the right of the Commission to submit observations should extend also to a power to verify how fines are executed by national authorities. To exclude this would imply denial of the fact that fines constitute an indispensable tool for the application of those articles. This is all the more important as the regulation containing the provision in question marks the turning point from a particularly centralised application of Articles 81 EC and 82 EC to a decentralised application of competition law. This requires the setting up of mechanisms capable of ensuring an application which, as indicated in the Regulation No 1/2003, must be, not only 'coherent' but also 'uniform.'[17]

## The Different Language Versions of Article 15 of Regulation No 1/2003

As to point b) above, it must be noted that, even if, despite what has been stressed, one would prefer a merely literal interpretation of the provision in question, it would, first of all, be necessary to consider that it authorises the Commission to submit observations, on its own initiative, to national courts when this is demanded by a coherent 'application', and not 'interpretation', of Articles 81 EC and 82 EC. Whilst the word 'interpretation' would have more easily been prone to confine the possibility of intervention of the Commission to national judicial litigation addressing these articles, the word used in Article 15 of Regulation No 1/2003 concerns, in a broader sense, also litigation related to provisions of national law raising incidental questions of the understanding of Community provisions (such as those defining the nature of the fines to be imposed in the framework of Community competition law).

A broad meaning of the term 'coherent application' is, moreover, confirmed by the different language versions. If, in fact, the French text of this provision uses the adjective 'cohérente', the adjective 'uniform' is used in the Danish ('ensartede'), Italian ('uniforme') and Swedish ('enhetliga') versions and the word 'einheitliche' is found in the German version of the recitals 1, 14, 17, 21 and 22 of Regulation No 1/2003.

As the expression 'coherent application' (of Articles 81 EC and 82 EC) is used in the same sense as the expression 'uniform application' (which, undoubtedly, has a broader meaning), one must consider that the Commission is entitled to

[17] The word 'uniform' is used in the recital 22 and the title of Art 16 of Reg No 1/2003. On the passage from one to another type of application of these provisions see LF Pace, *Fondamenti del diritto antitrust europeo* (Milano, Giuffrè, 2005); A Adinolfi *et al*, *L'applicazione del diritto comunitario della concorrenza. Commentario del Regolamento n. 1/2003 del Consiglio del 16 dicembre 2002* (Milano, Giuffrè, 2007).

submit observations on its own initiative to national courts at any stage when the latter must refer to these provisions, including the situation in which they have to decide on a dispute of national law involving the scope of a concept of Community law, such as, for instance, that of fines imposed by the Commission in the framework of Articles 81 EC and 82 EC.

## Concluding Remarks

The above considerations lead me to think that the difficulties in giving a broad interpretation to the third sentence of Article 15(3) of Regulation No 1/2003 can be overcome. This is even more so because only such an interpretation can guarantee that the determination of an infringement of Articles 81 EC and 82 EC and the imposition of a fine is not frustrated by an inadequate interpretation of the concept of fine by a national court, when the latter is not a court of last instance and does not make use of its right to request a preliminary ruling from the ECJ on this point.

# 5

# *The Difficult Relationship between National Health Systems and EU Competition Rules*

OTTÓ CZÚCZ

## INTRODUCTION

Although Article 152(5) EC foresees that the organisation and provision of health care services is the responsibility of each Member State,[1] and before the entry into force of the Amsterdam Treaty in 1999 Community institutions had not even had a complementary role as regards national healthcare policies, certain Community norms have more recently started to penetrate these fields. It has been the Court of Justice of the European Communities (hereinafter ECJ) that has played a decisive role in this process. Particularly through the judicial application of the Treaty articles on fundamental freedoms, concerning the free movement of workers, goods, services and capital, and of EC competition law provisions, it has become obvious that national healthcare systems are also operating within a framework determined by Community norms. Thus such Community norms indirectly influence the functioning of these national structures. The resulting situation may be a source of serious uncertainty and controversy. It raises a question related to the ambiguity of shared responsibility between the European Community and its Member States, namely: how freely can a Member State make decisions when it intends to provide a widely accessible, effective and high quality healthcare system for its citizens? To what extent does a Member State need to take into consideration certain Community law provisions?

In this chapter I try to summarise – mainly on the basis of some landmark ECJ judgments – the conclusions that can be drawn so far as regards the application of EC competition rules to the functioning of healthcare systems. This may also help to predict the direction in which the relevant case-law is likely to evolve in the future.

The questions examined should be divided into two groups. First, the chapter provides an overview of the case-law relating to the conditions under which various healthcare systems should be regarded as undertakings. Later I shall examine how EC competition law may affect certain components of health care systems that otherwise are not considered as undertakings. The chapter will concentrate on cases concerning healthcare institutions. However, some exceptions will be made, as the ECJ has worked out important methods and assessment criteria while examining other insurance branches or social institutions as well.

## CASES WHERE NATIONAL HEALTHCARE SYSTEMS CAN OR CANNOT BE REGARDED AS UNDERTAKINGS

### The Basic Assessment Criteria...

Since the judgment in *Höfner and Elsner*[2] case in 1991, it has been clear that the competition law provisions can only be applied to organisations entrusted with the operation of services of general economic interest[3] if they are considered as undertakings. As Community law does not define the notion of 'undertaking', this task was left to the Community Courts. Although *Höfner and Elsner* case does not concern healthcare services, its study is still indispensable because this precedent was later used in many litigations related to healthcare services.

In Germany, the Bundesanstalt für Arbeit (BA), according to the legislation then in force, enjoyed exclusive rights to employment procurement. The financing of this activity was organised through the collection of contributions from employers and employees.

In the case of certain professions (which were determined by previous arrangement), however, the BA could also entrust other institutions or persons with employment procurement. Especially in the case of business executives, a special branch made up by recruitment consultants came into being. The BA issued a circular in which it declared that – under certain circumstances – it tolerated the activity of such consultants.

In this case, the ECJ had to give an answer to the question as to whether a recruitment consultancy entrusted with the operation of services of general economic interest which held exclusive rights granted by national legislation was to be regarded as an undertaking subject to EC competition law. The ECJ's answer was that

> in the context of competition law, first that the concept of an undertaking encompasses every entity engaged in an economic activity, regardless of the legal status of the entity and the way in which it is financed and, secondly, that employment procurement is an economic activity.[4]

[1] This was also reaffirmed by the ECJ in Case 238/82 *Duphar and Others* [1984] ECR 523 para 16.
[2] Case C-41/90 *Höfner and Elser* [1991] ECR I-1979.
[3] Art 86(2) EC.
[4] Case C-41/90 *Höfner and Elser*, n 2 above, para 21.

It added:

> [t]he fact that employment procurement activities are normally entrusted to public agencies cannot affect the economic nature of such activities. Employment procurement has not always been, and is not necessarily, carried out by public entities. That finding applies in particular to executive recruitment.[5]

What all this means is that in the eyes of the ECJ, it is not the legal status of the organisation providing services of general economic interest nor the institutional framework or the method of financing that is decisive in determining whether, from the point of view of competition law, an undertaking should be regarded as a public service, but the way in which it functions in practice. What proved to be a decisive factor was whether employment procurement could in practice be handled by other private institutions or not (despite the fact that legal provisions granted exclusive rights to certain institutions). This approach was confirmed by the *SAT Fluggesellschaft*[6] and the *Diego Calì & Figli*[7] judgments. In the first case, the ECJ ruled that '[t]aken as a whole, Eurocontrol's activities, by their nature, their aim and the rules to which they are subject, are connected with the exercise of powers relating to the control and supervision of air space which are typically those of a public authority.'[8] Furthermore, the ECJ noted that '[s]uch surveillance is connected by its nature, its aim and the rules to which it is subject with the exercise of powers relating to the protection of the environment which are typically those of a public authority'. On this basis, it came to the conclusion that '[i]t is not of an economic nature justifying the application of the Treaty rules on competition.'[9] This functional approach – as Lenaerts notes[10] – became problematic when it was applied to social security institutions.

## …and Its Use in Basic National Healthcare Institutions…

The first case in which the ECJ had to decide on the status of a healthcare system (social security system) under community competition law was *Poucet and Pistre* case.[11] In this case, two French citizens (without actually disputing the legality of an insurance obligation) raised objections to the fact that they had to fulfil their obligations with a certain insurance company and they were prevented from choosing another one. The ECJ stated that:

> [s]ickness funds, and the organisations involved in the management of the public social security system, fulfil an exclusively social function. That activity is based on

[5] *Ibid* para 22.
[6] Case C-364/92 *SAT Fluggesellschaft* [1994] ECR I-43.
[7] Case C-343/95 *Diego Calì & Figli* [1997] ECR I-1547.
[8] Case C-364/92 *SAT Fluggesellschaft,* n 6 above.
[9] *Ibid* para 23.
[10] K Lenaerts, 'Droit communautaire et soins de santé: Les grandes lignes de la jurisprudence de la Cour de Justice des Communautés européennes'( www.ose.be/workshop/files/LenaertsFR.pdf).
[11] Joined Cases C-159/91 and C-160/91 *Poucet and Pistre* [1993] ECR I-637.

> the principle of national solidarity and is entirely non-profit-making. The benefits paid are statutory benefits bearing no relation to the amount of the contributions [...] that activity is not an economic activity and, therefore, the organisations to which it is entrusted are not undertakings.[12]

It follows from the reasoning of the ECJ that Community competition law rules do not apply to these national institutions, if and only if they fulfil the following criteria:

> i. Those schemes pursue a social objective and embody the principle of solidarity.
>
> ii. They are intended to provide cover for all the persons to whom they apply, against the risks of sickness, old age, death and invalidity, regardless of their financial status and their state of health at the time of affiliation.
>
> iii. The principle of solidarity is, in the sickness and maternity scheme, embodied in the fact that the scheme is financed by contributions proportional to the income from the occupation and to the retirement pensions of the persons making them; only recipients of an invalidity pension and retired insured members with very modest resources are exempted from the payment of contributions, whereas the benefits are identical for all those who receive them. Furthermore, persons no longer covered by the scheme retain their entitlement to benefits for a year, free of charge. Solidarity entails the redistribution of income between those who are better off and those who, in view of their resources and state of health, would be deprived of the necessary social cover [...].
>
> iv.Finally, there is solidarity between the various social security schemes, in that those in surplus contribute to the financing of those with structural financial difficulties.

The ECJ confirmed this case-law in several later judgments.

In *García and Others*,[13] for example, the ECJ had to decide, whether the scope of the EC directive concerning direct insurance other than life assurance[14] also comprises insurance related to self-employment in non-agricultural production on French territory. The plaintiffs, disputing the legality of the decisions that required the payment of their contributions, alleged that the monopoly in the field of social security created by French lawmakers was incompatible with Community norms. They argued that in many other countries the same goal is achieved partly or fully through private voluntary insurance in contrast to the French compulsory insurance system.

The ECJ – referring to the *Poucet and Pistre* judgment – reiterated its position by ruling that

> social security schemes which are based on the principle of solidarity, require compulsory contributions in order to ensure that the principle of solidarity is applied

[12] *Ibid* para 18.

[13] Case C-238/94 *García and Others* [1996] ECR I-1673.

[14] Council Directive 92/49/EEC of 18 June 1992 on the coordination of laws, regulations and administrative provisions relating to direct insurance other than life assurance and amending Directives 73/239/EEC and 88/357/EEC (third non-life insurance Directive) [1992] OJ L/228/1.

and that their financial equilibrium is maintained. If Article 2(2) of Directive 92/49/EEC were to be interpreted in the manner contemplated by the national tribunal, the obligation to contribute would be removed and the schemes in question would thus be unable to survive.[15]

On this basis, the ECJ considered that the social insurance schemes that satisfy the above criteria do not qualify as an undertaking and thus do not fall within the scope of the private insurance directive.

On the basis of these judgments, it appears that the ECJ created an unambiguous and consistent case-law as regards schemes belonging to national basic healthcare services ('first pillar systems'): these structures do not fall within the scope of EC competition law. The picture is, however, more complex (as Jacquemin[16] also notes) where institutions belonging to the complementary ('second pillar') systems are concerned.

## ...and Their Application to the Complementary (Second Pillar) Insurance Institutions

The judgment in *Fédération française des sociétés d'assurance and Others*[17] *(FFSA)* case followed the *Poucet and Pistre* logic. This was the first case where the ECJ had to decide whether an institution belonging to the second pillar was to be considered as an undertaking. The plaintiffs requested the annulment of the provisions concerning the voluntary supplementary retirement insurance for self-employed farmers (Coreva scheme), arguing that the new institution that had been granted monopoly (the 'Caisse Centrale de la Mutualité Sociale Agricole' or CCMSA) had obtained such a competitive advantage, through the granting of tax benefits to its members, that rival insurance companies were threatened with bankruptcy.

The ECJ first of all stated that the new institution was characterised by the following features:

> membership of the Coreva scheme is optional, that the scheme operates in accordance with the principle of capitalisation, and that the benefits to which it confers entitlement depend solely on the amount of contributions paid by the recipients and the financial results of the investments made by the managing organisation. The CCMSA therefore carries on an economic activity in competition with life assurance companies.[18]

So the so-called solidarity principle plays a very restricted role in this structure because:

> the principle of solidarity is reflected in this case by the fact that contributions are not linked to the risks incurred, by the placing of resources corresponding to the

[15] Case C-238/94 *García and Others*, n 13 above, para 14.
[16] A Jacquemin, 'Le droit de la concurrence et les systèmes de soins de santé' in P Nihoul and A-C Simon (eds), *L'Europe et les soins de santé* (Brussels, Larcier, 2005) 236.
[17] Case C-244/94 *Fédération française des sociétés d'assurance and Others* [1995] ECR I-4013.
[18] *Ibid* para 17.

> contributions paid at the disposal of the scheme in the event of the premature death of a member, by a mechanism for granting exemption from payment of contributions in the event of illness, and by the temporary suspension of payment of contributions for reasons connected with the economic situation of the holding. Such provisions already exist in certain group life assurance policies, or may be included therein.[19]

Based on the foregoing, it came to the conclusion that such institutions, despite the fact that they pursue social aims, do qualify as undertakings from the point of view of EC competition law.

Although *Albany*[20] was not concerned with healthcare either, it should nevertheless be mentioned, because it later proved to be a guide in the shaping of the case-law in this field. In this case a Dutch textile company refused to pay the contribution due to a supplementary pension fund that embraced the whole textile sector and was made compulsory by a collective agreement. It argued that on the one hand, this would be contrary to Community competition law and that, on the other hand, it would result in less favourable conditions than under a previous voluntary insurance scheme. The ECJ, after taking into consideration that '[t]he sectoral pension fund itself determines the amount of the contributions and benefits and the Fund operates in accordance with the principle of capitalisation,'[21] concluded: 'the fact that the fund is non-profit-making and the manifestations of solidarity are not sufficient to deprive the sectoral pension fund of its status as an undertaking within the meaning of the competition rules of the Treaty.'[22]

The *Cisal*[23] case produced the same result. In this case the ECJ had to consider a compulsory insurance scheme designed for non-agricultural employees against accident and occupation related diseases that forms a part of the Italian social welfare system.

The litigation in question arose from the fact that in 1998 Cisal refused to pay the compulsory accident insurance contribution for one of its staff, Mr Battistello, on the grounds that since 1986 Mr Battisello had already been insured by another private insurance company and thus Italian law was granting INAIL (Istituto Nazionale per l'Assicurazione contro gli Infortuni sul Lavoro) a monopoly incompatible with EC competition law.

After examining the system's characteristic features, the ECJ held that this structure pursues social objectives because

> [s]uch a scheme is intended to provide all the persons protected with cover against the risks of accidents at work and occupational diseases, irrespective of any fault which may have been committed by the victim, or by the employer, and therefore without any need for civil liability to be incurred by the person drawing benefits in respect of the risk activity.[24]

[19] *Ibid* para 19.
[20] Case C-67/96 *Albany* [1999] ECR I-5751.
[21] *Ibid* para 81.
[22] *Ibid* para 85.
[23] Case C-218/00 *Cisal* [2002] ECR I-691.
[24] *Ibid* para 35.

It added that

> the social aim of that insurance scheme is highlighted by the fact that benefits are paid even when the contributions due have not been paid, which obviously contributes to the protection of all insured workers against the economic consequences of accidents at work or occupational diseases.[25]

Furthermore, it maintained that the elements of solidarity can be identified in the system as:

> [t]he insurance scheme is financed by contributions the rate of which is not systematically proportionate to the risk insured. For example, it is clear from the case file that the rate may not exceed a maximum ceiling, even where the activity carried out entails a high risk, the balance of financing being born by all the undertakings in the same category as regards the risk run. Furthermore, contributions are calculated not only on the basis of the risk linked to the activity of the undertaking concerned but also according to the insured persons' earnings. Second, the amount of benefits paid is not necessarily proportionate to the insured persons' earnings, since, for the calculation of pensions, only salaries situated between a minimum and a maximum corresponding to the average nationwide salary, decreased or increased by 30 %, may be taken into consideration.[26]

On these grounds, the ECJ came to the conclusion that the INAIL has an exclusively social function and thus cannot be regarded as an undertaking under EC competition law.

The *Brentjens'*[27] and *Drijvende Bokken*[28] cases were also related to fields outside healthcare provisions yet they carry important information on the reasoning of the ECJ in qualifying as undertakings institutions of supplementary pension fund insurance made obligatory by collective contracts.

In both cases the litigation arose from the fact that the companies in question refused for a certain period of time to pay the compulsory contributions to insurance companies assigned to them, arguing that they had already had a more advantageous insurance with another company and that the assigned insurance company's monopoly was incompatible with EC competition law rules.

First, the ECJ held that the Dutch pension system is composed of a three-pillared structure, in which the first pillar is formed by the statutory basic pension. The second pillar is additional to the first, it embraces pensions for both employees and the self-employed, generally organised by sectors of the economy and on the basis of collective negotiations. The third pillar consists of voluntary individual pension or life insurance. The pension structures concerned in the case belonged to the second pillar.

Secondly, the ECJ yet again summed up the *FFSA* test and held that:

> [o]ptional affiliation, application of the principle of capitalisation and the fact that benefits depended solely on the amount of the contributions paid by the beneficiaries

[25] *Ibid* para 36.
[26] *Ibid* paras 39 and 40.
[27] Joined Cases C-115/97 to C-117/97 *Brentjens'* [1999] ECR I-6025.
[28] Case C-219/97 *Drijvende Bokken* [1999] ECR I-6121.

> and on the financial results of the investments made by the managing organisation implied that that organisation carried on an economic activity in competition with life assurance companies. Neither the social objective pursued, nor the fact that it was non-profit-making, nor the requirements of solidarity, nor the other rules concerning, in particular, the restrictions to which the managing organisation was subject in making investments altered the fact that the managing organisation was carrying on an economic activity.[29]

Thirdly, after examining the system's general characteristics, it stated that:

> [t]he sectoral pension fund itself determines the amount of the contributions and benefits and the Fund operates in accordance with the principle of capitalisation.[...] the amount of the benefits provided by the Fund depends on the financial results of the investments made by it, in respect of which it is subject, like an insurance company, to supervision by the Insurance Board.[30]

On the basis of the above, it concluded that the Dutch complementary pension funds operating within the system's second pillar were to be regarded as undertakings from the point of view of EC competition law.

The ECJ reached a similar conclusion in *Pavlov and Others*,[31] in which it examined whether a supplementary pension fund was to be considered as an undertaking, and held that:

> [a] pension fund, such as that in question in the main proceedings, which itself determines the amount of the contributions and benefits and operates on the basis of the principle of capitalisation, which has been made responsible for managing a supplementary pension scheme set up by a profession's representative body and membership of which has been made compulsory by the public authorities for all members of that profession, is an undertaking within the meaning of Articles [81 EC, 82 EC and 86 EC].[32]

Finally, a very recent case should be mentioned, in which the ECJ examined whether the German institutions providing insurance against accidents at work and occupational diseases, to which affiliation is compulsory, are to be regarded as undertakings. In the *Kattner Stahlbau*[33] judgment, the ECJ first of all stated that:

> [e]mployers' liability insurance associations such as MMB are involved, as public law bodies, in the management of the German social security system and that, in this respect, they fulfil a social function, which is entirely non-profit-making.[34]

Furthermore it held that:

> [t]he scheme is intended to provide all the persons protected with cover against the risks of accidents at work and occupational diseases, irrespective of any fault which may

[29] Joined Cases C-115/97 to C-117/97, *Brentjens'*, n 27 above, para 79.
[30] *Ibid* paras 81 and 82.
[31] Joined Cases C-180/98 to C-184/98 *Pavlov and Others* [2000] ECR I-6451.
[32] *Ibid* para 119.
[33] Case C-350/07 *Kattner Stahlbau*, judgment of 5 March 2009 nyr.
[34] *Ibid* para 35.

> have been committed by the victim or by the employer and therefore without any need to examine the question of the civil liability of the person drawing benefits in respect of the risk activity. [...] the social aim of such a scheme is also highlighted by the fact that, as the documents before the [ECJ] show, benefits are paid even when the contributions due have not been paid.[35]

To sum up the above, it is clear that, when examining the applicability of EC competition law to national institutions providing healthcare services, the central issue in the ECJ's analysis is whether those institutions can be regarded as undertakings. In the case of national institutions which provide basic services that reflect elements of solidarity (meaning that they strive to provide services to all the insured members regardless of their financial or health-related situation or the length of time they have been members), the ECJ consistently rules out the application of EC competition law. In these structures strong redistribution mechanisms are present (as the affiliated persons contribute proportionally while they obtain healthcare services according to their physical state; thus people with higher income take a bigger part in the financing of the healthcare system). In order to maintain the balance in the system, the use of state power for public purposes (compulsory membership, collection of contributions in the way tax is collected) is indeed indispensable. Institutions that display these characteristics are not considered to be undertakings.

The situation is more complex in countries where the healthcare system is structured horizontally or vertically and in which there is competition between the services of healthcare institutions belonging to the second or the third pillar. It appears that in these cases the ECJ also makes its decision based on the extent to which the principle of solidarity and the redistribution are present. In the case of institutions where redistribution is highly characteristic, that is there is no correlation between the contribution paid by the insured person and the accessible supplementary or additional services, hence their functioning cannot be ensured without state power, the ECJ usually holds that they are not undertakings.

On the other hand when it comes to institutions where there is a better balance between contributions and accessible services, and thus no intervention of state power is required (even if in some cases the scheme also follows social aims), the ECJ usually comes to the conclusion that such an institution is to be qualified as an undertaking subject to EC competition law.

There has not yet been any litigation before the ECJ concerning a voluntary supplementary healthcare institution belonging to the third pillar, but there is little doubt that the ECJ would qualify it as an undertaking.

[35] *Ibid* paras 40 and 41.

## COULD CERTAIN ELEMENTS OF THE HEALTHCARE SYSTEM BE CONSIDERED SEPARATELY?

The question has arisen whether, in the case of a healthcare institution which as a whole is not qualified as an undertaking, certain constituent parts could be detached and be subjected to the application of EC competition law. The ECJ has dealt with several such cases and this chapter will provide a brief overview of three of them.

First, the *Ambulanz Glöckner*[36] judgment must be mentioned. The litigation arose from a dispute concerning a modification in German legislation that allowed the local authorities to refuse to deliver service authorisations for companies active in traditional patient transportation services, in situations where the reserve capacity of public emergency ambulance service providers in the same area was sufficient to satisfy demand, not only for the latter services but also for traditional patient transportation services which could be calculated in advance.

In 1994, following an inquiry by the relevant authorities, emergency services in the given area had declared that their reserve capacities were not sufficiently used and thus Ambulanz Glöckner's service authorisation was not renewed as it had been in previous years. The explanation for the refusal was that the granting of the authorisation would have resulted in unused capacities which would have damaged the profitability of companies obliged to provide emergency services. The ECJ held in its judgment that: '[t]he [...] emergency transport services and patient transport service [...] have not always been, and are not necessarily, carried on by public authorities' [37] and so 'the provision of emergency transport services and patient transport services, [entities such as the medical aid organisations] must therefore be treated as undertakings within the meaning of the competition rules laid down by the Treaty.'[38]

The ECJ moreover declared that:

> an abuse within the meaning of Article 86 of the Treaty is committed where, without any objective necessity, an undertaking holding a dominant position on a particular market reserves to itself an ancillary activity which could be carried out by another undertaking as part of its activities on a neighbouring but separate market, with the possibility of eliminating all competition from that undertaking.[39]

In this judgment the ECJ thus considered that the patient transportation services in question were detachable from the healthcare services and so fell under the control of EC competition law.

In *AOK Bundesverband and Others*[40] the question was whether a new German healthcare law provision obliging healthcare funds to pay fixed maximum

[36] Case C-475/99 *Ambulanz Glöckner* [2001] ECR I-8089.

[37] *Ibid* para 20.

[38] *Ibid* para 22.

[39] *Ibid* paras 40 and 43.

[40] Joined Cases C-264/01, C-306/01, C-354/01 and C-355/01 *AOK Bundesverband and Others* [2004] ECR I-2493.

amounts when purchasing certain pharmaceutical products was against Community norms or not. The pharmaceutical companies and distributors found this legal practice injurious. In this case too, the ECJ had to answer whether the healthcare funds or their association could be regarded as an undertaking within the meaning of Articles 81 EC and 82 EC. The pharmaceutical companies considered that the healthcare funds are clearly undertakings, as they are in intense competition with each other in three areas, namely: the amount of contributions; the definition of the services provided; and the organisation and management of services.

Having examined the specific details of the German healthcare structure, the ECJ –contrary to Advocate General Jacobs' opinion[41] – held that:

> they fulfil an exclusively social function, which is founded on the principle of national solidarity and is entirely non-profit-making. [...] the sickness funds are compelled by law to offer to their members essentially identical obligatory benefits which do not depend on the amount of the contributions. The funds therefore have no possibility of influence over those benefits. [...] the sickness funds are joined together in a type of community founded on the basis of solidarity ('Solidargemeinschaft') which enables an equalisation of costs and risks between them. In accordance with Paragraph 265 et seq. of SGB V, an equalisation is thus effected between the sickness funds whose health expenditure is lowest and those which insure costly risks and whose expenditure connected with those risks is highest. [...] The sickness funds are therefore not in competition with one another or with private institutions as regards grant of the obligatory statutory benefits in respect of treatment or medicinal products which constitutes their main function.[42]

The ECJ ruled that the German healthcare funds could not be regarded as undertakings.

The ECJ then examined whether the definition of the fixed maximum amounts by the fund association is linked with its social functions or should be rather qualified as external economic activities. The ECJ concluded that:

> in determining the fixed maximum amounts, the fund associations merely perform a task for management of the German social security system which is imposed upon them by legislation and that they do not act as undertakings engaging in economic activity.[43]

In other words, the ECJ did not find the activity detachable from the basic function.

The ECJ reached a similar conclusion in the *FENIN v Commission*[44] case. In this particular case both the Court of First Instance of the European Communities (hereinafter CFI) and the ECJ had to give an answer to the question of whether an abuse of dominant position was present if Spain's national healthcare system (SNS) made a substantially delayed payment for pharmaceuticals and medical

[41] *Ibid* Opinion of Advocate General Jacobs.

[42] Joined Cases C-264/01, C-306/01, C-354/01 and C-355/01 *AOK Bundesverband and Others*, n 40 above, paras 51–54.

[43] *Ibid* para 64.

[44] Case C-205/03 P *FENIN v Commission* [2006] ECR I-6295.

devices bought from FENIN's trade unions. Before taking a decision, both Courts had to decide whether the SNS could be qualified as an undertaking. Following a negative conclusion, the Courts also had to decide whether the SNS was regarded as an undertaking when it appeared on the market as a buyer of healthcare products necessary for its activities. The CFI stated that:

> an organisation which purchases goods - even in great quantity - not for the purpose of offering goods and services as part of an economic activity, but in order to use them in the context of a different activity, such as one of a purely social nature, does not act as an undertaking simply because it is a purchaser in a given market.[45]

The ECJ agreed[46] - in this case also contrary to Advocate General Poiares Maduro's opinion.[47] The Courts thus considered that the purchasing activity could not be detached from the basic functions of healthcare providers.

These three judgments do not form a case-law solid enough to draw any definitive conclusions. However, it can be stated that the ECJ regards certain elements of the national healthcare system's activity as detachable only if they have already appeared as independent undertakings in the practice of the given country. On the other hand, when the activities in question are closely connected to the functioning of the given healthcare institution's activity, the ECJ refuses this separation. If a Member State is obliged to ensure a wide range of healthcare services, (even if the demand is uncertain and the funding is limited), the institutions have to face a multitude of difficult decisions. In such cases, regarding their responsibility for their service's 'downstream' side, they are not in a position to decide as freely as other market participants. However, according to the abovementioned ECJ judgments, the same applies to the so-called 'upstream' side of their functioning, when they appear as buyers of healthcare goods and services on the market. Their freedom to make decisions is also limited in this respect, therefore this part of their activity can not be regarded separately either.

## SUMMARY

It emerges from this brief overview that the relationship between national healthcare systems and EC competition law is very complex. On the basis of the existing case-law, it can be concluded that the ECJ classifies national basic healthcare institutions that follow the principle of solidarity and carry out extensive redistribution as 'services of general economic interest' and thus it exempts them from a competition law examination. This case-law is likely to continue in the foreseeable future. The assessment of institutions belonging to the second pillar is somewhat more complex. Finally, the situation is again simpler in the case of the institutions which are part of the third pillar and which

[45] Case T-319/99 *FENIN v Commission* [2003] ECR II-357 paras 36 and 37.
[46] Case C-205/03 P *FENIN v Commission*, n 44 above, para 28.
[47] *Ibid* Opinion of Advocate General Poiares Maduro.

provide supplementary services on a voluntary basis. They have to be regarded as part of the competitive sector.

Of all the questions examined, as seen from some Advocate Generals' opinions, the most difficult is to determine whether certain elements can be detached. One might expect that the ECJ will refine its case-law in this regard in the future.

New questions will, however, surely arise. According to certain experts,[48] the triggering event may be that many Member States want to reform the efficacy and the cost-efficiency of the healthcare system with partial privatisation, through the introduction of so-called 'public-private partnerships'.

Other experts[49] take the view that following the ECJ's *Watts*[50] judgment, a patient migration might occur, making it necessary to put an end to the immunity of general solidarity-based national healthcare schemes to EC competition law. Whatever direction these challenges may take in the future, it will clearly be the ECJ (and in certain cases the CFI) that has to find a solution until the EU legislator provides an adequate legal framework.

[48] J Lear and E Mossialos, 'Competition law and health services' (2008) 3 *Euro Observer* 5.

[49] A Cygan, 'Public healthcare in the European Union: Still a service of general interest' (2008) 57 *International and Comparative Law Quarterly* 529.

[50] Case C-372/04 *Watts* [2006] ECR I-4325.

6

# *Obsession with Justice – Competition Law Infringements and Their Perpetrators*

NILS WAHL

## INTRODUCTION

Not so long ago competition law infringements in the European Union were punished by fines that were perceived as high compared to punishments meted out for infringements of other economic rules. Yet, the fines might not have been high compared to the potential gains or the losses inflicted upon economic efficiency. Nowadays, fines for competition law infringements in the European Union have lost all contact with the financial consequences for infringements of other economic rules within the Union or in its member States. In fact, on occasion it would seem as if the fines imposed would measure up to the potential or actual deterioration of economic efficiency multiplied with the risk of detection, thus bordering on what could be labelled as optimal sanctions.[1]

To some extent this development could be explained as a consequence of an increased awareness of the importance of a competition policy for the well-functioning of an economy, and – perhaps – given this, the idea that no one should escape conviction nor fines.[2]

All the same, the Community legal system is based upon the rule of law. From this follows that infringements need to be proven to the requisite legal standard. Given the magnitude of sanctions that might follow infringements, the Court of Justice of the European Communities (hereinafter ECJ) has repeatedly explained

[1] Cf G Becker, 'Crime and Punishment: an Economic Approach' (1968) 2 *The journal of Political Economy* 169, and G Stigler, 'The Optimum Enforcement of Law' (1970) 3 *The journal of Political Economy* 526.

[2] See, eg Joined Cases 29/83 and 30/83 *Compagnie royale asturienne des mines and Rheinzink v Commission* [1984] ECR 1679 paras 6–9.

that this implies a presumption of innocence for those subject to investigation.[3] However, every presumption of innocence also entails a clear definition of what is prohibited. Without a clear and concise view on the content of a prohibition a presumption of innocence is meaningless. Moreover, it has to be clear beyond doubt who should be held accountable for proven infringements.

Although the competition rules of the EC Treaty are fairly understandable when it comes to what they actually prohibit, notwithstanding the occasional need for interpretation, clear definitions of the perpetrators are lacking. Thus it has been for the Community judiciary, and especially the ECJ to clarify who should be held liable for infringements of Community competition law. These clarifications – it is submitted – follow different roads. On occasion the ECJ takes a more formal approach and on others a practical or functional one. The question now is whether these clarifications also follow different rationales.

This article deals with the question of who should be held accountable and responsible for competition law infringements and to what extent the clarifications are mutually coherent. As examples some recent judgments by the ECJ and the Court of First Instance of the European Communities (hereinafter CFI) will be used. The subject in itself can be divided into three interrelated, but distinct questions: under which circumstances may an entity fall outside the scope of the competition rules due to its field of activity, who should be held accountable for competition law infringements although not being a competitor and, finally, who should pay the fines.

## FIRST QUESTION – THE FORMAL APPROACH

The Community competition rules only apply to *undertakings*, a term not defined in the EC Treaty. However, as follows from the well known case of *Höfner and Elser*,[4] the term 'undertaking' encompasses all entities which are engaged in economic activity, no matter their legal form and method of finance. Economic activity as such has been defined by the ECJ as 'any activity consisting in offering goods and services on a given market'.[5] Although the definition in itself would seem to be all encompassing, it is clear from case-law that certain undertakings and certain activities fall outside. It is equally clear that the definition of an undertaking tends to lay focus on the activity (economic or non-economic) performed rather than on the entity itself.

Generally speaking state activities have been held by the ECJ to fall outside the definition if the activities constitute the essential function of a state, thus commercial activities are not included in the exception merely because they are carried out by the state.[6] Other exceptions are activities based on principles of

[3] Case C-199/92 P *Hüls v Commission* [1999] ECR I-4287 paras 149 and 150, and Case C-235/92 P *Montecatini v Commission* [1999] ECR I-4539 paras 175 and 176.

[4] Case C-41/90 *Höfner and Elser* [1991] ECR I-1979 para 21.

[5] Case 118/85 *Commission v Italy* [1987] ECR 2599 para 7.

[6] Case C-343/95 *Diego Calì & Figli* [1997] ECR I-1547 paras 22–24.

solidarity and of a social character, which are generally to be considered to be outside the scope of economic activity.[7]

The first exception concerning state activities would seem to be rather clear cut – if the activity in question forms part of the essential function of a state, it cannot at the same time constitute an economic activity even if it would happen to involve economic transactions.[8] The behaviour of an entity engaged in such activity is not guided by concerns related to competition, wherefore an application of competition law would not render the desired results, while at the same time possibly jeopardising the other objectives.

The other exemption is less self-explanatory; or perhaps more correctly, the way the exemption is applied is less unambiguous. As stated certain activities of a purely, or mainly social character fall outside the definition of the competition rules since the entity in question is not considered to be an undertaking. Some of the leading cases in this respect are the joint cases of *Poucet and Pistre*, in which the ECJ declared that:

> [s]ickness funds, and the organisations involved in the management of the public social security system, fulfil an exclusively social function. That activity is based on the principle of national solidarity and is entirely non-profit-making. The benefits paid are statutory benefits bearing no relation to the amount of the contributions. Accordingly, that activity is not an economic activity and, therefore, the organisations to which it is entrusted are not undertakings within the meaning of Articles [81 EC and 82 EC].[9]

Subsequent developments included cases such as *Fédération française des sociétés d'assurance and Others*[10] and *Albany*.[11] In these cases the ECJ can be said to have confirmed its ruling in *Poucet and Pistre*, although the outcomes were the opposite given the diminished degree of solidarity in the systems in question. No matter what one's beliefs are as concerns the applicability of Article 86 EC (and the possibility of granting exemptions for certain activities) to situations like the ones now in question, it would seem clear that competition law should not be the guiding principle in these cases. In fact, an application of competition law principles to these activities could jeopardise the activities, without necessarily bringing the benefits normally associated with a strict competition law regime. The question remains, however, if the same could also be said about the case of *FENIN v Commission* decided in July 2006.[12]

The facts of *FENIN v Commission* were fairly clear. An association of undertakings selling medical equipment (FENIN) tried to interest the European Commission to take action against several bodies or organisations providing health care (SNS), for an alleged abuse of a dominant position regarding their

[7] Joined Cases C-264/01, C-306/01, C-354/01 and C-355/01 *AOK Bundesverband and Others* [2004] ECR I-2493 paras 51–55.

[8] Case C-364/92 *SAT Fluggesellschaft* [1994] ECR I-43.

[9] Joined Cases C-159/91 and C-160/91 *Poucet and Pistre* [1993] ECR I-637 paras 18 and 19.

[10] Case C-244/94 *Fédération française des sociétés d'assurance and Others* [1995] ECR I-4013.

[11] Case C-67/96 *Albany* [1996] ECR I-5751.

[12] Case C-205/03 P *FENIN v Commission* [2006] ECR I-6295.

purchasing practices. The Commission refused for the reason that SNS in the Commission's view did not act as an undertaking. According to the Commission, the purchasing activities of the SNS could not be dissociated from the subsequent use of the purchased equipment, that is, the provision of free health care which was considered a non-economic activity. On appeal the CFI accepted this reasoning and stated that:

> [i]t is the activity consisting in offering goods and services on a given market that is the characteristic feature of an economic activity [...] not the business of purchasing, as such. Thus, as the Commission has argued, it would be incorrect, when determining the nature of that subsequent activity, to dissociate the activity of purchasing goods from the subsequent use to which they are put. The nature of the purchasing activity must therefore be determined according to whether or not the subsequent use of the purchased goods amounts to an economic activity.[13]

Upon appeal the ECJ confirmed the approach of linking purchasing activity with subsequent use as done by the CFI.[14]

Taking as a starting point that some activities should not be subject to competition law, notably in this case the provision of free health care on the basis of principles of solidarity, does this really explain why also the preceding activity of purchasing should be exempted?

In its judgment, as confirmed by the ECJ, the CFI put emphasis on what actually constitutes economic activity – namely the activity of offering goods and services, not necessarily purchasing activity. The latter activity would instead be categorised according to its subsequent use. Although the reasoning follows from case-law invoked by the CFI, it does not really give any reasons for treating purchasing differently as compared to selling, and admittedly previous case-law concerning economic activity did not purport to give an exhaustive answer on what would constitute economic activity.[15] One possibility is of course that the CFI and the ECJ were of the opinion that all purchasing activity for final use should be outside the scope of competition law, as would seem to have been suggested by the Advocate General.[16] Another, and it is submitted more likely, explanation is that the ECJ did not rule out competition law implications for all kinds of purchasing activities for final use. Instead the ECJ made a clear connection with the subsequent use and indicated that the nature of that use should be the decisive factor. Thus, if the later use is not of an economic nature, the purchasing activity is neither.

This approach may be perceived as formalistic since it gives more weight to the formal circumstances of the case, without really paying any attention to potential effects on competition. It is of course possible to say that notwithstanding

[13] Case T-319/99 *FENIN v Commission* [2003] ECR II-357 para 36.

[14] Case C-205/03 P *FENIN v Commission*, n 12 above, para 26.

[15] W-H Roth, 'Case annotation C-205/03 Fenin' (2007) 44 *Common Market Law Review* 1131, at 1136 *ff*.

[16] Opinion of Advocate General Poiares Maduro in Case C-205/03 P *FENIN v Commission*, n 12 above, point 66.

any potential competition problems, these should not play any role when it comes to activities clearly outside the sphere of economic activity. In fact, the potential problems should perhaps not be classified as competition problems since competition does not play its usual role within this field, just as the case with activities constituting the essential function of a state. All the same, it is submitted that competition law problems might occur in connection with purchasing activity connected to non-economic activity.[17] However, by excluding an application of the competition rules by means of not classifying the entities in question as undertakings, the ECJ drew a clear line for the benefit of legal certainty. No doubt, it is easier for all parties concerned to know the limits for the applicability of the competition rules if something is clearly outside as compared to simply being granted an exemption according to Article 86 EC.

## SECOND QUESTION – THE TELEOLOGICAL APPROACH

In spite of its approach towards activities constituting the essential function of a state or to activities of a social character, the Community judiciaries' approach towards granting other exemptions from the applicability of the competition rules have in legal literature been perceived as reluctant.[18] Be that as it may, it is by all accounts evident that not many potential activities by an undertaking escape scrutiny under the competition rules. On the other hand it has often been thought that in order to infringe the competition rules, notably Article 81 EC, by means of entering into an agreement with someone else, the perpetrators need to be at least potential competitors. In a recent case from the CFI, that was, however, not the situation. If the CFI's acceptance of the Commission's approach is accepted by the ECJ, not in this case, since it was not appealed, but on a later occasion, the boundaries for the applicability of the competition rules will have been stretched quite considerably.

In the case of *AC-Treuhand v Commission*[19] the Commission had fined the company AC-Treuhand for taking part in cartel activities. The Commission did so even though AC-Treuhand was neither a producer of the products in question nor a producer of any substitute product. Instead AC-Treuhand fulfilled certain secretarial and administrative duties for the cartel members. AC-Treuhand was thus not part of the cartel agreement, although it was the legal successor of a company that had agreed with the cartel members to administer certain parts of the illegal activities, primarily statistical matters. AC-Treuhand had also on occasion participated in meetings of the cartel members and functioned as moderator or chairman of certain meetings, although the extent of this was disputed between the parties.

[17] FM Scherer and D Ross, *Industrial Market Structure and Economic Performance*, 3rd edn (Boston, Houghton Mifflin, 1990) 519 *ff*.

[18] J Faull and A Nikpay, *The EC Law of Competition*, 2nd edn (London, Oxford University Press, 2007) 190.

[19] Case T-99/04 *AC-Treuhand v Commission*, judgment of 8 July 2008 nyr.

On appeal to the CFI, the applicant's primary argument was that the Commission in finding AC-Treuhand responsible for the cartel infringement as such had violated the principle of *nullum crimen, nulla poena sine lege.* According to the applicant the Commission should have taken account of the fact that AC-Treuhand did not act as a perpetrator, but merely as an accomplice, something that according to AC-Treuhand should not be punishable.

Following the applicant's line of argumentation the CFI set out first to determine to what extent it was necessary to make a distinction between a perpetrator and an undertaking whose role is that of an accomplice, by means of a literal interpretation and a contextual/teleological interpretation of Article 81 EC.

Regarding the literal interpretation[20] the CFI dismissed the argument that in order to qualify as an undertaking under Article 81 EC the undertaking in question had to be active on the same market as all the other participants. According to the CFI it follows from case-law that in order to fall within the ambit of the prohibition the agreement has to restrict competition. However, from this did not follow that all the participants needed to be active within one and the same market. From this followed in turn, according to the CFI, that the term 'agreements between undertakings' does not require a restrictive interpretation of the notion of perpetrator.

As for the contextual and teleological interpretation[21] of Article 81 EC the CFI investigated several different aspects invoked by the applicant. As regards the idea that one has to restrict its own commercial freedom in order to fall foul of the prohibition, the CFI found that such an interpretation would restrict the scope of the prohibition laid down in Article 81 EC and consequently its useful effects and its main objectives as read in the light of Article 3(1)(g) EC.

Concerning the requirements for participation in the cartel as such, the CFI found that the normal rules for fining participation in cartel, that is, participation in meetings and so on, did apply also in this particular case.

The next argument by the applicant, namely that the Commission's unitary interpretation of Article 81 EC was contrary to the principal *nullum crimen, nulla poena sine lege* had possibly a greater potential for success than the others previously invoked. However, the CFI found that although the principle as such requires clear and unambiguous wording, the principle does not exclude an interpretation of the legislation in question. According to the CFI the term 'agreements between undertakings' constituted a sufficiently precise expression of the notions of cartel and perpetrator of an infringement, in that the term covers any undertaking which acts in a collusive manner, irrespective of the sector of activity or of the relevant market on which it is active, to insure that such an undertaking cannot be unaware, or even fail to recognise, that it is exposing itself to legal action if it adopts such conduct. Thus according to the CFI the liability in question was foreseeable.

[20] *Ibid* paras 115–123.
[21] *Ibid* paras 124–128.

Finally, as concerns the actual participation by AC-Treuhand in the cartel infringement it was according to the CFI established that they had participated and actively contributed to the cartel objectives. For all those reasons the CFI upheld the Commission decision.

The decision by the Commission and the judgment of the CFI can, it is submitted, be regarded as a teleological delimitation of the scope of the competition rules. It is a teleological decision in the sense that the assistance of an accomplice was no doubt positive for the other cartel members (that is why it was an accomplice!) wherefore it should also be held accountable for the infringement – as indicated; no one should escape conviction nor fines. The outcome is also teleological in the sense that it gives the Commission an additional tool in its endeavours of prosecuting cartel infringements. By sanctioning undertakings fulfilling only secondary services for the cartel these undertakings would also qualify for leniency. Thus the numbers of potential leniency applicants have increased and not just concerning anyone but presumably concerning undertakings knowing more or less the whole story – at least to the extent they are fulfilling services such as AC-Treuhand.

On the other hand, given the need for clear delimitations of the scope of the competition rules, it would seem doubtful if the judgment provides such clear guidance. Are there in fact any clear limits to competition law responsibility? May all sorts of undertakings somehow implicated in the working of a cartel, such as legal advisers, auditing firms and so on be fined for their participation? Even if the principles underlying the judgment may not be transposed to undertakings even further away from the cartel activities as such, does the judgment imply that unilateral activity by one undertaking, not being in a dominant position but assisted by someone such as AC-Treuhand, constitute a prohibited agreement, or may an accomplice only be held accountable if there is a fully fledged infringement apart from its own conduct? Indeed, it could here be said that in order for someone to be held an accomplice in criminal law matters, there needs to be an infringement. On the other hand, Community competition law is not criminal law and it does not require an anti-competitive effect or an effect at all, wherefore in that sense also attempts to commit infringements are prohibited (just as, for that matter, criminal law on occasion condemns acts without actual effects).

Obviously, it is not my intention to criticise the CFI for not having provided clear guidance. The CFI, just as the ECJ, in these matters only have to check the legality of a particular decision – not to formulate a coherent policy. It is, however, clear that the teleological delimitation of the scope has certain drawbacks when it comes to providing guidance.

THIRD QUESTION – THE FUNCTIONAL APPROACH

As results from the above, the Community judiciary on occasion follows what has here been labelled a formal approach and on other occasions a more teleological approach for the delimitation of the competition rules. On the other hand, a rather functional approach would seem to be most common, here illustrated by its approach towards responsibility for competition law infringements by subsidiaries. The term functional approach is here used to describe an approach that assigns liability for infringements based upon rebuttable presumptions.

As is well known the concept of undertaking in Community competition law (as well as in other areas of law) is supplemented by the idea that several undertakings might be considered as forming a single economic entity. Thus, another company than the one held accountable for an infringement is ultimately held responsible for paying the fines. There are two clear advantages with this for the Commission. First of all it gives the Commission an opportunity to charge the company that it considers being the one to blame in a more general sense. Furthermore – and given that a parent company (including its subsidiaries) always will have a higher turnover than any one of its subsidiaries seen in isolation – it grants the possibility of increasing the fines without the risk of running foul of the 10 %-rule in Article 23(4) of Regulation No 1/2003.[22] Under the assumption that higher fines give incentives to avoid infringing the rules, the presumption of liability for the behaviour of subsidiaries increases the effectiveness of the prohibitions. An additional benefit is that the Commission may invoke recidivism more often for a parent company than for several different subsidiaries. As a general observation it would seem plausible that the increase in fines during later years is at least in part attributable to an increased use of parental responsibility, which in turn generates case-law on the subject when parental companies litigate in order to rebut the presumption.

Consequently, what we are talking about here is not the direct liability for a parent company that is aware of an infringement of the competition rules on behalf of its subsidiaries, such liability being of the same character as any other direct liability. Rather what is of interest is the responsibility even absent of all knowledge of the infringement and only based on the structural links between two companies. Already in 1972 the ECJ hold that:

> the fact that a subsidiary has separate legal personality is not sufficient to exclude the possibility of imputing its conduct to the parent company […] in particular where the subsidiary, although having separate legal personality, does not decide independently upon its own conduct on the market, but carries out, in all material respects, the instructions given to it by the parent company.[23]

[22] Council Regulation (EC) No 1/2003 of 16 December 2002 on the implementation of the rules on competition laid down in Articles 81 and 82 of the Treaty [2003] OJ L/1/1. See Faull and Nikpay, n 18 above, 994.

[23] Case 48/69 *Imperial Chemical Industries v Commission* [1972] ECR 619 paras 132 and 133.

The formula and its implicit (which later became explicit[24]) presumption of liability for parent companies has since then been repeated on numerous occasions, and undoubtedly it now constitutes consistent case-law, notwithstanding references in later case-law to other aspects pointing in the direction of actual control of a subsidiary, as well.[25] The presumption of parent-company control implies not only as in merger control a *possibility* of control, but moreover that this control has been exercised. The control does not, however, have to have been exercised in relation to the actual conduct giving rise to fines (such control implying a more direct responsibility), but only in more general terms.

Notwithstanding the well established character of this case-law, the very presumption has as such been frequently questioned during later years. As of now there are several cases before the CFI and others are before the ECJ, all in essence alleging that the presumption shall not apply in their particular case or alternately that the presumption of liability is as such impossible to rebut and therefore not in conformity with applicable standards of legal certainty.

Clearly the presumption of liability serves as a functional delimitation of responsibility. The functionality of the competition rules, or at least its sanctions, would work less well if it was not possible to assign responsibility to the one company that stands the most to lose and therefore also has the strongest incentives to take action against infringements. On the other hand it is clear that a presumption of liability will on occasion not be a true reflection of the actual situation.

Larger undertakings are often divided into several divisions, which might or might not have been given legal personality. In those cases where all subdivisions together have one and the same legal personality, the question of imputation of liability does not arise. The legal person as such is held responsible no matter if its direction knew what was going on in lower echelons or not. It is here submitted that there is a clear logic behind this in the sense that it is the duty and prerogative of the direction of a company to set up a system of control in order to avoid mismanagement on lower levels, be these of a commercial or of a legal character. In addition, gains from illegal activities will also benefit one and the same legal person which carried out the illegal activities. In fact, the same policy considerations might be invoked also when it comes to illegal activities of subdivisions having a legal personality of its own.

First of all it is readily apparent that the owner of an undertaking might impose on that undertaking a control system of its choosing. It has been argued that the absence of such a control system or a system not adequately adapted should not free it from liability any more than it should shield it from liability in other respects.[26] In addition it could be remarked that the reasons for using

[24] Case 107/82 *AEG-Telefunken v Commission* [1983] ECR 3151 para 50.

[25] Case C-286/98 P *Stora Kopparbergs Bergslags v Commission* [2000] ECR I-9925 paras 27–29.

[26] WPJ Wils, 'The undertaking as subject of EC Competition law and the imputation of infringements to natural or legal persons' (2000) 2 *European Law Review* 99.

subdivisions having a legal personality or simply letting them be integrated in one and the same undertaking, would rarely seem to be connected to competition law considerations. If that is so, why make a distinction from a competition law perspective if the idea is to make a functional delimitation?

However, even if logic would seem to demand a coherent approach towards subdivisions – no matter if they have a legal personality of their own or not – that is not really the position of applicable case-law. In fact, it would seem as if the total absence of any kind of control of a subsidiary would in fact relieve the parent company of its responsibility for competition law infringements of the subsidiary. On the other hand at least the Commission would seem to be of the opinion that such absence of control is rather unusual, if not highly unlikely. In reality, and if for no other reason, a parent company often needs to monitor the financial results of a subsidiary for tax and company law reasons. In actual fact, control demanded by, for instance, tax legislation or company law, has been considered by the Commission to be sufficient to incur liability upon the parent company. To a certain extent this approach has also been confirmed by the CFI. The question would therefore seem to be: what kind of control may be exercised while at the same time being able to rebut the presumption of parental liability?

In the recent case of *Schunk and Schunk Kohlenstoff-Technik v Commission*[27] the undertaking in question, Schunk, was a so called financial holding company which according to its statutes had as its object the 'acquisition, the sale, the administration, in particular strategic management of industrial participations'. In finding that the corporate objective of Schunk, that is, to manage shareholdings in other companies, was not sufficient in itself to reverse a presumption of liability, the CFI thereby invoked the fact that according to its statutes Schunk was competent to take 'all actions that are appropriate to serve, directly or indirectly the above mentioned purpose'; that Schunk had told the Commission that intra-group sales should be excluded for the calculation of the turnover; that according to German corporate law share holders exert strong control over the management of a company; and finally that Schunk had not been able to prove that there was no overlapping of staff between Schunk and its subsidiaries.[28]

As follows from *Schunk and Schunk Kohlenstoff-Technik v Commission* it would seem clear that the requirements for reversing a presumption of parent company liability, in all those cases where there is a 100 % ownership of the subsidiaries, is not an easy task. However, as with the practical delimitation regarding the responsibility for accomplices, the functional delimitation of parental responsibility begs certain questions, primarily in this situation if the presumption implies that voluntary absence of control is in itself proof of control, thereby making the presumption impossible to reverse, or if only the circumstances under which the presumption may be rebutted has as of yet failed to occur?

[27] Case T-69/04 *Schunk and Schunk Kohlenstoff-Technik v Commission*, judgment of 8 October 2008 nyr.

[28] *Ibid* paras 58 *ff*.

## CONCLUSIONS – RATIONALES FOR DELIMITATION

As discussed above there are different ways of delimiting the scope of the Community competition rules as concerns their applicability to different situations and perpetrators. Terms as formal, teleological and functional delimitations have been used, but it would seem clear that the labelling is in itself non-conclusive. Evidently, one might describe all situations as functional in their approach,[29] or for that matter teleological in the result they try to achieve. The important conclusion to be drawn would seem to be that there are in fact limits to the applicability of the competition rules. Furthermore, it would seem clear that the limits are more clearly defined when it comes to situations where the underlying situation is of a non-economic nature. In those circumstances the Community judiciary would appear to accept more readily that other values do play a role, wherefore competition rules should not apply. In other situations the Community judiciary is more reluctant to find that the competition rules do not apply.

The non-applicability of the competition rules to activities of a non-economic nature serves the purpose of drawing a line between economic activities and activities of another character, be it state activities or others. The reason for this (besides following from the EC Treaty rules as such) derives from an insight that competition in the sense of providing an increased economic efficiency is not of principal concern within these other activities. It would thus seem as if the scope of competition law is defined by, and dependent of, whether or not an application of competition law may increase economic efficiency. It is here submitted that this explanation holds good for the situation in *FENIN v Commission*, but not as concerns the judgments of *AC-Treuhand v Commission* and *Schunk and Schunk Kohlenstoff-Technik v Commission*.

First as concerns *AC-Treuhand v Commission* it is clear that the extension of liability also to an accomplice not being active on the market (not even potentially) in no way increases economic efficiency. In fact, the participation of AC-Treuhand did not affect economic efficiency as such, since all the functions could have been performed by the participants themselves. The effects of the participation of AC-Treuhand are thus in no way comparable to the effects of the inclusion of an additional competitor within the cartel. In a similar way assigning parental liability for subsidiaries' infringements of the competition rules does not affect economic efficiency. The actual or potential damage done to the markets is in no way connected to the proprietor of the infringer, but the size and market share of the perpetrator only are relevant for that assessment. Parental liability will thus not affect economic efficiency. Consequently, the effects on economic efficiency are not the only determining factor when it comes to the limits of Community competition law.

That other determining factor could possibly be the efficiency of the competition rules from the point of view of surveillance. Clearly, both *AC-*

[29] So eg O Odudo, *The Boundaries of EC Competition Law* (Oxford, Oxford University Press, 2006) 24 *ff*.

*Treuhand v Commission* and *Schunk and Schunk Kohlenstoff-Technik v Commission* increases the possibilities of detection and deterrence. In fact, as concerns *Schunk and Schunk Kohlenstoff-Technik v Commission* and similar case-law, it could be said that the task of surveillance is externalised to parental companies. By fining parental companies for the activities of their subsidiaries the Commission gives incentives (and during later years, substantial incentives) for these parental companies to control the activities of their subsidiaries. Instead of trying to deter a multitude of smaller companies by means of fines adapted to their (presumably) modest size, the Commission can deter parental companies by fines adequately adapted to their (presumably) larger size, which in turn will ensure that the parental companies take action against their subsidiaries.

Although both approaches serve to delimit the scope of competition law, it is here submitted that when enforcement efficiency decides the scope of competition law it is not always clear where that will lead, or for that matter if other interests are fully respected. A case such as *AC-Treuhand v Commission* plainly diminishes legal certainty without any apparent gain for economic efficiency, while at the same time reducing the scope for other professional rules. Even if no one should escape liability nor fines for distortions of economic efficiency, competition law is not supposed to be a remedy for all problems in a society.

7

# *EU Competition Law and International Maritime Transport: How to Create a Level Playing Field?*

JAN VANHAMME

## INTRODUCTION

This contribution being part of a compilation of essays in honour of Judge *Virpi Tiili*, it is appropriate to draw inspiration from at least one of her habits: the effort to handle competition cases not purely on the basis of legal and procedural technicalities, but within the broader context of the market elements at hand.

In this article I shall examine how EU competition law is applied to maritime transport services. This economic activity is of considerable importance for the European economy. A substantial part of the volume of goods transported between the Member States is handled by sea shipping. And more than 80 % of all freight trade between the EU and the rest of the world is seaborne.[1]

Shipping is a fascinating area of study for lawyers. Because of some peculiar characteristics, such as extraterritoriality and the widespread practice of operators to fly flags of convenience, it raises difficult issues for regulators and practitioners in terms of international law, law of contracts, insurance and commerce, environmental law and labour law. Over the last decades, public authorities, especially the European Commission, have discovered that, besides the areas of law already mentioned, competition law is a useful instrument as well in regulating maritime transport.

As of 18 October 2008, the application of EU competition law to maritime transport services has profoundly changed. On that day, Regulation No 4056/86 laying down detailed rules for the application of competition rules to maritime

[1] See the 1st recital of the Community guidelines on State aid to maritime transport [2004] OJ C/13/3, as well as the Community report 'Maritime Transport Strategy 2009-2018' (www.ec.europa.eu/transport/citizen/doc/2009_maritime_policy_space_en.pdf).

transport and providing, amongst other things, for a block exemption of liner shipping conferences, ceased to apply.[2] The liner shipping market is a major component of maritime transport, covering all scheduled transport of cargo on pre-determined sea routes. The exemption had allowed – under certain conditions – for price fixing, capacity regulation and market sharing. Now that it has disappeared, only some forms of cooperation remain legal, that is, those falling under the liner consortia block exemption.[3]

Despite their importance, these recent changes are not the main focus of this contribution. The EU competition standards currently applicable to shipping companies have been described in considerable detail by the Commission in its Guidelines on the application of Article 81 EC to maritime transport services.[4] Moreover, they have been analysed in an outstanding monography.[5]

Instead, this essay aims to discuss the application of EU competition law within the broader and rather problematic context in which maritime transport takes place. Many shipping companies operating on international routes suffer a lack of competitiveness because a great number of their competitors register vessels in third countries that have lenient policies.

Other competitors, though also sailing to and from EU ports, enjoy the unfair advantage of being themselves established in a third country that has poorly developed competition rules and does not help the EU to enforce its own standards.

There is, in other words, no 'level playing field' in maritime transport, that is, no environment in which all companies in the same geographic and product market follow the same rules and are given an equal ability to compete.

A little more than two decades ago, the Council adopted a Regulation that enables the Community to impose compensatory duties on non-Community shipowners that apply unfair pricing practices,[6] as well as a Regulation allowing

[2] Council Regulation (EC) No 1419/2006 of 25 September 2006 repealing Regulation (EEC) No 4056/86 laying down detailed rules for the application of Articles 85 and 86 of the Treaty to maritime transport, and amending Regulation (EC) No 1/2003 as regards the extension of its scope to include cabotage and international tramp services [2006] OJ L/269/1.

[3] Commission Regulation (EC) No 823/2000 of 19 April 2000 on the application of Article 81(3) of the Treaty to certain categories of agreements, decisions and concerted practices between liner shipping companies (consortia) [2000] OJ L/100/24. Reg No 823/2000, as amended in 2005 (OJ L/101/10), is currently scheduled to remain into force until 25 April 2010. Consortia rationalise shipping through structural cooperation such as vessel sharing, common investments in containers, etc. For more analysis, see F Dinger, *What shall we do with the drunken sailor? EC Competition Law and Maritime Transport* (Basel, Europainstitut der Universität Basel, 2002) 22–33, and R Eriksson, 'EC Maritime Competition Law Reform: opportunities and Options' (2005) 3 *Competition Law Insight* 3, at 5.

[4] [2008] OJ C/245/2. Commentary by A Lista, 'Trick or Treat? Commission Guidelines on Maritime Transport Competition' (2008) 7 *Shipping & Trade Law* 1.

[5] A Pozdnakova, *Liner Shipping and EU Competition Law* (Alphen aan den Rijn, Kluwer Law International, 2008).

[6] Council Regulation (EEC) No 4057/86 of 22 December 1986 on unfair pricing practices in maritime transport [1986] OJ L/378/14. According to its 1st, 3rd and 4th recital, this Reg is based on the finding that 'the competitive participation of Community shipowners in international liner shipping is adversely affected by certain unfair practices of shipping lines of third countries', which consist of 'continuous charging of freight rates for the transport of selected commodities

*Cont.*

the Member States to take countermeasures against companies established in countries that, by legislative or other acts, distort fair and free competition in shipping.[7] However, these instruments are scarcely applied[8] and have not created a level playing field.

Hereafter, the lack of a level playing field in maritime transport will be further analysed, with an emphasis on legal techniques that may or may not be available to the EU in order to attain a more uniform application and enforcement of its competition rules in this sector.

## EU COMPETITION LAW AND MARITIME TRANSPORT: APPLICABILITY

The focus in this article is entirely on *international* maritime transport. The application of EU competition law in the area of cabotage, that is, transport between ports in one Member State, will not be discussed.

In international maritime transport, most routes linking a Member State's port to foreign destinations have a major component outside the EU. The transport vessels sail the high seas and, in many cases, start or finish their journey in an Asian, African or American port. How, then, do European competition rules apply?

The answer to this question lies in the territoriality principle. According to public international law, the State has the right to legislate for all persons within its territory. This jurisdiction extends to citizens and companies inside the territory engaging in conduct that is consummated or has its main effects outside the territory. It also extends to conduct initiated abroad but having effects within the territory. The latter rule, also called 'effects doctrine', has been controversial but is now widely accepted, especially since it enables authorities to keep an eye on transnational business.[9]

The Court of Justice of the European Communities (hereinafter ECJ) expressly endorsed the territorial principle and implicitly supported the effects doctrine in the *wood pulp* cases. It held that when producers established outside the European Community sell to purchasers established in the Community, concertation between those producers on the prices to be charged to their EC customers has the object and effect of restricting competition within the common market.[10] The ECJ emphasised that, 'if the applicability of prohibitions laid down

which are lower than the lowest freight rates charged for the same commodities by established and representative shipowners' and 'are made possible by non-commercial advantages granted by a State which is not a member of the Community'.

[7] Council Regulation (EEC) No 4058/86 of 22 December 1986 concerning coordinated action to safeguard free access to cargoes in ocean trades [1986] OJ L/378/21.

[8] For an isolated example, see Council Regulation (EEC) No 15/89 of 4 January 1989 introducing a redressive duty on containerized cargo to be transported in liner service between the Community and Australia by Hyundai Merchant Marine Company Ltd of Seoul, Republic of Korea [1989] OJ L/4/1.

[9] See V Lowe, *International Law* (Oxford, Oxford University Press, 2007) 172 and 173.

[10] Joined Cases 89/85, 104/85, 114/85, 116/85, 117/85 and 125/85 to 129/85 *Ahlström Osakeyhtiö and Others v Commission* [1988] ECR 5193 paras 12 and 13.

under competition law were made to depend on the place where the agreement, decision or concerted practice was formed, the result would obviously be to give undertakings an easy means of evading those prohibitions. The decisive factor is therefore the place where it is implemented'.[11]

The ECJ repeated this position several times, most recently in the proceedings between the French municipality of Mesquer and the oil company Total concerning compensation for the damage caused by the hydrocarbon waste spread on the territory of that municipality following the sinking of the tanker Erika. The ECJ ruled that the applicability of EU legislation should not be called into question by the fact that the spillage of hydrocarbons took place in the exclusive economic zone of France.[12] The ECJ again implicitly applied the effects doctrine. It held that, 'without there being any need to rule on the applicability of the [relevant EU] directive at the place where the ship sank, it suffices to observe that hydrocarbons thus accidentally spilled drifted along the coast until they were washed up on it, so being discharged on the Member State's land territory'.[13]

Case-law thus suggests that shipowners and operators, regardless where they are based and in which State they register their vessels, fall under EU competition rules whenever their conduct affects competition within the common market. This was aptly illustrated by the Court of First Instance of the European Communities (hereinafter CFI) in the *Atlantic Container* cases, concerning the Commission's decision to impose fines on operators of containerised liner services between North America and Europe on the ground of their participation to a 'Trans-Atlantic Conference Agreement' (TACA) that exceeded the scope of the exemption granted by Regulation No 4056/86. The CFI explained that 'TACA, as a liner conference operating on the transatlantic trade, is governed both by Community competition law under Articles [81 EC and 82 EC] and by US law, in particular the US Shipping Act'.[14] It also upheld the Commission's description of the relevant geographic market as being the area in which the maritime transport services are marketed, that is, the catchment area of the Member States' ports at hand.[15] In an earlier case between the same parties, the CFI had already explained that restrictions of competition had occurred within

[11] *Ibid* para 16. According to Whish, the ECJ did not fully and explicitly adopt the effects doctrine, since it based its conclusion on the mere fact that the agreement had been 'implemented' within the Community; R Whish, *Competition Law*, 6th edn (Oxford, Oxford University Press, 2009) 479 and 480.

[12] Within the exclusive economic zones of the Member States, EU law does not apply, unless it is related to the activities of exploration and exploitation listed in the United Nations Convention on the Law of the Sea with regard to this maritime area (Case C-111/05 *Aktiebolaget NN* [2007] ECR I-2697 paras 59 and 60).

[13] Case C-188/07 *Commune de Mesquer* [2008] ECR I-4501 paras 60 and 61.

[14] Joined Cases T-191/98, T-212/98 to T-214/98 *Atlantic Container Line and Others v Commission* [2003] ECR II-3275 para 1129.

[15] Para 519 of Commission Decision of 16 September 1998 relating to a proceeding pursuant to Articles 85 and 86 of the EC Treaty (Case No IV/35.134 - Trans-Atlantic Conference Agreement) [1999] OJ L/95/1. In an earlier decision, the Commission had noted, for example, that the catchment areas of Northern European ports cover Ireland, the United Kingdom, Denmark, the Netherlands, Belgium, Luxembourg, most of Germany and Northern and central France (this was before the accession of Finland, Sweden, Poland and the Baltic States to the EU).

the common market because it was there that the members to the agreement were in competition to sell their services to clients, namely shippers, established in the Community.[16]

## EU COMPETITION LAW AND MARITIME TRANSPORT: ENFORCEMENT

EU competition rules may well be applicable to international maritime transport, but how to enforce them when the company targeted by an EU competition authority is established outside the EU?

Regulation No 4056/86 being no longer applicable, the implementation of Articles 81 EC and 82 EC in this sector is now fully governed by the rules of Regulation No 1/2003.[17] This Regulation explains, as a matter of course, that infringements must be proven and it gives the necessary investigative and decision-making powers to the Commission in order to fulfil that requirement. Inevitably, several of these powers are exclusively designed to be exercised within the European Union itself. Surely, the Commission can send requests for information and statements of objections to undertakings based outside the EU.[18] It can also address final decisions to undertakings that are established overseas.[19] However, one of the Commission's major weapons for the collection of evidence, namely its powers of inspection, is only available for use on the territory of a Member State. This follows both from international law[20] and from Articles 20 and 21 of Regulation No 1/2003.[21]

Moreover, the enforcement of orders included in decisions addressed to companies established outside the EU and of penalties imposed by those decisions, heavily depends on the willingness of the authorities of the non-member country in question to give assistance.

[16] Case T-395/94 *Atlantic Container Line and Others v Commission* [2002] ECR II-875 para 72.

[17] Council Regulation (EC) No 1/2003 of 16 December 2002 on the implementation of the rules on competition laid down in Articles 81 and 82 of the Treaty [2003] OJ L/1/1.

[18] Case 52/69 *Geigy v Commission* [1972] ECR 787 para 11. See also Case T-338/94 *Finnboard v Commission* [1998] ECR II-1617 para 48. In *Geigy v Commission*, the ECJ held that, 'since there is no convention on the matter between the Community and the Swiss Confederation, the question how this notice is to be served on interested parties established outside the territory of the Community depends on international practice and must be resolved with mutual regard to the spheres of jurisdiction both of the Community and of the third State concerned. [...] [I]nternational law cannot be invoked in order to deny the Community the power to take the necessary steps to [...] [curtail] conduct adversely affecting competition which has arisen in the common market.'

[19] See, inter alia, Dec 1999/243, n 15 above. The ECJ has recognised that decisions can be served directly on undertakings established outside the Community (Case 6/72 *Europemballage and Continental Can v Commission* [1973] ECR 215 paras 9 and 10).

[20] Clearly, under the sovereignty principle, the Commission is unable to carry out inspections outside the EU unless it has the approval of the third State concerned. This is illustrated by Art 7(2)(b) of Reg No 4057/86. According to that provision, 'the Commission shall, after consultation, carry out investigations in third countries, provided that the firms concerned give their consent and the government of the country in question has been officially notified and raises no objection'.

[21] These provisions require close cooperation between the Commission and the Member State authorities as regards inspection of the premises and other property of undertakings and their members of staff.

These handicaps are to some extent mitigated if the targeted company is established in a State that has concluded a cooperation agreement with the EU in the area of competition. At the time of writing of this contribution, such agreements were in force between the EU and, respectively, Canada, Japan and the United Sates of America.[22] They are based on rules of comity, in that each party must take account of the other's significant interests when enforcing competition rules. In the near future, a similar agreement with Korea may enter into force.[23] Enforcement of competition rules is also well regulated between the EU and its partners of the European Economic Area (amongst which are Iceland and Norway) and, to some lesser extent, between the EU and some of its other associated partners.[24] In general, however, co-ordination of competition law enforcement is weak. In the Cotonou Agreement between the EU and a great number of African, Caribbean and Pacific countries, for example, the parties have only agreed 'to reinforce cooperation in this area with a view to formulating and supporting effective competition policies [...]. Cooperation in this area shall, in particular, include assistance in the drafting of an appropriate legal framework and its administrative enforcement with particular reference to the special situation of the least developed countries'.[25]

If no agreement with the non-member country exists and no spontaneous assistance is given, it may still be possible for the Commission to collect evidence, for example at the premises of the company's European subsidiaries – if these exist – or at the premises of any other entity related to the infringement.[26] Enforcement of final decisions is not excluded either, but becomes difficult and greatly depends on the presence of relevant entities and assets within the EU.

If the overseas company has a subsidiary in a Member State, the Commission may even consider to target that subsidiary directly and to impose penalties upon it, especially when it is clear that the subsidiary does not determine its market behaviour autonomously but essentially follows the directives of the parent company.[27]

[22] Agreement between the European Communities and the Government of Canada regarding the application of their competition laws [1999] OJ L/175/50; Agreement between the EU and Japan concerning cooperation on anti-competitive activities [2003] OJ L/183/12; Agreement between the Government of the United States of America and the Commission of the European Communities regarding the application of their competition laws [1995] OJ L/95/47; Agreement between the European Communities and the Government of the United States of America on the application of positive comity principles in the enforcement of their competition laws [1998] OJ L/173/28.

[23] www.ec.europa.eu/comm/competition/international/bilateral/index.html.

[24] See, eg Decision No 1/2004 of the EU-Morocco Association Council of 19 April 2004 adopting the necessary rules for the implementation of the competition rules [2005] OJ L/165/10.

[25] Art 45(3) of the Partnership agreement between the members of the African, Caribbean and Pacific Group of States of the one part, and the European Community and its Member States, of the other part, signed in Cotonou on 23 June 2000 [2000] OJ L/317/3.

[26] For example, in a case brought against the shipping group Ventouris, which is established in Panama, the Commission found evidence in the premises of a 'European Trust Agency', which was based in Athens and acted on behalf of Minoan Lines, a company linked to the same cartel as Ventouris. The CFI considered that such an exercise of inspection powers is legal (Case T-59/99, *Ventouris v Commission* [2003] ECR II-5257 paras 141–163).

[27] Case 6/72 *Europemballage and Continental Can v Commission*, n 19 above, para 15. See also, albeit in a different factual context, Case C-280/06 *ETI and Others* [2007] ECR I-10893 para 49.

Another strategy may consist of addressing the decision to the company established outside the EU and of subsequently proceeding, in cooperation with Member State authorities, to the seizure of assets present within the EU. In the case of shipowners, the ships themselves and their cargo can under some circumstances be considered to be such assets.[28]

## FLAGS OF CONVENIENCE

As has been documented by non-governmental organisations[29] and recognised by international organisations including the EU,[30] compliance with legal rules is undermined by the use of 'flags of convenience' (hereinafter FOC). This term refers to the widespread practice in the shipping industry to register vessels in a State that has an 'open registry' and therefore accepts that ships flying its flag are owned and controlled by foreigners who do not necessarily have a genuine connection with its territory. Often it is not required either that the ship itself and its crew present a substantial link with the country in question. FOC countries attract foreign shipowners by offering them low registration fees and tax exemptions or/and leniency in terms of protection of the environment and working conditions.[31]

Because FOC countries do not require a genuine link, it is difficult for them to exercise effective control over the ships they register, and often they do not have the ambition to do so.[32] FOCs are now offered by some twenty to thirty countries,[33] which makes it easy for shipowners and operators to change the nationality (and the names) of vessels frequently and thus reduce even further the chance of law infringements being discovered.[34]

Under international law, registries requiring no link with the country of registration are illegal. It has been emphasised by the International Court of Justice (ICJ) that, although every State is free to determine its nationality conditions, a genuine link between the State and its nationals is required.

[28] Case C-286/90 *Poulsen and Diva Navigation* [1992] ECR I-6019 paras 28–34.

[29] Foremost by the International Transport Workers' Federation (www.itfglobal.org/flags-convenience).

[30] www.ec.europa.eu/fisheries/cfp/external_relations/illegal_fishing/flags_convenience.

[31] A Mandaraka-Sheppard, *Modern Maritime Law and risk management*, 2nd edn (Abingdon, Routledge Cavendish, 2007) 278 and 279.

[32] As the Commission puts it: 'The States concerned are often developing countries lacking the means (or the will) to set in place effective control systems and even less so if the resources concerned are not theirs. Use of a flag of convenience constitutes a pernicious practice that drags the entire control system downwards' (www.ec.europa.eu, *loc. cit.*). See also the European Parliament's Working Document on the Common Maritime Policy, ch 2, para 3 (www.europarl.europa.eu/workingpapers/tran/w14/2_en.htm).

[33] There are different blacklists in literature and in policy documents. For two examples, see Mandaraka-Sheppard, n 31 above, 279 n 7, and www.itfglobal.org/flags-convenience/flags-convenien-183.cfm.

[34] P Gautier, 'L'État du pavillon et la protection des intérêts liés au navire' in MG Kohen (ed), *Promoting Justice, Human Rights and Conflict Resolution through International Law* (Den Haag, Martinus Nijhoff, 2007) 718.

Therefore, 'a State cannot claim that the rules it has thus laid down are entitled to recognition by another State unless it has acted in conformity with this general aim of making the legal bond of nationality accord with the individual's genuine connection with the State'.[35] In the same line of thought, Article 91 of the United Nations Convention on the Law of the Sea (UNCLOS[36]), codifying custom, obliges every State to make sure that only ships having a genuine link with it fly its flag. Article 94 of UNCLOS adds that '[e]very State shall effectively exercise its jurisdiction and control in administrative, technical and social matters over ships flying its flag'.

Multilaterally agreed systems such as the International Safety Management Code (ISM) and Port State Control (PSC) have counterbalanced somewhat the damage caused by the FOC practice, but have not solved the problem.[37] A more effective reaction would consist of unilaterally assimilating ships sailing under a flag of convenience to ships without nationality. The impunity of the owners and operators of those ships would thus be pierced. The pressure for such an interpretation of UNCLOS and of the customary rules enacted by it is increasing and is inspired by the aforementioned ICJ's *Nottebohm* judgment, but in a high profile case the International Tribunal for the Law of the Sea has refused to endorse such an approach. That case concerned the seizure, by Guinea, of the Saiga, an oil tanker registered in Saint Vincent and the Grenadines. Demands by the flag State to release the ship were ignored on the basis that, in the absence of any genuine link between the ship and Saint Vincent and the Grenadines, that State's claims were not relevant. The Tribunal dismissed this argument, saying that 'the purpose of the provisions of [UNCLOS] on the need for a genuine link between a ship and its flag State is to secure more effective implementation of the duties of the flag State, and not to establish criteria by reference to which the validity of the registration of ships in a flag State may be challenged by other States'.[38]

[35] *Nottebohm Case, Liechtenstein v Guatemala, ICJ Rep.* (1955) 23.

[36] [1998] OJ L/179/3.

[37] The ISM-code was adopted within the framework of the International Maritime Organization and later incorporated in the International Convention for the Safety of Life at Sea (SOLAS). PSC allows port States to detain ships that do not comply with international safety standards. For a discussion of its merits and deficiencies, see Mandaraka-Sheppard, n 31 above, 279–281. In general, as one author puts it, there has been 'a shift away from attempts to use the genuine link to limit re-flagging of ships to open registries to the question of adopting more stringent international norms for safety of ships and vessel-source pollution' [AG Oude Elferink, 'The Genuine Link Concept: Time for a Post Mortem?' in IF Dekker and HHG Post (eds), *On the Foundations and Sources of International Law* (Den Haag, Asser, 2003) 46].

[38] *The M/V Saiga (No 2), Saint Vincent and the Grenadines v Guinea, ITLOS Rep.* (1999), at 37, para 83. Similarly, the ECJ stated in a preliminary ruling that European regulations could not be applied to the Danish owner and crew of a ship flying the Panamanian flag, even though that ship had no genuine link with Panama and was obviously used to circumvent Community regulations as well as international agreements concluded by the EC (Case C-286/90, *Poulsen and Diva Navigation*, n 28 above). The flags of convenience issue reappeared in Case C-410/03 *Commission v Italy* [2005] ECR I-3507, as well as in Case C-438/05 *International Transport Workers' Federation and Finnish Seamen's Union* [2007] ECR I-10779.

## DEREGULATION: THE MAGIC FORMULA FOR OBTAINING A LEVEL PLAYING FIELD?

When the Council abolished Regulation No 4056/86 and thereby submitted maritime transport services to unrestricted competition, it reasoned this decision by pointing out that '[u]nder current market conditions price stability and the reliability of services are brought about by individual service agreements. The alleged causal link between the restrictions [brought about by liner conferences] (price fixing and supply regulation) and the claimed efficiencies (reliable services) therefore appears too tenuous'.[39] It also found that 'a thorough review of the industry carried out by the Commission has demonstrated that liner shipping is not unique as its cost structure does not differ substantially from that of other industries. There is therefore no evidence that the industry needs to be protected from competition.'[40]

These statements are most likely correct, but do not mention the wider context in which competition takes place when it comes to international maritime transport. As indicated in the previous sections of this contribution, attempts to create a level playing field in this economic sector are hindered by two obstacles.

Firstly, as is shown above, the enforcement of competition rules is difficult when the shipowner or operator is based in a non-member country that does not have competition law standards similar to those of the EU. Typically, countries with high standards are prone to conclude cooperation agreements on competition matters with the EU, whereas States with poorly developed competition rules see no need for such an agreement. As a result, the market behaviour of companies established in such States is difficult to catch under EU competition rules, even though the latter rules may very well be applicable in light of the territorial principle. This concern has become more important after the disappearance of the block exemption of liner conferences. Indeed, now that maritime transport is submitted to full competition, establishment in countries with sub-standard competition rules is more appealing than ever to companies that wish to engage in inappropriate market behaviour on routes to and from EU ports. This may lead to the unfair situation in which companies registered within the EU or in one of the EU's most reliable partner countries, abstain from the formerly well-established but now forbidden practice of concluding liner conference agreements, whereas companies registered in countries with a bad reputation of law enforcement continue to make and apply such deals.

Secondly, as is shown in section concerning FOCs, the existence of a level playing field in maritime transport is compromised by the possibilities nowadays widely available to any shipping company, based within the EU or elsewhere, to flag out its vessels.[41]

[39] The 4th recital of Reg No 1419/2006.

[40] *Ibid* 3rd recital.

[41] The problem has recently been highlighted again in the document 'Maritime Transport Strategy 2009-2018', which is a communication from the Commission to the Council, the European Parliament, the European Economic and Social Committee and the Committee of the Regions (www.ec.europa.eu/transport/citizen/doc/2009_maritime_policy_space_en.pdf).

Moreover, shipowners and operators may combine both strategic benefits, by officially – but not always substantially – establishing themselves in a FOC country with poor competition standards and registering their vessels there. Efforts to tackle anti-competitive behaviour within the internal market committed by such undertakings will almost inevitably remain in vain. Companies of this type do not tend to open subsidiary branches in the EU and sometimes set up an exceedingly complex company structure, making it difficult to link a particular vessel to a particular owner or operator.

Against this background, what does it precisely mean when the EU stipulates, in agreements with non-member countries, that competition in the maritime transport sector must be 'free and fair'?[42] In its recently concluded agreement on maritime transport with China, the EU has accepted that the rights convened under that agreement with regard to unrestricted access and non discriminatory treatment of ships extend to 'vessels flying the flag of a third country but owned or operated by a shipping company of China or a Member State of the Community'.[43] Provisions like these have a profound liberalising effect, since they convey the message that, regardless if a shipping company has a FOC policy or not, free trade and non discriminatory treatment are available to it.

In the meantime, several non-FOC countries, including a number of EU Member States, have relaxed their own rules applicable to ships and crews, thus trying to make their own flags more 'convenient' and to reduce the number of vessels flagged out to core FOC countries. Denmark and Germany, for example, have created 'international registers' that offer some advantages in comparison to pre-existing ship registers. Some other Member States have tried to attract shipping companies to 'offshore registers' that belong to one of their overseas territories.[44]

Will all this deregulation lead to fair competition? Liberalisation often seems to be a proper way for obtaining a level playing field, but when it comes to international maritime transport, this does not appear to be entirely true. The recent abolishment of the specific framework designed by Regulation No 4056/86 may, in fact, deepen the gap between market participants that will have no choice but to comply with Articles 81 EC and 82 EC and those, operating on the same routes, that do not have to fear enforcement.

It thus seems to this author that the recent decision of the Community legislator to bring maritime transport under the general scope of EU competition rules, though in itself justified and to be welcomed, should be accompanied by a more stringent approach regarding jurisdiction and enforcement.

[42] See, eg Annex to the Framework agreement for cooperation between the European Economic Community and the Federative Republic of Brazil [1995] OJ L/262/65.

[43] Art 3 of the Agreement on maritime transport between the European Community and its Member States, of the one part, and the government of the People's Republic of China, of the other part [2008] OJ L/46/25.

[44] See the introductory part of the Community guidelines on State aid to maritime transport [2004] OJ C/13/3.

## CONCLUSIONS

It is not surprising that in an international business such as shipping, operators establish themselves in places where competition as well as other crucial aspects of commerce are under-regulated. As is discussed above, extraterritorial application of EU competition rules can, on a case by case basis, restore some fairness in the maritime transport sector, that is, when the Commission finds evidence within the EU of anticompetitive behaviour committed by an overseas company and subsequently succeeds to enforce its decision. However, these occasional hits are insufficient to create a level playing field.[45]

It has long been understood that, in order to bring about fair competition, cooperation with non-member countries on competition policy is essential. This, of course, is known not only by the EU and its close partners of the European Economic Area and North America, but also by third State governments that want to continue to attract foreign businesses to their shores by typical flag of convenience advantages, including sub-standard competition rules and weak law enforcement. Even though the development of competition law in non-member countries is progressing,[46] bilateral cooperation with FOC countries is rather unpromising and multilateral negotiations on the harmonisation of competition rules have not led to satisfactory results so far.[47]

A more assertive approach of the part of the EU may offer better perspectives.

Why, for example, would the EU, as a major economic power, not act more vigorously towards obtaining better commitments from its trading partners? Considering, for example, the fact that many FOC countries are bound by the Cotonou Agreement, the EU may consider to monitor more sharply the implementation of Article 45 of that Agreement regarding competition[48] and of other provisions that are now undermined by the FOC policies of the countries in question.

The EU could also choose to base its policies more directly on the fact, discussed above, that the registration of vessels lacking a genuine link with the country of registration, is contrary to international law. Once the EU would take effective countermeasures or even decide to refuse entry to such vessels, this would have a profound, deterring effect on shipowners considering FOC practice. It would, at the same time, inspire FOC countries to make their flag less convenient in terms of competition, environmental and social criteria, to create a true link of control and enforcement with the vessels they register, and to attract shipowners by techniques that are less problematic and that are also in use in some EU Member States, such as low tax rates.[49]

[45] On the potential of extraterritoriality to correct under-regulation, as well as the limits of this potential, see M Taylor, *International Competition Law* (Cambridge, Cambridge University Press, 2006) 65–67.

[46] *Ibid* 72–76.

[47] B Zanettin, 'International Aspects' in G Amato and C-D Ehlermann (eds), *EC Competition Law – A Critical Assessment* (Oxford, Hart Publishing, 2007) 785–796.

[48] See n 25 above.

[49] For an example, see Commission Decision of 30 June 2004 concerning a series of tax measures which Belgium is planning to implement for maritime transport [2005] OJ L/150/1.

In this regard, the EU could draw inspiration from its Directive 2005/35/EC on ship-source pollution.[50] That Directive has boosted law enforcement in the field of environmental protection, by bringing an end to the impunity of shipowners sailing under flags of convenience.[51]

Directive 2005/35 is based on the finding that rules of maritime safety and environmental protection 'are being ignored on a daily basis by a very large number of ships sailing in Community waters, without corrective action being taken',[52] and obliges every Member State to regard ship-source discharges of polluting substances into the sea as criminal offences if committed with intent, recklessly or by serious negligence. Its rules are applicable not only in the internal waters, territorial seas and exclusive economic zones of the Member States, but also on the high seas, and they apply on every ship 'irrespective of its flag'.[53] Although it only allows for detention and penalties under well-defined circumstances, the Directive has been fiercely opposed by the International Association of Independent Tanker Owners (Intertanko), the International Association of Dry Cargo Shipowners (Intercargo) and other interest groups. In a combined effort, these associations brought a case before the High Court of Justice of England and Wales in which they questioned the validity of the Directive under international law, especially with regard to the right of innocent passage. However, in its preliminary ruling, the ECJ upheld the legality of the Directive.[54]

[50] Directive 2005/35/EC of the European Parliament and of the Council of 7 September 2005 on ship-source pollution and on the introduction of penalties for infringements [2005] OJ L/255/11.

[51] *Ibid.*

[52] 2nd recital of Dir 2005/35.

[53] Arts 2 and 3 of Dir 2005/35.

[54] Case C-308/06 *The International Association of Independent Tanker Owners and Others* [2008] ECR I-4057.

# 8

# *Article 82 EC – When Is a Price so High that It Becomes Abusive? An Appreciation of a Particularly Subjective Character*

BO VESTERDORF

## INTRODUCTION

Article 82 EC which prohibits abuse of a dominant position gives the European Commission broad powers to intervene vis-à-vis dominant undertakings in cases where it finds it necessary in order to prevent the dominant undertaking from restricting, distorting or preventing competition on the market in question.

This is without doubt important and necessary, at least from time to time, as has been demonstrated by a number of famous Commission and Court decisions in the case-law over the years. Suffice it to mention cases such as *Parke Davis and Co.*[1] regarding a patent protected product and its price, *Hoffmann-La Roche v Commission*[2] on exclusivity, *Hilti v Commission*[3] on illegal bundling, *AKZO v Commission*[4] on predatory pricing, *Michelin v Commission*[5] and *British Airways v Commission*[6] on rebates, or *Microsoft v Commission*[7] on refusal to deliver and illegal tying.

However, as important and powerful a tool as this is for the Commission, it is also a tool which – I submit – should only be used after careful consideration

[1] Case 24/67 *Parke Davis and Co.* [1968] ECR 81.
[2] Case 85/76 *Hoffmann-La Roche v Commission* [1979] ECR 461.
[3] Case T-30/89 *Hilti v Commission* [1991] ECR II-1439.
[4] Case C-62/86 *AKZO v Commission* [1991] ECR I-3359.
[5] Case T-203/01 *Michelin v Commission* [2003] ECR II-4071.
[6] Case T-219/99 *British Airways v Commission* [2003] ECR II-5917.
[7] Case T-201/04 *Microsoft v Commission* [2007] ECR II-3601.

and only when the facts of the case are very clear and consequently such that they provide solid and cogent evidence that all the conditions for the application of the provision are present. There must be clear evidence of dominance which implies that the relevant market definition must be based on a solid factual basis and economic analysis and that the position on that market of the undertaking in question and of any competitors is such that there can be no reasonable question as to its dominance. On top of that, the behaviour of the dominant undertaking on that market must, in my submission, be demonstrated to be clearly abusive.[8]

The reason why I – as can be seen from the preceding paragraph – think that both the Commission and the Community Courts should only apply Article 82 EC very carefully and only when all the conditions are very clearly met is that the two important legal notions – dominance and abuse – are vague and imprecise notions and as such can in fact be used very liberally or very restrictively and intervention by the competition authorities will normally have an important impact on the market in question and sometimes on the economy in general. The definition of dominance is by no means clear, but is and will always be a question of a more or less subjective appraisal of a number of factual and sometimes complex circumstances and economic analysis. The same applies, and even more so, to the notion of abuse. What one competition authority may think is abuse is not necessarily what another authority would find abusive. That this is so, is not really changed by the attempts by the Court of Justice of the European Communities (hereinafter ECJ) and the Court of First Instance of the European Communities (hereinafter CFI) to define or indicate what dominance or abuse is.

This is illustrated by the definition of dominance given by the ECJ. It has defined dominance as a position of economic strength enjoyed by an undertaking, which enables it to prevent effective competition being maintained on a relevant market, by affording it the power to behave to an appreciable extent independently of its competitors, its customers, and ultimately of consumers.[9] This definition, however, begs the questions of what is for example 'effective competition' or how 'independent' must it be before it is to an 'appreciable extent'? The same applies to the definition of abuse given by the ECJ in *Hoffmann-La Roche v Commission*[10] which – while indicating that the notion is an objective one – refers to behaviour which because of its nature may influence the market and which is not 'normal competition on the merits'. What kind of behaviour is it and what is 'normal competition on the merits'? The answer to these questions depends on an appreciation by someone and his appreciation

[8] By clearly abusive I want to stress that in my opinion intervention should be avoided in cases where the abusive character of the examined behaviour is open for discussion, in other words not evidently abusive. See in that regard Case 26/75 *General Motors v Commission* [1975] ECR 1367 in which the ECJ – in spite of accepting the Commission's finding of 5 instances of clearly excessive prices having been charged – declared the conduct to be non-abusive in light of the particular attenuating circumstances (few instances, new activity, lowering prices before intervention by Commission etc.).

[9] Case 27/76 *United Brands and United Brands Continentaal v Commission* [1978] ECR 207, and Case 85/76 *Hoffmann-La Roche v Commission*, n 2 above.

[10] See n 2 above.

does not necessarily correspond to what you may think or may not really convince you. Who is right? Is there any objectively correct answer? The answers must, however, be given by competition authorities controlled in the last resort by the Community Courts. Since the answers cannot be claimed to be strictly objective answers, the power to rule on such questions and to find a violation must be used only after very careful consideration and on the basis of very solid facts and economic analysis, especially since a finding of violation opens the door for sanctions and in particular potentially very large fines.[11]

When fines, which in Community competition law are at least of a quasi-penal character, can be imposed, it is a principle of fundamental character that what is 'punishable' must be described clearly in advance in the law[12] in order that people and undertakings may know how not to behave. I refer in that respect to the judgments by the ECJ in *Gondrand and Garancini*,[13] *X*[14] and by the CFI in *Schunk and Schunk Kohlenstoff-Technik v Commission*.[15]

Much has been written in the legal literature about predatory pricing and other sorts of exclusionary abuse but not that much about exploitative abuse in the form of 'unfair' prices.[16] In this intervention I shall therefore – without pretending this contribution to be more than some reflections on the subject – limit myself to discuss the notion of abuse in the form of imposing 'unfair' high prices which is directly prohibited by Article 82(a) EC. When discussing this kind of abuse, besides having to examine the already vague and imprecise notions of 'dominance' and 'abuse', we also have to examine the vague and imprecise notion of 'unfair', 'unreasonable' or 'excessive' combined with the condition that such prices must be 'imposed' on customers by the dominant undertaking which in such a case is exploiting its market power.

[11] See J Temple Lang, 'Fundamental Issues Concerning Abuse under Article 82 EC', in *Regulatory Police Institute Oxford, Annual Competition Policy Conference* (Oxford, 2005) (www.rpieurope.org/2005%20Conference/Temple_Lang_Abuse_under_article_82EC.pdf). See also in that sense D Waelbroeck, 'The Notion of Dominant Position: a Different Approach under Article 82 of the EC Treaty and Merger Control?' in *Liber Amicorum in Honour of Bo Vesterdorf* (Brussels, Bruylant, 2007) 569; in the same sense D Gerardin, 'The Necessary Limits to the Control of "Excessive" Prices by Competition Authorities – A View from Europe' (2007, Tilburg University Legal Studies Working Paper, available at SSRN: http://ssrn.com/abstract=1022678).

[12] See Waelbroeck, n 11 above: 'it is vital to carefully delineate all the elements that constitute the offence, not only the abuse but also the notion of dominant position'.

[13] Case 169/80 *Gondrand and Garancini* [1981] ECR 1931 para 17.

[14] Joined Cases C-74/95 and C-129/95 *X* [1996] ECR I-609 para 25.

[15] Case T-69/04 *Schunk and Schunk Kohlenstoff-Technik v Commission*, judgment of 8 October 2008 nyr, paras 28 and 29.

[16] However, some very interesting contributions can be found for example in: Temple Lang, n 11 above; S Kon and S Turnbull, 'Pricing and the Dominant Firm: Implications of the Competition Commission Appeal Tribunal's Judgment in the Napp Case' (2003) 2 *European Competition Law Review* 70; M Glader and S Chabert Larsen, 'Article 82: Excessive Pricing' (2006) 7 *Competition Law Insight* 3 (see critical comments on this D Gerardin and M Rato 'Article 82, IP Rights and Industry Standards: In Reply', 2006, available at SSRN: http://ssrn.com/abstract=950215); M Furse, 'Excessive Prices, Unfair Prices and Economic Value: the Law of Excessive Pricing under Article 82 EC and the Chapter II Prohibition' (2008) 1 *European Competition Journal* 59; see Gerardin, n 11 above; M van der Houde, 'Unfair and Excessive Prices in the Energy Sector' in C-D Ehlermann and M Marquis (eds), *Europea. Competition Annual 2007: A Reformed Approach to Article 82* (2008) 617, and P Akman, 'Exploitative Abuse in Article 82 EC: Back to Basics?' (2008, ESRC Centre for Competition Policy CCP Working Paper No. 09-1, available at SSRN: ssrn.com/abstract=1328316 Available).

This kind of exploitative abuse has only been dealt with rarely in the case-law, probably for two reasons: 1) it does not occur often because excessively high prices will normally lead the customers to seek other suppliers (if other suppliers can be found) and/or to expansion by existing non-dominant competitors or to the entry of new competitors; 2) it will normally only be possible to demand such prices for a short period of time due to the factors mentioned under point 1 and authorities will therefore either not detect the case, consider the problem to have been solved by the market or that it will eventually be solved by the market.

However, where the dominant undertaking enjoys a legal or de facto monopoly[17] it may be able to charge 'unfair' or 'excessive' prices for some time, especially if its product is a *must have product*. It may only be stopped eventually either by the competition authority or by losing its de facto monopoly if for example new entrants manage to break existing high barriers to entry. If it does not enjoy monopoly power legally or de facto, charging very high prices will – as mentioned above – normally lead existing competitors to try to take advantage of this by expanding their business or lead to new entrants into the market. Either or both of these effects would normally lead the dominant undertaking to reduce its prices in order not to lose its market share.

## BRIEF RESUME OF THE EXISTING CASE-LAW ON EXCESSIVE PRICES

Only few cases regarding excessive prices have been decided by the ECJ and the CFI; and the Commission itself has also only dealt with a few cases of this kind.

Among the cases decided, one may distinguish between different types of cases. Firstly, instances where the 'unfair' high prices were used for exclusionary purposes for example in the form of discrimination, see, for instance *British Leyland v Commission*[18] in which case British Leyland charged much higher prices for the issuance of type-approval certificates for parallel imported cars than for other cars in order to prevent parallel imports and exports. In this case, however, the real question was not so much the question of the excessiveness as such but the fact of discrimination by imposing higher prices in certain cases without any objective reason for doing so. In this case we find only little help in trying to define how high prices must be to become 'unfair'. One could also mention *General Motors Continental v Commission*[19] in that context.[20] In these two cases the ECJ made its first attempt at indicating how to determine whether a price might be considered unfair. It stated that an abuse under Article 82 EC 'might lie, inter alia, in the imposition of a price which is excessive in relation

[17] In this specific context the notion of a de facto monopoly may include the existence of competitors being able only to supply an insignificant part of the total demand on a market with important barriers to entry and expansion, like substantial investments to finance, legal obstacles like IP-rights, or legislative barriers, leaving the dominant undertaking with the remaining, uncontested part of the market.

[18] Case 226/84 *British Leyland v Commission* [1986] ECR 3263.

[19] See n 8 above.

[20] It is noteworthy that both British Leyland and General Motors held legal monopolies.

to the economic value of the service provided'. Another famous case of this type is *United Brands and United Brands Continentaal v Commission.*[21] In this case the dominant undertaking, United Brands, applied different prices for different markets without any objective reason which in principle amounted to illegal discrimination. But in that case the Commission and consequently later also the ECJ examined not only the question of discrimination but also the question of whether, in this specific context, the high prices imposed could be characterised as excessively high and as such be in violation of Article 82 EC.

Secondly, cases where the alleged unfair price was not used for exclusionary purposes but nevertheless examined along with another type of alleged abuse, for instance, discrimination. An important example of this type of case is the *Scandlines* case.[22] The complaint concerned the alleged 'unfairly' high prices charged by the undertaking Helsingborg Havn for the use of the facilities of the harbor which was the sole property of that undertaking. The Commission defined the harbor as the relevant market and the undertaking therefore necessarily was dominant and thus subject to the application of Article 82 EC. The Commission rejected the complaint having found that even if the price was very high compared with the direct costs it was not excessively high since the price should be compared to the economic value and not just with direct costs.

In *Scandlines* the Commission also importantly stated that the ECJ regrettably in *United Brands and United Brands Continentaal v Commission* had omitted to give further details on how to determine the economic value with which the prices charged should be compared. The Commission on its hand stated that the economic value of a specific good covers more than just costs and that it in particular also covers non-cost related elements such as demand and that a comparison with prices charged by competitors could also be a relevant factor to consider.

A third type of cases might be cases in which the alleged unfair high prices stand alone, in other words they are not connected with other anticompetitive elements, such as discrimination or other exclusionary elements. In this category[23] we do not, however and unfortunately, find any judgment by either the ECJ or the CFI.

## GENERAL CONSIDERATIONS

It is regrettable that the case-law is so sparse on the question of unfair pricing.[24] Dominating undertakings must be careful not to violate Article 82 EC when

[21] See n 9 above.

[22] COMP/35.658 – Scandlines Sverige v Port of Helsingborg.

[23] In this category I do not include cases where dominance is based on IP-rights because of the special nature of that kind of cases. See, however, in that respect, eg Case 238/87 *Volvo* [1988] ECR 6211.

[24] In the relatively few cases regarding excessive prices decided by the ECJ after Case 27/76 *United Brands and United Brands Continentaal v Commission*, n 9 above , the ECJ and the CFI have constantly just referred to the test indicated in *United Brands* without adding anything to or clarifying the test. This is regrettable but probably due to the fact that the two courts have not been presented with sufficiently detailed and well motivated questions in that regard by the referring national courts.

setting their prices and unfortunately can only seek little guidance in the case-law. As the Commission has stated in its recent Communication on its future application of Article 82 EC, the purpose of the Communication is to give guidance to the undertakings in order to increase predictability and thereby legal security. However, the Communication does not deal with the question of excessive pricing or other types of exploitative abuse.

As mentioned above, clear and precise definitions and therefore a high degree of predictability is, indeed, very important when violation of the rules in question may be sanctioned severely as is the case with violations of the Community competition rules. The Commission should as a consequence – at least in my opinion – also consider sending out a communication with guidance to the undertakings concerning exploitative abuse.

In trying to set their prices without risking violating competition law the undertaking needs to know first whether it is in a position of dominance. In order to know that, it needs to know which are the relevant product or service market and the correct geographical market. To answer these questions is not necessarily easy but assistance can be found in the Commission's Communication on definition of the relevant market.[25] It is, in any event, a wise strategy for the undertaking in question to take into account not the widest possible market definition but a more narrow market definition since that will be what the Commission – if in doubt – would tend to opt for were it to find it desirable to intervene. Secondly, if on the basis of such a more narrow market definition the undertaking finds itself in doubt, it would be the wise thing to do to base itself on dominance.

Third, the dominant undertaking needs to know the benchmark with which it must compare its price. Once the benchmark has been found it needs to know how much higher it can set its price before its price can be claimed to be 'unfair'.

Neither Community legislation nor the case-law gives us any answer to these last *two questions*. We have some indications by the Commission as regards the benchmark in the *Scandlines* case and some indications regarding benchmark and the mark-up that can be used in *United Brands and United Brands Continentaal v Commission* which used the wording 'no reasonable relation' to the economic value. In the doctrine, words like 'particularly high', 'excessive', and 'disproportionate' have been used to illustrate the gap between the benchmark and the charged price which makes the latter illegal under Article 82 EC.

Knowing that it is a risky affair trying to determine which are the, or at least some important and relevant, parameters which should normally be considered when trying to make an assessment of whether a specific price might violate Article 82 EC, I shall nevertheless try to explain how to determine the relevant benchmark and how to appreciate how big the gap between the benchmark and the price must be before it may be reasonably characterised as 'excessive' and therefore 'unfair' *unless* there are good objective reasons as an explanation.

[25] Commission Communication of 9 December 1997 [1997] OJ C/372/5.

## BENCHMARK

If the prices of the dominant undertaking are not substantially higher than those of its competitors on the same or neighboring markets,[26] there should not normally be any reason for the dominant undertaking to worry about Article 82(a) EC. The market price can then be assumed to be the relevant benchmark[27] and the prices of the dominant undertaking cannot in practice exceed that benchmark – at least for longer periods – because of the competitive pressure from its competitors or new entrants to the market.

If, on the other hand, the prices of the dominant undertaking having a de facto or legal monopoly are actually much higher than those of the competitors (that is, much higher than the general market price) – or there is no price to compare with – the dominating undertaking – if in doubt – should try to assess whether there is a risk of violating Article 82(a) EC. In that case (in which the general benchmark, the market price, cannot be used because exceeded considerably) the dominant undertaking – or the competition authority examining the case – must start by trying to see whether there exist objective reasons for the difference. In such a situation it will become necessary to look at the particular circumstances of the dominant undertaking in question and determine the specific economic value of its goods or services. This means that it will be necessary to establish a specific benchmark with which the price should be compared to see whether there is a substantial, inexplicable difference between that benchmark and the price charged.

This part of the exercise – determining the economic value – should in principle be the easiest since the idea in this respect is to try and determine which are the costs and other elements that from an economical, rational point of view may be legitimately included in the benchmark calculation.

These include without any doubt the following:

- Fixed costs (caution is necessary regarding right allocation of fixed costs)
- Variable costs
- Cost of capital

In calculating the above costs it may be necessary to include for example a mark-up to finance future capital investment to replace existing assets (an

[26] It may happen in practice that the smaller competitors take advantage of price increases from the dominant undertaking to raise their own prices as a consequence. If that is the case, it may render the value of price comparisons less instructive.

[27] From a purely economic point of view it might be said that the market price, ie the price which the customers accept to pay, equals the economic value of the particular good or service. In other words, if the customers accept to pay the price claimed by a dominant undertaking, there is no difference between the economic value of the good and the price paid and therefore no excessive price and no abuse. While this may apply for free markets, it is not convincing in relation to legal and de facto monopolies, especially in relation to *must have* products. This means that in such cases it is necessary to look at the price charged by competitors on neighboring markets (or if only a de facto quasi monopoly, competitors on the same market) and/or earlier or on other markets by the dominant undertaking. If such comparisons are not possible (eg because of too big differences between markets or competitors), an individual benchmark for the goods or services sold by the dominant undertaking must be established as proposed in the following text.

economically much more relevant cost factor than just depreciation costs) as well as to finance future new technology and/or business activities, opportunity costs (the fact that the goods might have been lawfully used for another more profitable purpose), and as the case may be, a mark-up to cover earlier suffered loss.

In determining the level of the variable costs of a particular good or service it may also in certain circumstances be relevant to include the costs for non-sold goods. That may be the case for example if the undertaking in question is in a position where it is necessary to maintain a certain high level of permanently replaced running stock (for example if the good in question can only be stocked for a short time) to meet demand of a cyclic and not, or not totally, predictable character. In such a situation the undertaking may frequently end up with a certain amount of unsold and unsellable goods. If such costs are not taken into account, the undertaking would necessarily incur future losses.

As concerns capital costs, it is obviously necessary to add a *reasonable profit*. What this may be is of course not easy to answer. While the average profit of the industry of the country in question may be an element relevant for comparison, one cannot always use that since – as the Commission said in the *Scandlines* case – it is well known that some sectors are structurally more profitable than others. It is therefore necessary to examine what is the average profit in the industry in question or in any comparable industry. An element which should normally lead to the acceptance of a higher price or even much higher profit that normal in the industry might for instance also be the need to be able to remunerate the shareholders or owners more generously for investing in higher risk activity in order to attract investment in such activity.

Furthermore, it will be of importance to consider *non-cost based factors such as demand characteristics* (*must have* factors, brand strength, luxury character, and for example temporary imbalance between supply possibilities and demand – a situation in which price increase may be a relevant and acceptable way of distributing too few goods between too many would-be buyers).

The *total sum of all these factors* may then constitute a sufficiently good proxy for the *economic value* of the good or service in question. It must, however, be repeated that even in trying to calculate the benchmark, several appreciations of a more or less subjective character must be made which means that all the individual non-objective elements should be calculated on the safe side.

The result should normally be the relevant benchmark with which the price charged or to be charged must be compared in order to see if the price is so much higher that it may clearly be characterised as excessive.

HOW HIGH TO BECOME EXCESSIVE?

In trying to answer this question it is – I think – necessary to stress that

1) dominance as such is not illegal under the EC competition law as appears from Article 82 EC itself and as it has been repeatedly stated by the Community Courts,

2) dominant undertakings are entitled to compete, even vigorously, but only as long as it is competition on the merits, and

3) also dominant undertakings are entitled to try to maximise their profits which is an inherent part of competition. What is forbidden is not large or very large *profits*[28] but only excessive prices which are *unfair*. If a dominant undertaking because of high efficiency is able to generate very large profits, this is consequently not unlawful but simply an important part of the economics and competition spurring other undertakings to try to achieve the same by being dynamic, efficient and creative.

High prices charged by the dominant undertaking is therefore not illegal per se even if it may mean high or even very high profits for the undertaking in question. Furthermore, it should not be forgotten that the mere fact that the undertaking in question is in a position of dominance will normally have as a consequence that it is a price *setter* and not a price taker. If, however, these prices become too high for the market, the market forces will normally correct the price level,[29] unless – as mentioned above – the undertaking in question is not exposed to any competition at all or any competition of importance, for example if it enjoys de facto monopoly power and the product is one that the consumers cannot do without. It should also be kept in mind that only in this latter situation will the dominant undertaking be able to *impose* the unfair price which is one of the conditions for applying Article 82 EC.

High prices only become contrary to competition law when they have 'no reasonable relation' to the economic value;[30] when they are excessive or exorbitantly high. But how high do they have to be to enter the illegal zone? How big a gap must there be between the price and the economic value as we have just defined and calculated it?

In *General Motors Continental v Commission* and *United Brands and United Brands Continentaal v Commission* the ECJ respectively stated that the price had to be 'excessive' and 'had no reasonable relation' to the economic value of the product. Already this way of indicating the level means that the price must exceed the economic value considerably.

[28] See Akman, n 16 above, at 13.

[29] In other words make it virtually impossible for the dominant undertaking to impose excessive prices.

[30] See Case 26/75 *General Motors Continental v Commission*, n 8 above, and Case 27/76 *United Brands and United Brands Continentaal v Commission*, n 9 above.

In a draft 'Competition Law Guideline'[31] the Office of Fair Trading (OFT) says that it would usually look for evidence that prices are 'substantially' higher than would be expected in a competitive market and look at whether there is any effective competitive pressure to bring the prices down. The OFT also stresses, however, that it is necessary to distinguish excessive prices from seemingly high prices that may be an integral part of the competitive process. That is necessary because high prices may just reflect for instance short term shifts in demand and supply or for example provide a fair return for earlier significant investments or losses.

In an interesting paper given at the Annual Competition Policy Conference in Oxford, July 2005, John Temple Lang has discussed 'Fundamental issues concerning abuse under Article 82 EC'. He starts off by stating that even though the concept of 'abuse' has given rise to much difficulty which according to him has been largely unnecessary as – if the law were properly understood – it is clear and satisfactory.[32] I cannot say that I agree with him, even though as regards for instance predatory pricing and discrimination it is not that difficult to apply the abuse test. However, as regards 'unfair high prices' it is by no means easy to determine when a price should be considered to be 'unfair' and if so whether intervention by the authorities is really useful and/or necessary.

The following discussion in his paper, in particular when discussing 'unfair' prices, is very interesting but is far from demonstrating that the concept of 'abuse' is clear. This appears clearly from his discussion of how to find out whether a price is 'unfair' because of being 'excessive' where he writes that 'no quantified test to say how much a price must exceed any of (five different levels mentioned earlier by Temple Lang) has been suggested'. He goes on to say that 'if possible more than one test should be used cumulatively' which indicates that this exercise is not simple and easy.

However, as regards the level of the price for it to be excessive, he writes that 'a price is not excessive merely because it is above the levels' he had indicated. 'It must be so substantially above as to be unreasonable, shocking and exceptional'. He finally mentions that most national cases in which excessive prices have been found involved an excess of over 100 %.

Concerning the question of when a price may be found to be 'unfair' and thus an abuse, the OFT Guidelines on abuse of dominant position indicate that 'prices would have to allow profits which significantly and persistently exceeded costs of capital before an abuse could be established'. It is noteworthy that not only must the price significantly but also *persistently*[33] exceed costs of capital.

[31] See: www.oft.gov.uk/shared oft /business leaflets/competition law/oft424a.pdf.

[32] It is, of course, correct that in the end it is for the competition authority and ultimately the courts to decide whether the concrete price charged was excessive and that that is a decision to be based on the particular circumstances of that case and in some cases the facts may be such that there can be little doubt either way. The big problem is, however, for the undertakings to get sufficient guidance from the case-law or guide lines from the Commission to help them avoid being charged with charging excessive prices. Such guidance does not exist at present.

[33] See in that connection Case 26/75 *General Motors Continental v Commission*, n 8 above, in which 5 instances of excessive prices did not amount to abuse because of attenuating circumstances.

I agree that normally only persistently excessive prices should be considered abusive, thereby allowing for the odd and perhaps rare case of a more random character which may happen for various and not necessarily unethical reasons.

As the words 'excessive' and with 'no reasonable relation' used by the ECJ in its case-law combined with the notion 'unfair' used by Article 82 EC indicate, I agree with Temple Lang and the OFT that for a price to become 'unfair' as being 'excessive' it must be far, or quite substantially, higher than the benchmark with which it must be compared. To demand such a difference or gap is not only a necessary consequence of the wording used by the EC Treaty and by the ECJ in its case-law, it is also necessary in order to take account of the lack of clear, simple, and exact methods for establishing the benchmark and the 'acceptable' profit in view of the particular circumstances of the market in question and of the (may be) dominating undertaking.

From a practical point of view I think it would be advisable for an undertaking or a competition authority, if in doubt concerning the question of whether a very high price demanded is not only very high but so high that it should be characterised as abusive, to do as the United Kingdom Competition Appeals Tribunal (CAT) did in the *NAPP* case[34] in order to examine whether the price demanded in that case could be characterised as abusive as found by the OFT.

As found by the CAT, it might in such a situation be very useful to compare the dominant undertaking's prices to those of its most profitable competitor, those of its competitors in general, and with the prices charged by the dominant undertaking in other markets. Furthermore it might be useful to examine whether the dominant undertaking's price has been increased significantly recently and, in particular, if that might be after important changes in the market, in other words after the exit of one or more of its competitors or undue advantage has been taken of a sudden imbalance between supply possibilities and demand.

If the dominant undertaking's prices are not significantly higher than those of its competitors, there would normally be no reason for concern. If they are significantly higher, one should examine whether that situation is of a more lasting character or just momentary. If they are just momentarily much higher, there would normally not be any reason to consider intervention unless customers had no alternative supplier because only in that situation can the unfair price be *imposed* on the customer and on top of that only if it is a *must have* product. If the price of the legal or de facto monopolist is persistently significantly higher, the benchmark test should be used to examine the case more closely to see if there is any objective explanation other than excessive pricing behind the price.

## CONCLUSION

The European Union is economically based on a market economy, in principle and largely also effectively leaving supply and demand to regulate the market. It

[34] *Napp Pharmaceutical Holdings v Director OFT*, 15 January 2002, case 100/1/1/01.

is generally acknowledged in theory – and in practical life it has proved to be the case – that this is by far the best way to generate growth and welfare for society in general and consumers in particular. This principle and the principle of the rule of law have been, are and should continue to be cornerstones of the Union's economic policy.

The respect of these two principles implies as little public intervention in the market as possible normally leaving it to the market to correct itself. Intervention by competition authorities should therefore also be kept at the minimum level necessary to avoid the unfortunate occasional excesses and when intervention must happen, it should be on the basis of legislation which is so clear that a *bonus pater familias,* and any reasonable undertaking on the market is able in advance to know what is illegal.

In that respect it is unfortunate that Article 82 EC, and in particular Article 82(a) EC, with the imprecise concepts of dominance, abuse and unfair prices – as has been demonstrated above – is in no way a clear and unequivocal legal text. Competition authorities, which furthermore are not well equipped to be price regulators, should therefore only intervene when strictly indispensable to avoid risk of serious negative changes of the market structure and/or serious lasting other consumer harm, remembering that competition law is there to protect consumers and not just competitors. Furthermore, intervention should only happen on the basis of very clear evidence and sound economic analysis regarding that kind of risk. As far as 'unfair' high prices are concerned, there is probably normally only reason to consider intervention if the dominant undertaking is not exposed to any real competitive pressure and if, at the same time, there are important barriers to entry, in other words only in situations where the dominant undertaking effectively is in a *position* to *impose* the excessive price and does so. Otherwise the market can be expected to correct itself within a reasonable time and force the 'unfair' prices down, perhaps not to the level that would exist on a market with perfect competition but at least to a more acceptable level.

As mentioned in the beginning, the above is only the result of some reflections on what 'abuse' may mean in regard of high prices. The notions of dominance and abuse in Article 82(a) EC are vague and imprecise and if coupled with the notion of 'unfairness' or 'excessiveness' it becomes less than clear when violations occur leading eventually to severe sanctions. Fortunately it seems that the Commission is conscious of this and therefore only may be expected to intervene if there is clear evidence of 'excessive' prices and if there is insufficient competitive pressure on the dominant undertaking which can be expected to correct the situation by way of forcing the high prices down again.

# 9

# *Object and Effects-Based Approaches in Identifying Abuses of a Dominant Position under Article 82 EC*

ARJEN W.H. MEIJ & TRISTAN BAUMÉ*

## INTRODUCTION

Throughout her tenure as a judge at the Court of First Instance of the European Communities (hereinafter CFI) *Virpi Tiili* has shown a keen interest in the intricacies of competition law and perhaps more particularly in the judicial approaches to economic appraisals involved in that part of the law.[1]

As it so happens, an observer of case-law in this area does not seem to have a very high perception of judges' understanding of the economics of competition law. As legal doctrine in this area is not always of particular assistance in this regard, the present contribution to the Liber Amicorum dedicated to our highly esteemed and warmly appreciated colleague and friend purports to examine whether it is feasible to reduce a complex economic notion within the framework of Article 82 EC to a slightly more simplified legal scheme which might even serve as a (non-binding) guideline for judges.

Within the system established by the EC Treaty ensuring that competition in the internal market is not distorted,[2] Articles 81 EC and 82 EC are the two provisions directed at undertakings. They pursue an identical aim, that is, the maintenance of effective competition within the common market.[3] Basically, the two provisions are of a complementary nature as they focus on two categories of restrictions on competition caused by undertakings – agreements between

* The views expressed herein are strictly personal and do not have any bearing on any pending case before the Court.

[1] V Tiili and J Vanhamme, 'The "Power of Appraisal" (pouvoir d'appréciation) of the Commission of the European Communities vis-à-vis the Powers of Judicial Review of the Communities' Court of Justice and Court of First Instance' (1999) 3 *Fordham International Law Journal* 885.

[2] Art 3(1)(g) EC.

[3] Case 6/72 *Europemballage and Continental Can v Commission* [1973] ECR 215 para 25.

undertakings, decisions by associations of undertakings, and concerted practices on the one hand, and the abuse of a dominant position by one or more undertakings on the other. One might have expected some parallelism in the wording of Articles 81 EC and 82 EC, given their complementary character and common purpose. It is, however, remarkable that the wording of Articles 81 EC and 82 EC differs far more than is arguably required by their respective targets. Indeed, Article 81 EC includes a reference to the object or effect of the agreements, decisions or concerted practices at issue. Also its third paragraph provides conditions which must be met for such agreements, decisions or concerted practices to escape from the scope of the prohibition. In contrast, Article 82 EC simply prohibits 'any abuse by one or more undertakings of a dominant position', without any reference to the object or effect of the abusive conduct at issue and without providing for any kind of escape clause similar to Article 81(3) EC.

The reason for such a difference in wording is rather obscure. Regarding the omission in Article 82 EC of the object or effect of the dominant undertaking's behaviour, there is no ground to suggest that the provision was originally designed to catch solely exploitative abuses. Nothing in the drafting of that provision permits such a conclusion, as each of the examples provided at Article 82 (a) through (d) EC may constitute either exploitative or exclusionary abuses, depending on the context to the particular behaviour. Indeed, if it appears that the conducts mentioned by Article 82 EC consist of the simple exploitation of market power to the detriment of consumers, the abuse is of an exploitative nature. Conversely, if those conducts harm competitors and therefore influence the competitive process on the market, either by excluding or disciplining rivals, the abuse is considered to be of an exclusionary nature.

Already in *Europemballage and Continental Can v Commission*, one of its first cases relating to an abuse of a dominant position, the Court of Justice of the European Communities (hereinafter ECJ) made it clear that Article 82 EC was also applicable to exclusionary abuses. It held that Article 82 EC was 'not only aimed at practices which [could] cause damage to consumers directly, but also at those which [were] detrimental to them through their impact on an effective competition structure, such as is mentioned at Article [3(1)(g) EC]'.[4] Further, whereas exploitative abuses are characterised by the fact that the abuse occurs through the use of economic power by a dominant position, the ECJ held that Article 82 EC does not require any strict link between the dominant position and its abuse.[5] This finding was confirmed in *Hoffmann-La Roche v Commission*.[6] Consequently, Article 82 EC prohibits: (i) exploitative abuses which presuppose the use of market power; (ii) exclusionary abuses through recourse to market power; and (iii) exclusionary conducts which do not require the use of market power.

[4] *Ibid* para 26; see also the reaffirmation of that principle in, inter alia, Case C-95/04 P *British Airways v Commission* [2007] ECR I-2331 para 106.

[5] *Ibid* para 27.

As a consequence of the inclusion of exclusionary abuses into the scope of Article 82 EC, two issues arose. First, since competitive interaction is itself likely to modify the structure of the market, for instance, through the ousting of a less efficient rival market player, it became necessary to distinguish abusive practices from those constituting 'legitimate competition'. Second, once a given behaviour is held not to belong to legitimate competition, it becomes relevant to assess to what extent the appraisal of the abuse should take into account its restrictive effect on competition. As will be suggested below, the examination of the effects may give rise to concerns where the line between a practice that may be permitted and a practice that should be prohibited is rather thin indeed. Despite the different wording of Articles 81 EC and 82 EC, the very fact that the scope of Article 82 EC encompasses exclusionary practices raises the issue of the assessment of the object or effect of the conduct considered.

## DEFINITION OF EXCLUSIONARY ABUSE

In its seminal case, *Hoffmann-La Roche v Commission*, the ECJ endeavoured to shed some light on these two issues by providing the following definition of an exclusionary abuse of a dominant position. It held: '[t]he concept of abuse is an objective concept relating to the behaviour of an undertaking in a dominant position which is such as to influence the structure of a market where, as a result of the very presence of the undertaking in question, the degree of competition is weakened and which, through recourse to methods different from those which condition normal competition in products or services on the basis of the [performances][7] of commercial operators, has the effect of hindering the maintenance of the degree of competition still existing in the market or the growth of that competition'.[8] This is still the prevailing definition of an exclusionary abuse under Article 82 EC today. In *Michelin I*, the ECJ specified that irrespective of the reasons why the undertaking has such a dominant

[6] Case 85/76 *Hoffmann-La Roche v Commission* [1979] ECR 461 para 91.

[7] The English version of this judgment appears to result from an inappropriate translation. The German version, which is the authentic language of the case, reads: '[…] welche von den mitteln eines normalen Produkt- oder Dienstleistungswettbewerbs auf der Grundlage der *Leistungen* der Marktbürger abweichen'. In French, the same passage reads: '[…] par le recours à des moyens différents de ceux qui gouvernent une compétition normale des produits ou services sur la base des *prestations* des opérateurs économiques' (emphasis added). The words 'Leistungen' or 'préstations' have been translated into English by the word 'transactions' (the relevant passage therefore reads: 'through recourse to methods different from those which condition normal competition in products or services on the basis of the *transactions* of commercial operators'). We consider that a correct translation into English would have led to use the word 'performances'. This translation is all the more regrettable given that this phrase identifies for the first time the notion of 'competition on the merits'. Further, it may be noted that the English version of the ECJ's judgment in Case 322/81 *Nederlandsche Banden-Industrie Michelin v Commission* [1983] ECR 3461, which repeats, at para 70, para 91 of Case 85/76 *Hoffmann-La Roche v Commission*, n 6 above, does use the word 'performances'. For the purposes of this article, we have adapted the quotation of para 91 of the Case 85/76 *Hoffmann-La Roche v Commission*, cited above, accordingly.

[8] Case 85/76 *Hoffmann-La Roche v Commission*, n 6 above, para 91.

position, the undertaking concerned has a special responsibility not to allow its conduct to impair genuine undistorted competition on the common market.[9]

The definition of exclusionary abuses in *Hoffmann-La Roche v Commission* includes three essential elements, that is, (i) the abuse of a dominant position is an objective concept, (ii) it is identified by reference to the concept of 'competition on the merits', (iii) which, in turn, relates to practices having the effect of hindering competition.

## Objective Concept of Abuse

In *Hoffmann-La Roche v Commission*, the ECJ made clear that the concept of abuse is an objective one. This finding entails two consequences. First, it suggests that the anticompetitive character of a given practice is to be assessed objectively, taking into consideration the context within which the conduct takes place. Second, dominant undertakings may not escape from the scope of Article 82 EC simply by claiming the absence of any subjective intention to restrict competition through improper practices. Neither the dominant undertaking's own knowledge of the abusive nature of its conduct[10] nor its intention to cause harm[11] are required for behaviour to be regarded as abusive. The fact that an undertaking did not have the intention to discourage or weaken competition has, in principle, no bearing on the classification of conduct as abusive.[12]

Nevertheless, it is incorrect to suppose that the subjective dimension of an abuse is entirely irrelevant. On the contrary, in some cases, proof of intention to have recourse to improper means in order to weaken or eliminate competition may constitute further incriminating evidence leading to the classification of a conduct as abusive and may eventually have significant consequences on the level of fine imposed. Therefore, while proof of intention may militate against a dominant undertaking, absence of intention will not exempt it from the rigours of Article 82 EC.

In that respect, a distinction should be made between the intention to exclude competitors and the intention to exclude them through improper means. Arguably, the former should not be incriminated under competition law, as by its very nature the game of competition accepts that rivals may have as a goal to win to the detriment of their competitors. The intention to use improper means in order to harm competition should therefore be the only relevant subjective element that could be taken into account when analysing a potential abuse. However, the Community Courts have not always followed such an approach. On occasion, they have taken into consideration the intention to exclude competitors. For example, in the context of predatory pricing, the ECJ has

[9] Case 322/81 *Nederlandsche Banden-Industrie Michelin v Commission*, n 7 above, para 57.

[10] Case T-271/03 *Deutsche Telekom v Commission* [2008] ECR II-477 para 327.

[11] Case T-128/98 *Aéroport de Paris v Commission* [2000] ECR II-3929 para 173.

[12] Case T-65/89 *BPB Industries and British Gypsum v Commission* [1993] ECR II-389 para 70.

developed a test that posits subjective intent as a requirement for considering that the impugned conduct constitutes an abuse. It held that prices below average total costs (that is fixed costs plus variable costs), but above average variable costs (those which vary depending on the quantities produced), are to be regarded as abusive if they are part of a plan to eliminate a competitor.[13] Also in *Compagnie maritime belge transports and Others v Commission,*[14] the ECJ referred to the intention of the liner conference to exclude the only competitor on the market in order to justify that price cuttings with a view to match competitor's rates may be regarded as an abuse.

## Competition on the Merits

In *Hoffmann-La Roche v Commission*, the ECJ identified for the first time the criterion for distinguishing practices acceptable under competition law from those that may be prohibited, that is, the 'recourse to methods different from those which condition normal competition in products or services on the basis of the traders' performances'. The ECJ has subsequently stated, in numerous cases, that 'Article [82 EC] prohibits a dominant undertaking from eliminating a competitor and thereby reinforcing its position by having recourse to means other than those within the scope of competition on the merits'.[15] Even though the ECJ appeared to identify the notion of competition on the merits, it did not so far get to define what this comprised. As a result, the scope of the concept is still largely unclear. The case-law of the ECJ has therefore been criticised for not providing legal certainty,[16] a shortcoming that was to a large extent already in-built in the text of Article 82 EC itself.

It may be emphasised in this context that the notion of competition on the merits is closely related to the concept of consumer welfare and, more broadly, to the very aim of competition law. Indeed, competition on the merits is probably best understood through a teleological approach since the concept is key to

[13] Case C-62/86 *AKZO v Commission* [1991] ECR I-3359 para 72.

[14] Joined Cases T-24/93 to 26/93 and T-28/93 *Compagnie maritime belge transports and Others v Commission* [1996] ECR II-1201 paras 147 and 148; Joined Cases C-395/96 P to C-396/96 P *Compagnie maritime belge transports and Others v Commission* [2000] ECR I-1365 para 119.

[15] See, eg Case C-62/86 *AKZO v Commission*, n 13 above, para 70, and Case T-228/97 *Irish Sugar v Commission* [1999] ECR II-2969 para 111. There again, while both judgments display an identical phrase in their French versions, which use the expression 'concurrence par les mérites', the English versions differ in wording. Para 70 of Case C-62/86 *AKZO v Commission*, cited above, reads: 'Article [82 EC] prohibits a dominant undertaking from eliminating a competitor and thereby strengthening its position by using methods other than those which come within the scope of competition on the basis of *quality*' (emphasis added). We consider that the English version of para 111 in Case T-228/97 *Irish Sugar v Commission*, cited above, which is quoted above in the main text, has the correct wording.

[16] See F Jenny, 'Abus de position dominante et modernisation de l'article 82 du traité CE' in F Brunet and G Canivet (eds), *Le nouveau droit communautaire de la concurrence* (Paris, LGDJ, 2008) 281, at 284 and para 660, where the author notes that the notion of competition on the merits serves rather to justify the merits of the competition authorities' decisions rather than to provide useful guidance to traders.

distinguishing what should be prohibited from what should be permitted or even ultimately promoted under competition law. As consumer welfare constitutes the ultimate concern underlying competition policy, competition on the basis of traders' performances may only be understood as consisting of behaviours that are beneficial to consumers – in terms of price, output, quality, variety, innovation, and so on.

It is interesting to note that the European Commission's stated aim regarding exclusionary conduct is 'to ensure that dominant undertakings do not impair effective competition by foreclosing their competitors in an anticompetitive way, thus having an adverse impact on consumer welfare, whether in the form of higher price levels than would have otherwise prevailed or in some other form such as limiting quality or reducing consumer choice.'[17] This statement shows that the prohibition of exclusionary abuses is meant to protect consumer welfare, an approach that mirrors the ECJ's finding in *Europemballage and Continental Can v Commission*, where it held that Article 82 EC is aimed at practices that are detrimental to consumers through their impact on the competitive structure.[18]

It should be borne in mind that the competitive structure is more often impaired through means which display clear efficiencies for the benefit of consumers, that is, through practices that are not manifestly outside the scope of competition on the merits. Therefore, the impairment of the competitive structure will, in principle, trigger the application of Article 82 EC where the conduct at issue not only offers efficiencies but also consists in the exercise by a dominant undertaking of its market power. Indeed, the special responsibility that Article 82 EC imposes on dominant undertakings allows them to alter the competitive structure exclusively and purely on the basis of their performances, without their market power playing any role in the further reduction of the level of competition. However, although Article 82 EC requires the dominant position to play a neutral role in the competitive process, such market power may nonetheless impact the undertaking's efficiency, which constitutes precisely the basis on which the dominant undertaking is allowed to compete. A competition authority may therefore be faced with the uncomfortable case of a dominant undertaking which is reducing the level of competition to the detriment of consumer welfare purely on the basis of efficiencies that competitors are not able to meet precisely because they do not enjoy equivalent market power. In such a case, the dominant undertaking is not departing from competition on the merits but consumer welfare may eventually be harmed.

## Effect of Restricting Competition

Finally, the definition of exclusionary abuse given by the ECJ in *Hoffmann-La Roche v Commission* makes the finding of an abuse dependant on the conduct's

[17] Guidance on the Commission's enforcement priorities in applying Art 82 EC to abusive exclusionary conduct by dominant undertakings, COM(2009) 864 final, para 19.

[18] Case 6/72 *Europemballage and Continental Can v Commission*, n 3 above, para 26.

restrictive effect. It should be stressed right away that this requirement should not be construed as obliging the Commission to wait for the anticompetitive effects to arise before taking action on the impugned practices. Nevertheless, this requirement makes the finding of abuse conditional to the likelihood of the practice's restrictive effect, which necessarily raises the issue of how such likelihood is to be determined.

The requirement that an abuse must have a restrictive effect has triggered enormous controversy as regards the standard to be applied in order to find anticompetitive effect. Many commentators have criticised the case-law of the Community Courts and the decisional practice of the Commission, which they consider to be inconsistent.[19] Whereas in some cases an analysis of the effects of the dominant undertaking's practices has been conducted in order to demonstrate the existence of an abuse, in other cases, the Commission and the CFI contented themselves with just noting the implementation of the practice itself.

For example, in *BPB Industries and British Gypsum v Commission*[20] and in *Van den Bergh Foods v Commission*,[21] the CFI held that a conduct which constitutes a usual practice on the market should not be prohibited as a matter of principle. However, 'those considerations, which are applicable in the normal situation of a competitive market, cannot be accepted without reservation in the case of a market on which, precisely because of the dominant position held by one of the traders, competition is already restricted'. Hence, in order to appraise whether, respectively, an exclusive purchasing commitment and the provision of refrigerators by a dominant undertaking on the condition that they are used exclusively for that firm's products, constitute abuses of a dominant position, an assessment of the restrictive effects on competition is required.[22]

It may also be noted that the relevance of the conducts' restrictive effects has often been understated, as the main focus was on its abusive nature. In the first case relating to a refusal to deal, *Commercial Solvents v Commission*, the ECJ concentrated its attention on the fact that an undertaking which is dominant on a raw material market may not cease to supply that raw material to its customer in order to reserve that input for itself. The fact that such behaviour was at risk of eliminating competition on the downstream market was mentioned but not further discussed, arguably because it was not really a controversial issue.[23]

In some other cases, the relevance of the conducts' actual effects has been left aside, in favour of a more formal approach to the abuse. This approach was

[19] See J Temple Lang and R O'Donoghue, 'The Concept of an Exclusionary Abuse under Article 82 EC' in *GCLC Research Papers on Article 82 EC* (Bruges, July 2005) 38; J Padilla and D Slater, 'Rebates as an Abuse of Dominance under Article 82 EC' in *GCLC Research Papers on Article 82 EC* (Bruges, July 2005) 84, and D Waelbroeck, 'Michelin II: a per se rule against rebates by dominant companies?' (2005) 1 *Journal of Competition Law and Economics* 149.

[20] Case T-65/89 *BPB Industries and British Gypsum v Commission*, n 12 above.

[21] Case T-65/98 *Van den Bergh Foods v Commission* [2003] ECR II-4653.

[22] Case T-65/89 *BPB Industries and British Gypsum v Commission*, n 12 above, paras 65–67, and Case T-65/98 *Van den Bergh Foods v Commission*, n 21 above, paras 159 and 160.

[23] Joined Cases 6/73 and 7/73 *Commercial Solvents v Commission* [1974] ECR 223 para 25.

crystallised in the CFI judgment in *Michelin II,*[24] where it found that '[f]or the purpose of establishing an infringement of Article 82 EC, it is sufficient to show that the abusive conduct [...] tends to restrict competition or, in other words, that the conduct is capable of having that effect'.[25] The CFI also held that '[for] the purpose of applying Article 82 EC, establishing the anti-competitive object and the anti-competitive effect are one and the same thing [...]. If it is shown that the object pursued by the conduct of an undertaking in a dominant position is to limit competition, that conduct will also be liable to have such an effect'.[26]

In the same vein, in *British Airways v Commission,*[27] the CFI held that 'for the purposes of establishing an infringement of Article 82 EC, it is not necessary to demonstrate that the abuse in question had a concrete effect on the markets concerned. It is sufficient in that respect to demonstrate that the abusive conduct of the undertaking in a dominant position tends to restrict competition, or, in other words, that the conduct is capable of having, or likely to have, such an effect'.[28] It added that 'where an undertaking in a dominant position actually puts into operation a practice generating the effect of ousting its competitors, the fact that the hoped-for result is not achieved is not sufficient to prevent a finding of abuse of a dominant position within the meaning of Article 82 EC'.[29] This case attracted all the more attention as a parallel case in the United States resulted in a different outcome. Indeed, concomitant to the complaint lodged before the Commission, Virgin Atlantic also lodged a complaint before the Southern District Court of New York, arguing that British Airways' commission system constituted an attempt of monopolisation, infringing Sections 1 and 2 of the Sherman Act. Both the District Court and, on appeal, the Court of Appeals for the 2nd Circuit, rejected Virgin Atlantic's complaint, on the basis that it had failed to discharge its burden of proof of showing below cost pricing. The 2nd Circuit noted, in particular, that 'the decision to offer incentives was nothing more than an attempt to generate increased business on the whole by limiting profitability on selected sales. We must be mindful that low prices are a positive aspect of a competitive marketplace and are encouraged by the antitrust laws'.[30]

In 2005 the Commission initiated a review of its policy under Article 82 EC in order to bring it more in line with an economic and effects-based approach. This review led to the adoption of the Commission's Guidance on its enforcement priorities in applying Article 82 EC to abusive exclusionary conduct by dominant undertakings (hereinafter Commission Guidance on Article 82 EC). In the wake of the important discussion which this pursued modernisation of Article 82 EC has triggered, the following analysis makes an endeavour to identify a rationale behind a possible object/effect interplay in identifying abuses of a dominant position.

[24] Case T-203/01 *Michelin v Commission* [2003] ECR II-4071.
[25] *Ibid* para 239.
[26] *Ibid* para 241.
[27] Case T-219/99 *British Airways v Commission* [2003] ECR II-5917.
[28] *Ibid* para 293.
[29] *Ibid* para 297.
[30] *Virgin Atlantic Airways Ltd. v British Airways Plc*, 257F. 3d 256 (2d Cir.2001) para 57.

Before actually considering the application of an 'object or effect' approach in relation to Article 82 EC, the mechanism of the analogous test under Article 81 EC will be briefly outlined, since this test is traditionally applied in the context of Article 81 EC.

## Object or Effect under Article 81 EC

In relation to Article 81 EC, three basic observations may be made. First, as the ECJ made it clear in early judgments relating to this Article, the requirements that an agreement be restrictive of competition by its object or by its effect are not cumulative but alternative. Hence, once an agreement is held to be restrictive by its object, there is no need to examine its concrete effects.[31] Second, the ratio lying behind the classification of restrictions by object is related to a presumption that some particularly pernicious clauses can only result in restriction of competition and should therefore be banned as a matter of law. As the Commission has put it in its guidelines for the application of Article 81(3) EC, 'restrictions of competition by object are those that by their very nature have the potential of restricting competition'. These restrictions 'have such a high potential of negative effects on competition that it is unnecessary for the purposes of applying Article 81(1) [EC] to demonstrate any actual effects on the market'.[32] Third, and importantly, the restrictive object of an agreement is nonetheless to be appraised within the actual context in which it is to be applied. To that extent, the economic and legal environment in which the undertakings operate, the products or services covered by the agreement, the structure of the market concerned and the actual conditions in which it functions need to be taken into account.[33]

Yet, the dichotomy between object and effect is not always easy to handle, as the line to be drawn between restrictions by object and restrictions by effect may in some situations be unclear. In essence, the classification of an agreement as being restrictive of competition by its object depends on whether the purpose of that agreement, as objectively appraised within the relevant economic context, must be regarded as restricting competition.[34] When the objective purpose of

[31] Case 56/65 *LTM* [1966] ECR 337 para 249, and Joined Cases 56/64 and 58/64 *Consten and Grundig v Commission* [1966] ECR 429 para 342.

[32] See para 21 of the Commission's Guidelines on the application of Article 81(3) EC [2004] OJ C/101/97.

[33] Case 56/65 *LTM*, n 31 above, para 249; Joined Cases 56/64 and 58/64 *Consten and Grundig v Commission*, n 31 above, para 343; Joined Cases 29/83 and 30/83 *Compagnie Royale Asturienne des Mines and Rheinzink v Commission* [1984] ECR 1679 para 26, and Case T-168/01 *GlaxoSmithKline Services v Commission* [2006] ECR II-2969 para 110. See also para 22 of the Commission's Guidelines on the application of Article 81(3) EC, n 32 above.

[34] See Joined Cases 29/83 and 30/83 *Compagnie Royale Asturienne des Mines and Rheinzink v Commission*, n 33 above, para 26. The subjective intention of the parties to that agreement is therefore of limited significance. An agreement may have the object of restricting competition even though the parties to it are pursuing another objective.

an agreement, as assessed within its factual, economic or legal background, is held not to be directed toward the restriction of competition, the competition authority should still enquire whether it is liable to have such an effect. In that respect, the competition authority may hold that, taking into account the context within which it is to operate, such an agreement is still liable to have the effect of significantly restricting competition. This does not mean that such effects must already have arisen, their emergence often being conditional on the reaction of the market, that is, on reactions of third parties which are beyond the control of the parties to the agreement. However, the degree of uncertainty relating to the actual occurrence of restrictive effects does not prevent the agreement to be classified as restrictive by its effect, as long as the likelihood that this agreement will produce harmful effects is substantiated, taking into account the actual context within which it operates.

## Principles Governing an 'Object or Effect' Test under Article 82 EC

It is to be noted, first of all, that the issue whether the identification of the abuse should rest on the object or the effect of the conduct at stake does not arise in relation to exploitative abuses. Indeed, as far as this type of abuse is concerned, the identification of the conduct as such is sufficient to find an abuse of a dominant position, as this type of abuse is directly related to misuse of market power and directly detrimental to consumer welfare. The most obvious example of this is provided by Article 82(a) EC, which concerns in particular the imposition of unfair purchase or selling prices. Once the competition authority has been able to demonstrate that prices have been raised at supra-competitive levels, it has by the same token demonstrated consumer harm. Hence, in case of exploitative abuse, the object of the conduct and its effect amount necessarily to one and the same thing. To that extent, a per se approach to exploitative abuses is in principle admissible, simply because by their very nature such abuses cannot present any kind of efficiencies in the interest of consumer welfare. This is however without prejudice to the much more delicate and debated issue of the grounds on which a given price should be regarded as excessive.

Conversely, the issue of whether an object or effect-based test is to be adopted does arise in relation to exclusionary abuses. We suggest that the extent to which an object-based test may be adopted is a function of the notion of competition on the merits, which, as we have argued above, is in turn to be understood in light of consumer welfare.

### *Practices Manifestly Outside Competition on the Merits*

In an approach based on competition on the merits, an object-based test is sufficient to identify an abuse of a dominant position when the practice at issue, as considered objectively within its actual context, bears no relation with competition on the merits, in that it shows no efficiency whatsoever for the benefit of consumers while striving for the exclusion of competitors or, at least, for a reduction of the level of competition. The adoption of a purely object-based or formal approach to such restrictive practices does not, however, mean that the anticompetitive capacity or potential of the conduct at issue does not need to be demonstrated. On the contrary, the anticompetitive potential of the conduct should be investigated and demonstrated by reference to the economic or legal context in which it is to take place. If that were not so, a conduct which is incapable of excluding competitors or otherwise lessening the level of competition would be liable to be classified as an abuse only because of the subjective intention of the dominant undertaking.

Once it is established that, considered within its context, a dominant firm's conduct is likely to restrict competition through means that are manifestly outside the realm of competition on the merits, there should be no need to examine the effects of such conduct in view of its classification as abuse.[35] In this perspective, proof of lack of actual restrictive effect should not have an impact on the finding of abuse where it does not affect the grounds which led to the conclusion that the practice at stake was likely to produce anticompetitive effects through wholly improper means. That may well be the case where the results hoped for failed to materialise as a result of the interference of events which were beyond the dominant undertaking's control, such as the action of third parties jeopardising the results pursued by the abusive practices. Article 82 EC is indeed to be construed so as sanctioning exclusionary practices even if the dominant undertaking's improper actions have failed to reach their goals. As it is established in such cases that the restrictive effects on competition have not occurred and are not going to occur anymore, Article 82 EC is applied here solely for pedagogical purposes, the dominant undertaking being prosecuted as a matter of principle, for having conducted itself in a way which was particularly pernicious to competition while producing no added value of any type for the benefit of consumer welfare.

The Commission has identified this kind of abuse in its Guidance on enforcement priorities in applying Article 82 EC. At paragraph 22, it states:

> There may be circumstances where it is not necessary for the Commission to carry out a detailed assessment before concluding that the conduct in question is likely to result in consumer harm. If it appears that the conduct can only raise obstacles to competition and that it creates no efficiencies, its anti-competitive effect may be inferred. This could be the case, for instance, if the dominant undertaking prevents its customers from testing the products of competitors or provides financial incentives to its customers on condition that they do not test such products, or pays a distributor or a customer to delay the introduction of a competitor's product.

As the use by the Commission of the expression 'for instance' shows, the prevention of the testing by customers of competing products or the provision of

[35] It should be noted that the assessment of the abuse's effects may well become relevant in relation to the calculation of the fine.

financial incentives with a view to excluding or delaying the entry of competing products are far from being considered the only practices manifestly outside the scope of competition on the merits.

*The Uneasy Line between Competition on the Merits and Improper Competition*

Nevertheless, many, if not most, of the practices that are likely to exclude competitors or to otherwise reduce the level of competition may not be considered as entirely foreign to competition on the merits, as they may just as well be regarded as stemming from the traders' performances and as offering efficiencies for the benefit of consumer welfare. In those cases, it will be more difficult to determine whether the exclusionary effect of the conduct at stake is caused by the efficiency offered to customers or consumers (lower price, better quality, and so on) or also by the undertaking's market power. As we have emphasised above, the combination of the practice in question with the undertaking's market power may impair the competitive structure by pushing competitors out of the market. Tying and bundling offer a good example of such practices. The tying or bundling of two different, but complementary, products or services may create, or may stem from, certain efficiencies which are of direct benefit to consumer welfare. Yet, such practices are liable to restrict competition because of the very presence of the undertaking's dominant position on at least one of the relevant markets. In view of their potential positive effect on consumer welfare, an object-based analysis would be at risk of ignoring such efficiencies.

Other practices, such as predatory pricing, tend to restrict competition by following mechanisms that are identical to those by which competition increases. In those cases, the exclusionary effect finds its cause in the offering of efficiencies to consumers which competitors are often not able to meet, at least not without incurring losses. Arguably, such efficiencies are not based on the trader's performance, as they are not offered on the basis of the undertaking's actual production costs. Nevertheless, even if predatory pricing may be regarded as not being based on competition on the merits, the direct benefits which are offered to consumers may require some extent of an effect-based approach in the assessment of its abusive character. Indeed, a purely formal approach would be at risk of prohibiting behaviours which antitrust rules are precisely intended to promote.[36] Consequently, the dominant undertaking should be able to escape the scope of Article 82 EC in situations where it can prove that it has not been able to recover its losses because of the competitive constraints still existing on the market.

A similar consideration applies in relation to conditional rebates, which may have loyalty enhancing effects restricting competition when applied by undertakings enjoying market power. Such practices also display efficiencies for

[36] See, on this point, the cautious attitude of United States authorities toward aggressive price cuttings in OECD Policy round tables, Competition on the merits, Directorate for Financial and Enterprise Affairs Competition Committee DAF/COMP(2005)27, 22 December 2005, unclassified, 216, to be found at: www.oecd.org/dataoecd/7/13/35911017.pdf (last visited on March 24, 2009).

the benefit of consumer welfare, the most basic aspect of which consisting in lowering the price.[37] Since such pricing practices may well belong to commercial usages and offer efficiencies, which make them sometimes difficult to distinguish from competition on the merits, an analysis of their effects on competition is advisable. There again, a purely formal approach would be at risk of prohibiting behaviour which is to the benefit of consumer welfare and which competition policy should consequently promote.

As has been mentioned above, in cases of practices displaying efficiencies to the benefit of consumer welfare, the alteration of the competitive structure is not only caused by the dominant undertaking's performance, but also to a significant extent by its market power. Therefore, even in those situations where conduct offering efficiencies to the benefit of consumer welfare is held to constitute an abuse of a dominant position, the notion of competition on the merits never entirely loses its relevance. If Article 82 EC prohibits a dominant undertaking from implementing certain practices, it is because such practices would allow it to alter the structure of competition and, indirectly, consumer welfare, on grounds that are not purely related to the conduct's purported efficiencies. Considered in that perspective, Article 82 EC is therefore, in principle, a tool aimed at restricting the dominant undertaking's behaviour to means which do not consist in the use of its market power.

A conspicuous variation on this theme may be found in *Compagnie maritime belge transports and Others v Commission.*[38] That case was concerned with several conducts considered abusive by the Commission, one of them consisting in a price diminution designed to meet the rates offered by the only rival. This price diminution did not, however, constitute predation, as it was not found to be below variable or total production costs. Consequently, the applicants alleged that the sole reduction of profit margins could not be regarded as exceeding what is normal in competition. The CFI and the ECJ replied that this price diminution should be regarded as an abuse as it was established that it had been carried out with a view to excluding the only competitor on the market.[39] It should be borne in mind that the undertakings which were part of the liner conference at issue collectively enjoyed super dominance, with a market share of 90 %, as the ECJ was keen to underline.[40] By selectively cutting its prices in order to match those of the only competitor on the market, the liner conference endeavoured to eliminate the only source of competition on the market in order to continue to require its users to pay higher prices for the services which were not threatened by that competition.[41] As appears from the CFI's and ECJ's

[37] For a discussion of the potential efficiencies created by conditional rebates, see, eg Padilla and Slater, n 19 above, at 87.

[38] Joined Cases T-24/93 to 26/93 and T-28/93 *Compagnie maritime belge transports and Others v Commission*, n 14 above; Joined Cases C-395/96 P and C-396/96 P *Compagnie maritime belge transports and Others v Commission*, n 14 above.

[39] *Ibid* paras 147 and 148 of the CFI's judgment and para 119 of the ECJ's judgment.

[40] *Ibid* para 119 of the ECJ's judgment.

[41] *Ibid* para 117 of the ECJ's judgment.

judgments, focus was exclusively on the preservation of the market structure, presumably in order to eventually secure consumer welfare. This approach is reminiscent of the Freiburg's ordoliberal school of thought,[42] which has exerted a considerable influence on European competition policy until at least the late 1990s. It may strike the innocent observer that this reasoning did not take account of the notion of competition on the merits, the focus being solely placed on the likely effects of the practice at stake on the competitive structure. Although one may accept that situations of super dominance may justify an even closer scrutiny of the dominant undertakings' conduct, in terms of competition policy, the question remains whether conduct which is purely based on the trader's performance should be regarded as abusive. This issue may be all the more delicate where the dominant position confers a greater efficiency allowing the dominant undertaking to exclude competitors from the market and to subsequently maximise its profit to the detriment of consumer welfare.

Essentially, the interplay between the object and the effects-based approaches may be compared to the tipping of weighing scales which incline one way or the other according to whether the practice at issue gives rise to prima facie efficiencies. Where it is clear that there is no competition on the merits, because the impugned conduct produces no efficiencies, the scales will incline towards an object-based approach. Conversely, where conduct results from or could be justified on the basis of efficiencies, the scales will tilt towards an effects-based approach, which focuses on consumer welfare. In those circumstances where it is considered that conducts remaining entirely within competition on the merits could also constitute abuses of a dominant position, as in *Compagnie maritime belge transports and Others v Commission*, a purely effect-based approach should then be adopted.

The question whether the prohibition of conduct pertaining to competition on the merits is compatible with *Hoffmann-La Roche v Commission* remains however controversial, since the latter defines abuse of a dominant position as a behaviour which is not based on trader's performances. The notion of competition on the merits could well be regarded as an impediment to the classification of a practice as an abuse, even where the practice in question may eventually be detrimental to consumer welfare because the alteration of the

[42] In this school of thought, competition is understood as a process of economic coordination based on the operators' economic freedoms of action, which requires close supervision on the part of public authorities. In this conception, the focus is on the protection of individual economic freedom of action in the interest of a free and fair political, social and economic order. The protection of such individual economic freedom of action against collusion and dominant undertakings' exclusionary practices becomes an aim in itself in the interest of an open market. Therefore, the focus is not directly on economic efficiency, which is regarded to result indirectly from the successful maintenance of an open and free market. For some brief accounts of the Freiburg school of thought, see, eg R O'Donoghue and AJ Padilla, *The Law and Economics of Article 82 EC* (Oxford, Hart Publishing, 2006) 8 and 9; J Faull and A Nikpay, *The EC Law of Competition*, 2nd edn (Oxford, Oxford University Press, 2007) 218 and 219; W Wurmnest, 'The Reform of Article 82 EC in the Light of the "Economic Approach"' in M-O Mackenrodt, B Conde Gallego and S Enchelmaier (eds), *Abuse of Dominant Position: New Interpretation, New Enforcement Mechanisms?* (Berlin, Springer, 2008) 10 and 11.

competitive constraints exerted on the dominant undertaking will allow it to raise its profits subsequently.

*Analysis of Restrictive Effects; a Focus on Consumer Welfare*

The standard to be applied in order to establish anticompetitive effects constitutes certainly the most delicate issue in identifying abuses of a dominant position.

When the ECJ extended the scope of Article 82 EC to exclusionary abuses in *Europemballage and Continental Can v Commission*, the wording used clearly suggested that focus on the competitive structure is justified to the extent that impairment of that structure is liable to be detrimental to consumer welfare.[43] The latter notion thus appears to remain the ultimate objective of competition policy. Hence, the appraisal of a practice's negative effects should in principle focus on its impact on consumer welfare, rather than on the exclusionary effect as such. In this view, a deterioration of the competitive structure cannot, conceptually, be equated with consumer harm.

In any event, it may be presumed to some extent that once the competitive structure on the market is damaged, detrimental effects will be felt on consumer welfare at some point, as no competitive constraints will exert any disciplining effect on the dominant undertaking's behaviour, which is supposed to maximise its profits to the largest possible extent. Thus, basically, the appraisal of the effects on consumer welfare consists in assessing the extent to which the impairment of the competitive structure will permit the dominant undertaking to take advantage of the decreased competitive pressures in order to maximise its own benefits to the detriment of consumers. Such an examination necessarily entails a degree of margin of appraisal, as it calls for a 'complex economic analysis' as well as some competition policy choices, for instance inasmuch as it requires the competition authority to determine the period of time within which the net effect on consumer welfare is to be appraised. The choice of the relevant period of time may vary according to the specificities of the market in issue.

As Article 82 EC should be capable of being applied in a preventive manner, the Commission must be able to prohibit practices before the impairment of the competitive structure has properly occurred, which requires it to appraise the practices' likely effects. Such an exercise will certainly also includes complex assessments requiring the use of economic tests displaying relative advantages and disadvantages.[44] Presumably, the appraisal of practices' likely effects is a difficult exercise which will never be entirely free from some degree of uncertainty. At least and in any case, in order to demonstrate the likelihood of the practices' anticompetitive effects and their not merely hypothetical nature, the Commission should nevertheless justify its finding on the basis of concrete

[43] See n 4 above.

[44] For discussions of such tests, see, in particular, Jenny, n 16 above, and Temple Lang and O'Donoghue, n 19 above.

features of the market as well as on sound economic theory. Admittedly, the Community Courts are not to substitute their views to that of the Commission with regard to the choice of the test used. However, if so requested by the applicant, the CFI does verify whether such a test does not lead to manifestly inappropriate conclusions.

The principle according to which competition law is to focus primarily on consumer welfare would find appropriate expression in situations where, while the Commission could have considered prima facie that a given practice was likely to impair the competitive structure on the market, hard facts show that the positions of some competitors have actually been reinforced or that newcomers have appeared on the market, thus indicating that the competitive pressure on the dominant firm has increased notwithstanding the exclusionary practices. When the exclusionary practices display immediate efficiencies to the benefit of consumer welfare, proof of actual and definitive absence of damage to the competitive structure may lead to the conclusion that the practices at stake have had only pro-competitive rather than anticompetitive effects. To take but one straightforward example in this approach, blunt predatory pricing would be able to escape the scope of Article 82 EC when the dominant undertaking can prove that its practice has actually failed in lowering the competitive pressure exerted against it and, therefore, in diminishing the discipline competition imposes on the dominant firm's behaviour. In this context, it should however be noted that the only fact that predatory pricing has not pushed competitors out of the market does not necessarily imply that the competitive constraint exerted on the dominant firm's behaviour has not diminished, as the practices in question may deter rivals from competing too harshly with the dominant undertaking in the future.

The extent to which the appraisal of restrictive effects has been focused on consumer welfare rather than on the competitive structure is, however, not always very apparent from the Commission's practice or, for that matter, from the case-law. In an approach possibly following the lines of Freiburg ordoliberal thinking, the emphasis has sometimes been put on the protection of the market structure. Such a tendency has been more particularly apparent in those cases where it was not contested that the practices at stake did not have the exclusionary effects sought, and where the structure of the market actually displayed increased competition. For instance, in *Michelin II*, in answer to the argument according to which Michelin's market shares and prices had been falling steadily while its competitors had reinforced their position on the market and new manufacturers had entered the market, the CFI stated that it was very probable that the fall in Michelin's market share and sales prices would have been even greater if the loyalty enhancing rebates had not been put into practice.[45] Likewise, in *British Airways v Commission*, the CFI held that in the absence of the dominant undertaking's rebates system, the competitors' market shares would have been able to grow even more significantly.[46] In *Compagnie*

[45] Case T-203/01 *Michelin v Commission*, n 24 above, para 245.
[46] Case T-219/99 *British Airways v Commission*, n 27 above, para 298.

*maritime belge transports and Others v Commission*, where the abusive nature of the impugned conduct was controversial, the CFI was faced with a similar argument of the applicant, which alleged a lack of effect on the competitive structure. The CFI did consider, however, that the fact that the result sought was not achieved was not sufficient to avoid the practice being characterised as an abuse and that the rival's market share might have increased more significantly if the practice had not been implemented.[47]

In view of the foregoing, it may be considered that the CFI focused on what the competitive structure would have been, had the abusive practices not been implemented, rather than on the practices' net negative impact on consumer welfare. Whereas the abuses consisted in practices displaying prima facie efficiencies for the immediate advantage of consumers, that is price reductions, the evolution of the market structure showed an increasing degree of competition (increasing market shares for competitors and new rivals entering the market).

It should be noted that the competitive structure that would have existed in the absence of the abuse and, thus, the impact of the dominant firm's practices on the evolution of the competition level may be relevant to the extent that it reveals an effect on the evolution of the competitive constraints exerted against the dominant undertaking. Indeed, in some cases the disciplining effects of competitive constraints might have been more effective if the abusive practices had not been implemented. Hence, even where the competitive structure has improved to some extent notwithstanding the abusive practices, such practices may nonetheless have prevented or delayed a further intensification of competitive constraints on the dominant undertaking, to the net detriment of consumer welfare. In any case, variations of competitors' market shares and market entry or exit of rivals are to be considered with caution, as they may not necessarily be unfailing indicators for measuring the variation of the competitive constraints exerted on the dominant undertaking. Moreover, even though the increase of the competitors' market shares could have been greater in the absence of the abusive practices, the prevention of intensification of competitive pressure on the dominant undertaking may be irrelevant when the existing competitive constraints are in any event sufficient to discipline the dominant firm's behaviour for the benefit of consumer welfare.

At this point, a few remarks should perhaps be devoted to the burden of proof which is to govern the assessment of a possibly abusive conduct. At paragraphs 30 and 31 of its Guidance on Article 82 EC, the Commission states that it is up to the dominant undertaking to demonstrate that consumer welfare will eventually not be damaged by the potentially abusive behaviour. To that end, the dominant undertaking should demonstrate, on the basis of verifiable evidence, the fulfilment of four cumulative conditions directly inspired from Article 81(3) EC, that is first, the conduct in question offers efficiencies, second, the conduct is indispensable to the realisation of those efficiencies, third, those efficiencies

[47] Joined Cases T-24/93 to T-26/93 and T-28/93 *Compagnie maritime belge transports and Others v Commission*, n 14 above, para 149.

outweigh the likely negative effects on 'competition and consumer welfare' and, fourth, the conduct does not eliminate effective competition.

The issue of the burden of proof has never been very simple and any proper analysis of that question would require much more space than is available for the present contribution. For the purpose of the present reflection, we limit ourselves to observing that as soon as a given practice displays some efficiencies, which may be either recognised by the competition authority itself or demonstrated by the dominant undertaking, the competition authority will need to engage in an effect-based analysis. The extent of that analysis will depend on the capacity of the dominant undertaking to show convincingly that the efficiencies brought about by its conduct will not be outweighed by a reduction in the competitive pressure exerted against it and which would subsequently allow it to derive supra-competitive revenues or to behave in such manner.

It should be noted, in this connection, that the application of the four conditions inspired from Article 81(3) EC is by no means a guarantee for an appropriate effective result of the effect-based analysis. It only provides an analytical framework within which the assessment of a conduct's effect on consumer welfare is to take place. Therefore, the debate relating to the sometimes controversial validity of some of the presumptions or economic tests which the competition authority is to use as proxies for assessing the conducts' restrictive effects on competition remains unaffected.

## CONCLUSION

The purpose of the present chapter is to outline a theoretical framework governing an 'object or effect test' under Article 82 EC. It is suggested that the notion of competition on the merits, which is to be understood in the light of what is beneficial to consumer welfare, should play a determinative role. Indeed, those types of conduct which are by their very nature such as to only restrict the level of competition while providing no efficiency of any kind to the benefit of consumer welfare, that is to say practices which do clearly not fall within the ambit of competition on the merits, may be categorised as abuses on the basis of an object-based analysis. Conversely, the abusive character of those types of conduct which display efficiencies likely to benefit consumer welfare should be assessed according to an effect-based analysis. Such an effect-based analysis implies in principle focusing on consumer welfare, as the latter constitutes the proclaimed ultimate goal of competition policy.

As emerges from the above, the assessment of a practice's net effects on consumer welfare constitutes a delicate exercise which is subject to a significant degree of uncertainty. Such uncertainty is mainly related to the difficulty in quantifying the likely negative and positive effects of a given behaviour on consumer welfare. The difficulty of such an assessment may indeed risk rendering the effectiveness of any effect-based approach illusory and bringing the analysis closer to an object-based approach. The use of proxies, such as the evolution of the market structure, will therefore often be inevitable. In any case, regardless of the degree of uncertainty in the analysis of a given practice's effects on consumer welfare, it remains essential to keep in mind the relevant framework within which any assessment is to take place and the background against which the Community Courts are to appraise the arguments put forward by the parties while exercising control of the legality of Commission decisions in Article 82 EC cases. Obviously, object and effect-based approaches do not constitute a panacea to all problems inherent to cases on abuses of dominant positions. However, they may be of some assistance to clarify the analytical process involved.

# 10

# *Product Safety and Antitrust – Focus on Enforcement Networks*

MAIJA LAURILA

## INTRODUCTION

Both consumer law/policy and competition law/policy (here for convenience referred to as the 'two areas' or 'both areas') are central in *Virpi Tiili's* professional experience. Consumer product safety and antitrust are at the heart of the two areas and they have a lot in common. The two policies seek to enhance consumer welfare. In both areas, investigation into business practices and individual enforcement decisions are key to achieving results in the marketplace. The substantive rules in the two areas are harmonised, as far as cases with cross-border dimension in the European Union are concerned, but procedures and sanctions are regulated nationally.

The purpose of this chapter is to compare product safety enforcement with antitrust enforcement and in particular the enforcement networks and consider to what extent antitrust can serve as a model or inspiration. One can imagine a degree of cross-fertilisation between the competent authorities, which in some European countries are the same in both areas, and one should also recognise the ever closer relations between different authorities both within the EU and also globally. Moreover, the purpose is to discuss where the limits of such developments seem to be and, finally, the further common challenges which lie ahead.[1]

[1] This chapter is based on my experience in the implementation, monitoring and development of these policies in the European Commission, first as regards competition and subsequently non-food product safety. I chose to write about enforcement and not the law itself so as to widen the perspectives (how competition law and policy permeates other areas) represented in the book. The views are purely personal and do not engage the European Commission. I would like to express my sincere thanks to my colleagues Stefano Soro (European Commission DG Health and Consumers) and Dorothe Dalheimer (European Commission DG Competition) for their valuable comments on the chapter; any errors are however still mine.

The business environment is currently particularly demanding. The greatest economic crisis during the history of the EU is testing industry and also the public authorities. The authorities must ensure that this situation is not used, by economic operators, as a pretext or excuse for escaping the basic rules of antitrust and consumer laws. The authorities must for instance be vigilant so as to check that the costs of compliance (product safety checks), which the whole industry incurs due to external elements are not, by collusive agreement, passed on to consumers. Such practices have been seen in the antitrust area but they are not excusable. The economic operators' awareness of their duties towards the consumer is important and the authorities need to consider how best to harness the business sector in an exercise to ensure compliance by the whole industry sector.

## LEGAL ENVIRONMENT

The legal environment is well established but not simple, given that economic operators in the business of manufacturing, importing and/or distributing consumer products must be fully aware of several sets of legal requirements. These have their roots in the EC Treaty, which provides for undistorted competition (Article 81 EC) and a high level of consumer protection (Article 153 EC), as well as for a well-functioning internal market and certain fundamental rights. Therefore, from this perspective, businesses face challenges especially in the areas of antitrust, product safety (recalls and other corrective measures), product liability (for damages) and a spectrum of consumer rights. Finally, consumer access to justice and redress is an important complement to public enforcement by the competent authorities.

The enforcement networks in the two areas have developed greatly in recent years, especially since the major EU enlargement in 2004. The relevant networks, that is, in antitrust the European Competition Network[2] (hereinafter ECN) and in consumer product safety the RAPEX (Community rapid alert system for non-food consumer products) network, have both been in operation since 2004. The legal framework in the two areas was also recently revised and the current rules apply in both areas since 2004.

In antitrust, at the time of writing, the European Commission is taking stock of the experiences under the Network Notice[3] and the implementation of Regulation No 1/2003 on the implementation of the rules on competition laid down in Articles 81 and 82 of the Treaty[4] to see the strengths and possible weak points of the system over the last five years. In particular, it will be interesting to see if the intended flexibility in a system of parallel EU and Member State

[2] See http://ec.europa.eu/competition/ecn/index_en.html and www.ec.europa.eu/rapex.

[3] Commission Notice on cooperation within the Network of Competition Authorities [2004] OJ C/101/43.

[4] Council Regulation (EC) No 1/2003 of 16 December 2002 on the implementation of the rules on competition laid down in Articles 81 and 82 of the Treaty [2003] OJ L/1/1.

competences has been achieved. Also, hopefully, the stocktaking gives some indication as to the extent the authorities have used the possibilities – such as sectoral subgroups – to discuss upfront their enforcement priorities and strategies in order to gain synergies and avoid unnecessary duplication.

In the area of consumer product safety, Europe has the General Product Safety Directive (hereinafter GPSD)[5] which sets the general obligation for businesses to place on the market only safe consumer products. From this broad obligation, also known as the 'general safety provision', stem accessory obligations for the producer to be informed and monitor the risk their product may pose to the health and safety of consumers and to take appropriate action including, if necessary, to avoid these risks, withdrawal from the market, adequately and effectively warning consumers or recall from consumers. The main obligation of the enforcement authorities of the Member States, correspondingly, is to make sure that economic operators fulfil these obligations. More detailed safety requirements exist for certain products (such as toys, cosmetics, electrical appliances), which are therefore in the harmonised area and to which the GPSD applies in a complementary manner. The RAPEX network processes the obligatory notifications under Articles 11 and 12 of the GPSD: a notification, sent to the Commission for validation and circulation to other Member States and network members, is required in cases of a serious risk to consumer health and safety from a consumer product, if there is a cross-border dimension, and the other Member States are required to follow-up and take measures if the same product is found on their territory.[6] In addition, Article 10 establishes a European network to exchange information and expertise, undertake joint surveillance and testing projects, and improve co-operation at Community level. The workings of this administrative cooperation network are not regulated in further detail. The recent report of the Commission on the implementation of the Directive[7] identified possible scope for improvement in the area of market surveillance. This related to the implementation of commonly-agreed best practices, increased exchange of information across the EU and a stronger role for the Commission in setting up market surveillance priorities.

As of 1 January 2010, this framework will be complemented by the entry into force of the market surveillance system provided for by Regulation No 765/2008 setting out the requirements for accreditation and market surveillance relating to the marketing of products and repealing Regulation No 339/93.[8] This framework

[5] Directive 2001/95/EC of the European Parliament and the Council on general product safety [2002] OJ L/11/4.

[6] RAPEX Guidelines, see Corrigendum to Commission Decision 2004/418/EC of 29 April 2004 laying down guidelines for the management of the Community Rapid Information System (RAPEX) and for notifications presented in accordance with Article 11 of Directive 2001/95/EC ([2004] OJ L/151), [2004] OJ L/208. These guidelines are currently being reviewed.

[7] Report from the Commission to the European Parliament and to the Council, 14.1.2009 COM(2008) 905 final.

[8] Regulation (EC) No 765/2008 of the European Parliament and of the Council of 9 July 2008 setting out the requirements for accreditation and market surveillance relating to the marketing of products and repealing Regulation (EEC) No 339/93 [2008] OJ L/218/30.

also establishes a Community Rapid Information System (Article 22) based on the RAPEX model but of a wider application than the GPSD as it covers a wider range of products (not only defined by their use by consumers) and other risks and it will need to start network-building.

The articulation between these two horizontal frameworks relevant for product safety is still being clarified by the Commission, and the market surveillance and enforcement network(s) are facing a learning process which, by definition, offers opportunities. It appears that the Member States are today more than ever open to coordination and cooperation in this field, which is an interesting development considering that, in the past, national attitudes on market surveillance have been usually based on the subsidiarity principle.

## POINTS OF CONVERGENCE: PAST, PRESENT AND (POSSIBLY) FUTURE

### Internal Market Needs Proper Enforcement and Awareness

The objective and the mission to guarantee the safety of consumer products in the internal market is a necessary corollary to the objectives of competition policy, aiming at creating scope for innovation, more choice and better value for money. A level playing field is important in both areas: the internal market must not be distorted as a result of uneven enforcement of either of these policies.

There is a clear need for a credible threat to achieve a deterrence effect. Authorities need to be able to show adequate competence and indicators of the use of their powers to act in the public interest. Scoreboards and other information about the ability to detect infringements and to punish them are helpful in this regard. Both areas have in common the fact that sanctions and procedures are still national. This leads to a certain extent to a less than level playing field, although there is currently no comparative information indicating if certain Member States are applying more severe sanctions than others.

In both areas, the authorities are seeking ways to advocate for and promote compliance. Corporate compliance programmes are important to create a competition and safety culture within companies. In antitrust, the leniency policy has paid off and the authorities across the network which implement leniency are able to better use their resources as they can focus on cases which are easier to prove. In product safety, a prominent example of a tool to sensitise businesses was the evaluation project into business safety measures in the toy supply chain.[9] If in product safety the act of voluntarily coming forward when a problem is identified is already required by law and not thus comparable to a leniency application, it is likely to be relevant in the determination of the sanction (by the Member State authorities) and in any case an irreproachable recall management record is part of the goodwill and reputation of any business.

[9] http://ec.europa.eu/consumers/safety/projects/docs/safety_measures_toy_supply_chain.pdf.

When enforcement action has proportionality (to risks in the large sense) as one of its guiding principles, it will not stifle entrepreneurship and innovation but ensure that market players respect the European rules so that both European consumers and compliant businesses enjoy the benefits of the single market. Thus, when working to guarantee consumer welfare, it is important that authorities stay clear of any excessive red-tape actions and explain their policy to facilitate compliance. Public opinion will show how well the authorities are able to strike this balance.

In addition to the external facets, there is also an internal dimension. The building of trust and solidarity in the network is essential in the enforcement of the same substantive rules in an area of 30 countries (the EU Member States and EFTA/EEA countries). The ECN is a relatively structured network thanks to the instruments (especially the Commission Notice) which govern it and which all Network members have committed to respect. The ECN members meet also regularly at different levels – from Director-Generals to desk officers. The functioning of the RAPEX network under the GPSD is helped by guidelines (adopted in the form of a Commission Decision) containing practical rules and criteria in order to facilitate consistent implementation. In addition to these guidelines, 'networking' takes place in meetings of the GPSD Committee and the RAPEX contact points. Unlike the ECN authorities, the RAPEX network does not have the benefit of an important body of case-law and decades of experience in the same area. The enforcers have therefore been granted important financial support from the EU for joint, cross-border relevant market surveillance actions and capacity building (5.4 million euros from 2004 to 2008 for joint actions, of which almost half in 2008 only, which can be interpreted as a sign of the growing interest of authorities to cooperate across borders and consequently present more meritorious applications for support).

## Global Governance Benefits from Global Forums

It is often said that global challenges require global cooperation and, where possible, global solutions. Products often span the globe before they arrive at retail outlets and components can travel even more before they reach the final consumer as part of a product. If a problem occurs in any part of this value chain (such as collusion to fix price of raw materials or replacement of a safe material by a toxic one), it is difficult to remedy in one jurisdiction only and certainly it is much more efficient if the jurisdictions cooperate and have shared values. This has led to the development of cooperation networks on an international level, at which the European Commission, sometimes with colleagues from the Member States, participates to represent the European views.

The International Competition Network (ICN) provides antitrust agencies from developed and developing countries with a focused network for addressing practical antitrust enforcement and policy issues of common concern. It facilitates procedural and substantive convergence in antitrust enforcement through a results-oriented agenda and informal, project-driven organisation. The ICN brings international antitrust enforcement into the 21st century. By enhancing convergence and cooperation, the ICN promotes more efficient, effective antitrust enforcement worldwide. Consistency in enforcement policy and elimination of unnecessary or duplicative procedural burdens stands to benefit consumers and businesses around the globe.[10]

The ICPSC (International Consumer Product Safety Caucus) is a platform to facilitate the exchange of information on consumer product safety issues in the area of governmental policy, legislation and market surveillance with a view to strengthening the collaboration and cooperation among governments and regulatory agencies around the world. Current active members of the ICPSC are representatives from several countries in Asia, from Australia, North America and Europe. Regulators of several countries in South America have shown interest in becoming active in ICPSC. The sharing and dissemination of information, the collaboration and the co-operation will be in accordance with applicable statutes of the respective government or regulatory agency.[11]

The OECD Committee on Consumer Policy (CCP) works to increase trust in the global economy. It has a mandate to develop principles leading to a fair and transparent marketplace, and seeks to ensure their effective implementation online and across borders. A product safety roundtable organised by the CCP in 2008 focused on non-food items. In light of recent developments and trends, participants examined the challenges in domestic and international consumer product safety regimes and identified ways to address the problems, including through enhanced international information sharing - product safety was chosen for the work programme 2009-2010.[12] It is thus catching up with the antitrust related debate which the OECD had taken up much earlier.

These multilateral fora have their value especially in highlighting certain issues common to most, if not all, jurisdictions and facilitating contacts to learn from one another. There are also demands to go further to gain concrete efficiencies in enforcement; currently such developments are mostly bilateral.

## Legal Limitations Affect Public Disclosure and Exchange of Information among Authorities

Professional secrecy and confidentiality protection are particularly important when considering exchanges of information in multi-jurisdiction situations. One specific issue relates to the fact that some jurisdictions may impose criminal penalties for violations of antitrust and also of product safety laws.

*Sharing of information for enforcement purposes* is a question of major interest in enforcement networks. In antitrust, Article 12 of Regulation No 1/2003 allows

[10] http://www.internationalcompetitionnetwork.org/.
[11] http://www.icpsc.org/.
[12] http://www.oecd.org/topic/0,3373,en_2649_34267_1_1_1_1_37441,00.html.

for information exchange and the use in evidence of information collected by other ECN members (in certain conditions).[13] In addition, Article 22 of the same Regulation allows explicitly for mutual assistance in fact-finding.[14] This latter possibility has been used in a few dozen cases and has proven helpful in concluding investigations.

Article 24(2) of Regulation No 765/2008, which will apply from 2010 to the market surveillance with respect to harmonised products, stipulates that the competent authorities of one Member State shall give the market surveillance authorities of other Member States assistance on an adequate scale by supplying information or documentation, by carrying out appropriate investigations or any other appropriate measure and by participating in investigations initiated in other Member States. Moreover, under Article 25, market surveillance initiatives designed to share resources and expertise between the competent authorities of the Member States may be set up by the Commission or the Member States concerned, and are coordinated by the Commission. This is to some extent comparable to the principle in the ECN that the national authority's arm's reach is extended by way of a possibility to get investigation assistance from other Member States, but is less specific and its practical application is still to be developed. This

[13] Art 12 of Reg No 1/2003:
Exchange of information
1. For the purpose of applying Articles 81 and 82 of the Treaty the Commission and the competition authorities of the Member States shall have the power to provide one another with and use in evidence any matter of fact or of law, including confidential information.
2. Information exchanged shall only be used in evidence for the purpose of applying Article 81 or Article 82 of the Treaty and in respect of the subject-matter for which it was collected by the transmitting authority. However, where national competition law is applied in the same case and in parallel to Community competition law and does not lead to a different outcome, information exchanged under this Article may also be used for the application of national competition law.
3. Information exchanged pursuant to paragraph 1 can only be used in evidence to impose sanctions on natural persons where:
– the law of the transmitting authority foresees sanctions of a similar kind in relation to an infringement of Article 81 or Article 82 of the Treaty or, in the absence thereof,
– the information has been collected in a way which respects the same level of protection of the rights of defence of natural persons as provided for under the national rules of the receiving authority. However, in this case, the information exchanged cannot be used by the receiving authority to impose custodial sanctions.

[14] Art 22 of Reg No 1/2003:
Investigations by competition authorities of Member States
1. The competition authority of a Member State may in its own territory carry out any inspection or other fact-finding measure under its national law on behalf and for the account of the competition authority of another Member State in order to establish whether there has been an infringement of Article 81 or Article 82 of the Treaty. Any exchange and use of the information collected shall be carried out in accordance with Article 12.
2. At the request of the Commission, the competition authorities of the Member States shall undertake the inspections which the Commission considers to be necessary under Article 20(1) or which it has ordered by decision pursuant to Article 20(4). The officials of the competition authorities of the Member States who are responsible for conducting these inspections as well as those authorised or appointed by them shall exercise their powers in accordance with their national law.
If so requested by the Commission or by the competition authority of the Member State in whose territory the inspection is to be conducted, officials and other accompanying persons authorised by the Commission may assist the officials of the authority concerned.

possibility is particularly relevant where the responsible economic operator or the evidence is located in a country other than that where an infringement is detected. The future use of this possibility in market surveillance related to the free movement of goods would benefit from cross-fertilisation with the ECN.

In RAPEX, the principle of information sharing applies extensively and includes product (laboratory) test reports and information about product sources and the supply chain. However, use in evidence is not regulated as clearly as in antitrust. Depending on national rules, in carrying out their enforcement work some authorities may be able to use as evidence of non-compliance test reports issued in other countries, while others carry out their own testing. The Commission has no competence to decide that one test result is more reliable than another, and it can only seek consensus or, in the most extreme case, consider initiating infringement proceedings, in particular in relation to a safeguard clause notification, against a Member State which would base its enforcement decision on a manifestly erroneous test report and thereby unjustifiably restrict the free movement of goods in the internal market. Thus the practical value of exchanging such information is still dependent on national rules.

As regards *information sharing with third countries,* the same benefits can be expected in both areas: cartels and breaches of product safety requirements regularly have features involving other, third country jurisdictions. The EU antitrust enforcement regime is better suited than the product safety setup to make use of such exchanges, given that by initiating antitrust proceedings (or even already by commencing investigative measures) in a case where there is a need to engage in cooperation with, for example, the US or the Japanese administration, the Commission is able (if its enforcement priorities permit it) to ensure it is in charge of the case and can keep the sensitive information confidential as necessary. In product safety, since the Commission does not have enforcement competence, it is obliged to relay the information to the Member States in order for action to be taken. Although all authorities must have equally effective professional secrecy rules, it is understandable that foreign jurisdictions ask for more reassurances about the capability of the enforcement network to duly protect the information that they envisage to give to the Commission.

The GPSD provides that access to the RAPEX system can be granted to applicant countries, third countries or international organisations, within the framework of agreements between the Community and those countries and organisations.[15] This must be based on reciprocity and include provisions on confidentiality. Of course, there are also less extensive ways of exchanging relevant information that can still be helpful in improving understanding of issues in other jurisdictions and even in certain ways to enforcement activities. In particular, in the product safety area where new risks may emerge from innovation by companies (such as the aquadots case[16]), sharing experiences with

[15] Art 12(4).

[16] In the EU RAPEX notification No 1171/07, see http://ec.europa.eu/consumers/dyna/rapex/create_rapex_print.cfm?rx_id=158; in the United States http://www.cpsc.gov/cpscpub/prerel/prhtml08/08074.html. Also on Wikipedia.

newly identified risks is invaluable, so that the same risk does not materialise in all markets before authorities act against it. The case of finding the harmful substance called dimethyl fumarate, or DMF,[17] in consumer products and addressing related risks is another example where authorities from the early stages of the risk assessment and consequently of risk management shared information and sought mutually acceptable solutions.

In antitrust, there are no legal provisions comparable to the above-mentioned possibility in the GPSD to grant, under certain conditions, formal access to third countries to the enforcement data system. Nonetheless, formal agreements have been concluded with certain countries, but these are more limited in scope and do not enable the third countries to act as network members. Moreover, waivers from the parties to the antitrust case are needed for such information exchanges.

The Commission makes *available to the public certain information,* under Article 16 of the GPSD, in order to increase awareness and empower consumers to take decisions for themselves: brand name of dangerous product, photo, risk description and information about corrective measures. For the national authorities, there is more information in the RAPEX system, which is helpful in their cooperation with producers (including importers) and distributors. For instance, the identification of suppliers is protected as a business secret and therefore it is not public, save in circumstances of proven overriding public interest.

The competition authorities cooperating within the ECN are under professional secrecy rules and cannot disclose outside the Network any information received pursuant to Regulation No 1/2003, unless it is necessary to prove an infringement of Articles 81 EC and 82 EC. They must in particular protect the business secrets and other confidential information of companies from being unduly disclosed to anyone outside the Network. Nonetheless, the authorities cooperating within the ECN select ECN-related information that does not fall under the professional secrecy rule and can thus be communicated to the outside in order to increase transparency where possible. A concrete result is the regular publication of aggregate figures of new investigations in the Network and of envisaged decisions of which the national competition authorities have informed the Commission pursuant to their legal obligation. This information is available on the Commission/DG Competition Internet website. The results of the individual case investigations, insofar as they have lead to published decisions, are however not collected centrally and must be searched via the responsible authorities' websites.

## LIMITS OF CONVERGENCE AND REFLECTIONS ON DIFFERENCES

Article 85 EC determines that in antitrust the Commission is empowered to take decisions and enforce the law and that, in exercising these powers, it is

[17] See Commission IP/09/190, 29 January 2009.

not submitted to any regulatory committee but only to a *sui generis* advisory committee (not under 'comitology'). In product safety, the secondary legislation is based on Article 95 EC and thus also the internal market objective. The Commission takes implementing measures in accordance with the comitology rules. For instance, when the Commission intends to adopt a (temporary) decision banning the presence of a particular substance in consumer products (phthalates or, more recently, DMF mentioned above and pending at the time of writing), it must get the qualified majority of the Member States behind the decision and the European Parliament (as co-legislator of the basic act) can exercise scrutiny before the Commission can adopt such a decision. Subsequently, the Member States must take measures at the national level to enforce the ban, and the Commission can only envisage infringement proceedings if a Member State does not respect it.

The question can be asked if there are perspectives to see the development of a product safety enforcement capacity at the Community level. It must be remembered that this is an area where subsidiarity arguments are strongly present. The 'summer of recalls' in 2007, when millions of toys and other everyday consumer products were taken off the markets in Europe and other continents, hit hard consumer confidence in product safety enforcement and the safety of products available on the market. It triggered questions on the legal framework and its implementation. The conclusions drawn from the management of the crisis did not pertain to any shift in powers but more to the substantive requirement that products must be made safe and that the Member States' enforcement authorities must improve cooperation and carry out market surveillance. It is difficult to imagine another crisis that would trigger any such shift in powers in favour of centralised action (by the Commission). Therefore, there is always tension in international relations: the Commission is the entity in the EU that has centralised information about product safety breaches and the competence to share it with third countries (on the basis of agreements), but it is not an enforcement agency which can discuss as such on an equal footing with other agencies in the international arena.

It is arguable that some considerations would speak in favour of a system of parallel Community and national competences, in the product safety area as well as the antitrust area, but with obvious differences. Where the same product is distributed in more than three (to use the criteria applying in antitrust) EU countries, the European importer would arguably benefit if it could discuss and agree the nature and scope of the needed corrective action with one authority (the Commission) rather than with the competent authorities in all the different Member States. This would ensure that there are no 'conflicting' decisions in different Member States such as a requirement to recall a product in one territory and just a requirement to stop its sale in another. This has potentially large economic consequences and a risk of a less than level playing field. However, product safety enforcement is an area that requires permanent presence on the market of each Member State and, as pointed out earlier, the development of a product safety enforcement authority at the Community level is unlikely.

The practical value of a well-functioning network is not only in efficient work allocation (where this applies, like in antitrust). It can be seen, as the Commissioner for Consumer Affairs Meglena Kuneva has said, to be about 'solidarity'. This refers to the fact that where one Member State identifies a product posing a serious risk to the health and safety of consumers and takes it off the market, this information benefits also the other authorities and the citizens in all European countries. The authorities in other Member States can to some extent base their market surveillance actions on the indications from other members of the network. Thus even the less resourced, less equipped authorities have at their disposal information that allows them to target action and protect the consumers in that country from a dangerous product. However, the Commission does not have the competence under the GPSD to take on the case, even if a Member State authority adopts a line in contradiction with the established practice, and it cannot take enforcement action should a Member State fail to do so on its market. This is possible in antitrust.[18] Thus the means to guarantee coherent practice throughout the network are less developed in product safety than in antitrust.

When comparing the ECN rules to the product safety enforcement, the 'pre-decision' stage cooperation is also much less developed in product safety. In antitrust, the national authority must inform the Commission of its envisaged decision before it can be adopted, and this information may also be made available to the competition authorities of the other Member States (Article 11(4) of Regulation No 1/2003). In product safety, there is no obligation but only an option (third paragraph of Article 12(1) of the GPSD) to inform the Commission of envisaged decisions, which would often be helpful especially when the risk from the product is very serious or in the case of an emerging risk where there is no legislation and no standard as a benchmark (such as the above-mentioned DMF case) and the only basis for action is the 'catch-all' general safety provision. Of course, discussions between a Member State and the Commission are possible and can also take place in the network meetings, but only pre-decision information, if passed on to other network members, would allow all network members to act simultaneously on their respective territories.

The stage after notification in the two areas is also regulated differently, and this is for good reason. In product safety this triggers an obligation for other Member States to follow-up and take measures if they find the same non-compliance on their territory or else justify non-action, whereas in antitrust this is not the case. By contrast, in antitrust, the *ne bis in idem* principle would even prevent double action (punishment) if the second authority would address the same case. Moreover, according to the ECN network principles (paragraph 5 of the Network Notice), national authorities retain full discretion in deciding whether or not to investigate a case.

[18] In antitrust, the Commission can take over the enforcement task in a particular case, in other words de-seize a national authority of its competence, pursuant to Art 11(6) of Reg No 1/2003 in the situations referred to in point 54 of the Network Notice, which include a reference to a situation where 'Network member(s) is (are) unduly drawing out proceedings in the case'.

Information to the public has arguably a much more practical value and impact in the product safety area than in antitrust. Most importantly, the information concerns very direct, serious threats to the physical health and safety. Additionally, individual consumers have a clear role in making the policy effective. It is true that consumer complaints have relevance in both areas, but it is only in product safety that the enforcement decision's effectiveness, in terms of protecting their health and safety, may depend on how well the consumers return the dangerous product to the seller.

It can also be argued that information to consumers has more direct perceived relevance in the product safety field than in antitrust. At least there is evidence in a recent Eurobarometer survey[19] that with respect to non-food product safety, 17 % of consumers (and 25 % of retailers) think that, essentially, all products are safe. 48 % of consumers (and 55 % of retailers) think that a small number of products are unsafe. As many as 75 % of EU27 consumers had heard of non-food products being recalled from the market, and 10 % had been directly or indirectly affected by such a product recall. These percentages are significant and it can be partly due to the 'summer of recalls' media attention and partly to the fact that part of corrective measures taken in product safety violations is often in the form of information to consumers. In any event, practically every corrective measure which relates to a product sold in more than one Member State is listed, along with details such as brand name and description, photos and explanation of serious risk, on the Commission website. In antitrust, public awareness is guaranteed in cases where the Commission imposes high fines on undertakings (such as Microsoft cases) but the Network members' enforcement actions are less known.

## FINAL REMARKS

Scarce enforcement resources are under strain, and efficient and effective use of these resources, linked with proactive advocacy and other actions, requires creative thinking and the sharing of best practices. Are there any elements which product safety enforcers could, more than today, take as best practices – or more – from competition enforcers?

Inspiration for further developing product safety enforcement can be sought from further, structured coordination of enforcement priorities as well as structured sharing of best practices in areas such as investigation techniques, similarly to antitrust, to see collectively how best to allocate the scarce resources. The existence of a well-structured and well-functioning network, where discussions are a common feature and sectoral specialists get together so that they are at least as well coordinated and know each other as business people of

[19] Eurobarometer on Consumer Protection in the Internal Market, survey interviews of 26,746 European citizens from all 27 Member States, see http://ec.europa.eu/consumers/strategy/docs/eurobar_298_report_final_en.pdf for more details.

the same sector, is currently not a luxury but a simple necessity. Enforcement of a policy across Europe is only efficient if it is not done merely according to national traditions and priorities that, in the worst case, are determined locally and ignore developments in other EU countries. The more there is coordinated and joint priority setting, joint actions, sharing of knowledge and, if possible, also evidence, the better the results are likely to be. Policy-makers in areas where a competent authority in one Member State cannot ask the competent authority in another Member State to take investigative actions or enforcement action on its behalf where the latter is well placed, could look into the experience in those areas where this is possible. If the experience is positive, policy-makers could consider the extension of the model, thus working towards the realisation of the internal market also in this wider sense.

Europe speaking with one voice, even where there is no exclusive EU competence, is also essential in the global networks, as that gives it much more weight than any European country alone can have.

It is also worth noting that, in antitrust, closer cooperation in policy-making and enforcement coordination has, over and above legal obligations, brought about a trend towards greater approximation of national procedural laws and policies.[20] Hence, there is reason to believe that in product safety closer cooperation can produce similar trends and show ever greater overall coherence.

In conclusion, the key to optimising product safety enforcement is not to try to transpose the antitrust model in full but to invest in coordinating the network members, who take decisions independently and defend them if challenged, to achieve the best possible coherent practice. If there are cases of under-enforcement or differences in the level of enforcement, these are to some extent taken care of by the fact that the Commission invests in preventive actions (better legislation, better information, 'safety pacts' to share best practices etc).

Regarding the common challenges ahead from the European executive perspective, one can start a list with the need for businesses to simultaneously comply with the laws of many jurisdictions, the long and sophisticated supply chains where different business cultures also meet and must find a way to deal with inevitable differences, and the question where and how information is stored and whether it is available to authorities when required (traceability of products versus concealing information relating to antitrust violations).

When the RAPEX network becomes fully mature and less investment is needed in capacity-building type work, which ensures that all members can make a useful contribution to the network, it can arguably get further inspiration from the methods of multilateral and bilateral exchanges between ECN members. The strengths of the ECN model in terms of close practical cooperation and thereby

[20] A prime example of this trend towards further convergence is in the ECN model leniency programme (http://ec.europa.eu/competition/ecn/documents.html) and another example is that a large number of national competition authorities have received the power to adopt commitment decisions based on the model of Reg No 1/2003 but not mandatory in national systems.

consistent application of Community law are truly worth considering in other enforcement networks on the way to 'A Europe of results'.[21]

Finally, although this chapter discusses the cross-fertilisation from the benchmark values of antitrust to the neighbouring and developing area of product safety and the RAPEX network, it is reasonable to add that the consumer information and empowerment dimension of product safety is a value that might be a potential benchmark also for the ECN. Though the ECN is well known to, and has credit among, antitrust specialists, wider public recognition of its merits would benefit from such closeness to the citizen.

[21] Commission Communication of 5 September 2007 COM(2007) 502 final. 'The European Union is founded in law, pursues many of its policies through legislation and is sustained by respect for the rule of law. Its success in achieving its many goals as set out in the Treaties and in legislation depends on the effective application of Community law in the Member States. Laws do not serve their full purpose unless they are properly applied and enforced.'

# 11

# *Consumer Protection and EU Competition Law*

SARI HAUKKA*

## INTRODUCTION

During the last years, consumer interests have been invoked frequently as one of the most important objectives in the context of competition law enforcement. However, in the competition rules of the Treaty, the consumer is rarely mentioned. It is certainly true that Article 153(2) EC stipulates that consumer protection requirements shall be taken into account in defining and implementing other Community policies and activities. Likewise, Article 38 of the Charter of Fundamental Rights of the European Union requires that 'Union policies shall ensure a high level of consumer protection'.[1] Nevertheless, the role of consumers in the 'pure' competition rules is less outstanding. Pursuant to Article 81(3) EC, derogation from paragraph 1 is possible if the practice contributes to improving the production or distribution of goods or to promoting technical or economic progress, while allowing consumers a fair share of the resulting benefit. Consumers are also mentioned in Article 82(b) EC in the list of possible abuses namely when describing that 'limiting production, markets or technical development to the prejudice of consumers' is considered as abuse. In addition, pursuant to Article 87(2)(a) EC, a State aid, having a social character, granted to individual consumers, is compatible with the common market provided that such aid is granted without discrimination related to the origin of the products concerned. Furthermore, the Merger Regulation cites 'the interests of the intermediate and ultimate consumers' among interests to be taken into account in the appraisal of the compatibility of a notified merger.[2]

* The views are purely personal and do not engage the European Chemicals Agency.
[1] [2007] OJ C/303/1.
[2] Art 2(1)(b) of Council Regulation (EEC) No 4064/89 of 21 December 1989 on the control of concentrations between undertakings (corrected version) [1990] OJ L/257/13.

The purpose of this chapter is to analyse recent competition case-law of the Community Courts in order to see whether and to what extent consumer interests are taken into account in the application of competition law.[3] Consumer protection has been recognised as one, if not even the ultimate goal, of competition law in some recent cases. The Court of First Instance of the European Communities (hereinafter CFI) has underlined that 'the rules designed to ensure that competition is not distorted in the internal market are ultimately intended to enhance the well-being of consumers'.[4] Equally, Advocate General Jacobs stated in his Opinion in *Bronner* that the primary purpose of Article 82 EC 'is to prevent distortion of competition — and in particular to safeguard the interests of consumers — rather than to protect the position of particular competitors'.[5] This chapter seeks to elucidate whether or not these statements have turned into reality in the application and interpretation of competition law.

In relation to Article 81 EC, the consumers have not been in a very visible role in competition law enforcement at the Community level during the last five years. This is due to the decentralisation of competition law enforcement to national authorities by Regulation No 1/2003.[6] As Member States' courts and competition authorities now have the power to apply Article 81 EC in its entirety, the questions of consumer interests in the context of competition law application will be less visible at the EU level unless the national courts refer these questions to the Court of Justice of the European Communities (hereinafter ECJ) in accordance with Article 234 EC. Furthermore, the European Commission now focuses on cartels which by definition are harmful for consumers because they lead to higher prices, less quality and less innovation. Where cartels exist, the consumer interests for applying competition law are evident and normally do not require separate evaluation.

Consumer interests have been most noticeable in recent years in court cases concerning Article 82 EC, in particular with regard to the concept of abuse of dominant position. When publishing guidance on its enforcement priorities in applying EC Treaty rules on abuse of a dominant market position, the Commission has also stated that consumer welfare will be at the heart of the fight against abuses by dominant undertakings and that it will prioritise 'those cases where the exclusionary conduct of a dominant undertaking is liable to have harmful effects on consumers.[7] Moreover, it stated that the focus of the Commission's enforcement policy should be on protecting consumers and the process of competition and not on protecting individual competitors.

The possibility of individual consumers and consumer organisations to take part in competition law enforcement is an important aspect in this respect.

[3] The cases have thus been selected mainly from 2006 onwards.

[4] Joined Cases T-259/02 to T-264/02 and T-271/02 *Raiffeisen Zentralbank Österreich and Others v Commission* [2006] ECR II-5169 para 99.

[5] Opinion of Advocate General Jacobs in Case C-7/97 *Bronner* [1998] ECR I-7791 point 58.

[6] Council Regulation (EC) No 1/2003 of 16 December 2002 on the implementation of the rules on competition laid down in Articles 81 and 82 of the Treaty [2003] OJ L/1/1.

[7] Press release IP/08/1877, 3 December 2008.

In fact, the more consumers have a possibility to participate in competition proceedings, the better their voice on issues of what is to be considered as a genuine consumer interest will probably be taken into account. In this respect, the case-law on legal standing as far as consumers are concerned will be reviewed.

## CONSUMER PROTECTION BY COMPETITION LAW

Even though the focus of this chapter is to examine to what extent competition rules promote consumer interests, it is also important to recall that competition law does not provide adequate protection to consumers in all circumstances. For example, competition rules do not offer any protection where a potential anti-competitive situation is created by measures taken by a Member State. An example can be found in the *Cipolla and Others* judgment.[8] The ECJ was asked in an Italian case whether Articles 10 EC, 81 EC and 82 EC preclude a Member State from adopting a legislative measure which approves, on the basis of a draft produced by a professional body of lawyers, a scale fixing a minimum fee for members of the legal profession from which there can generally be no derogation in respect of either services reserved to those members or services such as out-of-court services which may also be provided by any other economic operator not subject to that scale.

The ECJ recalled that Articles 81 EC and 82 EC have solely to do with the conduct of undertakings and not with laws or regulations emanating from Member States. However those articles, read in conjunction with Article 10 EC, which lays down a duty to cooperate, none the less require Member States not to introduce or maintain in force measures, even of a legislative or regulatory nature, which may render ineffective the competition rules applicable to undertakings. Consequently, as the Italian State had not required or encouraged the adoption of agreements, decisions or concerted practices contrary to Article 81 EC or reinforced their effects nor had it divested its own rules of the character of legislation by delegating to private economic operators responsibility for taking decisions affecting the economic sphere, it was not precluded from fixing a minimum fee for legal services.

However, from a consumer perspective the solution appears extremely unsatisfactory as a minimum fee from which there can generally be no derogation seems not only to restrict competition but also to exclude all competition on prices below a certain level. Hence, if the goal of the competition rules is to encourage competitive processes and consequently consumer welfare, the result is most inadequate.

Nevertheless, the ECJ also examined whether Article 49 EC precluded legislation containing an absolute prohibition of derogation, by agreement, from the minimum fees set by the scale in question. The submissions by the Italian

[8] Joined Cases C-94/04 and C-202/04 *Cipolla and Others* [2006] ECR I-11421.

Government and the Commission are interesting examples how differently consumer interests can be presented. The Italian Government argued that excessive competition between lawyers might lead to price competition which would result in deterioration in the quality of the services provided to the detriment of consumers. The Commission was of the opinion that no causal link can be established between the setting of minimum levels of fees and a high qualitative standard of professional services provided by lawyers. Instead, the quality should be controlled by setting up appropriate deontological rules.

The ECJ seems to have accepted both lines of argumentation, at least partially. The ECJ did accept that a scale imposing minimum fees cannot prevent members of the profession from offering services of mediocre quality. However, the ECJ stated that such a scale can serve to prevent lawyers from being encouraged to compete against each other by possibly offering services at a discount, with the risk of deterioration in the quality of the services provided. On the other hand, the ECJ also recalled that even an informed consumer cannot assess the quality of the service provided because lawyers have a high level of technical knowledge which consumers may not have (so-called asymmetry of information between 'client-consumers' and lawyers).

The ECJ decided, nevertheless, that the objectives of protection of consumers and the proper administration of justice may be regarded as overriding requirements relating to the public interest capable of justifying a restriction on freedom to provide services. The ECJ left it to the national court to decide whether professional rules in respect of lawyers, in particular rules relating to organisation, qualifications, professional ethics, supervision and liability, suffice in themselves to attain the objectives of the protection of consumers and the proper administration of justice.[9]

The guidelines given to the national court for the assessment of the factual situation leave several questions open as far as consumer interests are concerned. It would have been interesting if the ECJ had for example explained further how preventing competition with prices prevents the deterioration of the quality of legal services if an asymmetry of information between client-consumers and lawyers exists. Thus, even though the ECJ acknowledges that consumers often are not able to judge the quality of the services provided, it is still presumed that a guarantee of a certain price level would ensure the quality of the services. However, even if lawyers are not allowed to compete with prices, there is no guarantee that the quality of the service offered is better than without the price competition. In other terms, if consumers are not able to judge the quality of the services, nothing assures that quality instead of price would be used to compete. In fact, it could equally be argued that not allowing a scale of minimum fees would enhance competition in the field of legal services and would therefore lead to a situation where consumers benefited from competition through lower prices, better quality and a wider choice of new or improved services which is what competition normally brings about. The justification according to which

[9] *Ibid* para 69.

the scale of minimum fees also promotes the proper administration of justice would have been less convincing.

It could even be argued that if consumer interests had been further examined, it might have revealed that, in fact, there were no overriding requirements relating to the public interest capable of justifying a restriction on freedom to provide services. Consequently, if the assessment of what actually serves best the interests of consumers would have been different, a similar result could have been achieved by combining the application of Article 153(2) EC with Article 49 EC instead of competition rules. In fact, if consumer interests are not properly examined, this may easily lead to a situation which affects the interests of consumers adversely and does not bring about the positive effects presumed. To the contrary, if consumer interests are thoroughly examined, this could even lead to a situation where consumer protection favours competition and not only the other way around, that is, that competition benefits consumers.

The effectiveness of consumer protection by means of competition policy is also linked to the manner in which competition law is interpreted. The significance of competition law for consumers was raised by Advocate General Kokott in her Opinion in *T-mobile Netherlands and Others*.[10] She underlined the need of uniform interpretation of Community competition law under the new, decentralised system by pointing out the risks for the internal market and for the European consumer which could result from any relaxation of the rules on competition laid down in the EC Treaty. She recalled that '[n]ot only the fundamental objective of equal conditions of competition for undertakings on the single market but also the concern for uniform protection of consumer interests in the entire Community would be undermined if in the enforcement of the competition rules of Articles 81 EC and 82 EC significant disparities occurred between the authorities and courts of the Member States'.[11]

In this case, she discussed the different consequences which would follow if the infringement of Article 81(1) EC were dependent of demonstrating anti-competitive effects even in cases where the anti-competitive object is established. Of particular interest from consumers' point of view are her remarks on how Article 81(1) EC would be deprived of an element of its practical effectiveness should the prohibition of a practice simply by reason of its anti-competitive object not be allowed. She underlined that 'it goes too far to make the finding of an anti-competitive object dependent on an actual determination of the presence or absence of an anti-competitive impact in an individual case, irrespective of whether that impact relates to competitors, consumers or the general public. Instead, for the prohibition of Article 81(1) EC to be triggered it is sufficient that a concerted practice has the potential – on the basis of existing experience – to produce a negative impact on competition.'[12]

[10] Opinion of Advocate General Kokott in Case C-8/08 *T-Mobile Netherlands and Others*, judgment of 4 June 2009 nyr.

[11] *Ibid* points 3 and 85.

[12] *Ibid* points 42–46.

Competition law can protect consumer interests also by securing a sufficiently high level of sanctions with sanctions having a deterrent effect. Preventing anti-competitive measures is best not only for competition but also for consumers because if the anti-competitive behaviour can be avoided, no adverse effects can alter the market before possible intervention of competition authorities. In that regard, the 1998 Guidelines on the method of setting fines provide that, in addition to the nature of the infringement, its actual impact on the market and the size of the relevant geographic market, it is necessary to take account of the effective economic capacity of offenders to cause significant damage to other operators, in particular consumers, and to set the fine at a level which ensures that it has a sufficiently deterrent effect (Section 1 A, fourth paragraph).[13] This consideration was recently recalled by Advocate General Trstenjak in case *Archer Daniels Midland v Commission* when examining why an increase in the level of fines is necessary.[14] She stated that a higher level of fines was particularly necessary for the most serious infringements where the principal aim of the infringement is to maintain a higher level of prices for consumers. She also reminded that many undertakings carry on conduct which they know to be contrary to Community law because the profit which they derive from their unlawful conduct exceeds the fines so far imposed. Conduct of that kind could only be deterred by fines which are heavier than in the past.

## WHAT ARE CONSUMER INTERESTS?

An evident problem when taking consumer interests into account in competition policy context is to define what is meant by consumer interests or even by the concept of consumer.[15] The concept of consumer may include all direct and indirect users of a product or service or only the final consumers in the sense of traditional consumer protection, that is, persons who acquire goods or services for private use.[16] It is this latter definition which should be used because it is the one that best guarantees that the interests taken into account are actually those

[13] Guidelines on the method of setting fines imposed pursuant to Article 15 (2) of Regulation No 17 and Article 65 (5) of the ECSC Treaty [1998] OJ C/9/3. The 2006 Guidelines do no longer refer to consumers and their interests. Nevertheless, the same need for deterrent effect is mentioned in points 4, 30, 31 and 37 of the 2006 Guidelines. See Guidelines on the method of setting fines imposed pursuant to Article 23(2)(a) of Regulation No 1/2003 [2006] OJ C/210/2.

[14] Opinion of Advocate General Trstenjak in Case C-510/06 P *Archer Daniels Midland v Commission*, judgment of 19 March 2009 nyr, point 67.

[15] See generally E Buttigieg, 'Consumers Interests under the EC's Competition Rules on Collusive Practices' (2005) *European Business Law Review* 643.

[16] See *Guidance on the Commission's enforcement priorities in applying Article 82 of the EC Treaty to abusive exclusionary conduct by dominant undertakings* C(2009) 864 final, footnote 15 (http://ec.europa.eu/competition/antitrust/art82/guidance_en.pdf). According to the Commission, 'The concept of "consumers" encompasses all direct or indirect users of the products affected by the conduct, including intermediate producers that use the products as an input, as well as distributors and final consumers both of the immediate product and of products provided by intermediate producers. Where intermediate users are actual or potential competitors of the dominant undertaking, the assessment focuses on the effects of the conduct on users further downstream'.

of consumers and not those of competitors. However, the concept of consumer is often either not defined in the case-law or the definition is only implicit.

Different consumers may well have different preferences and their needs may also vary over time. A good example of this is price discrimination.[17] The question of what is the maximum benefit for the largest group of consumers will not be discussed in this chapter.[18] However, it is important to note that, in relation to the exemptions of Article 81(3) CE, the ECJ defined in its *Asnef-Equifax and Administración del Estado* judgment that it is the beneficial nature of the effect on all consumers in the relevant markets that must be taken into consideration, not the effect on each member of that category of consumers.[19]

Competition law enforcement in the field of abuses of dominant position has, over the recent years, increasingly taken into account consumer interests. However, it is not always easy to determine what kind of an effect those interests should have on the outcome of a competition case. An interesting example can be found in the field of predatory pricing.

In *France Télécom v Commission*, the Commission found that the prices charged by Wanadoo Interactive (hereinafter WIN) for its asymmetric digital subscriber line services did not enable it to cover its variable costs until August 2001 or to cover its full costs between then and October 2002. Consequently, the Commission considered the pricing predatory and part of a plan to pre-empt the market in high-speed Internet access during a key phase in its development. Accordingly, the conduct was considered as an abuse of its dominant position. WIN lodged an action against that decision before the CFI.

One of the legal questions was whether the Commission needed to prove that recoupment of losses was later possible. The CFI held that the Commission was correct in taking the view that proof of recoupment of losses was not a precondition to make a finding of predatory pricing and that the Commission was able to regard prices below average variable costs as abusive. Thus, the eliminatory nature of such pricing was presumed. In relation to full costs, the Commission had also to provide evidence that WIN's predatory pricing formed part of a plan to 'pre-empt' the market. However, in neither of those two situations was it necessary to prove, in addition, that WIN had a realistic chance of recouping its losses.[20]

In its appeal, France Télécom asked the ECJ to set aside the CFI's judgment. The Opinion of Advocate General Mazák raised several interesting issues from the perspective of consumers.[21] In fact, at the heart of the dispute was the question whether the CFI had erred in law considering that no proof of the

[17] Report by the EAGCP, *An economic approach to Article 82* (2005) 30–34 (http://ec.europa.eu/competition/publications/studies/eagcp_july_21_05.pdf). See also P Akman, 'To Abuse, or not to Abuse: Discrimination between Consumers' (2007) 32 *European Law Review* 492.

[18] See generally J Stuyck, 'EC Competition Law after Modernisation: More Than Ever in the Interest of Consumers' (2005) *Journal of Consumer Policy* 1.

[19] Case C-238/05 *Asnef-Equifax and Administración del Estado* [2006] ECR I-11125 para 70.

[20] Case T-340/03 *France Télécom v Commission* [2007] II-107 para 228.

[21] Opinion of Advocate General Mazák in Case C-202/07 P *France Télécom v Commission*, judgment of 2 April 2009 nyr.

possibility of recoupment of losses were required. The CFI justified its opinion by stating that 'it must be possible to penalise predatory pricing whenever there is a risk that competitors will be eliminated'. It added that 'the aim pursued, which is to maintain undistorted competition, rules out waiting until such a strategy leads to the actual elimination of competitors'. [22] Advocate General Mazák did not agree with the CFI's interpretation but considered that the possibility of recoupment of losses must be proven.[23] Apart from a question of how *AKZO v Commission*[24] and *Hoffmann-La Roche v Commission*[25] case-law should be interpreted, he considered that 'where there is no possibility of recouping losses, consumers and their interests should, in principle, not be harmed'.[26]

The difference between the two opinions can be seen as a divergence between the short-term and long-term interests of consumers. In the short-term scenario, the consumers never suffered because they had the benefit of low prices produced by the fierce price competition. However, in the long run the consumers would suffer as the competition would be structurally diminished. These two different approaches seem to be intertwined by the requirement of proof of recoupment of losses. In fact, it could be argued that the long-term harm will occur only if the recoupment of losses is possible, that is, if elimination of competitors has been successful and the prices can subsequently be raised above the level they would have had, had the competition stayed effective. On the contrary, if the recoupment of losses were not possible, then the only result of pricing below costs would have been that the consumers benefit from lower prices.

The different approach can also be argued as a difference between the concept of attempt and result. Following the line of argumentation of the CFI, the predatory pricing is in itself anti-competitive and there is no need to wait whether the aim sought with the predatory pricing is achieved, namely the elimination of competitors, which in turn allows for recouping the losses. The CFI seems to take a view that already the attempt to eliminate competitors is anti-competitive. To the contrary, the other approach would be that the anti-competitive 'crime' must be successful because, from the consumer point of view, if it was only an attempt then the consumers would not suffer but benefit from the lower prices and competition would prevail as earlier.

In this respect, a similarity could be found in the application of Article 81 EC where an anti-competitive object and anti-competitive effects constitute not cumulative but alternative conditions, meaning that regardless of their effects, concerted practices are prohibited if they pursue an anti-competitive purpose.[27] An interesting example can be found in Advocate General Kokott's Opinion in *T-mobile Netherlands and Others*. She argued that even in the absence of a direct

[22] Case T-340/03 *France Télécom v Commission*, n 20 above, para 226.

[23] Opinion of Advocate General Mazák in Case C-202/07 P *France Télécom v Commission*, n 21 above, point 69.

[24] Case C-62/86 *AKZO v Commission* [1991] ECR I-3359.

[25] Case 85/76 *Hoffmann-La Roche v Commission* [1979] ECR 461.

[26] Opinion of Advocate General Mazák in Case C-202/07 P *France Télécom v Commission*, n 21 above, point 74.

[27] Case C-49/92 P *Commission v Anic Partecipazioni* [1999] ECR I-4125 para 123.

influence on consumers and the prices payable by them, a concerted practice may have an anti-competitive object. She justified her opinion by referring to the objectives of competition law which is designed to protect competition within the internal market from distortions (Article 3(1)(g) EC). In this respect, she referred to her Opinion in *British Airways v Commission* where she stated that

> Accordingly, Article 82 EC, like the other competition rules of the Treaty, is not designed only or primarily to protect the immediate interests of individual competitors or consumers, but to protect the structure of the market and thus competition as such (as an institution), which has already been weakened by the presence of the dominant undertaking on the market. In this way, consumers are also indirectly protected. Because where competition as such is damaged, disadvantages for consumers are also to be feared. [28]

The obligation to prove the possibility or not to recoup losses is also linked to the question who bears the burden of proof. This in turn may have an effect on consumer interests. If the Commission is required to demonstrate that the recoupment of losses is possible, it makes the identification of an abuse more difficult and may lead to situations where a negative effect on consumers escapes antitrust control because of the impossibility to provide the evidence, at least before the harm has occurred in form of diminished competition.[29] In some cases the Commission would perhaps be able to prove the possibility of recouping the losses only ex post, that is, after the harm to the competitive structure has already occurred. Thus, not only would some abuses escape competition control but the harm for the competitive structure could be irreversible before the competition authorities were able to intervene into the anti-competitive behaviour. The problem could be avoided without abandoning the need to address the recoupment of losses issue by presuming that a pricing below costs is an abuse unless the dominant undertaking is able to prove that it will not be possible to recoup the losses. Thus, the company would carry the risk of not being able to demonstrate that its pricing below costs is driven by other than anti-competitive reasons.[30]

[28] Opinion of Advocate General Kokott in Case C-8/08 *T-Mobile Netherlands and Others*, n 10 above, point 58. See also Opinion of Advocate General Kokott in Case C-95/04 P *British Airways v Commission* [2007] I-2331 point 68.

[29] See also Opinion of Advocate General Geelhoed in Case C-407/04 P *Dalmine v Commission* [2007] ECR I-829 points 136 and 137, where he considers that if an object based approach to Art 81 EC was not accepted, it would signify 'a considerable increase in the burdens of investigation and proof placed on the Commission since it will also have to investigate and substantiate the effects of such infringements of Article 81(1) EC, which are already serious in themselves'. Consequently, it would severely impair the effectiveness of that core provision of the EC Treaty.

[30] See generally *Guidance on the Commission's enforcement priorities in applying Article 82 of the EC Treaty to abusive exclusionary conduct by dominant undertakings*, n 16 above, point 71. The Commission has taken the position that it will not only intervene 'if the dominant undertaking would be likely to be able to increase its prices above the level persisting in the market before the conduct. It is sufficient, for instance, that the conduct would be likely to prevent or delay a decline in prices that would otherwise have occurred. Identifying consumer harm is not a mechanical calculation of profits and losses, and proof of overall profits is not required. Likely consumer harm may be demonstrated by assessing the likely foreclosure effect of the conduct, combined with consideration of other factors, such as entry barriers. In this context, the Commission will also consider possibilities of re-entry'.

In addition, the requirement to produce evidence of the possibility of recouping the losses is based on an assumption that a rational company would not engage itself in unprofitable prices unless it foresees a possibility to cover those losses later in a better market situation or that if it does so, it only aligns its prices to those of its competitors. Yet, is this presumption always true? In fact, if consumer welfare is at the heart of competition policy, should not then also the presumption be the one which is more harmful for consumers, that is, that assumed predatory pricing is meant to eliminate the competitors of the market and not that the unprofitable prices are just a way of aligning the company's prices to those of its competitors. The assumption would then cover the situation where the dominant undertaking is unsuccessful in predation, for instance, where the elimination of competitors proves more costly than expected but it is still rational to continue the predatory strategy in order to minimise the losses.[31]

In *France Télécom v Commission*, the ECJ aligned with the CFI's decision and dismissed the appeal. The ECJ recalled that 'it does not follow from the case-law of the Court that proof of the possibility of recoupment of losses suffered by the application, by an undertaking in a dominant position, of prices lower than a certain level of costs constitutes a necessary precondition to establishing that such a pricing policy is abusive'.[32] The ECJ added that

> Moreover, the lack of any possibility of recoupment of losses is not sufficient to prevent the undertaking concerned reinforcing its dominant position, in particular, following the withdrawal from the market of one or a number of its competitors, so that the degree of competition existing on the market, already weakened precisely because of the presence of the undertaking concerned, is further reduced and customers suffer loss as a result of the limitation of the choices available to them.[33]

Thus an argument that consumers never suffered because they had the benefit of low prices is not sufficient to rule out damage to the competitive process and consequently harm caused to consumers in the long-term.

## PROTECTING CONSUMERS OR COMPETITORS

It is often difficult to balance consumer interests with the rights of undertakings when an undertaking exercises its right to dispose freely of its property or to choose its trading partners, which in turn may lead to a refusal to supply.[34]

The interplay between these different objectives can be seen in the CFI's *Microsoft v Commission* judgment, in particular with regard to the refusal to supply the interoperability information.[35] The CFI recalled that although

[31] *Ibid* footnote 46.

[32] Case C-202/07 P *France Télécom v Commission*, n 21 above, para 110.

[33] *Ibid* para 112.

[34] See also *Guidance on the Commission's enforcement priorities in applying Article 82 of the EC Treaty to abusive exclusionary conduct by dominant undertakings*, point 75.

[35] Case T-201/04 *Microsoft v Commission* [2007] II-3601.

undertakings are, as a rule, free to choose their business partners, in certain circumstances a refusal to supply on the part of a dominant undertaking may constitute an abuse of a dominant position. It also underlined that before a refusal by the holder of an intellectual property right to license a third party to use a product can be characterised as an abuse of a dominant position, three conditions must be satisfied: the refusal must relate to a product or service indispensable to the exercise of an activity on a neighbouring market; the refusal must be of such a kind as to exclude any effective competition on that market; and the refusal must prevent the appearance of a new product for which there is potential consumer demand.[36]

The CFI stated that the work group server operating systems of Microsoft's competitors must be able to interoperate with Windows domain architecture on an equal footing with Windows operating systems if they are to be capable of being marketed viably. The CFI emphasised that the absence of such interoperability with the Windows domain architecture has the effect of reinforcing Microsoft's competitive position on the work group server operating systems market, particularly because it induces consumers to use its work group server operating system in preference to its competitors', although its competitors' operating systems offer features to which consumers attach great importance.[37] Therefore, when assessing the circumstance relating to the appearance of a new product, the CFI placed that assessment in the context of the damage to the interests of consumers. The CFI emphasised that in the balancing of the interest in protecting the intellectual property right and the economic freedom of its owner against the interest in protecting free competition, the latter can prevail only where refusal to grant a licence prevents the development of the secondary market, to the detriment of consumers.[38]

However, concerning the balancing of the immediate consumer interest in having more technical choices with what might be less social welfare (consumer and producer benefits) in the long-term in form of reduced incentive to innovate, the CFI's arguments seem quite straightforward. The CFI rejected Microsoft's arguments to the effect that the refusal is objectively justified because the technology concerned is covered by intellectual property rights by noting that such justification would render ineffective the principles established in the case-law.[39] According to the CFI, Microsoft had also failed to show that if it were required to disclose the interoperability information, this would have a significant negative effect on its incentives to innovate.[40]

From a consumer perspective these kinds of conclusions are fully justified only if the short-term positive effects were clear, in other words, that there will be more technical choice, and if the long-term harm is not likely, in other words, that the likelihood that innovation is diminished is low. In fact, for consumers in

[36] *Ibid* paras 331 and 332.
[37] *Ibid* para 422.
[38] *Ibid* para 646.
[39] *Ibid* para 690.
[40] *Ibid* paras 701 and 711.

general it is more detrimental if companies limit their investments in innovation because of the fear that upon request they are obliged to share the benefits of their investments with their competitors.[41] Consequently, when evaluating what the long-term interests of consumers are, attention should be paid also to the impact the decision may have outside the specific case. It could even be argued that if these kind of 'violations' of intellectual property rights in the form of competition law enforcement become frequent, the negative effects on innovation in general are more likely. This in turn would reduce the innovative incentives and economic efficiency which are probably more important to the consumers' long-term interests than an increased choice of products or services in an individual case.

In the *Microsoft v Commission* judgment, the CFI also scrutinised the bundling of the Windows client PC operating system and Windows Media Player. When examining whether consumers had a choice to obtain the tying product without the tied product, the CFI observed that, in consequence of the tying, consumers were unable to acquire the Windows operating system without simultaneously acquiring Windows Media Player. In this regard, the CFI considered that neither the fact that Microsoft did not charge a separate price for Windows Media Player, nor the fact that consumers were not obliged to use the media player, was relevant for the purposes of the examination of the harmful consequences of tying.[42]

When examining if the practice was able to foreclose the market, the CFI considerations seemed, at first sight, to focus on the viewpoint of Microsoft's competitors. The CFI found that offering original equipment manufacturers (hereinafter OEM) only the version of Windows bundled with Windows Media Player had the inevitable consequence of affecting relations on the market between Microsoft, OEMs and suppliers of third-party media players by appreciably altering the balance of competition in favour of Microsoft and to the detriment of the other operators. The CFI considered that that practice enabled Microsoft to obtain an unparalleled advantage with respect to distribution of its product and to ensure the ubiquity of Windows Media Player on client PCs throughout the world, thus providing a disincentive for users to use third-party media players and for OEMs to pre-install such media players on client PCs. The CFI concluded that the Commission was correct to find that there was a significant risk that the tying would lead to a weakening of competition in such a way that the maintenance of an effective competitive structure would not be ensured in the near future.[43]

Here again, it is difficult to balance the consumers' short and long-term interests. In close sight, it would seem to be in the consumers' interest to have a free Media Player when acquiring the Windows operating system even if it was not intended to be used. However, when the viewpoint is set on protecting the

[41] See also Opinion of Advocate General Jacobs in Case C-7/97 *Bronner*, n 5 above, points 57 and 61.

[42] Case T-201/04 *Microsoft v Commission*, n 35 above, paras 969 and 970.

[43] *Ibid* paras 1037–1055.

process of competition and, consequently, in protecting that the consumers have also in the future a choice between different products and therefore a structural guarantee of existing competition which in turn is necessary to secure reasonable prices, good quality and new innovations, the emerging picture protects not only competitors, but also consumers.

Consequently, protecting consumer interests by protecting competitive processes leads to some extent also to the protection of competitors. The recent case-law demonstrates that bringing consumer interests into competition law enforcement enlarges the scope of its application. In particular, this is the case concerning refusal to supply and exclusive dealing where the basic rights of property and the contractual rights are restricted by competition rules and where the applicability of competition rules over above-mentioned basic rights is justified on the basis of consumer welfare grounds. Nevertheless, there seems to be less discussion whether consumer welfare is such an important value that it justifies the restrictions that are imposed on the other rights equally protected by basic principles of Community law. Yet, as Advocate General Jacobs noted in the *Bronner* case 'the justification in terms of competition policy for interfering with a dominant undertaking's freedom to contract often requires a careful balancing of conflicting considerations'.[44]

In the *Sot. Lélos kai Sia and Others* judgment, the ECJ seems to have shifted the balance between consumer interests and the commercial interests of an undertaking slightly more towards protecting the incentive for innovations and protection of property rights.[45] The preliminary question was whether a pharmaceutical company abuses its dominant position on the national market for certain medicinal products if it refuses to meet wholesalers' order because those wholesalers were involved in parallel exports of those products to other Member States where the price of the products were higher. The ECJ acknowledged that such parallel exports of medicinal products from a Member State where the prices are low to other Member States in which the prices are higher open up an alternative source of supply to buyers of those products in the States where the prices were higher and that it necessarily brings some benefits to the final consumers of those products.[46] Nevertheless, the ECJ decided that a pharmaceutical company may, in order to protect its own commercial interests, refuse to supply orders from wholesalers involved in parallel exports if those orders are out of the ordinary. For the context of this article, the most interesting part of the ECJ judgment is where the ECJ justified the right to refuse to supply orders which are out of ordinary. The ECJ observed that 'in the light of the Treaty objectives to protect consumers by means of undistorted competition and the integration of national markets, the Community rules on competition are also incapable of being interpreted in such a way that, in order to defend its own

[44] Opinion of Advocate General Jacobs in Case C-7/97 *Bronner,* n 5 above, point 57.

[45] Joined Cases C-468/06 to C-478/06 *Sot. Lélos kai Sia and Others,* judgment of 16 September 2008 nyr, paras 49–52.

[46] *Ibid* para 53.

commercial interests, the only choice left for a pharmaceuticals company in a dominant position is not to place its medicines on the market at all in a Member State where the prices of those products are set at a relatively low level'.

The link between the protection of consumers and the protection of commercial interests of a company is somewhat difficult to understand in the above-mentioned case. The ECJ may have meant that if the only choice left for a pharmaceuticals company in a dominant position is not to place its medicines on the market at all in a Member State where the prices of those products are set at a relatively low level, the consumers of that Member State would then suffer for not having access to the medicines in question or for having to pay a higher price for those products if they then needed to be exported from another Member State where the price level was higher. This would make sense in a hypothesis where the pharmaceuticals company would completely stop provisioning the Member State where the prices of those products are set at a relatively low level. In fact, in such a situation, the final consumers in the other Member States would neither profit from the lower prices generated by the parallel import as there would not be any alternative source of supply. Thus, consumer interests in all Member States concerned would be harmed. If this was the logic followed by the ECJ, it would have been useful if it was written out more clearly. However, as this was not the case, the judgment is also open to other interpretations of which one could be that the ECJ wanted to limit the applicability of competition law when interfering with a dominant undertaking's freedom to contract or with its intellectual property rights.

## CONSUMERS' LEGAL STANDING IN COMPETITION CASES

Consumers are more and more seen as active enforcers of competition law. However, it is rare that consumers are applicants or even interveners in competition cases at the Community Court level even though that right has been recognised by the Community Courts.

The right of consumer associations to intervene in competition cases was recognised by the ECJ already in 1984 when Bureau Européen des Unions des Consommateurs was admitted to intervene in a case concerning selective distribution system in the car industry.[47]

The possibility of a consumer association to lodge a complaint in a competition case and, consequently to contest the Commission decision, was accepted in judgment *BEUC and NCC v Commission*.[48] More recently, the approach has been formalised by the Commission in its notice on the handling of complaints by the Commission under Articles 81 and 82 of the EC Treaty.[49] It is stated in point 37 of the notice that consumer associations can lodge complaints with the Commission. Furthermore, the Commission holds the view that individual

[47] Joined Cases 228/82 and 229/82 *Ford of Europe and Ford-Werke v Commission* [1984] ECR 1129. See also Case T-23/90 *Peugeot v Commission* [1991] ECR II-653.

[48] Case T-37/92 *BEUC and NCC v Commission* [1994] ECR II-285 para 36.

[49] [2004] OJ C/101/65.

consumers whose economic interests are directly and adversely affected insofar as they are the buyers of goods or services that are the object of an infringement can be in a position to show a legitimate interest.

The Commission also accepted as complainant an individual consumer in the Greek Ferries case. Following a complaint from a customer to the effect that ferry tariffs were very similar on routes between Greece and Italy, the Commission opened a formal investigation which led to a decision.[50] The complainant's status of an individual consumer was not disputed in the actions which were brought before the CFI against the Commission decision.

The right of a final consumer to participate as complainant in proceedings relating to infringements of competition rules was raised in the Austrian Bank case relating to bank fees for national currency/euro exchange transactions. During the administrative procedure, an Austrian political party, the Freiheitliche Partei Österreichs (hereinafter FPÖ) requested to have access to the statements of objections claiming that the party had suffered economic harm as a result of the impugned practices. The banks under investigation objected to the statements of objections being sent to the FPÖ because, in their contention, the FPÖ could not be regarded as a complainant with a legitimate interest.

In its judgment *Österreichische Postsparkasse v Commission,*[51] the CFI confirmed that nothing prevents a final customer who purchases goods or services from being able to satisfy the notion of legitimate interest within the meaning of Article 3 of Regulation No 17.[52]

The CFI considered that a final customer who shows that he has sustained or is likely to sustain harm to his economic interests owing to the restriction of competition in question has a legitimate interest for the purposes of Article 3 of Regulation No 17 in lodging an application or a complaint with the aim of securing a finding by the Commission that there has been an infringement of Articles 81 EC and 82 EC. Of particular interest in the context of this article is the CFI's statement that 'the ultimate purpose of the rules which seek to ensure that competition is not distorted in the internal market is to enhance the welfare of consumers'. It added that the recognition that final customers have a legitimate interest helps to achieve the objectives of competition law.

However, the CFI also stated that recognition of a final customer's status as an applicant or complainant depends on the likelihood that the latter will suffer economic damage as a result of the anti-competitive practices. This requirement is necessary in order not to render the notion of legitimate interest meaningless by making it excessively broad or pave the way for an alleged 'actio popularis'.[53]

[50] Commission Decision 1999/271/EC of 9 December 1998 relating to a proceeding pursuant to Article 85 of the EC Treaty (IV/34.466 - Greek Ferries) [1999] OJ L/109/24.

[51] Joined Cases T-213/01 and T-214/01 *Österreichische Postsparkasse v Commission* [2006] ECR II-1601.

[52] Regulation No 17: First Regulation implementing Articles 85 and 86 of the Treaty [1962] OJ L/13/204. A similar provision can be found in Art 7(2) of Reg No 1/2003: 'Those entitled to lodge a complaint for the purposes of paragraph 1 are natural or legal persons who can show a legitimate interest and Member States.'.

[53] Joined Cases T-213/01 and T-214/01 *Österreichische Postsparkasse v Commission*, n 51 above, paras 114–118, 124 and 131.

The question of legal standing of individual consumers or consumer associations in State aid cases does not seem to have been examined by the Community Courts so far. The closest example can perhaps be found in *Commission v Aktionsgemeinschaft Recht und Eigentum*.[54] Aktionsgemeinschaft Recht und Eigentum (hereinafter ARE), an association of groups dealing with issues relating to property ownership in the agricultural and forestry sectors wanted to challenge a State aid decision. In the contested decision, the Commission, without initiating the formal examination procedure provided for in Article 88(2) EC, raised no objection to the aid embodied in certain modifications to the German Indemnification and Compensation Act. Under this Act, certain agricultural land situated in the former German Democratic Republic could be acquired by various categories of persons for less than half of its actual market value. According to ARE, the land acquisition scheme was discriminatory by reason of the requirement of possession of a long-term lease, a requirement which would have the same effect of a residence criterion, in other words that the (principal) place of residence of the beneficiaries needed to be in the territory of the German Democratic Republic.

The CFI had considered the action by ARE admissible. However, the ECJ did not share CFI's opinion, but took the view that the mere fact that an applicant may be regarded as concerned within the meaning of Article 88(2) EC cannot suffice to render the action admissible. According to the ECJ, the applicant must further demonstrate that it has a particular status within the meaning of *Plaumann v Commission*[55] case-law.[56] The ECJ stated that an association set up to promote the collective interests of a category of persons can therefore only be regarded as being individually concerned to the extent to which the position of its members in the market is substantially affected by the aid scheme covered by the contested decision. That is not the case, even if certain members of such an association are economic operators who may be regarded as direct competitors of beneficiaries of the aid provided for and, therefore, their competitive position is necessarily affected by the contested decision, where it appears to be accepted that all operators in the relevant sector in the European Union may be regarded as competitors of the beneficiaries of that aid.[57]

This case demonstrates, as was noted by the Advocate General Jacobs in his Opinion, that the Community Courts have taken a broader view of the test for standing of complainants in other related areas, namely under the competition rules applying to undertakings (Articles 81 EC and 82 EC) and in cases of dumping than in State aid cases.[58]

However, it should be questioned whether the legal standing of consumers should differ between antitrust and State aid cases. In fact, if the protection of consumers is one of the ultimate goals of competition law, then the same

[54] Case C-78/03 P *Commission v Aktionsgemeinschaft Recht und Eigentum* [2005] ECR I-10737.
[55] Case 25/62 *Plaumann v Commission* [1963] ECR 197.
[56] Case C-78/03 P *Commission v Aktionsgemeinschaft Recht und Eigentum*, n 54 above, para 37.
[57] *Ibid* paras 70–72.
[58] *Ibid* Opinion of Advocate General Jacobs point 142.

justification which confers a right to stand as an interested party in Articles 81 EC and 82 EC cases should also be applied to State aid cases. Like any other anticompetitive measure, also State aid has a negative effect on the structure of the market, impairing the competition between companies and thus ultimately affecting consumer welfare.

## CONCLUSIONS

The Community Courts seem to have taken consumer protection as one of their guiding principles in competition cases, at least in some of them. Nevertheless, the Community Courts do not as a rule clearly define what their definition of consumers or of consumer interests is when applying competition law to specific cases. In particular, it would be useful if the Courts would spell out in a more extensive way the different considerations they have taken into account when balancing the different interests consumers may have. In fact, as can be seen from the case-law studied above, consumer interests change, for instance, depending on the timeframe examined. If the varying interests are not assessed thoroughly enough, it may well be that consumer protection in EU competition law is nothing more than a different name for protecting efficient competition and may sometimes even lead to protecting competitors more than consumers. Clear definitions would improve consumer protection because efficient competitive processes do not always automatically result in long-term consumer benefits being materialised. In addition, if protecting consumers is the main goal or one of the main objectives of competition law enforcement, should the Courts then not assess in each competition case whether the proposed application and interpretation of competition rules really lead to the protection of consumer interests. In other terms, the Courts should not restrain their examination of consumer interests only to those competition cases where such arguments are raised by the parties but should themselves evaluate the effects of competition judgments for the consumers if there is any doubt that the outcome would be different if consumer interests were taken into account.

Furthermore, not only substantial rules of competition law should be applied with consumer interests in mind but attention should also be paid to the fact that procedural issues can have an effect on how efficiently competition law protects consumers. The economic approach to competition law is illustrative. Emphasising economic evidence in the application of competition rules may lead to situations where the burden of proof placed on competition authorities is such that harmful behaviour escapes the net of antitrust measures.[59] Consequently, in some cases, the protection of consumers is more efficient if a combination of form-based and effects-based approaches is used. Combining an economic approach with clear rules on who bears the burden of proof is hence of utmost

[59] But see LL Gormsen, 'Article 82 EC: Where are we coming from and where are we going to?' (2006) *The Competition Law Review* 5.

importance. The competition authorities should be able to rely on the most likely economic scenarios and the company would have to prove otherwise, a principle regularly applied in consumer protection law.

It will be interesting to see whether other Community policies, such as enhancing European competitiveness, gain more importance in the enforcement priorities of competition law in the aftermath of the current financial crisis. Of particular interest will thus be the cases where the protection of competitive process as a method of promoting consumer interests will be in conflict with the competitive strength of European industry, in other words, when the economic considerations do not coincide with consumer interests. It may well be that, in the present economic situation, the definition of consumer interests will be enlarged not only to encompass the traditional consumer interests but consumer interests will be seen in a larger context of social welfare, hence avoiding a confrontation between different competition policy goals.

# 12

# *Unfair Competition and Trade Marks*

NINA KORJUS*

## INTRODUCTION

Trade mark owners may have invested a lot in their marks and, consequently, it is in their interest to have as much protection as possible against unfair use of their trade marks. In particular as regards luxury products or other products covered by a trade mark with a reputation, the attempts to take unfair advantage of the image may go very far. Concretely, the legal issues raised by the extensive protection claimed by such brands can result, inter alia, in the following questions: can L'Oréal prevent companies marketing 'smell-alike' versions of Trésor, Noa or Anaïs-Anaïs perfumes? Can Louis Vuitton prevent Google from selling its brand names as keywords? Can Christian Dior prevent the resale of its luxury corsetry goods by discount stores? Some of these questions do not yet have definite answers, but they illustrate well what trade mark owners may face in the context of unfair competition.

Unfair competition law – in contrast with antitrust law – is not directly regulated in the EC Treaty. However, the system for the protection of competition required of the Community as a result of Article 3(1)(g) EC covers not only measures against behaviour that falls within classical antitrust law, but also infringements of unfair competition law including, for instance, the creation of a likelihood of confusion and dilution.[1]

Trade mark rights are an essential element in the system of undistorted competition which the EC Treaty seeks to establish and maintain. Under such a system, an undertaking must be in a position to keep its customers by virtue of the quality of its products and services, something which is possible only if there are distinctive marks which enable customers to identify them.[2]

* All views expressed in this paper are strictly personal.

[1] See, eg J Glöckner, 'The Law Against Unfair Competition and the EC Treaty' in RM Hilty and F Henning-Bodewig (eds), *Law Against Unfair Competition* (Berlin, Springer, 2007) 77.

[2] See, eg Case C-10/89 *Hag GF* [1990] ECR I-3711 para 13; Case C-206/01 *Arsenal Football Club* [2002] ECR I-10273 para 47, and Case C-228/03 *Gillette Company and Gillette Group Finland* [2005] ECR I-2337 para 25.

The EC Treaty does not contain any explicit provisions concerning trade marks or unfair competition, and traditionally trade mark cases were solved notably under provisions on the free movement of goods[3] until the adoption of Directive 89/104/EEC to approximate the laws of the Member States relating to trade marks[4] (hereinafter Directive 89/104 or Trade Mark Directive). In 1994 a unitary Community trade mark was created by Regulation No 40/94 on the Community Trade Mark[5] (hereinafter Regulation No 40/94 or Community Trade Mark Regulation).

Unfair competition protection serves as a complement to special rights such as trade mark rights. The Community Trade Mark Regulation and the Trade Mark Directive expressly reserve the application of national laws against unfair competition.[6] The law of unfair competition is left to the Member States as far as there is no harmonisation by Community secondary law.[7]

The underlying principles of unfair competition law can be found in the Paris Convention.[8] According to Article 1(2) of the Paris Convention, the repression of unfair competition is a part of the protection of industrial property. Article 10bis of the Paris Convention obliges, inter alia, the Member States of the European Union,[9] to grant an effective protection against unfair competition. This Article defines unfair competition as 'any act of competition contrary to honest practices in industrial or commercial matters'. In particular, acts of confusion, of denigration and of misleading indications shall be prohibited.

[3] See, eg CN Kakouris, 'La concurrence déloyale dans la jurisprudence de la Cour de Justice des Communautés Européennes' in *La responsabilité non-contractuelle en matière commerciale* (Heidelberg, Heidelberg Verlag Recht und Wirtschaft GmbH, 1995). Of course trade mark rights were also treated under the competition rules; see, eg WA Rothnie, 'EC Competition Policy, the Commission and Trade Marks' (1991) *International Business Lawyer* 495. See also L Focsaneanu, 'La jurisprudence de la Cour de Justice des Communautés européennes en matière de concurrence. IV. – Propriété intellectuelle et concurrence (brevets, marques, appellations d'origine, droits d'auteur)' (1975) 187 *Revue du Marché Commun* 343.

[4] Council Directive 89/104/EEC of 21 December 1988 to approximate the laws of the Member States relating to trade marks [1989] OJ L/40/1. Dir 89/104 has been repealed and replaced by Directive 2008/95/EC of the European Parliament and of the Council of 22 October 2008 to approximate the laws of the Member States relating to trade marks [2008] OJ L/299/25, which entered into force on 28 November 2008. In this chapter, reference is made to the old Directive.

[5] Council Regulation (EC) No 40/94 of 20 December 1993 on the Community trade mark [1994] OJ L/11/1. Reg No 40/94 has been repealed and replaced by Council Regulation (EC) No 207/2009 of 26 February 2009 on the Community trade mark [2009] OJ L/78/1, which entered into force on 13 April 2009. The codified version brings no substantive legal changes but the numbers of many of the Articles change. In this chapter, reference is made to the old Regulation.

[6] See Art 14(1) of Reg No 40/94 and recitals of Dir 89/104.

[7] See also F Henning-Bodewig and G Schricker, 'New Initiatives for the Harmonisation of Unfair Competition Law in Europe' (2002) *European Intellectual Property Review* 271.

[8] Paris Convention for the Protection of Industrial Property of 20 March 1883, as revised at Brussels on 14 December 1990, at Washington on 2 June 1911, at the Hague on 6 November 1925, at London on 2 June 1934, at Lisbon on 31 October 1958, and at Stockholm on 14 July 1967, and as amended on 28 September 1979.

[9] See contracting parties to the Paris Convention (total 173) at www.wipo.int/treaties/en/ShowResults.jsp?lang=en&treaty_id=2.

The harmonisation work at the European Union level started in the 1960s[10] but it was only in 1984 that it resulted in Directive 84/450/EEC on Misleading Advertising,[11] which was amended in 1997 in order to include comparative advertising[12] (hereinafter Directive 84/450 or Directive on Misleading and Comparative Advertising).[13] Directive 84/450 establishes minimum criteria for harmonising legislation.

In 2005 the harmonisation work resulted in Directive 2005/29/EC concerning unfair business-to-consumer commercial practices in the internal market[14] (hereinafter Directive 2005/29 or Unfair Commercial Practices Directive).[15] Directive 2005/29 fully harmonises the rules on unfair commercial practices at the Community level and, accordingly, Member States may not adopt stricter rules than those provided for in the Directive, even in order to achieve a higher level of consumer protection.[16] This Directive directly protects consumer economic interests from unfair business-to-consumer commercial practices and

[10] The harmonisation work was prepared by Eugen Ulmer in the Max Planck Institute. He proposed a harmonisation of unfair competition law in the broad sense, ie, including trade names, famous trade marks and indications of geographical origin, under a general clause based on Art 10bis of the Paris Convention. See, eg E Ulmer, 'Le droit de la concurrence déloyale et le Marché commun' (1963) *La Propriété industrielle* 33, and E Ulmer, 'Unfair Competition Law in the European Economic Community' (1973) *International Review of Industrial Property and Copyright Law* 188. See, for the history, eg C Wadlow, 'Unfair Competition in Community Law: Part 1: the Age of the "Classical Model"' and 'Part 2: Harmonisation Becomes Gridlocked' (2006) *European Intellectual Property Review* 433 and 469, and F Henning-Bodewig, 'Secondary Unfair Competition Law' in RM Hilty and F Henning-Bodewig (eds), *Law Against Unfair Competition* (Berlin, Springer, 2007) 111. See also A Robertson and A Horton, 'Does the United Kingdom or the European Community Need an Unfair Competition Law?' (1995) *European Intellectual Property Review* 568.

[11] Council Directive 84/450/EEC of 10 September 1984 relating to the approximation of the laws, regulations and administrative provisions of the Member States concerning misleading advertising [1984] OJ L/250/17.

[12] Directive 97/55/EC of European Parliament and of the Council of 6 October 1997 amending Directive 84/450/EEC concerning misleading advertising so as to include comparative advertising [1997] OJ L/290/18.

[13] Dir 84/450 has been repealed and replaced by Directive 2006/114/EC of the European Parliament and of the Council of 12 December 2006 concerning misleading and comparative advertising [2006] OJ L/376/21 which entered into force on 12 December 2007. This is simply a codified version, in the interests of clarity and rationality, of the provisions in Dir 84/450. Since the case-law so far concerns the old Directive, reference is made to it in this chapter.

[14] Directive 2005/29/EC of the European Parliament and of the Council of 11 May 2005 concerning unfair business-to-consumer commercial practices in the internal market and amending Council Directive 84/450/EEC, Directives 97/7/EC, 98/27/EC and 2002/65/EC of the European Parliament and of the Council and Regulation (EC) No 2006/2004 of the European Parliament and of the Council [2005] OJ L/149/22.

[15] See generally B Dutoit, 'Un nouveau droit européen (tronqué) de la concurrence déloyale' in A Epiney, M Haag and A Heinemann (eds), *Die Herausforderung von Grenzen: Festschrift für Roland Bieber* (Baden-Baden, Nomos Verlagsgesellschaft, 2007) 645; R García Pérez, 'Las disposiciones generales y la cláusula general de la Ley de Competencia Desleal a la luz de la Directiva sobre practicas comerciales desleales' (2006) 242 *Gaceta juridical de la Unión Europea y de la competencia* 60, and C Handig, 'The Unfair Commercial Practices Directive – A Milestone in the European Unfair Competition Law?' (2005) 16 *European Business Law Review* 1117.

[16] See Joined Cases C-261/07 and C-299/07 *VTB-VAB and Galatea*, judgment of 23 April 2009 nyr, para 52. This is the first case concerning interpretation of Dir 2005/29. According to this judgment, Community law precludes national legislation which, without taking account of the specific circumstances, prohibits any combined offer made by a vendor to a consumer.

thereby it also indirectly protects legitimate businesses from their competitors who do not play by the rules of this Directive and thus guarantees fair competition in fields covered by it. The Unfair Commercial Practices Directive does not cover or affect the provisions of the Directive on Misleading and Comparative Advertising on advertising which misleads business but which is not misleading for consumers and on comparative advertising.[17]

For the purposes of this chapter unfair competition is envisaged in a broad sense, that is, not limiting the examination only to cases relating to the application of the Unfair Commercial Practices Directive or the Directive on Misleading and Comparative Advertising. In fact, the Trade Mark Directive and the Community Trade Mark Regulation already include several provisions which can be understood as protecting trade mark owners against unfair competition.[18] The recent case-law of the Court of Justice of the European Communities (hereinafter ECJ) has been particularly interesting in that regard and, therefore, this chapter will focus on it. The case-law of the Court of First Instance of the European Communities (hereinafter CFI) concerning, for instance, likelihood of confusion, is already well developed but will not be examined here.

In this chapter I will examine the following recent judgments or pending cases: *Intel Corporation*,[19] *O2 Holdings and O2 (UK)*,[20] *L'Oréal and Others*,[21] *Google and Google France*,[22] and *Copad*.[23] I will first deal with dilution and free-riding, secondly, with the relationship between trade mark protection and comparative advertising, thirdly, with the specific question concerning the use of trade marks by search engines and, finally, with the question of the effects of a licence agreement on the exhaustion of trade mark rights.

## DILUTION AND FREE-RIDING

### Protection under Article 5(2) of the Trade Mark Directive

Article 5(2) of the Trade Mark Directive establishes, for the benefit of trade marks with a reputation, a form of protection whose implementation does not require the existence of a likelihood of confusion. Article 5(2) applies to situations in which the specific condition of the protection consists of a use of the sign in question without due cause which takes unfair advantage of, or is detrimental to, the distinctive character or the repute of the trade mark.[24]

[17] See recitals 8 and 6 in the preamble to Dir 2005/29.

[18] See, eg Arts 4 and 5 of Dir 104/89 and Arts 8 and 9 of Reg 40/94.

[19] Case C-252/07 *Intel Corporation*, judgment of 27 November 2008 nyr.

[20] Case C-533/06 *O2 Holdings and O2 (UK)* [2008] ECR I-4231.

[21] Case C-487/07 *L'Oréal and Others*, judgment of 18 June 2009 nyr.

[22] Joined Cases C-236/08 to C-238/08 *Google and Google France* pending. The oral hearing was held on 17 March 2009.

[23] Case C-59/08 *Copad*, judgment of 23 April 2009 nyr.

[24] See, eg Case C-102/07 *adidas and adidas Benelux* [2008] ECR I-2439 para 40. It has been stated that since the wording of Arts 4(4)(a) and 5(2) of Dir 89/104 is essentially identical, they are designed

*Cont.*

The ECJ has stated, interpreting it not solely on the basis of its wording, but also in the light of the overall scheme and objectives of the system of which it is a part, that Article 5(2) of the Trade Mark Directive also applies in respect of goods and services identical with or similar to those covered by the registered mark.[25]

There are three types of injury against which Article 5(2) of the Trade Mark Directive ensures such protection for the benefit of trade marks with a reputation. They are, first, detriment to the distinctive character of the trade mark, also referred to as dilution, whittling away or blurring; second, detriment to the repute of that mark, also referred to as tarnishment or degradation, and, third, unfair advantage taken of the distinctive character or the repute of that mark, also referred to as free-riding or parasitism.[26] Any of those three types of injury suffices for that provision to apply.

First, dilution, or detriment to the distinctive character of the trade mark, is caused when that mark's ability to identify the goods or services for which it is registered and used as coming from the proprietor of that mark is weakened, since use of an identical or similar sign by a third party leads to dispersion of the identity and hold upon the public mind of the trade mark. That is notably the case when the trade mark with a reputation, which used to arouse immediate association with the goods and services for which it is registered, is no longer capable of doing so.[27]

to give trade marks with a reputation the same protection. See Case C-252/07 *Intel Corporation,* n 19 above, para 24. The corresponding provisions of Reg 40/94 are Arts 8(5) and 9(1)(c). There is, though, one essential difference: according to Art 4(4)(a) of Dir 89/104 and Art 8(5) of Reg 40/94, the use 'would take' unfair advantage or 'be' detrimental, while according to Art 5(2) of Dir 89/104 and Art 9(1)(c) of Reg 40/94, the use 'takes' unfair advantage or 'is' detrimental. This could be explained by the fact that the former provisions concern refusal to register a later mark for which it would be difficult to show that it 'takes' or 'is' something, since it may not have been used at all yet. However, these provisions also cover applications for a declaration of invalidity of a trade mark already registered and, supposedly, already used.

[25] See Case C-292/00 *Davidoff* [2003] ECR I-389 para 30; Case C-408/01 *Adidas-Salomon and Adidas Benelux* [2003] ECR I-12537 para 22, and Case C-102/07 *adidas and adidas Benelux,* n 24 above, para 37. *Davidoff* has been criticised since it extended the protection under Art 5(2) of Dir 89/104 against dilution to all situations, whether the goods are similar or dissimilar or whether they are competitive or non-competitive. It has been argued that 'dilution' should be defined as a separate and clearly distinctive part of the whole scope of protection that the trade mark law can give or it will lose its usefulness as a legal concept and as a helpful instrument in legal practice. According to critics, mixing 'likelihood of confusion' and 'dilution' together is bound to result in legal frustration with the possibility of making wrong decisions and harming the balance of free and fair competition. See J Jensen, 'Trademark dilution law in the European Community' (2008) 5 *Nordiskt Immateriellt Rättsskydd* 444, at 450 and 459.

[26] See Case C-252/07 *Intel Corporation,* n 19 above, paras 27 and 29, and Opinion of Advocate General Sharpston in that case points 11 and 12. As the Advocate General points out, in the United States Trademark Dilution Revision Act of 2006, the term dilution covers both blurring and tarnishment. This Act is designed to protect famous marks from uses that blur their distinctiveness or tarnish their reputation but it does not involve free-riding.

[27] Case C-252/07 *Intel Corporation,* n 19 above, para 29. See also Opinion of Advocate General Jacobs in Case C-408/01 *Adidas-Salomon and Adidas Benelux,* n 25 above, point 37 citing Frank Schechter from year 1927. In the US Trademark Dilution Revision Act of 2006 blurring (corresponding dilution in *Intel Corporation*) is defined as an 'association arising from the similarity between a mark or a trade name and a famous mark that impairs the distinctiveness of the famous mark'.

Second, tarnishment, or detriment to the repute of the trade mark, is caused where the goods or services covered by the identical or similar sign by a third party may be perceived by the public in such a way that the trade mark's power of attraction is diminished. The risk of detriment can, inter alia, occur where those goods or services have a characteristic or a quality which may have a negative influence on the image of the trade mark with a reputation on account of its being identical or similar to the sign.[28]

Third, free-riding, or the concept of the unfair advantage taken of the distinctive character or the repute of the mark, encompasses instances where there is a clear exploitation and free-riding on the coat-tails of a famous mark or an attempt to trade upon its reputation.[29] In other words, it implies that the image of the mark with a reputation or the characteristics which it projects are transferred to the goods covered by the other sign, with the result that the marketing of those goods is made easier by that association with the mark with a reputation.[30] In simple terms, what is prohibited is the drawing of benefit from the mark with a reputation by the proprietor of the other sign.[31] This concept thus does not relate to the detriment caused to the mark but to the advantage taken by the third party as a result of the use of the identical or similar sign.[32]

According to established case-law, the types of injury referred to in Article 5(2) of the Trade Mark Directive, where they occur, are the consequence of a certain degree of similarity between the mark and the sign, by virtue of which the relevant section of the public makes a connection between those two marks, that is to say, establishes a link between them even though it does not confuse them.[33]

In the absence of such a link in the mind of the public, the use of the sign is not likely to take unfair advantage of, or be detrimental to, the distinctive character or the repute of the trade mark. However, according to the ECJ, the existence of such a link is not sufficient, in itself, to establish that there is one of the types of injury referred to in Article 5(2) of the Trade Mark Directive, which constitute the specific condition of the protection of trade marks with a reputation laid down by that provision.[34]

The existence of such a link must be subject to an overall assessment, taking into account all factors relevant to the circumstances of the case and, in

[28] Case T-215/03 *Sigla v OHIM - Elleni Holding (VIPS)* [2007] ECR II-711 para 39. See also Opinion of Advocate General Jacobs in Case C-408/01 *Adidas-Salomon and Adidas Benelux,* n 25 above, point 38. In the US Trademark Dilution Revision Act of 2006 tarnishment is defined as an 'association arising from the similarity between a mark or trade name and a famous mark that harms the reputation of the famous mark'.

[29] See Opinion of Advocate General Jacobs in Case C-408/01 *Adidas-Salomon and Adidas Benelux,* n 25 above, point 39.

[30] See Case T-215/03 *Sigla v OHIM - Elleni Holding (VIPS),* n 28 above, para 40, and Case T-21/07 *L'Oréal v OHIM - Spa Monopole (SPALINE),* judgment of 25 March 2009 unreported, para 19.

[31] See Case C-252/07 *Intel Corporation,* n 19 above, para 36.

[32] Case C-487/07 *L'Oréal and Others,* n 21 above, para 41.

[33] See, eg Case C-102/07 *adidas and adidas Benelux,* n 24 above, para 41, and Case C-252/07 *Intel Corporation,* n 19 above, para 30. See, concerning Reg 40/94, eg Case T-137/05 *La Perla v OHIM - Worldgem Brands (NIMEI LA PERLA MODERN CLASSIC),* judgment of 16 May 2007 unreported, para 34, and Case C-320/07 P *Antartica v OHIM,* judgment of 12 March 2009 unreported, para 43.

[34] Case C-252/07 *Intel Corporation,* n 19 above, paras 31 and 32.

particular, the degree of similarity between the marks at issue; the nature of the goods or services for which the marks at issue were registered, including the degree of closeness or dissimilarity between those goods or services, and the relevant section of the public; the strength of the earlier mark's reputation; the degree of the earlier mark's distinctive character, whether inherent or acquired through use and the existence of the likelihood of confusion on the part of the public.[35]

According to the case-law, the stronger the trade mark's distinctive character and reputation are, the easier it will be to accept that detriment has been caused to it. The more immediately and strongly the mark is brought to mind by the sign, the greater the likelihood that the current or future use of the sign is taking, or will take, unfair advantage of the distinctive character or the repute of the mark or is, or will be, detrimental to them.[36]

In order to enjoy protection given by Article 5(2) of the Trade Mark Directive, a trade mark must be known by a significant part of the public concerned by the products or services it covers in a substantial part of the territory of the Member State in question.[37] As regards Community trade marks, the question as to whether a Community trade mark enjoys a 'reputation in the Community' has not yet been given a definite answer. According to Advocate General Sharpston in the pending case *PAGO International,* the answer should be that a Community trade mark is protected in the whole of the Community on the ground that it has a 'reputation in the Community' within the meaning of Article 9(1)(c) of the Community Trade Mark Regulation if it has a reputation in a substantial part of the Community. In her view, what constitutes a substantial part of the Community for that purpose is not dependent on national boundaries but must be determined by an assessment of all the relevant circumstances of the case, taking account, in particular, of, first, the public concerned by the products or services covered by the trade mark and the proportion of that public which knows of the mark and, secondly, the importance of the area in which the reputation exists, as defined by factors such as its geographical extent, population and economic significance.[38]

The ECJ's landmark judgment in *Intel Corporation*[39] of 27 November 2008 illustrates well the latest developments as regards dilution and offers some

[35] *Ibid* paras 41 and 42, and Case C-320/07 P *Antartica v OHIM,* n 33 above, para 45.

[36] See Case C-375/97 *General Motors* [1999] ECR I-5421 para 30; Case C-252/07 *Intel Corporation,* n 19 above, para 69, and Case C-487/07 *L'Oréal and Others*, n 21 above, para 44.

[37] See Case C-375/97 *General Motors*, n 36 above, paras 26, 28 and 31.

[38] Opinion of Advocate General Sharpston of 30 April 2009 in Case C-301/07 *PAGO International* pending, point 41. She suggests that a trade mark which has a reputation only in one Member State does not qualify as a trade mark with a 'reputation in the Community' within the meaning of Art 9(1)(c) of Reg 40/94, see point 43. The reference for a preliminary ruling in this case came from Austria. In that respect, it can be noted that the US Trademark Dilution Revision Act of 2006 introduced a strict standard of fame, requiring the mark to be known amongst the general consuming public of the entire United States. See, eg I Simon Fhima, 'The Fame Standard for Trademark Dilution in the United States and European Union Compared' (2008) 17 *Transnational Law and Contemporary Problems* 631.

[39] See n 19 above.

clarification on some specific questions such as the relevant public and the evidence required. In another landmark judgment, *L'Oréal and Others*,[40] of 18 June 2009, the ECJ had the opportunity to clarify, inter alia, the concept of free-riding.

### Case *Intel Corporation*

In the ECJ's judgment in *Intel Corporation*, the issue raised in the national proceedings was whether the owner of the trade mark INTEL, which has a huge reputation in the United Kingdom for microprocessor products as well as multimedia and business software, may obtain invalidation of the later mark INTELMARK, registered for marketing services.

After making some preliminary observations on the protection given by Article 4(4)(a) of the Trade Mark Directive,[41] the ECJ stated that the public to be taken into account varies depending on the type of injury alleged by the proprietor of the trade mark with a reputation. Accordingly, the ECJ distinguishes between the relevant public, which with regard to dilution or tarnishment is the public to which the trade mark with a reputation is addressed, while with regard to free-riding, it is the public to which the other sign is addressed.[42] Although this seems quite logical, this distinction is worth noting in so far as it is the first time the ECJ makes such an explicit distinction on the issue.[43]

The ECJ also made a general statement as to proof required by the proprietor of the trade mark with a reputation. According to the ECJ, the proprietor of the earlier trade mark 'is not required to demonstrate actual and present injury to its mark' for the purposes of Article 4(4)(a) of the Trade Mark Directive. The ECJ pursued that when it is foreseeable that such injury will ensue from the use which the proprietor of the later mark may be led to make of its mark, the proprietor of the earlier mark cannot be required to wait for it actually to occur in order to be able to prohibit that use. The proprietor of the earlier mark must, however, prove that there is a serious risk that such an injury will occur in the future.[44]

The requirement of a serious risk seems to go a bit further than the requirements set out in the established case-law of the CFI concerning the application of Article 8(5) of the Community Trade Mark Regulation, according to which 'the proprietor of the earlier mark is not required to demonstrate actual

[40] See n 21 above.

[41] Corresponding essentially, as stated before, to the protection given by Art 5(2) of Dir 89/104 described above.

[42] Case C-252/07 *Intel Corporation*, n 19 above, paras 33–36.

[43] It is interesting to note that later in Case C-320/07 P *Antartica v OHIM*, n 33 above, in dismissing the appeal against Case T-47/06 *Antartica v OHIM – Nasdaq Stock Market (nasdaq)*, judgment of 10 May 2007 unreported, the ECJ stated, clearly in order to comply with this distinction given earlier in *Intel Corporation*, that it was 'implicitly, but clearly, apparent from' the assessment of the CFI that, when assessing the existence of injury, it included in its examination, as the relevant public, the average customer of goods and services for which the later mark was requested; see paras 48–50.

[44] Case C-252/07 *Intel Corporation*, n 19 above, para 38.

and present harm to his mark, but must adduce prima facie evidence of a future risk, which is not hypothetical, of unfair advantage or detriment'.[45] It should be noted that in *Intel Corporation* Advocate General Sharpston agreed with the line taken by the CFI.[46]

The Advocate General correctly points out that the provisions concerned cater for two types of situation: existing use of a registered mark or other sign, and future use of a mark which has not yet been registered. Where the later mark or sign is already in use, it is likely to be possible for the owner of the earlier mark to obtain actual evidence of the existence of a link in the mind of the public, and of the alleged infringement, to support his case, in particular from consumer surveys or marketing figures, although it may not be practicable for each element to be exactly quantified. Where the later mark is merely at the stage of application for registration, such evidence is unlikely to be readily available. Whenever evidence of that kind can be presented, it will obviously carry considerable weight in the assessment. If it is not available, or if only limited evidence is available, inferences must necessarily be drawn from that which can be established. Evidence of the reputation, repute and distinctive character of the earlier mark should however always be available, and those characteristics should never need to be established by inference.[47]

So basically only a 'likelihood of dilution' and not an 'actual dilution' should be sufficient to obtain relief. Indeed, trade mark owners should be able to stop dilution in its inception, instead of waiting until there is actual harm to the distinctive character of the earlier trade mark with a reputation.[48]

However, as the ECJ went on in *Intel Corporation*, the existence of a link between the conflicting marks does not dispense the proprietor of the earlier trade mark from having to prove 'actual and present injury to its mark', or a 'serious likelihood that such an injury will occur in the future'.[49]

The ECJ acknowledged that although dilution may appear even if an earlier mark with a reputation is not unique, the more 'unique' the earlier mark is, the greater the possibility for dilution is. However, the brand owner must provide evidence showing a change or a serious likelihood that such a change will occur in the future in the economic behaviour of the average consumer of the goods or services for which the earlier mark was registered as a consequence of the

[45] See Case T-67/04 *Spa Monopole v OHIM – Spa-Finders Travel Arrangements (SPA-FINDERS)* [2005] ECR II-1825 para 40, and most recently T-21/07 *L'Oréal v OHIM – Spa Monopole (SPALINE)*, n 30 above, para 38.

[46] Opinion of Advocate General Sharpston in Case C-252/07 *Intel Corporation*, n 19 above, point 85.

[47] *Ibid* point 84.

[48] It should be noted that since the US Trademark Dilution Revision Act of 2006, only a likelihood of dilution (by blurring or by tarnishment) is needed. Before the revision the situation was unclear until a decision of the Supreme Court, which found that 'actual dilution' was the relevant standard (*Moseley v Victoria's Secret Catalogue, Inc*, 537 US 418 [2003]). Change was needed after that judgment. See, eg DM Cendali and BL Schriefer, 'The Trademark Dilution Revision Act of 2006: A Welcome – and Needed – Change' (2006) 105 *Michigan Law Review First Impressions* 108, and I Simon, 'Dilution in the US, Europe, and beyond: international obligations and basic definitions' (2006) *Journal of Intellectual Property Law & Practice* 406, at 409.

[49] Case C-252/07 *Intel Corporation*, n 19 above, para 71.

use of the later mark. In that respect, a first use of the later mark may suffice in some circumstances. According to the ECJ, dilution of a trade mark requires the dispersion of the identity and hold upon the public mind of the earlier mark.[50]

It seems that the ECJ has established a new requirement, that is, evidence showing a change in the economic behaviour of the average consumer of the goods or services for which the earlier mark with a reputation was registered as a consequence of the use of the later mark. In that respect, the ECJ also went further than its Advocate General, who considered that dilution need not necessarily involve economic detriment, so that a change in economic behaviour is not essential. As she pointed out, if the trade mark Coca-Cola, or a similar mark or sign, were used for a range of unrelated goods or services, its distinctiveness might well be lessened, but people might drink the beverage in undiminished quantities.[51] Of course, any evidence of actual negative change in consumer behaviour would support the right owner's case, but as mentioned before, concrete evidence can be quite difficult to produce.

The ECJ's approach in *Intel Corporation* may make dilution very hard to prove in practice. What constitutes sufficient evidence remains unclear. Concretely, it could mean that Intel has to show that its consumers are buying less of its goods and if customers keep buying Intel as much as they did before, probably no dilution would be accepted. Because of this heavy burden of proof on brand owners, the judgment clearly is a big disappointment for them, since they were probably hoping to secure extended protection for famous brands. It follows from that judgment that there is no automatic protection against the use of other trade marks applied by third parties to dissimilar goods purely on the basis of a huge reputation and uniqueness of the trade mark in question.

Although the questions referred in *Intel Corporation* also concerned free-riding, the ECJ concentrated mainly on aspects relating more directly to dilution. Further guidance on free-riding was obtained in *L'Oréal and Others*.[52]

## Case *L'Oréal and Others*

L'Oréal SA, Lancôme Parfums et Beauté and Laboratoire Garnier are members of the L'Oréal group, which produces and markets luxury fragrances. They are proprietors of the well-known trade marks Trésor, Miracle, Anaïs-Anaïs and Noa. Malaika and Starion marketed perfumes which were imitations of the fragrance of successful perfumes to wholesalers and hard discount stores in the United Kingdom, which were produced by Bellure. Those perfumes were sold at extremely low retail prices. The bottles and packaging used to market those imitations were generally similar in appearance to the bottles and packaging used by L'Oréal and protected by word and figurative trade marks, although that

[50] *Ibid* paras 72–77.
[51] *Ibid* Opinion of Advocate General Sharpston point 74.
[52] See n 21 above.

similarity was unlikely to mislead retailers or consumers as to the origin of the product. By packaging their products with a wink of an eye to L'Oréal's, Malaika and Starion were able to charge higher prices but without damaging sales of L'Oréal's products. Malaika and Starion also used comparison lists, which were provided to retailers and which indicated the word mark of the luxury fragrance of which the perfume being marketed was an imitation.

L'Oréal maintained, inter alia, that the imitation of the names, bottles and boxes of its perfumes and the sale of perfumes in such imitative bottles and boxes was contrary to Article 5(2) of the Trade Mark Directive. The questions relating to the comparison lists will be dealt later when examining the relationship between trade mark protection and comparative advertising.

It is worth presenting first Advocate General Mengozzi's interpretation of Article 5(2) of the Trade Mark Directive. According to him, that provision must be interpreted as meaning that where a trader uses a sign that is similar to another person's mark and derives an advantage from this originating in that similarity and in the consequential association of that sign with the positive qualities of that mark, such use may be prohibited if it is without due cause, which cannot be the advantage itself, or, where due cause is shown, if it is apparent, taking such due cause and all the relevant circumstances of the case into account, that that advantage is unfair; that prohibition cannot be precluded on account of the fact that there is no effect (or likelihood of any effect) on the mark's essential function of providing a guarantee of origin, no effect (or likelihood of any effect) on the mark's distinctive character or reputation and such use has no impact on the sales of the products identified by the mark or on the return on the investments made in connection with that mark.[53]

Thus, the Advocate General considered that the advantage which a trader gains from the use for his own products of a sign that is similar to another person's well-known mark may be classified as unfair within the meaning of Article 5(2) of the Trade Mark Directive. For him, it is sufficient to demonstrate that the sign used by the third party has a particular attraction for the consumer due to the fact that that sign is associated with positive qualities of the well-known mark in such a way as to induce the consumer to buy the products under that sign.[54]

As for the requirement of 'unfair' advantage, the Advocate General took the view that it comes to play only where due cause is demonstrated. Consequently, where the boost given to the third party's sign as a result of the connection with the well-known mark derives from a use of that sign for which there is due cause, it would still be necessary to determine whether or not the advantage taken by the third party is unfair. On the other hand, where due cause cannot be shown, the advantage taken of the reputation of the mark should be deemed to be unfair. Accordingly, where it is apparent that the only purpose of the use by a trader of a sign that is similar to another person's well-known mark in order to distinguish his own products is to exploit the reputation or particular image of that mark

[53] *Ibid* Opinion of Advocate General Mengozzi point 111.
[54] *Ibid* points 97 and 103.

in order to promote the sale of those products, the advantage which that trader thereby derives should be classified as unfair.[55]

In the concrete case, according to the Advocate General, the national court should verify whether the companies showed due cause for the use of bottles and boxes similar to those of the L'Oréal's trade marks and, if so, whether, taking that due cause and all the relevant circumstances of the case into account, the advantage drawn by those companies of the reputation of those marks was unfair.[56]

If the companies could not show due cause, they would automatically be considered as infringing L'Oréal's trade marks. The interpretation the Advocate General gave to Article 5(2) of the Trade Mark Directive favours the brand owners since it would fall for the companies using similar trade marks to justify their use.

Although the ECJ did not fully follow the Opinion of the Advocate General, its interpretation of that provision is also a clear victory for the brand owners. After reminding that just one of the three types of injury against which Article 5(2) of the Trade Mark Directive ensures protection suffices, it held that an advantage taken by a third party of the distinctive character or the repute of the mark may be unfair, even if the use of the identical or similar sign is not detrimental either to the distinctive character or to the repute of the mark or, more generally, to its proprietor.[57]

Despite that clear statement, the ECJ then went on by stating that the global assessment which must be undertaken in order to determine whether the use of a sign takes unfair advantage of the distinctive character or the repute of the mark, may also take into account, where necessary, the fact that there is a likelihood of dilution or tarnishment of the mark.[58]

It was indisputable that Malaika and Starion used packaging and bottles similar to the marks with a reputation registered by L'Oréal in order to market perfumes which constituted 'downmarket' imitations of the luxury fragrances for which those marks were registered and used. The referring court had held that there was a link between certain packaging used by Malaika and Starion, on the one hand, and certain marks relating to packaging and bottles belonging to L'Oréal, on the other. That link conferred a commercial advantage on Malaika and Starion. It was also clear that the similarity between those marks and the products marketed by Malaika and Starion was created intentionally in order to create an association in the mind of the public between fine fragrances and their imitations, with the aim of facilitating the marketing of those imitations.[59]

The ECJ stated that in the general assessment which the referring court will have to undertake in order to determine whether, in those circumstances, it can be held that unfair advantage is being taken of the distinctive character or the

[55] *Ibid* points 106–108.
[56] *Ibid* point 110.
[57] Case C-487/07 *L'Oréal and Others*, n 21 above, para 43.
[58] *Ibid* para 45.
[59] *Ibid* paras 46 and 47.

repute of the mark, that court will, in particular, have to take account of the fact that the use of packaging and bottles similar to those of the fragrances that are being imitated is intended to take advantage, for promotional purposes, of the distinctive character and the repute of the marks under which those fragrances are marketed.[60]

The ECJ continued that where a third party attempts, through the use of a sign similar to a mark with a reputation, to ride on the coat-tails of that mark in order to benefit from its power of attraction, its reputation and its prestige, and to exploit, without paying any financial compensation and without being required to make efforts of its own in that regard, the marketing effort made by the proprietor of that mark in order to create and maintain the image of that mark, the advantage resulting from such use must be considered to be an advantage that has been unfairly taken of the distinctive character or the repute of that mark.[61]

Therefore, according to the ECJ, Article 5(2) of the Trade Mark Directive must be interpreted as meaning that the taking of unfair advantage of the distinctive character or the repute of a mark, within the meaning of that provision, does not require that there be a likelihood of confusion or a likelihood of detriment to the distinctive character or the repute of the mark or, more generally, to its proprietor. The advantage arising from the use by a third party of a sign similar to a mark with a reputation is an advantage taken unfairly by that third party of the distinctive character or the repute of the mark where that party seeks by that use to ride on the coat-tails of the mark with a reputation in order to benefit from the power of attraction, the reputation and the prestige of that mark and to exploit, without paying any financial compensation, the marketing effort expended by the proprietor of the mark in order to create and maintain the mark's image.[62]

It follows from that judgment that well-known marks should have wide protection against competitors that take unfair advantage of the reputation of these marks. After the judgment in *Intel Corporation*,[63] which was not really in favour of brand owners, it gives a clear relief to them. Other aspects of that judgment, concerning comparative advertising, will be dealt with in the next chapter.

## TRADE MARK PROTECTION AND COMPARATIVE ADVERTISING

### Preliminary Observations

The relationship between trade mark protection and comparative advertising is an issue that has only recently been addressed by the ECJ.

[60] *Ibid* para 48.
[61] *Ibid* para 49.
[62] *Ibid* para 50.
[63] See n 19 above.

As regards, first, comparative advertising, it should be recalled that under Article 2(2a) of the Directive on Misleading and Comparative Advertising, 'comparative advertising' means any advertising which explicitly or by implication identifies a competitor or goods or services offered by a competitor. According to settled case-law, that is a broad definition covering all forms of comparative advertising, so that, in order for there to be comparative advertising, it is sufficient for there to be a statement referring even by implication to a competitor or to the goods or services which he offers.[64] The test for determining whether an advertisement is comparative in nature is thus whether it identifies, explicitly or by implication, a competitor of the advertiser or goods or services which the competitor offers.[65]

It is also settled case-law that the conditions required of comparative advertising must be interpreted in the sense most favourable to it since comparative advertising helps to demonstrate objectively the merits of the various comparable products and to stimulate competition between suppliers of goods and services to the consumer's advantage.[66]

As regards, secondly, trade mark law, it should be recalled that Article 5 of the Trade Mark Directive confers exclusive rights on the proprietor of a registered trade mark, including the right to prevent all third parties from using, in the course of trade, any sign which is identical to, or similar to, the trade mark in relation to identical goods or services or even, where appropriate, other goods.

As it is stated in recitals 14 and 15 in the preamble to the Directive on Misleading and Comparative Advertising, it may, however, be indispensable, in order to make comparative advertising effective, to identify the goods or services of a competitor, making reference to a trade mark or trade name of which the latter is the proprietor. Such use of another's trade mark, trade name or other distinguishing marks does not breach this exclusive right in cases where it complies with the conditions laid down by this Directive, the intended target being solely to distinguish between them and thus to highlight differences objectively.

[64] See Case C-112/99 *Toshiba Europe* [2001] ECR I-7945 paras 30 and 31 (first case dealing with comparative advertising); Case C-44/01 *Pippig Augenoptik* [2003] ECR I-3095 para 35 (according to that case stricter national provisions on protection against misleading advertising cannot be applied to comparative advertising as regards the form and content of the comparison); Case C-381/05 *De Landtsheer Emmanuel* [2007] ECR I-3115 para 16 (according to that case comparative advertising between products without designation of origin (beer) and products with such designation (champagne) is possible in certain cases; a reference in an advertisement to a type of product and not to a specific undertaking or product can be considered to be comparative advertising), and Case C-533/06 *O2 Holdings and O2 (UK)*, see n 20 above, para 42.

[65] Case C-112/99 *Toshiba Europe*, n 64 above, para 29; Case C-381/05 *De Landtsheer Emmanuel*, n 64 above, para 17, and Case C-533/06 *O2 Holdings and O2 (UK)*, n 20 above, para 43. See on comparative advertising also V Tiili, 'Viittaaminen toisen tavaramerkkiin markkinoinnissa' in *Tavaramerkki* (Vammala, Suomen Lakimiesliiton Kustannus Oy, 1983) 164, at 173 *ff*.

[66] See Case C-112/99 *Toshiba Europe*, n 64 above, paras 36 and 37; Case C-44/01 *Pippig Augenoptik*, n 64 above, para 42; Case C-356/04 *Lidl Belgium* [2006] ECR I-8501 para 22 (according to that case comparative advertising can relate collectively to selections of products; however, in certain cases such comparative advertising can be misleading), and Case C-381/05 *De Landtsheer Emmanuel*, n 64 above, paras 34 and 35. More generally, concerning the first cases, see S Fletcher, P Fussing and A Indraccolo, 'Comparisons and Conclusions: Welcome Clarification from the European Court of Justice on the Interpretation of the Comparative Advertising Directive' (2003) *European Intellectual Property Review* 570.

The relationship between these two Directives was, until recently, far from being clear. The first case dealing with that relationship is *O2 Holdings and O2 (UK)*,[67] where the ECJ had the opportunity to consider whether comparative advertising involving competitor's trade mark or a sign similar to that mark should be dealt with under the Trade Mark Directive, the Directive on Misleading and Comparative Advertising or a combination of the two. The second case is the above mentioned *L'Oréal and Others*.[68]

It should be noted that in his Opinion in *O2 Holdings and O2 (UK)*, Advocate General Mengozzi ruled out the application of the Trade Mark Directive in that case by interpreting recitals 14 and 15 in the preamble to the Directive on Misleading and Comparative Advertising in a way that the use of a competitor's trade mark in an advertisement which compares the characteristics of goods or services marketed by him under that mark with those of the advertiser is specifically and exhaustively covered by Article 3a of that Directive. According to him, it would be prohibited only if it did not comply with the conditions laid down in that Article and in that case, it would be prohibited under that Article and not under Article 5(1)(a) or (b) of the Trade Mark Directive. Conversely, if it would comply with those conditions, it could not be held to be prohibited under the provisions contained in the latter.[69]

Under Article 5(1)(a) and (b) of the Trade Mark Directive, the proprietor of a mark is entitled to prevent the use, in the course of trade, of a sign which is identical with the trade mark in relation to goods or services which are identical, and the use of a sign which is similar to the trade mark if there is a likelihood of confusion, which includes the likelihood of association between the sign and the trade mark.

Article 3a(1) of the Directive on Misleading and Comparative Advertising provides that comparative advertising is to be permitted under certain conditions. Those conditions are, inter alia, that it is not misleading, that it does not create confusion in the market place between the advertiser and a competitor or between trade marks, that it does not discredit or denigrate a trade mark, that it does not take unfair advantage of the reputation of a trade mark of a competitor and that it does not present goods or services as imitations or replicas of goods or services bearing a protected trade mark.

[67] See n 20 above.

[68] See n 21 above.

[69] *Ibid* Opinion of Advocate General Mengozzi of 31 January 2008, points 33 and 34. For criticism of that Opinion see, eg O Bray, 'O2 Holdings v Hutchison 3G Ltd: Advocate General's Opinion a backwards step for brand owners' (2008) *Entertainment Law Review* 120. See also Opinion of Advocate General Jacobs in Case C-2/00 *Hölterhoff* [2002] ECR I-4187 points 64–77, concerning the use of trade marks to describe the characteristics of gemstones, where the Advocate General discussed the relationship between those two directives, even though that case concerned only application of Dir 89/104. The ECJ held in that case that the proprietor of a trade mark cannot rely on his exclusive right under Article 5(1) of Dir 89/104 where a third party, in the course of commercial negotiations, reveals the origin of goods which he has produced himself and uses the sign in question solely to denote the particular characteristics of the goods he offers for sale, so that there can be no question of the trade mark used being perceived as a sign indicative of the undertaking of origin (para 17).

**Case *O2 Holdings and O2 (UK)***

O2 and O2 (UK) use bubble images in a host of ways to advertise their mobile telephone services and are the proprietors of two British national trade marks which consist of a static picture of bubbles.

In 2004, Hutchison 3G ('H3G'), a competitor of O2 and O2 (UK) which markets its services under the sign '3', launched an advertising campaign for its pay-as-you-go service known as 'Threepay'. To that end, it broadcasted a television advertisement in which it compared the price of its services with those of O2 and O2 (UK). That advertisement began by using the name 'O2' and moving black-and-white bubble imagery, followed by 'Threepay' and '3' imagery, together with a message that H3G's services were cheaper in a specific way.

O2 and O2 (UK) brought proceedings for infringement of their bubbles trade marks before the High Court of Justice of England and Wales, although they accepted that the price comparison in the advertisement was true and that that advertisement was not misleading. The action was dismissed. O2 and O2 (UK) therefore appealed against that judgment before the Court of Appeal (England and Wales), which asked the ECJ whether a proprietor of a mark is entitled to prevent the use of a sign which is identical with, or similar to, its mark in a comparative advertisement which does not give rise to a likelihood of confusion between the advertiser and a competitor or between the advertiser's marks, goods and services and those of a competitor. O2 and O2 (UK) claimed that the use, by H3G, of a sign similar to their bubbles trade marks in a comparative advertisement jeopardised the exclusive right granted to them by those marks.

*Relationship between the Trade Mark Directive and the Directive on Misleading and Comparative Advertising*

As a preliminary point, the ECJ sought to explain the interaction between the Trade Mark Directive and the Directive on Misleading and Comparative Advertising. It considered that the use, in a comparative advertisement, of a sign identical with, or similar to, a mark of a competitor for the purposes of identifying the latter's goods and services may constitute use within the meaning of Article 5(1) and (2) of the Trade Mark Directive and may therefore be prevented, where necessary, by virtue of those provisions.[70] By doing so, it clearly took a different view from Advocate General Mengozzi, who considered, as said before, that the Trade Mark Directive should not have applied at all to comparative advertising cases.

However, the ECJ recalled that the Community legislature sought to promote comparative advertising and, to that end, to limit to a certain extent the right conferred by the mark. It stated that when the use, in an advertisement, of a sign similar to the mark of a competitor of the advertiser is perceived by the average consumer as a reference to that competitor or to the goods and services which he

[70] Case C-533/06 *O2 Holdings and O2 (UK)*, n 20 above, paras 33–37.

offers, there is comparative advertising within the meaning of Article 2(2a) of the Directive on Misleading and Comparative Advertising.[71]

According to the ECJ, in order to reconcile the protection of marks and the use of comparative advertising, Article 5(1) and (2) of the Trade Mark Directive and Article 3a(1) of the Directive on Misleading and Comparative Advertising must be interpreted to the effect that the proprietor of a registered trade mark is not entitled to prevent the use, by a third party, of a sign identical with, or similar to, his mark, in a comparative advertisement which satisfies all the conditions, laid down in the latter provision, under which comparative advertising is permitted. However, where the conditions required in Article 5(1)(b) of the Trade Mark Directive to prevent the use by a third party of a sign identical with, or similar to, a registered trade mark are met, a comparative advertisement in which that sign is used cannot satisfy the condition, laid down in Article 3a(1)(d) of Directive on Misleading and Comparative Advertising, that comparative advertising do not create confusion. The ECJ considered that the same interpretation must be given to the term 'confusion' in both provisions.[72]

Thus, in the case where an advertiser uses, in a comparative advertisement, a sign identical with or similar to, a competitor's mark, the competitor either does not establish the existence of a likelihood of confusion and, consequently, is not entitled to prevent the use of that sign on the basis of Article 5(1)(b) of the Trade Mark Directive, or he establishes the existence of a likelihood of confusion and, consequently, the advertiser cannot challenge such prevention under Article 3a(1)(d) of the Directive on Misleading and Comparative Advertising, since the advertisement at issue does not satisfy all the conditions laid down in that provision.[73]

### *Interpretation of Article 5(1)(b) of the Trade Mark Directive*

In response to the question referred by the Court of Appeal, the ECJ pointed out that according to settled case-law[74] a proprietor of a mark may prevent the use of a sign which is similar to his mark under Article 5(1)(b) of the Trade Mark Directive only if four conditions are satisfied: that use must be in the course of trade; it must be without the consent of the proprietor of the mark; it must be in respect of goods or services which are identical with, or similar to, those for which the mark is registered; and it must affect or be liable to affect the essential function of the trade mark, which is to guarantee to consumers the origin of the goods or services, by reason of a likelihood of confusion on the part of the public.[75]

[71] *Ibid* paras 39 and 44.

[72] *Ibid* paras 45, 46, 49 and 51.

[73] *Ibid* para 50.

[74] Case C-206/01 *Arsenal Football Club*, n 2 above; Case C-245/02 *Anheuser-Busch* [2004] ECR I-10989; Case C-120/04 *Medion* [2005] ECR I-8551; Case C-48/05 *Adam Opel* [2007] ECR I-1017, and Case C-17/06 *Céline* [2007] ECR I-7041.

[75] Case C-533/06 *O2 Holdings and O2 (UK)*, n 20 above, para 57.

The ECJ noted that the first three conditions were satisfied in the case in the main proceedings. By contrast, in accordance with the referring court's own findings, the use by H3G of bubble images similar to the trade marks did not give rise to a likelihood of confusion on the part of consumers. The advertisement, as a whole, was not misleading and, in particular, did not suggest that there was any form of commercial link between O2 and O2 (UK) on the one hand, and H3G, on the other. Consequently, the fourth condition was not satisfied in the case in the main proceedings.[76]

In that regard, the ECJ stated that even though the notion of likelihood of confusion is the same in Articles 4(1)(b) and 5(1)(b) of the Trade Mark Directive, in the case provided for in the latter provision, the assessment must be limited to the circumstances characterising that use, without there being any need to investigate whether another use of the same sign in different circumstances would also be likely to give rise to a likelihood of confusion.[77] This seems logical, since infringement cases differ from registration cases. In the latter, a successful applicant will have the right to use his mark in any manner he wishes and therefore, it is necessary to assess likelihood of confusion with the opponent's earlier mark in all the circumstances in which the mark applied for might be used.

Consequently, the ECJ found that Article 5(1)(b) of the Trade Mark Directive was to be interpreted as meaning that the proprietor of a registered trade mark is not entitled to rely on his trade mark rights to prevent the use, by a third party, in a comparative advertisement, of a sign similar to that mark in relation to goods or services identical with, or similar to, those for which that mark is registered where such use does not give rise to a likelihood of confusion on the part of the public, and that is so irrespective of whether or not the comparative advertisement satisfies all the conditions laid down in Article 3a of the Directive on Misleading and Comparative Advertising under which comparative advertising is permitted.[78]

### *Comments*

This case shows the drafting problems of both the Trade Mark Directive and the Directive on Misleading and Comparative Advertising. In fact, despite the recitals of the latter, neither of these directives contains explicit rules about their relationship. As mentioned above, the Advocate General and the ECJ reached different conclusions regarding that relationship. The brand owners should be satisfied that the ECJ did not follow the Advocate General, since if all comparative advertising cases were to fall exclusively under the Directive on Misleading and Comparative Advertising, the trade mark owner would only have the ability to act to the extent that the national transposition of this Directive in

[76] *Ibid* paras 60–63 and 68.
[77] *Ibid* paras 65–67.
[78] *Ibid* para 69.

his home country allows him to. This might leave the trade mark owner with far less ability to protect his mark than he would have had under trade mark law.[79]

The judgment left many questions open, notably as to the nature of the relationship between the Directive on Misleading and Comparative Advertising and non-confusion based infringement under Article 5(1)(a) and Article 5(2) of the Trade Mark Directive. Because the H3G did not use the bubbles trade marks as registered by O2 and O2 (UK), but a sign similar to those marks, the ECJ did not interpret Article 5(1)(a) of the Trade Mark Directive. Therefore, the position in relation to identical use of a competitor's mark was still left open. The same goes as regards Article 5(2) of the Trade Mark Directive and trade marks with a reputation.

These questions were answered in another reference for a preliminary ruling from the same national court in *L'Oréal and Others*.[80] This case, as noted above, arises from a dispute relating to the referential use of well-known perfume trade marks in order to indicate the similarity of the brand owner's scent to that of a cheap smell-alike competitor. Advocate General Mengozzi delivered his Opinion on 10 February 2009 and the ECJ gave its ruling on 18 June 2009.

### Case *L'Oréal and Others*

As already mentioned above, Malaika and Starion distributed perfumes which were imitations of the fragrance of successful perfumes to wholesalers and hard discount stores in the United Kingdom. In marketing those perfumes, they made use of and supplied to their retailers comparison lists which made an analogy, in terms of similarity of smell, between each of those perfumes and a luxury perfume identified by reference to the word mark by which it is known. L'Oréal's word marks Trésor, Miracle, Anaïs-Anaïs and Noa appeared on those lists.

L'Oréal alleged that the use of comparison lists constituted trade mark infringement contrary to Article 5(1)(a) of the Trade Mark Directive.

The first four questions referred by the Court of Appeal related to the use by an advertiser of another person's trade mark in comparative advertising consisting, in particular, of comparison lists. In that context, another person's trade mark was used to identify goods which were in fact the goods of the proprietor of the trade mark itself and not those of the advertiser. The ECJ considered that the comparison lists may constitute comparative advertising within the meaning of Article 2(2a) of the Directive on Misleading and Comparative Advertising.[81]

[79] See, eg I Simon Fhima, 'Trade Mark Infringement in Comparative Advertising Situations: O2 v H3G' (2008) 10 *European Intellectual Property Review* 420, at 424. See also D Blankenburg, 'Neues zur vergleichenden Werbung, zur Verwechslungsgefahr und zur markenmäßigen Benutzung?' (2008) 10 *Wettbewerb in Recht und Praxis* 1294.

[80] See n 21 above.

[81] *Ibid* para 52.

*Interpretation of Article 5(1)(a) of the Trade Mark Directive*

By its first question, the referring court was asking whether Article 5(1)(a) or (b) of the Trade Mark Directive must be interpreted as meaning that the proprietor of a registered trade mark is entitled to prevent the use by a third party, in comparative advertising, of a sign identical with that mark in relation to goods or services which are identical with those for which that mark was registered, where such use is not capable of jeopardising the essential function of the mark, which is to indicate the origin of the goods or services. By its second question, which was considered together with the first question, the referring court was essentially asking whether the proprietor of a well-known mark can oppose such use, under Article 5(1)(a), where that use is not capable of jeopardising the mark or one of its functions but none the less plays a significant role in the promotion of the goods or services of the third party.

In the comparison lists relating to perfumes, Malaika and Starion had used the word marks Trésor, Miracle, Anaïs-Anaïs and Noa, as registered by L'Oréal, and not signs which were merely similar to those marks. Furthermore, that use was made in respect of products which were identical with those in respect of which those marks were registered, that is to say, perfumes. Such use fell thus within the scope of application of Article 5(1)(a) of the Trade Mark Directive and not that of Article 5(1)(b).

According to Advocate General Mengozzi, Article 5(1)(a) of the Trade Mark Directive must be interpreted as meaning that the proprietor of a trade mark is not entitled to prohibit use by a third party in comparative advertising of a sign that is identical with that mark for goods or services which are identical with those for which the mark is registered where such use does not affect or is not liable to affect the mark's essential function of providing a guarantee of origin or any of the mark's other functions. That is the case even if such use plays a significant role in the promotion of the advertiser's goods and, in particular, permits that advertiser to take unfair advantage of the mark's reputation.[82]

The Advocate General pointed out that in this case there was neither any likelihood of confusion on the part of the public as to the origin of the goods and, accordingly, no effect on the essential function of the trade marks for which protection was sought, nor any effect on the reputation of those marks and, accordingly, on the functions (of communication) which those marks perform as a result of that reputation. In reply to L'Oréal's arguments, he pointed out that the fact that unfair advantage may be taken does not mean, unlike in situations in which the reputation of a well-known mark is tarnished or degraded, that such a use undermines or is liable to undermine the communications functions which the marks in question perform as a result of that reputation.[83]

Luckily for the trade mark proprietors, the ECJ did not follow the Opinion of the Advocate General. It reminded that the exclusive right under Article 5(1)

[82] *Ibid* Opinion of Advocate General Mengozzi point 61.

[83] *Ibid* point 60.

(a) of the Trade Mark Directive was conferred in order to enable the trade mark proprietor to protect his specific interests as proprietor, that is, to ensure that the trade mark can fulfil its functions and that, therefore, the exercise of that right must be reserved to cases in which a third party's use of the sign affects or is liable to affect the functions of the trade mark.[84] According to the ECJ, these functions include not only the essential function of the trade mark, which is to guarantee to consumers the origin of the goods or services, but also its other functions, in particular that of guaranteeing the quality of the goods or services in question and those of communication, investment or advertising.[85] The express recognition of these alternative functions of a trade mark is important in the case of smell-alike perfumes, where it is clear that consumers are not confused by them.

The ECJ underlined that the protection conferred by Article 5(1)(a) of the Trade Mark Directive is thus broader than that provided by Article 5(1)(b), the application of which requires that there be a likelihood of confusion and accordingly the possibility that the essential function of the mark may be affected. By virtue of the 10th recital in the preamble to the Trade Mark Directive, the protection afforded by the registered trade mark is absolute in the case of identity between the mark and the sign and also between the goods or services, whereas, in case of similarity between the mark and the sign and between the goods or services, the likelihood of confusion constitutes the specific condition for such protection.[86]

The ECJ deducted from its earlier case-law that the proprietor of the mark cannot oppose the use of a sign identical with the mark on the basis of Article 5(1)(a) of the Trade Mark Directive if that use is not liable to cause detriment to any of the functions of that mark.[87] It reminded that certain uses for purely descriptive purposes are excluded from the scope of application of Article 5(1) of the Trade Mark Directive, because they do not affect any of the interests which that provision is intended to protect and accordingly do not constitute 'use' within the meaning of that provision.[88] However, in the present case, it was clear that the word marks belonging to L'Oréal were used in the comparison lists distributed by Malaika and Starion not for purely descriptive purposes, but for

[84] In that regard, the ECJ referred to Case C-206/01 *Arsenal Football Club*, n 2 above, para 51; Case C-245/02 *Anheuser-Busch*, n 74 above, para 59, and Case C-48/05 *Adam Opel*, n 74 above, para 21.

[85] Case C-487/07 *L'Oréal and Others*, n 21 above, para 58. It should be noted that in that regard the ECJ did not make any referrals to the case-law; in his Opinion, point 54, Advocate General Mengozzi referred to Case T-215/03 *Sigla v OHIM – Elleni Holding (VIPS)*, n 28 above, para 35, and to the Opinion of Advocate General Sharpston in Case C-252/07 *Intel Corporation*, n 19 above, points 8–13. According to him, the communications function is the capacity of the trade mark to communicate information, relating to non-physical characteristics which the image of the product or the company may generally be associated with, such as quality, trustworthiness and reliability, or particular attributes, such as a certain style, luxury and strength.

[86] Case C-487/07 *L'Oréal and Others*, n 21 above, para 59.

[87] *Ibid* para 60. See also Case C-206/01 *Arsenal Football Club*, n 2 above, para 54, and Case C-48/05 *Adam Opel*, n 74 above, para 22.

[88] Case C-487/07 *L'Oréal and Others*, n 21 above, para 61. The ECJ cited, to that effect, Case C-2/00 *Hölterhoff*, n 69 above, para 16.

the purpose of advertising. Now the referring court has to determine whether the use which is made of the marks belonging to L'Oréal is liable to affect one of the functions of those marks, such as, in particular, their functions of communication, investment or advertising.[89]

In conclusion, the ECJ held that Article 5(1)(a) of the Trade Mark Directive must be interpreted as meaning that the proprietor of a registered trade mark is entitled to prevent the use by a third party, in a comparative advertisement which does not satisfy all the conditions, laid down in Article 3a(1) of the Directive on Misleading and Comparative Advertising, under which comparative advertising is permitted, of a sign identical with that mark in relation to goods or services which are identical with those for which that mark was registered, even where such use is not capable of jeopardising the essential function of the mark, which is to indicate the origin of the goods or services, provided that such use affects or is liable to affect one of the other functions of the mark.[90] It follows that even if one of the functions of the mark is jeopardised, but all conditions laid down in Article 3a(1) of the Directive on Misleading and Comparative Advertising are satisfied, the trade mark proprietor cannot prevent the use by relying on Article 5(1)(a) of the Trade Mark Directive. The ECJ's interpretation of these conditions will be dealt below.

Furthermore, the ECJ noted that since those marks have a reputation, their use in the comparison lists may also be prevented under Article 5(2) of the Trade Mark Directive, the applicability of which does not necessarily require that there be a likelihood of detriment to the mark or its proprietor, provided that the third party takes unfair advantage of the use of that mark.[91] In the main proceedings, this provision was applied only to the use of similar bottles and packaging. Of course, in that regard it is also necessary that all the conditions laid down in Article 3a(1) of the Directive on Misleading and Comparative Advertising for comparative advertising to be permitted are not satisfied. However, since one of the conditions is 'not [to] take unfair advantage of the reputation of a trade mark,' logically it is not satisfied if Article 5(2) of the Trade Mark Directive can be applied. As it will be seen later, the concept of 'unfair advantage' should be interpreted in the same way in both provisions.

*Interpretation of Article 3a(1)(g) and (h) of the Directive on Misleading and Comparative Advertising*

By its third and fourth questions in *L'Oréal and Others*, the referring court was essentially asking whether Article 3a(1) of the Directive on Misleading and Comparative Advertising must be interpreted as meaning that where an advertiser indicates through a comparison list, without in any way causing confusion or deception, that his product has a major characteristic similar to that

[89] Case C-487/07 *L'Oréal and Others*, n 21 above, paras 62 and 63.

[90] *Ibid* para 65.

[91] *Ibid* para 64. See above the ECJ's view of the interpretation of that provision.

of a product marketed under a well-known trade mark, of which the advertiser's product constitutes an imitation, that advertiser takes unfair advantage of the reputation of that trade mark, within the meaning of Article 3a(1)(g) or presents 'goods or services as imitations or replicas' within the meaning of Article 3a(1)(h) of that Directive.

Article 3a(1)(a) to (h) of the Directive on Misleading and Comparative Advertising lists cumulative conditions which comparative advertising must satisfy in order to be permitted. The ECJ recalled that the purpose of those conditions is to achieve a balance between the different interests which may be affected by allowing comparative advertising. Thus, it is apparent from a reading of recitals 2, 7 and 9 in the preamble to this Directive that the aim of Article 3a is to stimulate competition between suppliers of goods and services to the consumer's advantage, by allowing competitors to highlight objectively the merits of the various comparable products while, at the same time, prohibiting practices which may distort competition, be detrimental to competitors and have an adverse effect on consumer choice.[92]

The ECJ reminded that the conditions listed in Article 3a(1) of the Directive on Misleading and Comparative Advertising must be interpreted in the sense most favourable to permitting advertisements which objectively compare the characteristics of goods or services, while ensuring at the same time that comparative advertising is not used anti-competitively and unfairly or in a manner which affects the interests of consumers.

As mentioned above, Article 3a(1) of the Directive on Misleading and Comparative Advertising makes the use of a competitor's trade mark in comparative advertising subject, inter alia, to four particular conditions, laid down in Article 3a(1)(d), (e), (g) and (h) respectively. It is thus provided that the use of the mark must not create a likelihood of confusion, it must not discredit or denigrate the mark, it must not take unfair advantage of the reputation of the mark and it must not present goods or services as imitations or replicas of goods or services bearing the mark.

According to the ECJ, the object of those conditions is to reconcile the interest of the proprietor of the mark in benefiting from protection of his exclusive right, on the one hand, and the interest of the proprietor's competitors and of consumers in having effective comparative advertising which objectively highlights the differences between the goods or services offered, on the other.[93]

The ECJ thus concluded that the use of a competitor's trade mark in comparative advertising is permitted by Community law where the comparison objectively highlights differences and the object or effect of such highlighting is not to give rise to situations of unfair competition, such as those described, inter alia, in Article 3a(1)(d), (e), (g) and (h) of the Directive on Misleading and Comparative Advertising.[94]

[92] *Ibid* paras 67 and 68.
[93] *Ibid* para 71.
[94] *Ibid* para 72. The ECJ referred, to that effect, to Case C-44/01 *Pippig Augenoptik*, n 64 above, para 49.

First, the ECJ examined the condition relating to Article 3a(1)(h) of that Directive, which provides that comparative advertising must not present goods or services as imitations or replicas of goods or services bearing a protected trade mark or trade name. To the ECJ it was clear that that condition applies not only to counterfeit goods but also to any imitation or replica. It was also clear that the conditions set out in Article 3a(1) are distinct and, thus, Article 3a(1)(h) of the Directive on Misleading and Comparative Advertising does not require either that the comparative advertising be misleading in nature or that there be a likelihood of confusion.[95]

The ECJ recalled that the particular object of the condition laid down in Article 3a(1)(h) of the Directive on Misleading and Comparative Advertising is to prohibit an advertiser from stating in comparative advertising that the product or service marketed by him constitutes an imitation or replica of the product or the service covered by the trade mark. In that respect, the ECJ followed the Advocate General and held that it is not only advertisements which explicitly evoke the idea of imitation or reproduction which are prohibited, but also those which, having regard to their overall presentation and economic context, are capable of implicitly communicating such an idea to the public at whom they are directed. The Advocate General was of the view that also situations in which formulas such as 'type' or 'style' are appended to that mark in describing the advertiser's product should be prohibited.[96]

The ECJ pointed out that the object and effect of the comparison lists was to draw the attention of the relevant public to the original fragrance of which the perfumes marketed by Malaika and Starion were purportedly an imitation. Those lists thus attested to the fact that those perfumes were imitations of the fragrances marketed under certain marks belonging to L'Oréal, and they consequently presented the goods marketed by the advertiser as being imitations of goods bearing a protected trade mark within the meaning of Article 3a(1)(h) of the Directive on Misleading and Comparative Advertising. Here again, the ECJ referred to the Opinion of the Advocate General and stated that it is irrelevant in that regard whether the advertisement indicates that it relates to an imitation of the product bearing a protected mark as a whole or merely the imitation of an essential characteristic of that product such as, in the present case, the smell of the goods in question.[97]

Secondly, the ECJ examined the condition relating to Article 3a(1)(g) of the Directive on Misleading and Comparative Advertising, which provides that comparative advertising must not take unfair advantage of the reputation of a trade mark. According to the ECJ, the expression 'take[s] unfair advantage' of that reputation, which is used both in that provision and in Article 5(2) of the Trade Mark Directive, must in principle be given the same interpretation.[98] The

[95] Case C-487/07 *L'Oréal and Others,* n 21 above, paras 73 and 74.

[96] *Ibid* para 75, and Opinion of Advocate General Mengozzi point 84.

[97] *Ibid* para 76, and Opinion of Advocate General Mengozzi point 88.

[98] *Ibid* para 77. The ECJ referred, by analogy, to Case C-533/06 *O2 Holdings and O2 (UK)*, n 20 above, para 49, where it had already held that the term 'confusion', which is used both in Art 5(1)(b) of Dir 89/104 and in Art 3a(1)(d) of Dir 84/450, must be given the same interpretation.

ECJ pointed out that since the comparison lists used by Malaika and Starion presented the perfumes which they marketed as being an imitation or a replica of goods bearing a protected trade mark within the meaning of Article 3a(1)(h) of that Directive, the third question had to be understood as meaning that it sought to ascertain whether, in such circumstances, the use of those lists resulted in the taking of an unfair advantage of the reputation of that protected mark for the purposes of Article 3a(1)(g).[99]

In that regard, the ECJ held that since, under the Directive on Misleading and Comparative Advertising, 'comparative advertising which presents the advertiser's products as an imitation of a product bearing a trade mark is inconsistent with fair competition and thus unlawful, any advantage gained by the advertiser through such advertising will have been achieved as the result of unfair competition and must, accordingly, be regarded as taking unfair advantage of the reputation of that mark.' Consequently, its answer to the third and fourth questions was that Article 3a(1) of that Directive must be interpreted as meaning that an advertiser who states explicitly or implicitly in comparative advertising that the product marketed by him is an imitation of a product bearing a well-known trade mark presents 'goods or services as imitations or replicas' within the meaning of Article 3a(1)(h). The advantage gained by the advertiser as a result of such unlawful comparative advertising must be considered to be an advantage taken unfairly of the reputation of that mark within the meaning of Article 3a(1)(g).[100]

The ECJ's reasoning might seem a little bit circular since it says that because the advertising was contrary to Article 3a(1)(h), it was unfair under Article 3a(1)(g) of the Directive on Misleading and Comparative Advertising even though it is sufficient that one of the conditions listed in Article 3a(1) is not satisfied in order for comparative advertising not to be permitted. It seems that the ECJ wanted to emphasise that the condition relating to 'not [to] take unfair advantage of the reputation of a trade mark' was also satisfied, since it would be possible to prevent the use by applying Article 5(2) of the Trade Mark Directive. In fact, the national court might take the view that the use in comparison lists did not affect any of the functions of the trade marks in question and, accordingly, the trade mark proprietor could not rely on Article 5(1)(a) of the Trade Mark Directive to prevent the use of its trade marks in comparison lists.

It is worth noting that the answer the Advocate General proposed was a little bit different. According to him, Article 3a(1)(g) of the Directive on Misleading and Comparative Advertising must be interpreted as meaning that it is not possible to conclude on the basis of the simple fact that a trader, in a comparison list, compares his product with a product identified by a well-known mark that the advertiser takes unfair advantage of that mark's reputation and that if, where such an advantage exists, it can be presumed that the public at whom the advertising is directed is caused to associate the proprietor of the well-known

[99] Case C-487/07 *L'Oréal and Others*, n 21 above, paras 77 and 78.
[100] *Ibid* paras 79 and 80.

mark with the advertiser in such a way that the public might associate by way of extension the reputation of the former's products with those of the latter, it is for the national court to determine whether that advantage is unfair in the light of all the relevant individual circumstances of the case.[101] This could have been understood in a way that the Advocate General considered that by using comparison lists, the companies' marketing and advertising policy should not have been permitted under Article 3a(1)(g) of the Directive on Misleading and Comparative Advertising since their aim was just to give the idea that you can smell good as if you used an expensive luxury perfume by buying the cheap smell-alike versions.

In conclusion, the ECJ's judgment in *L'Oréal and Others* seems a real victory for brand owners. The judgment gave quite clear answers although one might criticise some points. In any case the ECJ's view is much clearer than its Advocate General's, since it was sometimes difficult to see if the Advocate General was on the brand owners' side or on the side of those seeking to take advantage of those brands in some way.

## USE OF TRADE MARKS BY SEARCH ENGINES

One specific question in relation to unfair competition and trade marks is the use of trade marks by search engines.

In that respect, the pending battle between Google and Louis Vuitton[102] concerning keywords in the internet is worth mentioning. This is an important case for the electronic commerce industry since it is the first time the ECJ is invited to state whether companies in the EU can block search engines from using trade marked brand names to trigger results.

Search engines normally operate by selling advertising links to search terms (keywords). Under current Google practice, a user searching the site with trade marked keywords finds the name of advertisers appearing on top or on the right hand side of the screen under the heading 'sponsored links'. In the case of a search performed using Louis Vuitton's trade marks, the results could include links for companies marketing counterfeit or replica goods.[103] The case is a reference for a preliminary ruling from the French Cour de cassation lodged on 3 June 2008 asking, mainly, whether Google is under an obligation to grant rights owners exclusivity over certain keywords closely associated with a brand and looking for interpretation of Article 5(1)(a) and (b) and Article 5(2) of the Trade Mark Directive. The key question is whether the search engine uses the trade marks when it makes them available to advertisers and then displays a sponsored link.[104]

[101] *Ibid* Opinion of Advocate General Mengozzi point 80.

[102] Joined Cases C-236/08 to C-238/08 *Google and Google France*, n 22 above.

[103] It can be noted that when performing a search with 'Louis Vuitton', 'LV' or 'Vuitton' today, no sponsored links appear any more. The links for replica goods appear in the normal result list.

[104] More specifically, the first question is whether Art 5(1)(a) and (b) of Dir 89/104 and Art 9(1)(a) and (b) of Reg 40/94 should be interpreted as meaning that a provider of a paid referencing

*Cont.*

In such a case, the main arguments in favour of search engines could be that trade mark law is completely irrelevant because they are not making trade mark 'use' of the marks and that placing competitors' advertisements in a list of search results will not lead to consumers being confused that the advertisers are affiliated with the trade mark owner. On the other side, the trade mark owners' arguments could be that search engines are selling rights to their trade marks to third parties, and that under these circumstances they are intervening in the commercial transaction between the consumer and the trade mark owner. Trade mark owners believe that this sale, as well as the placement of competitor advertisements on the search results page, infringe and dilute their trade mark rights.[105]

In this pending case, Google claimed that it is not using the brand to identify its products or services and is not commercialising them either. According to Google, its service contributes towards increasing competition and the development of commerce online. In return, Louis Vuitton claimed that Google reaps a benefit from sellers paying to use keywords associated with well-established brands, whose image consequently suffers.[106]

In this respect, it should be noted that in the United States, where there has been a wealth of litigation on keyword advertising in various federal district and appeal courts, the rulings are inconsistent. It has been argued that in recent years, the US courts have mainly favoured search engines and keyword advertisers, rather than trade mark owners.[107] However, this seems to have changed with a ruling of 3 April 2009 in *Rescuecom v Google*,[108] where the Second Circuit Court

service who makes available to advertisers keywords reproducing or imitating registered trade marks and arranges by the referencing agreement to create and favourably display, on the basis of those keywords, advertising links to sites offering infringing goods is using those trade marks in a manner which their proprietor is entitled to prevent. According to the second question, in the event that the trade marks have a reputation, may the proprietor oppose such use under Art 5(2) of Dir 89/104 and Art 9(1)(c) of Reg 40/94? Finally, in the event that such use does not constitute a use which may be prevented by the trade mark proprietor under Dir 89/104 or Reg 40/94, may the provider of the paid referencing service be regarded as providing an information society service consisting of the storage of information provided by the recipient of the service, within the meaning of Art 14 of Directive 2000/31/EC of 8 June 2000 on certain legal aspects of information society services, in particular electronic commerce, in the Internal Market (Directive on electronic commerce) [2000] OJ L/178/1, so that that provider cannot incur liability until it has been notified by the trade mark proprietor of the unlawful use of the sign by the advertiser?

[105] See M Daly, 'An Analysis of the American and European Approaches to Trade Mark Infringement and Unfair Competition by Search Engines' (2006) 8 *European Intellectual Property Review* 413, 416.

[106] See, eg S Bodoni, 'Google, LVMH Clash over Keyword Rights at EU Court' *www.bloomberg.com* 17 March 2009. It can also be noted that in June 2008 a French court ordered auction site eBay to pay 38 million euros to LVMH Moet Hennessy Louis Vuitton SA for allowing online auctions of fake copies of its goods. On the contrary, in a judgment of 22 May 2009 of the High Court of Justice of England and Wales, High Court of London, eBay was not held jointly liable for trade mark infringements committed by its users selling L'Oréal's products. See *L'Oréal and Others v eBay International and Others* [2009] EWHC 1094 (Ch). However, the High Court decided to make a reference for a preliminary ruling in that case, not yet registered.

[107] See D Meale, 'The Online Advertising Free-riding Free-for-all' (2008) 12 *Journal of Intellectual Property Law & Practice* 779.

[108] *Rescuecom Corp. v Google Inc.* 562 F.3d 123 2d Cir. 3 April 2009. See also G Sterling, 'Court: Trademarked Keywords Can't Be Used By Third Parties In AdWords' *www.searchengineland.com* 6 April 2009.

of Appeals reversed the lower court ruling[109] and held that recommending and selling a mark to an advertiser to trigger a sponsored link could violate trade mark law. It considered that Google's keyword advertising practices constituted a 'use in commerce'.[110] This evolution in fact is quite close to the French one. Unlike earlier in the United States, the lower courts in France have not had particular difficulties with the invisible or internal use of the trade mark in keyword advertising considering such use straightforward use of an identical sign for identical goods or services.[111]

It remains to be seen how the ECJ will rule on the question as to whether keywords are protected under the Trade Mark Directive, which has been of great concern to brand owners.

## EFFECTS OF A LICENCE AGREEMENT ON THE EXHAUSTION OF THE RIGHTS CONFERRED BY A TRADE MARK

One last example of trade mark owners' rights concerns the effects of a licence agreement on the exhaustion of these rights. Even though this example is not so directly related to the concept of unfair competition and to unfair use by a third party of a trade mark identical or similar to another mark, it is worth mentioning in the context of luxury products.

It should be recalled that it follows from Article 7(1) of the Trade Mark Directive that the rights conferred on the proprietor of a trade mark are exhausted where goods have been put on the market in the Community by him or with his consent. However, according to Article 7(2) of that Directive, they are not exhausted where there exist legitimate reasons for the proprietor to oppose

[109] *Rescuecom Corp. v Google Inc.* 456 F.Supp.2d 393 NDNY 28 September 2006.

[110] Despite this ruling, Google announced on 4 May 2009 that it has modified its AdWords trade mark policy to allow bidding on trade marked terms in 190 new countries to conform to its current policy in the United States, Canada, Ireland and the United Kingdom. According to Google, this means that as of 4 June 2009, it will no longer investigate complaints relating to the use of trade marks as keywords as AdWords advertisers and that in the affected regions, a company advertising on Google will be able to select trade marked terms as keywords, and a user searching with a trade marked keyword may see a greater number of relevant ads in the sponsored links section, giving them greater choice. This trade mark policy does not apply to the Member States of the EU (except the United Kingdom and Ireland). See B Schwartz, 'Google AdWords Opens Up Trademarked Bidding To Most Countries' *www.searchengineland.com* 5 May 2009.

[111] See Daly, n 105 above, at 417, and Meale, n 107 above, at 781 and 784. Regarding the concept of 'use', see order of 19 February 2009 in Case C-62/08 *UDV North America* nyr, para 54, according to which the concept of 'use' for the purpose of Art 9(1)(a) and (2)(d) of Reg No 40/94 covers a situation in which a trade intermediary, which is acting in its own name but on behalf of the vendor and is thus not an interested party in relation to trade in goods in which it is itself a contractual party, uses, in its business papers, a sign which is identical with a Community trade mark in relation to goods or services which are identical with those for which the mark is registered. As regards the concept of 'intermediary' in the context of copyright and related rights in the information society, see order of 19 February 2009 in Case C-557/07 *LSG-Gesellschaft zur Wahrnehmung von Leistungsschutzrechten* nyr, para 46, according to which the term 'intermediary' includes an access provider who merely provides a user with access to the network by allocating him a dynamic IP address but does not himself provide him with any services such as e-mail or file-sharing services and does not exercise any control, either in law or in fact, over the services which the user makes use of.

further commercialisation of the goods, especially where the condition of the goods is changed or impaired after they have been put on the market.

Furthermore, according to Article 8(2) of the Trade Mark Directive, the proprietor of a trade mark which has been licensed may invoke his rights against a licensee who contravenes any provision in his licensing contract with regard, inter alia, the quality of the goods manufactured by the licensee.

The ECJ delivered, on 23 April 2009, an important judgment in *Copad*[112] which raises for the first time the question of the effects of a licence agreement on the exhaustion of the right of a proprietor of a trade mark. In this case the ECJ had to examine the extent to which the proprietor of the trade mark can stop goods bearing the mark from being 'dumped' in discount stores even though the licence agreement contains express provisions prohibiting sale by the licensee to discount stores. In particular, the case raised the issue whether and, as the case may be, in what circumstances the reputation of a good as a luxury product has to be considered to be an indication of quality.[113]

In 2000, Christian Dior couture SA concluded a trade mark licence agreement with Société Industrielle Lingerie ('SIL') in respect of the manufacture and distribution of luxury corsetry goods bearing the Christian Dior trade mark. That agreement stated that in order to maintain the repute and prestige of the Christian Dior trade mark SIL agreed not to sell, in particular, to discount stores outside the selective distribution network, without written agreement from Dior, and that the licensee was supposed to make all necessary provision to ensure that that rule was complied with by its distributors or retailers.

However, since it was faced with economic difficulties, SIL sold goods bearing the Christian Dior trade mark to Copad, a company operating a discount store business, despite Dior's explicit refusal. Taking the view that that resale was prohibited by the agreement, Dior brought an action against SIL and Copad for trade mark infringement. Before the French courts, the resellers pleaded exhaustion of Dior's trade mark rights, because the goods had been put on the market in the European Economic Area (EEA) with Dior's consent. The French Cour de cassation referred questions to the ECJ concerning the interpretation of Article 8(2) and Article 7(1) and (2) of the Trade Mark Directive.

First, the ECJ held that Article 8(2) of the Trade Mark Directive is to be interpreted as meaning that the proprietor of a trade mark can invoke the rights conferred by that trade mark against a licensee who contravenes a provision in a licence agreement prohibiting, on grounds of the trade mark's prestige, sales to discount stores, provided it has been established that that contravention, by reason of the situation prevailing in the case, 'damages the allure and prestigious image which bestows on those goods an aura of luxury'.[114]

Article 8(2) of the Trade Mark Directive entitles the proprietor of a trade mark to invoke the rights conferred by that trade mark against a licensee who

[112] See n 23 above.
[113] *Ibid*, see Opinion of Advocate General Kokott point 1.
[114] Case C-59/08 *Copad*, n 22 above, para 37.

contravenes any provision in his licensing contract with regard to its duration, the form covered by the registration in which the trade mark may be used, the scope of the goods or services for which the licence is granted, the territory in which the trade mark may be affixed, or the quality of the goods manufactured or of the services provided by the licensee. This list is exhaustive.[115]

The ECJ underlined that the quality of luxury goods is not just the result of their material characteristics, but also of the allure and prestigious image which bestows on them an aura of luxury.[116] In this respect, a selective distribution system which sought to ensure that the goods were displayed in sales outlets in a manner that enhanced their value, especially as regards positioning, advertising, packaging as well as business policy, contributed to the reputation of the goods at issue and therefore to sustaining the aura of luxury surrounding them.[117]

Therefore it was conceivable that the sale of luxury goods by the licensee to third parties that were not part of the selective distribution network might affect the quality itself of those goods, so that, in such circumstances, a contractual provision prohibiting such sale had to be considered to be falling within the scope of Article 8(2) of the Trade Mark Directive. It was for the national court to examine whether, taking into account the particular circumstances of the case before it, contravention by the licensee of the provision in question damaged the aura of luxury of the luxury goods, thus affecting their quality.[118]

Secondly, the ECJ held that a sale that takes place in disregard of a provision prohibiting resale to discount stores outside the selective distribution network may, for the purposes of the Trade Mark Directive, be considered to have taken place without the consent of the proprietor of the trade mark where it is established that such a breach contravenes one of the provisions listed in Article 8(2) of the Directive.

It should be recalled that Article 5 of the Trade Mark Directive confers on the trade mark proprietor exclusive rights which entitle him, inter alia, to prevent any third party from importing goods bearing the mark, offering the goods, or putting them on the market or stocking them for these purposes. Article 7(1) of that Directive contains an exception to that rule, in that it provides that the trade mark proprietor's rights are exhausted where the goods have been put on the market in the EEA by him or with his consent.[119]

The ECJ stated that where a licensee puts goods bearing the mark on the market he must, as a rule, be considered to be doing so with the consent of the proprietor of the trade mark, for the purposes of Article 7(1) of the Trade Mark Directive. However, the licence agreement does not constitute the absolute and unconditional consent of the proprietor of the trade mark to the licensee putting the goods bearing the trade mark on the market. Article 8(2) of that Directive

[115] *Ibid* paras 20 and 49.
[116] See also Case C-337/95 *Parfums Christian Dior* [1997] ECR I-6013 para 45.
[117] Case C-59/08 *Copad*, n 22 above, paras 24 and 29.
[118] *Ibid* paras 30 and 31.
[119] *Ibid* para 41. See also Joined Cases C-414/99 to C-416/99 *Zino Davidoff and Levi Strauss* [2001] ECR I-8691 para 40, and Case C-16/03 *Peak Holding* [2004] ECR I-11313 para 34.

expressly enables the proprietor of the mark to invoke the rights the trade mark confers on him against a licensee where the latter contravenes certain provisions in the licence agreement.[120]

Therefore, Article 7(1) of the Trade Mark Directive must be interpreted as meaning that a licensee who puts goods bearing a trade mark on the market in disregard of a provision in a licence agreement does so without the consent of the proprietor of the trade mark where it is established that the provision in question is included in those listed in Article 8(2) of that Directive.[121]

Thirdly, the ECJ examined the situation in which the national court finds that sale by the licensee to a third party is unlikely to undermine the quality of the luxury goods bearing the trade mark, so that it must be considered that they were put on the market with the consent of the proprietor of the trade mark. The ECJ held that damage done to the reputation of a trade mark may, in principle, be a legitimate reason, within the meaning of Article 7(2) of the Trade Mark Directive, allowing the proprietor of the mark to oppose further commercialisation of luxury goods which have been put on the market in the EEA by him or with his consent.[122]

It follows from the *Copad* judgment that the proprietor of a trade mark can oppose the resale of his luxury goods by discount stores in particularly where the discount store received the goods from a licensee in contravening of a licence agreement and where that contravention damages the allure and prestigious image which bestows on them an aura of luxury. This is an important case since it allows companies to defend their brands against discount sales. Before the judgment, the state of law was not clear on this point.

## CONCLUDING REMARKS

This chapter has discussed dilution and free-riding, the relationship between trade mark protection and comparative advertising, use of trade marks by search engines and, finally, effects of a licence agreement on exhaustion of the rights conferred by a trade mark. By my choice of these issues dealt with above, I have tried to illustrate what can be understood, in a broad sense, by trade mark protection in the context of unfair competition and, accordingly, in the context of competition law, following from the need to protect the system of undistorted competition. As can be seen, the subject is topical, since the case-law in this area is still evolving.[123]

[120] Case C-59/08 *Copad*, n 22 above, paras 46–48.

[121] *Ibid* para 51.

[122] *Ibid* para 55. See also Case C-337/95 *Parfums Christian Dior*, n 116 above, para 43, and Case C-63/97 *BMW* [1999] ECR I-905 para 49.

[123] However, nothing new under the sun: it is worth noting that already 30 years ago, Judge *Virpi Tiili* studied in her doctoral thesis whether the content of the truthfulness-principle of advertising had changed as the emphasis in Finland had shifted from the protection of competitors toward the protection of consumers; see V Tiili, *Deceptive Advertising – A Study of the Truthfulness Principle in Advertising from the Point of View of Market Law* (Vammala, Suomalainen Lakimiesyhdistys, 1979).

It seems that contrary to the current development in the United States,[124] the Community law, as interpreted by the ECJ, has not always given brand owners sufficient protection against unfair competition, as could be seen in *Intel Corporation*. As regards trade marks with a reputation, it is not sufficient to show that there was no due cause since in that judgment the ECJ introduced a new requirement of evidence of a change in economic behaviour on the part of the consumer which might be hard to prove.

However, after *Intel Corporation*, the outcome in *L'Oréal and Others* was a significant victory for the brand owners. This ruling confirmed that well-known brands have wide protection against competitors that take unfair advantage of the repute of their marks. In that regard, the brand owners do not have to show any damage to their brands. It suffices that the other party seeks to ride on the coat-tails of the mark with a reputation in order to benefit from the power of attraction, the reputation and the prestige of that mark and to exploit, without paying any financial compensation, the marketing effort expended by the brand owner in order to create and maintain the mark's image.

As regards comparative advertising and trade mark protection, already *02 Holdings and 02 (UK)* confirmed that the Trade Mark Directive could be applied even in cases of comparative advertising, even though the latter concept is covered by a broad definition and the conditions required of it must be interpreted in the sense most favourable to such advertising. However, since the condition relating to the likelihood of confusion was not satisfied in that case, the proprietor could not rely on Article 5(1)(b) of the Trade Mark Directive to prevent the use, by a third party, in a comparative advertisement, of a sign similar to that mark in relation to identical goods.

In *L'Oréal and Others* the ECJ gave further clarifications about the relationship between the Trade Mark Directive and the Directive on Misleading and Comparative Advertising, clearly in favour of the brand owners. It also explicitly held that Article 5(1)(a) of the Trade Mark Directive can be relied on, even if the essential function of the mark is not jeopardised by the use by a third party, in comparative advertisement which does not satisfy all the conditions laid down in Article 3a(1) of the Directive on Misleading and Comparative Advertising, of an identical sign for identical goods, provided that one of the other functions of the mark, such as the functions of communication, investment or advertising is liable to be affected. In any case, Article 5(2) of the Trade Mark Regulation could be relied on, provided that the third party takes unfair advantage of the use of that mark. Since the comparative advertising at issue presented the advertiser's products as an imitation of a product bearing L'Oréal's trade mark, any advantage gained by the advertiser through such advertising had been achieved as the result of unfair competition and had, accordingly, to be regarded as taking

[124] As the International Trademark Association has described, the passage of the US Trademark Dilution Revision Act of 2006 was 'a very important achievement in the protection of famous and well-known trademarks' and 'gives brand owners a powerful tool for protecting the trademarks they have worked so hard to build'. See 'Trademark Dilution Revision Act Passed by United States Congress' press release at www.inta.org 26 September 2006.

unfair advantage of the reputation of that mark. As already said, this judgment strengthens brand owners' position.

The pending case *Google and Google France* will show how far the brand owners, in that case Louis Vuitton, may require protection against unfair competition. A lot will depend on the ECJ's interpretation of the concept of 'use' in that case.

Finally, the *Copad* judgment is a positive sign for the brand owners in relation to the exhaustion of rights and effects of a licence agreement, underlining that the quality of luxury goods is also the result of the allure and prestigious image which bestows on them an aura of luxury.

Consequently, for the moment it seems that, according to the current case-law of the ECJ, the protection of well-known marks against unfair competition is quite wide. That evolution is extremely important for the brand owners. In fact, trade marks as intangible business have gained in importance over the years and trade mark rights are nowadays recognised as a property right which has an economic value and contributes to the overall value of a business and which can be owned and sold. Protection of trade mark rights is important not only for the right owners but also for the society as a whole. In fact, it is in the interest of countries to have the strongest possible enforcement mechanisms to protect the investment climate and labour markets and also to reduce the loss of tax revenues that are directly affected by the lack of efficient protection against, inter alia, trade mark counterfeiting.[125] Efficient protection of trade mark rights against unfair competition should thus be provided. It is, of course, not only trade marks with a reputation which should benefit from protection against unfair competition, but all the other trade marks as well, provided that the necessary conditions, such as the existence of likelihood of confusion, are established.

As the European Commissioner for Internal Market and Services Charlie McCreevy has stated, as a prime advertising tool, trade marks are of paramount importance in the marketing and commercialisation of goods and services, and therefore affordable and easy access to trade mark protection is vital for fostering innovation and competitiveness by encouraging the production and distribution of quality products.[126] At the same time trade marks are an essential element in the system of undistorted competition which the EC Treaty seeks to establish and maintain.

[125] See, eg T Su Aung, 'Education & Awareness-Building Initiatives of International Trademark Association (INTA) on Trademark Protection and Enforcement' WIPO/ACE/3/4 26 April 2006. See also, especially concerning goodwill, U Bernitz and V Tiili, *Suomalainen ja kansainvälinen markkinaoikeus* (Porvoo, Werner Söderström Osakeyhtiö, 1974) 188.

[126] C McCreevy, 'Affordable Trade Mark Protection for Europe' SPEECH/09/157 Brussels, 31 March 2009. That was in relation to a press conference on the reduction of the fees changed by the Office for Harmonisation in the Internal Market (trade marks and designs) but also qualifies as a general statement. See for a critical view about brands N Klein, *No Logo* (London, Flamingo, 2001). Klein argued almost a decade ago that global brands have resulted in the exploitation of third world workers, increased domestic unemployment and reduced domestic wages.

# 13

# *Sanctioning EC Competition Law Infringements: as Time Goes by...*

ARNAUD BOHLER*

## INTRODUCTION

'*Sed fugit interea fugit irreparabile tempus*'...[1] but it flees in the meantime, irretrievable time flees. Time is an inescapable fact, determining every aspect of human activity. As law is created by society with the aim of governing and organising relationships between individuals, subject to the passing of time, it is bound to take account of the latter and be, itself, subject to it.

Instinctively, one may associate the importance of the passage of time with the situation of natural persons. However, companies, as well as public authorities, are also crucially concerned by the time factor. Indeed, efficient and prosperous economic activity requires prompt business reactions and a legally stable environment. Accordingly, regulatory authorities, including competition authorities, are compelled to respect this necessity. In addition, in its mission to detect and sanction anti-competitive behaviour, a competition authority will find it both easier and more effective to act as soon as it can. It will find it easier because any piece of evidence it may want to rely upon undergoes, itself, the effect of the passage of time. It will also find it more effective, because a sanction produces a higher deterrent effect on both the undertaking in breach and on other undertakings potentially tempted to commit infringements, and more useful – as it will prevent possible irreversible effects on the market and allow the actors to adapt in due time to the legal environment – if it is imposed at an early stage.[2]

* All views expressed in this paper are strictly personal, and should not be construed as reflecting the opinion of the institution. The author is grateful to Massimo Marelli for his comments on this article.

[1] Virgil, *Georgics*.

[2] See G Canivet, 'Le temps: un impératif dans l'organisation des procédures', Ateliers de droit de la concurrence: le facteur temps (www.dgccrf.bercy.gouv.fr/fonds_documentaire/dgccrf/02_actualite/ateliers_concu/facteur_temps1.htm).

The purpose of the present discussion is to explore the way European Community law, as interpreted and applied by the case-law of the Court of First Instance of the European Communities (hereinafter CFI) and of the Court of Justice of the European Communities (hereinafter the ECJ), takes account of the passing of time when assessing the action of the European Commission, acting as a competition authority. The issue of the duration of judicial proceedings and the right to a fair trial is admittedly linked to this subject-matter. Such an issue would however, due to its somewhat different and multiple implications, merit a separate discussion. It will thus be touched upon only in so far as it is directly interrelated with the question of the duration of EC competition law administrative proceedings.

From the perspective of an undertaking subject to a Commission's enquiry against a breach of Articles 81 EC and/or 82 EC, the passage of time may be analysed as giving rise to the existence of two separate rights, both deriving from the objective obligation imposed on the Commission to act within a certain time-frame. On the one hand, relying on the rules on limitation periods, an undertaking is entitled to claim a 'right to oblivion'.[3] On the other hand, pursuant to the principle of reasonable delay, it may inversely legitimately request not to be forgotten.

## THE PASSING OF TIME AND THE RIGHT TO OBLIVION: THE RULES ON LIMITATION PERIODS

The notion of limitation period can be generally defined as the extinguishment of a right as a result of it not being exercised within a delay laid down by the law. According to the European Court of Human Rights,

> [l]imitation may be defined as the statutory right of an offender not to be prosecuted or tried after the lapse of a certain period of time since the offence was committed. Limitation periods, which are a common feature of the domestic legal systems of the Contracting States, serve several purposes, which include ensuring legal certainty and finality and preventing infringements of the rights of defendants, which might be impaired if courts were required to decide on the basis of evidence which might have become incomplete because of the passage of time.[4]

Applied to the action of a public authority, such as the Commission, it can thus be analysed as a mechanism by which this authority loses its power either to investigate or to sanction law infringements due to the passage of time.

[3] This description of the operation of limitation periods is debated in the literature. See L Jeannin, 'La prescription' in *La clémence saisie par le droit – Amnistie, prescription et grâce en droit international et comparé* (Paris, Société de Législation Comparée, 2007) 257, and H Letteron, 'Le droit à l'oubli' (1996) 2 *Revue de droit publique* 385. This theoretical issue is not, however, the focus of the present discussion.

[4] *Stubbings and Others v the United Kingdom* no IV (1996) EHRR 51.

As far as EC competition law is concerned, following the revealing by the ECJ of the existence of a legal vacuum,[5] the Council introduced in 1974 a first set of rules on limitation periods through Regulation No 2988/74 concerning limitation periods in proceedings and the enforcement of sanctions under the rules of the European Economic Community relating to transport and competition (hereinafter Regulation No 2988/74).[6] These rules have been, in essence, taken over and adapted to take account of the instauration of a system of parallel powers between national and EC competition authorities, in Regulation No 1/2003 on the implementation of the rules on competition laid down in Articles 81 and 82 of the Treaty (hereinafter Regulation No 1/2003).[7]

Although Regulation No 2988/74 indicates as the sole objective of limitation that of ensuring legal certainty,[8] in the national legal system of most Member States, this mechanism is, in fact, generally founded upon a wider range of fundamental considerations.[9] Two such considerations are particularly important for the purposes of the present discussion. Firstly, and this is particularly true in criminal matters, once a certain amount of time has elapsed between an infringement, the infringement is deemed to have been forgotten, so that the social need to punish it has faded away. Secondly, the evidence of the infringement may disappear with the passing of time, and the risk of erroneous or unjust findings grows accordingly.

The impact of these elements on the application of limitation to each specific area of law depends on both the kind of infringement and the nature of the defendant involved. As far as EC competition law is concerned, it should first be noted that this area is aimed at sanctioning business behaviour. In addition, any infringement of competition rules is likely to be difficult to uncover, and will involve the responsibility of companies or associations of companies rather than natural persons. This is probably why the competition law rules on limitation appear to be less restrictive than in other areas of law. However, it will be seen that the margin of manoeuvre granted to the Commission in its mission to detect, find and punish EC competition infringements is scrutinised by the

[5] See Case 41/69 *ACF Chemiefarma v Commission* [1970] ECR 661 paras 17–21, and Case 52/69 *Geigy v Commission* [1972] ECR 787 paras 20–22. See also HG Lyklema, 'La gravité des infractions au droit communautaire en rapport avec la prescription de leurs poursuites' (1971) 5 *Cahiers de droit européen* 522.

[6] Regulation (EEC) No 2988/74 of the Council of 26 November 1974 concerning limitation periods in proceedings and the enforcement of sanctions under the rules of the European Economic Community relating to transport and competition [1974] OJ L/319/1.

[7] Council Regulation (EC) No 1/2003 of 16 December 2002 on the implementation of the rules on competition laid down in Articles 81 and 82 of the Treaty [2003] OJ L/1/1.

[8] See 2nd recital to Reg No 2988/74. See also Case C-278/02 *Handlbauer* [2004] ECR I-6171 para 40, and Case 41/69 *ACF Chemifarma v Commission*, n 5 above, para 19. On its part, Reg No 1/2003 does not mention at all the objective of the limitation periods it provides for.

[9] Among which, as stated in Joined Cases T-22/02 and T-23/02 *Sumitomo Chemical and Sumika Fine Chemicals v Commission* [2005] ECR II4065 para 94, 'the requirement to prevent actions which are brought late and are motivated more by an intention to cause harm than by justice; the deterioration of evidence; the need to penalise a lack of diligence on the part of the person bringing the action; the eventual disappearance of the public interest in pursuing infringements and the requirement that the public authorities focus on current matters'.

Community Courts, which apply some limits aimed at preventing the abusive exercise of those powers. An analysis of the application of such limits will be carried out, successively, in relation to the powers which are explicitly subject to limitation periods by virtue of Regulation No 2988/74, and those which are implicitly not subject to such rules.

## The Powers Subject to Explicit Limitation Periods

Contrary to most national criminal jurisdictions,[10] in EC competition law enforcement, by virtue of Articles 25 and 26 of Regulation No 1/2003,[11] only the power to impose penalties and to enforce them are explicitly subject to limitation periods.

According to Article 25 of Regulation No 1/2003, in the case of infringements other than those of provisions concerning requests for information or the conduct of inspections – in which case the powers of the Commission is subject to a limitation period of three years – the power of the Commission to impose fines or periodic penalty payments is subject to a limitation period of five years.

### *Commencement of the Limitation Period*

The limitation period of five years begins to run on the day on which the infringement is committed. This relatively brief delay is, however, mitigated by the fact that, by virtue of the second sentence of Article 25(2) of Regulation No 1/2003, in the case of continuing or repeated infringements, time shall begin to run on the day on which the infringement ceases. Considering, firstly, that competition law infringements are generally commercial practices which are not committed once, but during a certain period of time and, secondly, the very broad approach to the notion of complex and continued infringement, the Commission can sometimes find itself in a position to sanction infringements committed decades before the finding of an infringement.

In fact, it must be recalled that, according to settled case-law, a single and continuous infringement of Article 81(1) EC could be deemed to arise from a series of acts or from continuous conduct which formed part of an 'overall plan' because they had the same object of distorting competition within the common market.[12] In the same vein, the ECJ has ruled, in response to a plea drawn from Regulation No 2988/74, that, if the notion of continued infringement varies somewhat between the various Member States' legal orders, it entails in any case a plurality of illegal behaviours or implementing acts of a single infringement,

[10] See L Idot, 'Le temps: une limite à l'action des autorités', Ateliers de droit de la concurrence: le facteur temps (www.dgccrf.bercy.gouv.fr/fonds_documentaire/dgccrf/02_actualite/ateliers_concu/facteur_temps2.htm), para 36.

[11] Which restate the rules previously set out in Arts 1 and 2 of Reg No 2988/74.

[12] Joined Cases C-204/00 P, C-205/00 P, C-211/00 P, C-213/00 P, C-217/00 P and C-219/00 P *Aalborg Portland and Others v Commission* [2004] ECR I-123 para 258.

joint by one common subjective element.[13] This subjective analysis of the link between successive illegal acts makes it difficult for an undertaking to show that the continuity of the infringement has been interrupted. Admittedly, with regard to the alleged duration of an infringement, it has been held that the principle of legal certainty requires that, if there is no evidence directly establishing the duration of the infringement, the Commission should adduce at least evidence of facts *sufficiently proximate* in time for it to be *reasonable* to accept that that infringement continued uninterruptedly between two specific dates (emphasis added).[14] Even if the burden of proof concerning the continuity of the infringement remains with the Commission, it is clear from this wording that the standard of proof required is not particularly high.

Thus, for instance, in *Degussa v Commission*,[15] the CFI found that, although the concerted practice had not been implemented and had experienced some wavering for a period of almost two years, due to the withdrawal of one of the participants and a change in the market conditions, since the participants had not explicitly manifested a will to put the concerted practice to an end, the latter could not be considered as interrupted. In particular, the CFI considered that it cannot be inferred from that brief period of disagreement between the participants that the collusion had come to an end, since not only did the meetings continue to be held regularly but, in addition, during those meetings an agreed reaction to new market data were adopted. The fact that Degussa temporarily lowered prices in order to regain customers and that it consistently rejected proposals not to lower prices could not, therefore, be taken to mean that it intended to distance itself from the content of the meetings and act independently, particularly since, according to certain documents, it intended to agree with the other participants on a price rise at a later stage. On the basis of this subjective examination of the intentions of the participants in the cartel, the infringement was consequently described as a single and continuous one from 1986 to 1999, despite this period of wavering of almost two years.

In *Peróxidos Orgánicos v Commission*,[16] the dispute was not in relation to a possible interruption of the limitation period, as in *Degussa v Commission*, but was, rather, based on the applicant's submission that the illegal conduct actually ceased earlier than alleged by the Commission. The CFI adopted a rather balanced approach as to the onus of proof in those circumstances. In particular, the CFI took the view that whilst the general principle that the Commission is required to prove the duration of the infringement is not called into question by the fact that the applicant raised a defence of limitation, it is incumbent upon the applicant to prove that the limitation period has expired. The result is therefore that the burden of proof is somewhat shared between the Commission and the applicant. Such apportionment of the burden of proof, according to the

[13] Case C-235/92 P *Montecatini v Commission* [1999] ECR I-4539 para 195.

[14] Case C-185/95 P *Baustahlgewebe v Commission* [1998] ECR I-8417 para 58, and Case T-43/92 *Dunlop Slazenger v Commission* [1994] ECR II-441 para 79.

[15] Case T-279/02 *Degussa v Commission* [2006] ECR II-897 paras 129 *ff*.

[16] Case T-120/04 *Peróxidos Orgánicos v Commission* [2006] ECR II-4441 paras 50 *ff*.

CFI, is likely to vary, inasmuch as the evidence put forward by one party may be of such a kind as to require the other party to provide an explanation or justification, failing which it is permissible to conclude that the burden of proof has been discharged, and thus may be sufficient to give rise to a – rebuttable – presumption.

It is not easy to determine the concrete implications of this composite approach but, at least in the case in question, it seems that the scrutiny with respect to the evidence submitted by the Commission was not very intense. In fact, after recalling the various probative elements taken into account by the Commission in its decision, the CFI concluded that this evidence is capable of corroborating the Commission's assessment regarding the applicant's continuing participation in the infringement beyond 1997. This was deemed to be sufficient to reverse the burden of proof, the CFI considering that, in the light of these *indicia*, it was next to be established whether the applicant had advanced arguments and provided evidence capable of contradicting those indicia or casting doubt on their probative value. In particular, the applicant was required to provide an alternative explanation or justification capable of contradicting the interpretation given by the Commission. To make things more clear, the CFI went on to conclude that, accordingly, the Commission's findings contained in the relevant recitals of the contested decision were not manifestly erroneous or unlawful, and that, therefore, the Commission's proceedings were not time-barred.

It can be drawn from the construction above that, even if the CFI ensures the right of the participants in procedure concerning Article 81 EC to contest either the continuity or the date of the cessation of that infringement, there is no perfect symmetry with regard to the standard of proof to be met by, on the one hand, the Commission, and, on the other hand, the undertaking concerned. In fact, as soon as the Commission adduces at least some evidence of events giving rise to a concerted practice, which are sufficiently proximate in time for it to be reasonable to accept that an infringement continued uninterruptedly between two specific dates, it is for the undertaking in question to provide the evidence, as difficult as it may be, supporting an alternative explanation, capable of rebutting this assumption, and, ultimately, to show a manifest error of appraisal on the part of the Commission. In reality, this conclusion should not come as a surprise, as it is an expression of the general presumption of validity enjoyed by Community measures.[17]

This indirect alleviation of the time constraints imposed on the powers of the Commission, which follows from a flexible application of the conditions for establishing the existence of a single and continuous illegal behaviour, is reinforced by several specific aspects pertaining to the interruption and the suspension of the limitation period as conceived by Regulation No 1/2003.

[17] See, inter alia, Case T-35/92 *Deere v Commission* [1994] ECR II-957 para 31.

*Interruption and Suspension of the Limitation Period*

Whilst the suspension of the limitation period has the effect that the lapse of time during which the limitation period is suspended is not taken into account in determining the end of the five-year period,[18] the interruption of the limitation period, on the basis of Article 25(5) of Regulation No 1/2003 makes the limitation period start running afresh. However, Article 25 also provides that the limitation period shall expire, in any event, at the latest, on the day on which a period equal to twice the limitation period (that is, ten years in the case of infringements other than those of provisions concerning requests for information or the conduct of inspections) has elapsed without the Commission having imposed a fine or a period penalty payment.

This means that the Commission has five years to take the first steps of an investigation after the ending of an infringement. As soon as it does so, it disposes of a fresh period of five years before it is required to take any new step in the procedure, with an absolute limit for taking a final decision of ten years from the day the infringement has ceased.

Thus, the rules concerning the interruption of the limitation period provide the Commission with crucial flexibility to set its competition policy and enforcement priorities, and to channel its resources towards particular sectors of investigation. It is all the more so since the steps capable of interrupting the limitation period are defined in particularly broad terms.

In particular, according to Article 25(3) of Regulation No 1/2003, a step capable of interrupting the limitation period can consist of any action adopted by the Commission or by the competition authority of a Member State for the purposes of the investigation or proceedings in respect of an infringement.[19] The possibility to take into account actions of national competition authorities, introduced by Regulation No 1/2003 in order to take account of the establishment of a system of parallel powers,[20] makes national competition authorities the permanent and local watchdog of the EC competition rules, multiplying the actions capable not only to detect infringements and initiate proceedings, but also to interrupt the course of limitation periods. Finally, it is worth noting that the interruption shall apply not only vis-à-vis the undertaking to which the action is notified, but also vis-à-vis all the undertakings which have participated in the infringement.

In this regard, in the recent case of *ArcelorMittal Luxembourg and Others v Commission*,[21] the CFI had occasion to clarify the effect, *ratione personae*, of the

[18] Pursuant to Art 25(6) of Reg No 1/2003, the limitation period for the imposition of fines or periodic penalty payments shall be suspended for as long as the decision of the Commission is the subject of proceedings pending the ECJ. By virtue of Art 25(5), the ten-year ceiling limitation period provided for in the case of an interruption shall be extended by the time during which limitation is suspended pursuant to Art 25(6). For an application of the equivalent provisions in Reg No 2988/74, see Case T-276/04 *Compagnie maritime belge v Commission*, judgment of 1st July 2008 nyr, paras 23 *ff*.

[19] Art 25(3) gives an indicative list of such actions, namely written request for information, written authorisations to conduct inspections, initiation of proceedings, and notification of the statement of objections.

[20] See Recital 31 of Reg No 1/2003.

[21] Case T-405/06 *ArcelorMittal Luxembourg and Others v Commission*, judgment of 31 March 2009 nyr.

interruption of the limitation period, on the one hand, and its suspension, on the other.

The applicant submitted that the limitation period could not have been interrupted in respect of its alleged infringement, since it had not been identified during the proceedings as an undertaking having participated in the infringement and it had not been addressed a statement of objections by the Commission. The CFI firmly rejected this argument and made it clear that the expression 'undertakings which have participated in the infringement' used in Article 25(4) of Regulation No 1/2003 comprises any undertaking identified in a Commission decision sanctioning an infringement.[22] The circumstance that an undertaking was not identified as such in the initial statement of objections or, more generally, during the administrative proceedings is not relevant if the undertaking is named in the decision.[23] According to the CFI, therefore, the limitation period is interrupted by any action of the Commission for the purposes of an investigation or the pursuit of the infringement, which is notified to at least one undertaking that the Commission considers has participated in the infringement, and it concerns every undertaking which is found as having participated in that infringement, including those which are still unknown by the Commission at the time it undertakes the first steps of an investigation. Indeed, the CFI considers that the expression used in the abovementioned provision implies an objective assessment, namely the participation in the infringement, and not a subjective and contingent one, such as the identification of that undertaking during the administrative proceedings.

Interestingly, the CFI followed the opposite approach in relation to the alleged suspensive effect of an action brought by an undertaking in respect of another undertaking fined by the contested decision but which did not contest the decision. Indeed, from a factual point of view, it should be recalled that the Commission had adopted an initial decision on 16 February 1994 fining a certain number of undertakings for their participation in a cartel on the beams market which ended on 17 January 1991. This decision was contested before the CFI by Arbed, ArcelorMittal's predecessor, on 8 April 1994 and, on appeal, before the ECJ – which finally annulled it by judgment of 2 October 2003 as far as Arbed was concerned.[24] Consequently, the Commission adopted a new decision on 8 November 2006, addressed to both Arbed and TradeArbed, its subsidiary. The latter submitted that the decennial limitation period had not been suspended in its respect since it had not brought the action for annulment of the initial decision and that, in consequence, the second Commission decision was time barred. Whilst the CFI underlined the objective nature of the mechanism of interruption as expressed by the wording of Article 25(4) of Regulation No 1/2003, justifying its *erga omnes* effect, it founded its reasoning concerning

[22] *Ibid* paras 143 *ff*.

[23] See also Case T-276/04 *Compagnie maritime belge v Commission*, n 18 above, para 31 and the case-law cited.

[24] Case T-137/94 *ARBED v Commission* [1999] ECR II-303, and Case C-176/99 P *ARBED v Commission* [2003] ECR I-10687.

suspension on the relative effect of the action brought before the EC judge. In the absence of an explicit answer to this problem in the text of Regulation No 1/2003, the CFI recalled the *inter partes* effect of the proceedings and their consequences, as stated by the ECJ in *Commission v AssiDomän Kraft Products and Others.*[25] Carrying out a teleological and comparative analysis, the CFI also considered that, contrary to the interruption the purpose of which is to allow the Commission to pursue and sanction efficiently competition law infringements – the suspension of the limitation period concerns, by definition, cases in which the Commission has already adopted a decision. It was not considered necessary to attach an *erga omnes* effect to the introduction, by one of the undertakings sanctioned, of an action before the EC jurisdiction. The CFI concluded from the foregoing that the action brought by an addressee against a decision cannot have any kind of incidence on the situation of the other addressees, so that the second decision had to be annulled in respect of TradeArbed.

In the light of the broad definition of the actions capable of interrupting the time periods, as much as the number of authorities entitled to do so, and the scope of the possible effects of interruption, it could be concluded that, as soon as the Commission or a national competition authority is aware of the existence of a potential infringement of EC competition law, there is little scope for undertakings to rely on limitation periods to escape a sanction.

However, this does not mean that the Commission can artificially keep its powers alive by taking actions aimed only at interrupting the elapsing of the limitation period. The CFI gave a clear indication in that sense in its *CMA CGM and Others v Commission* judgment.[26] In this case, the Commission had launched proceedings against members of a liner conference and independent shipping companies in respect of horizontal price-fixing agreements. The Commission sent a statement of objections to the parties to the agreements on 19 April 1994 in which it announced its intention to impose fines. The parties to the agreement sent their reply to the statement of objections on 16 September 1994. The Commission then sent a request for information on 24 March 1995 relating to the turnover figures of those parties for 1993 and 1994. However, the Commission had not subsequently adopted a final decision. Three years later, on 30 June 1998, it sent a further request for information relating to the turnover figures of the same parties for 1997 and not an additional one on 11 October 1999 to obtain turnover figures for 1998. A final decision imposing fines on the parties to the agreements was finally adopted on 16 May 2000. In their application for annulment of the Commission decision, the applicants submitted that the final step which validly stopped the time running for the purposes of the limitation period was the Commission's request for information of 24 March

[25] Case C-310/97 P *Commission v AssiDomän Kraft Products and Others* [1999] ECR I-5363 paras 49 *ff*.

[26] Case T-213/00 *CMA CGM and Others v Commission* [2003] ECR II-913. See, namely, M Rosado da Fonseca, 'Calculating time-limits for imposing fine under Article 81 EC' (2003) 10 *European Law Reporter* 387, and L Idot, 'Comm. 179' (2003) 5 *Europe* 22.

1995. Consequently, the five-year limitation period allegedly came to an end on 24 March 2000 and the final decision could not therefore lawfully impose fines on the applicants.

The CFI concluded, first, that, in order validly to interrupt the five-year limitation period laid down by Article 1(1)(b) of Regulation No 2988/74, a request for information must be necessary for the preliminary investigation or proceedings and, second, that, in the present case, the purpose of the requests for information of 30 June 1998 and 11 October 1999 was not to enable the Commission to calculate the maximal permitted fines and so they were not necessary for the conduct of the investigation. The CFI therefore annulled the contested decision in so far as it imposed fines, since they were imposed after the five-year limitation period had expired.

While the objective of limiting the Commission's powers by avoiding an abusive use of acts intended to interrupt the limitation period is wholly laudable, it is arguable whether the reasoning of the CFI can go free of any criticism.

In particular, the conclusion that, in order to interrupt the five-year limitation period, a request for information must be necessary for the preliminary investigation or proceedings, which is not explicitly provided for in Regulation No 2988/74, relies on a far-fetched interpretation of that Regulation and of Regulation No 17.[27]

Firstly, the initial assertion that the interruption of the limitation period constitutes an exception to the five-year limitation period, and thus must be interpreted narrowly, is not totally convincing. It is submitted that the mechanism of limitation periods is, in itself, a derogation to the principle according to which one is liable for its breaching the law, and an exception to the powers of the Commission to enforce the prohibition laid down in Articles 81 EC and 82 EC. In addition, it could be argued that the conceptual relationship between the five-year limitation period and its interruption is not, as such, one of exception, but rather one of condition. In other words, the absence of any interruptive action taken by the Commission for a period of five years could be analysed as a condition for depriving the Commission of its power to sanction EC competition law infringements.

Secondly, the CFI rightly points out that Article 2(1)(a) of Regulation No 2988/74 provides that in order to interrupt the limitation period, written requests for information must be *for the purposes* of the preliminary investigation or proceedings in respect of an infringement.[28] Similarly, the CFI underlines that, pursuant to Article 11 of Regulation No 17, a request for information must be necessary, which means, according to the case-law, that it may legitimately be regarded *as having a connection with the putative infringement*.[29] On the basis of these elements, one could infer that the essential criterion as to the question

[27] Regulation No 17: First Regulation implementing Articles 85 and 86 of the Treaty [1962] OJ L/13/204.

[28] Case T-213/00 *CMA CGM and Others v Commission*, n 26 above, para 485.

[29] *Ibid* para 486, and Case T-39/90 *SEP v Commission* [1991] ECR II-1497 para 29.

whether an action taken by the Commission will interrupt the five-year limitation period is that it can legitimately be regarded as having a connection with the putative infringement. Furthermore, the requirement that the written request for information be necessary in order to produce effects, is not the result of a restrictive interpretation of the term 'necessary', on the contrary. Therefore, the conclusion of the CFI according to which, in order to interrupt the five-year limitation period, the request for information *must be necessary for the preliminary investigation or proceedings* does not flow directly from Regulation No 2988/74 and Regulation No 17, or the case-law, but rather shows the willingness of the CFI to put tighter limits on a possible abusive exercise by the Commission of its powers. This appears quite clearly from developments where the CFI insists that the Commission cannot make requests for information the sole purpose of which is to prolong the limitation period artificially so as to preserve the power to impose a fine, and that the duration of the procedure in the case in question appeared, at least at first sight, to have been unreasonable.[30]

Thirdly, it must be noted not only that the requirements determined by the CFI result from a constructive interpretation, but also that the CFI exercised its judicial review role very thoroughly. Thus, it examined whether the requests, when they where sent in 1998 and 1999, were necessary for the Commission to be able to adopt a final decision imposing fines, or whether the circumstances surrounding the adoption of those requests show, on the contrary, on the basis of precise and consistent indicia, that they were not necessary. The CFI reached the latter conclusion on the basis of the fact that the Commission, in its analysis, already had all the information necessary for the adoption of a decision further to the replies to the first request for information, received from the applicants on 24 March 1995. One can see that, if the objective is legitimate, the way in which it is pursued leads the judge to undertake a detailed examination, liable to limit the broad power of appraisal of the Commission as to the way it deems appropriate to conduct its administrative proceedings. Furthermore, in that exercise, the CFI is called upon to make substantial and subjective ex post considerations that may not be wholly adapted to procedural matters,[31] as was illustrated in the appeal brought before the ECJ.[32] On this occasion, the question as to the legality of the

[30] Case T-213/00 *CMA CGM and Others v Commission*, n 26 above, paras 488 and 494.

[31] In that regard, it is worth noting that not all national courts competent in competition matters have followed such a substantive approach. For instance, the French Cour de cassation has recently quashed a judgment rendered by the Cour d'Appel de Paris, on the ground that it had erroneously considered that the limitation period had not been interrupted by an action taken by the rapporteur of the French competition authority which did not have the purpose of investigating, finding or sanctioning competition infringements, but of artificially prolonging the limitation period. According to the French Supreme Court, as soon as an action aims at investigating, finding or sanctioning competition infringements, it must be considered as an act interrupting the limitation period, without it being necessary to assess whether it pursued another objective (*Cass. Com.*, 6 November 2007, *Ministre de l'Économie v DBS, Sort et Chaste et Somoclest*, No 06-16194). See C Lemaire, 'Chronique-Procédures' (2008) 1 *Concurrence*s 166. See also, as concerns the appealed judgment of the Cour d'Appel de Paris of 23 May 2006, L Driguez, 'Le juge, garant de l'efficience du principe de prescription en droit français de la concurrence' (2006) 36 *La Semaine Juridique édition Entreprise et Affaires* 1472.

[32] Case C-263/03 P *Commission v France*, judgment of 12 October 2004 unreported.

principle established by the CFI was not settled. However, the ECJ considered that the CFI made erroneous assessments when ascertaining whether the requests for information were necessary for the proceedings. In particular, according to the ECJ, the CFI could not state, in such a categorical way, that the obligation to verify that the calculated fines did not exceed the ceiling authorised by the applicable legal provision could not explain the sending of the 1998 and 1999 requests for information, since the Commission did not have in its possession such information at the time when the contested decision was adopted. The ECJ even added that the turnover figures for 1998 might have been of some use in estimating the turnover for 1999 which, in the present case, was the reference year for the calculation of the maximum permitted amount of the fines, whilst it is much less plausible that the turnover figures for 1993 and 1994 were as useful for the purposes of such an estimate.[33]

It results from the foregoing that, in order to sidestep its inability to draw legal consequences from the length of administrative proceedings by resorting to the principle of reasonable delay,[34] the CFI carried out an uncomfortable appraisal of the subjective and substantive purpose of purely procedural administrative acts, almost amounting to a control of misuse of powers. The need to adopt this approach is even more questionable when considering that, in the case at hand, all evidence relating to the infringement had been collected within an uninterrupted five-year period running from the cessation of the infringement, and, on that basis, the principle of legal certainty, on which the notion of limitation periods is namely based, was not impaired.

### *Enforcement of Penalties*

Pursuant to Article 26 of Regulation No 1/2003, the power of the Commission to enforce decisions taken pursuant to Articles 23 (fines) and 24 (periodic penalty payments) shall be subject to a limitation period of five years, running from the day on which the decision becomes final. That limitation period may be interrupted by a notification of a decision varying the original amount of the fine or periodic penalty payment (or refusing to do so) or by any action of the Commission or of a Member State designed to enforce payment. The limitation period shall be suspended for as long as time to pay is allowed, or enforcement of payment is suspended pursuant to a decision of the ECJ.

At first sight, these clear and explicit rules would be unlikely to raise problems of interpretation. However, in an action for annulment brought against Commission acts concerning the outstanding balance of the fine imposed by a Commission decision in the Welded steel mesh case,[35] questions arose as to the jurisdiction competent to declare whether the enforcement of a Commission decision is time-barred, pursuant to Regulation No 2988/74.

[33] *Ibid* para 58.

[34] For further developments in this regard, see the 2nd part of the present chapter.

[35] Decision 89/515/EEC of 2 August 1989 relating to a proceeding under Article 85 of the EEC Treaty (IV/31.553 - Welded steel mesh) [1989] OJ L/260/1.

The facts of the dispute can be summarised as follows. The Commission adopted the Welded steel mesh decision on 2 August 1989, imposing on the applicant, Ferriere Nord, a fine of ECU 320,000. A bank guarantee was provided by the applicant for the duration of the proceedings before the CFI seeking annulment of the Commission decision. The action for annulment before the CFI as well as an appeal before the ECJ were dismissed, with final judgment delivered by the ECJ on 17 July 1997.[36] Due to the severe devaluation of the Italian lira between the date of the Commission decision and the date of the judgment on appeal, the applicant requested a reduction in the amount of the fine and interest, which was refused by the Commission by letter of 11 September 1997. Almost seven years later, on 5 February 2004, the Commission put the applicant on notice to settle the debt still owed by it as quickly as possible. On 13 April 2004, the Commission added that, failing payment before 30 April 2004, it would call on the bank to honour the guarantee. Those two acts of 5 February and 13 April 2004 were contested before the CFI by Ferriere Nord, which considered that they constituted enforcement acts adopted after the five years limitation period laid down in Article 4(1) of Regulation No 2988/74.[37]

On first instance, the Commission contended, primarily, that the action was inadmissible on the ground that the contested acts do not constitute decisions within the meaning of Article 249 EC, since those acts have no additional legal effect with regard to the amount of the fine owing pursuant to the Welded steel mesh decisions and the Commission's refusal of 11 September 1997.

The CFI addressed the admissibility issue only after having concluded that, since the contested acts had been adopted more than five years after the last interruptive act of 11 September 1997, the powers of the Commission to seek enforcement of the fine imposed to applicant were time-barred. As to the question whether the contested acts could be the subject of proceedings under Article 230 EC, the CFI simply recalled that according to constant case-law, a decision within the meaning of Article 249 EC is any act which clearly and definitively alters its addressee's legal position. Since the powers of the Commission to enforce the fine were time-barred, the applicant could regard itself as protected from any claim made by the Commission to this end. Thus, the contested acts, which demanded payment and threatened to take steps to enforce the bank guarantee, clearly and definitely altered the applicant's legal position, and the action seeking their annulment was deemed to be admissible.

This subjective and factual reasoning was not endorsed by the ECJ on appeal.[38] In a very straight-forward ruling, the ECJ stated that the contested acts must be regarded as giving notice of enforcement of a decision taken previously, that is to say the Welded steel mesh decision. The ECJ adopted a more orthodox approach

[36] See Case T-143/89 *Ferriere Nord v Commission* [1995] ECR II-917, and Case C-219/95 P *Ferriere Nord v Commission* [1997] ECR I-4411.

[37] Equivalent to Art 26 of Reg No 1/2003. See Case T-153/04 *Ferriere Nord v Commission* [2006] ECR II-3889.

[38] Case C-516/06 P *Commission v Ferriere Nord* [2007] ECR I-10685. See E Barbier de la Serre, 'Prescription de la récupération d'une amende' (2008) 15 *Revue Lamy de la concurrence* 81.

and analysed first the admissibility of the action, and found that the challenged acts, whether they occur before or after any limitation period has expired, cannot be regarded as having produced legal effects binding on, and capable of affecting the interests of, Ferriere Nord. In reality, according to the ECJ, they constituted acts which are purely preparatory to enforcement.

If this approach seems legally unquestionable, one could legitimately wonder what would be the right way for an applicant to contest clearly time-barred enforcement acts. The ECJ tackled this question in response to the applicant's arguments relating to the application of the right to effective judicial protection. It recalled that enforcement of a decision of the Commission which imposes a pecuniary obligation on a legal person such as Ferriere Nord is governed by Article 256 EC which, in its fourth paragraph, provides for effective judicial protection. At this stage, it is worth recalling that, by virtue of this Article:

> Decisions of the Council or of the Commission which impose a pecuniary obligation on persons other than States, shall be enforceable.
>
> Enforcement shall be governed by the rules of civil procedure in force in the State in the territory of which it is carried out. The order for its enforcement shall be appended to the decision, without other formality than verification of the authenticity of the decision, by the national authority which the government of each Member State shall designate for this purpose and shall make known to the Commission and to the Court of Justice.
>
> When these formalities have been completed on application by the party concerned, the latter may proceed to enforcement in accordance with the national law, by bringing the matter directly before the competent authority.
>
> Enforcement may be suspended only by a decision of the Court of Justice. However, the courts of the country concerned shall have jurisdiction over complaints that enforcement is being carried out in an irregular manner.

The ECJ's ruling on appeal suggests that the company could bring its case before the competent national jurisdiction in order to argue that the enforcement of the fine was time-barred. Whilst this approach is consistent with the last paragraph of Article 256 EC, it remains unclear whether the validity of the contested national enforcement measures could be assessed in respect of EC rules on limitation periods. Indeed, Article 256 EC explicitly provides that enforcement shall be governed by the rules of civil procedure in force in the State in the territory of which it is carried out. Should this be interpreted as excluding the application, by national jurisdictions, of the rules set out in Regulation No 2988/74 and Regulation No 1/2003, the EC provisions concerning enforcement limitation periods would be deprived of useful effect. Unless a distinction should be made between, on the one hand, the decision of the Community institution to proceed to enforcement in accordance with national law by bringing the matter before a national authority, within the meaning of the third paragraph of Article 256 EC, and, on the other hand, enforcement measures taken by those authorities, foreseen in the fourth paragraph of that Article.[39] Whilst the national measures would be governed by the national rules of civil procedure, the EC decision to demand such national measures could be the subject of an action for annulment on the basis of Article 230 EC before the CFI, on grounds drawn from EC limitation periods.

There is little case-law about the application of Article 256 EC. In *CESTAS v Commission*,[40] the CFI was asked to annul a debit note addressed by the Commission in the context of subsidies allowed by the European Development Fund which, if it was not honoured by the debtor, permitted the Commission to enforce a recovery decision by way of an enforceable decision under Article 256 EC. Responding favourably to the objection of inadmissibility raised by the Commission, the CFI stated that the contested act was a preparatory measure preceding the possible adoption of a decision by the Commission to continue the recovery procedure either by initiating legal proceedings or by adopting a decision under Article 256 EC, thus implying that the latter decision could be challenged, which, in a way, confirms the approach presented above.

## The Powers implicitly not Subject to Limitation Periods

### *Finding the Infringement*

Even though Regulation No 2988/74 did not explicitly provide for the power of the Commission to find an infringement, the ECJ, in *GVL v Commission*,[41] acknowledged the existence of an implied power of the Commission to do so, as implicit in the existence of the express powers to order cessation of the infringement and to impose fines, provided for in Regulation No 17. Thus, the ECJ held that the cessation of an infringement prior to the adoption of a decision by the Commission did not in itself constitute an obstacle to the Commission's exercise of its powers to find and punish an infringement of the competition rules, provided that the institution has a legitimate interest in so doing. This novelty was late included in Article 7(1), last sentence, of Regulation No 1/2003, by virtue of which '[i]f the Commission has a legitimate interest in doing so, it may also find that an infringement has been committed in the past'. However, the question whether the rules on limitation periods concerning the powers to impose fines and enforce them, set out above, were applicable to this implied

[39] The French wording of Art 256 EC could give support to this reading (emphasis added):
'Après l'accomplissement de ces formalités à la demande de l'intéressé, celui-ci *peut poursuivre l'exécution forcée en saisissant directement l'organe compétent*, suivant la législation nationale.
L'exécution forcée ne peut être suspendue qu'en vertu d'une décision de la Cour de justice. Toutefois, *le contrôle de la régularité des mesures d'exécution* relève de la compétence des juridictions nationales.'

[40] Case T-260/04 *CESTAS v Commission* [2008] ECR II-701.

[41] Case 7/82 *GVL v Commission* [1983] ECR 483 paras 23 and 24.

power remained unsolved until *Sumitomo Chemical and Sumika Fine Chemicals v Commission*.[42] In this case, heard by a chamber of five judges (extended composition), the CFI ruled, after a thorough textual, linguistic, systematic and teleological analysis, that a decision finding an infringement is not a penalty within the meaning of Article 1(1) of Regulation No 2988/74 and is not therefore covered by the limitation period laid down by that provision. As a consequence, the powers of the Commission to investigate and adopt a decision finding that an undertaking has taken part in a violation of Articles 81 EC and 82 EC are not subject to the EC limitation periods, even though the infringement itself is time-barred.

This apparently minor power can, in fact, prove to be a very efficient tool to circumvent the strict application of EC limitation periods and to obtain, indirectly, a both deterrent and punitive effect with respect to the undertakings which counted on a 'right to oblivion'. Indeed, even though the infringement in question might be outside the scope of the sanctioning powers of the Commission, it can still be subject to civil actions brought by private parties which suffered damages due to the illegal conduct of the undertakings concerned, at the national level and pursuant to national civil procedure laws. The time-limits applicable to these actions might be longer than those imposed on administrative actions. In addition, the ability of the national procedure provisions to safeguard the rights which individuals derive directly from Community law are subject to the scrutiny of the ECJ, which has declared that the full effectiveness of Article 81 EC and, in particular, the practical effect of the prohibition laid down in Article 81(1) EC would be put at risk if it were not open to any individual to claim damages for loss caused to him by a contract or by conduct liable to restrict or distort competition. Indeed, the existence of such a right strengthens the working of the Community competition rules and discourages agreements or practices, frequently covert, which are liable to restrict or distort competition. From that point of view, actions for damages before the national courts can make a significant contribution to the maintenance of effective competition in the Community.[43]

In this regard, it is worth recalling that, in accordance with the principle of procedural autonomy, in the absence of Community rules governing the matter, it is for the domestic legal system of each Member State to designate the courts and tribunals having jurisdiction to hear actions for damages based on an infringement of the Community competition rules and to prescribe the detailed procedural rules governing those actions, provided that the provisions concerned are not less favourable than those governing actions for damages based on an infringement of national competition rules (principle of equivalence) and that

[42] See n 9 above. Among the numerous comments on this case see namely C Harris, 'What are the Commission's limits in deciding competition cases' (2006) 1 *International Trade Law & Regulation* 34; E Barbier de la Serre, 'Droit à l'oubli en l'absence d'un intérêt légitime à constater une infraction' (2005) 5 *Revue Lamy de la concurrence* 69; L Idot, 'Compétence de la Commission et infractions passées' (2005) 12 *Europe* 22, and F Zivy, 'Chroniques Procédures' (2006) 1 *Concurrences* 173.

[43] Case C-453/99 *Courage and Crehan* [2001] ECR I-6297 paras 26 and 27.

those national provisions do not render practically impossible or excessively difficult the exercise of the right to seek compensation for the harm caused by an agreement or practice prohibited under Article 81 EC (principle of effectiveness).

As the ECJ indicated in *Manfredi and Others*,[44] this is applicable, in particular, to rules governing limitation periods. Thus, the ECJ held that it is for the national court to determine whether a national rule which provides that the limitation period for bringing an action seeking compensation for harm caused by an agreement or practice prohibited under Article 81 EC begins to run from the day on which that prohibited agreement or practice was adopted, particularly where it also imposes a short limitation period that cannot be suspended, renders it practically impossible or excessively difficult to exercise the right to seek compensation for the harm suffered. Whilst leaving this appraisal to the national judge, the ECJ gave clear indications as to what the assessment should be. In particular, it indicated that a national rule under which the limitation period begins to run from the day on which the agreement or concerted practice was adopted could make it practically impossible to exercise the right to seek compensation for the harm caused by that prohibited agreement or practice, particularly if the national rule also imposes a short limitation period which is not capable of being suspended. In such a situation, where there are continuous or repeated infringements, it is possible that the limitation period expires even before the infringement is brought to an end, in which case it would be impossible for any individual who has suffered harm after the expiry of the limitation period to bring an action[45].

Significantly, the Commission relied on that judgment in its 2008 White Paper on damages actions for breach of the EC antitrust rules,[46] when considering proposals for policy choices and specific measures that would ensure that all victims of infringements of EC competition law have better access to effective redress mechanisms. As far as limitation periods are concerned, the Commission proposed that, in the case of a continuous or repeated infringement, the limitation period should not start to run before the day on which the infringement ceases and before the victim of the infringement can reasonably be excepted to have knowledge of the infringement and of the harm it caused him.[47] The relation between this perspective and the allocation of Commission

[44] Joined Cases C-295/04 to C-298/04 *Manfredi and Others* [2006] ECR I-6619.

[45] *Ibid* paras 78 and 79.

[46] White Paper on Damages Actions for Breach of the EC antitrust rules, COM (2008) 165 2/4/2008.

[47] It must be noted that the latter condition contrasts with the EC case-law relating to action for damages brought before the Community judge on the basis of Art 288(2) EC. In that context, it has been held that the argument that the limitation period cannot begin until the victim has specific and detailed knowledge of the facts of the case is misconceived, since knowledge of the facts is not one of the conditions which must be met in order for the limitation period to run. In fact, the function of the limitation period is to reconcile protection of the rights of the aggrieved person and the principle of legal certainty. The length of the limitation period was thus determined by taking into account, in particular, the time that the party who has allegedly suffered harm needs to gather the appropriate information for the purpose of a possible action and to verify the facts likely to provide the basis of that action (Case C-136/01 P *Autosalone Ispra dei Fratelli Rossi v Commission* [2002] ECR I-6565

*Cont.*

resources appears when considering the Commission's suggestion as to the incidence of ongoing public enforcement on limitation periods concerning private actions.

Even if the Commission considered the possibility that the limitation periods applicable to private actions might simply be suspended from the date proceedings are instituted by the Commission or any of the EU national competition authorities, it eventually disregarded this option for three main reasons. Firstly, the opening of proceedings by competition authorities is rarely known by the public, which would make it difficult for them to calculate the period that remains once the competition authority has dealt with the case. Secondly, some competition authorities do not formally close proceedings, or do not make the closing of proceedings publicly known, with the consequence that claimants would not know when the remaining part of the limitation starts running again. It is submitted that none of these two obstacles would be insurmountable. Thus, the decisive element seems to have been the third one put forward by the Commission, namely the difficulties that could emerge in cases where suspension commences at a very late stage, when the limitation period has almost expired.

According to the Commission, after the conclusion of administrative proceedings, there might not be enough time left to prepare the claim. This would most often be the case where the power of the Commission to impose fines is time-barred by virtue of Regulation No 1/2003. The alternative option, which has the Commission's preference, would avoid this risk. It would consist of allowing a new two-year limitation period to start following the final infringement decision of a competition authority or, if challenged before a court, the date of the judicial review decisions. If this option were to be retained, it would mean that despite its sanctioning power being time-barred, the Commission could adopt and make public a decision finding an infringement of Articles 81 EC and 82 EC, virtually at any time since the *Sumitomo Chemical and Sumika Fine Chemicals v Commission* case[48] made it clear that no limitation period applied in that case. On the basis of such a decision, a private action could be brought before national competent jurisdictions within a two-year period. In that situation, undertakings having taken part in a cartel would, in reality, never be sheltered from having to answer for their wrongdoings, and the 'right to oblivion' which underpins the notion of limitation period would partly be deprived of its essence.

However, for the time-being, the question remains whether this possibility to allow private parties to bring civil proceedings would, in itself, justify a legitimate interest for the Commission to find an infringement after its power

paras 28 and 31, and Case T-140/04 *Ehcon v Commission* [2005] ECR II-3287 paras 57 and 58). This argument has however exceptionally been endorsed in Case 145/83 *Adams v Commission* [1985] ECR 3539 paras 50 and 51, where the ECJ, due to the specific circumstances of the case, noted that the applicant was prevented from bringing proceedings within a reasonable time because he only belatedly became aware of the event giving rise to the damage, so that the expiry of the limitation period had to be fixed at a date later than the normal date of expiry of that period.

[48] See n 9 above, paras 133–136.

to impose a fine has run out. In fact, whilst declaring that the power to find an infringement was not subject to the EC limitation periods rules, in the *Sumitomo Chemical and Sumika Fine Chemicals v Commission* case[49] the CFI nonetheless annulled the Commission decision since it held that the Commission had not sufficiently explained the legitimate interest in adopting such a decision, this being a condition for the Commission to make finding pursuant to the *GVL v Commission* case.[50] This lack of reasoning was held to amount to an error of law justifying, in itself, the annulment of the decision.

It results from the rest of the CFI's reasoning that the obligation bearing on the Commission is not only a formal one, but that the EC judge will scrutinise whether the justifications put forward by the Commission are sufficient to establish a legitimate interest. Thus, the CFI considered that the arguments of the Commission had not demonstrated the existence of such a legitimate interest, and required that this demonstration be done concretely and specifically.[51] Indications as to the elements which could justify the Commission interest were given by the CFI, namely the need to promote exemplary behaviour on the part of the undertakings, the interest in discouraging any repeat infringement, and the interest in enabling the injured parties to bring matters before the national civil courts. As far as the latter objective is concerned, the CFI however that the Commission had not given any indication, relating to the particular circumstances of the case, of legal proceedings undertaken or even capable of being envisaged by third parties injured by the infringements. It went even further in underlining that, on the contrary, the applicant even raised the question whether the desire to assist in the bringing of proceedings before national courts was in itself debatable, and that the Commission had not responded in detail to this objection.[52] Formally, therefore, the very principle whether the Commission can find an infringement with the sole purpose of helping private parties in their damages actions is thus not yet settled. Even if that principle was to be admitted, it seems that the CFI is willing to put limits to the powers I has granted to the Commission to find infringements of EC competition rules irrespective of limitation periods. However, this raises the question of the type of review, full or limited,[53] it should exercise in this regard.

### *Recidivism*

As set out above, the objective to avoid recidivism could, pursuant to the *Sumitomo Chemical and Sumika Fine Chemicals v Commission* case,[54] constitute a legitimate interest in finding an infringement despite the fining power of

[49] *Ibid.*
[50] See n 41 above.
[51] Joined Cases T-22/02 and T-23/02 *Sumitomo Chemical and Sumika Fine Chemicals v Commission*, n 9 above, para 138.
[52] *Ibid* para 139.
[53] In this regard, see Zivy, n 42 above.
[54] See n 9 above.

the Commission being time-barred.[55] Implicitly, this statement relies on the assumption that the Commission is entitled to take into consideration, when fining an undertaking for taking part in an infringement, the circumstance that the same undertaking was found to have taken part in an earlier similar infringement in respect of which the Commission's powers to impose fines were time-barred.[56]

While such a possibility could not be envisaged in legal systems where limitation periods are applicable not only to the sanctioning powers of the public authorities but also to their decisions finding an infringement,[57] it is consistent with the EC rules on limitation periods, as interpreted by the case-law, that a definitive decision solely finding an infringement may be the basis for aggravating the sanction of a later similar infringement. The ECJ unambiguously laid down this principle in *Groupe Danone v Commission*,[58] where it ruled that the CFI, in regard to the characteristics of the appellant's previous conduct, correctly noted that the concept of repeated infringement does not necessarily imply that a fine has been imposed in the past, but merely that a finding of infringement of Community law has been made in the past.

It results from the preceding developments that the power to find an infringement is not subject to a limitation period, on the condition that the Commission establishes a legitimate interest in so doing. Nevertheless, the question arises whether, should the Commission have adopted such a finding decision, the power to take this element into consideration for the purposes

[55] Concerning recidivism, the CFI did not provide substantial details as to the kind of evidence the general requirement that the legitimate interest in finding the infringement be established in concrete and specific terms would imply. The CFI simply stated that the Commission has adduced no evidence whatsoever of the risk of recidivism on the part of the applicants. It is submitted that, because of its hypothetical nature, such a risk can hardly be evidenced in terms other than speculative. The burden of proof bearing on the Commission will thus greatly depend on the type of control that the CFI intends to exercise in this regard.

[56] In this regard, it is worth noting that the conditions concerning the characteristics of the infringements for there to be a case of recidivism are broadly defined. Thus, in Joined Cases T-101/05 and T-111/05 *BASF and UCB v Commission* [2007] ECR II-4949, the CFI rejected at the outset the applicant's argument that a case of repeated infringement can be recognised only where the infringements relate to the same product market. The CFI considered that it is sufficient that the Commission is dealing with infringements falling under the same provision of the EC Treaty (para 64). This definition seems even wider than that provided for either in the 1998 Commission Guidelines on the method of setting fines imposed pursuant to Article 15(2) of Regulation No 17 and Article 65(5) of the ECSC Treaty [1998] OJ C/9/3, or the 2006 Commission Guidelines on the method of setting fines imposed pursuant to Article 23(2)(a) of Regulation No 1/2003 [2006] OJ C/210/2. Whilst the former Guidelines refers to 'repeated infringement of the same type by the same undertaking(s)', the latter could be interpreted as more restrictive in referring to the situation 'where an undertaking continues or repeats the same or a similar infringement after the Commission or a national competition authority has made a finding that the undertaking infringed Articles 81 and 82'.

[57] Which implies that the definition of recidivism refers to a penalty sentence. In this regard, it can be noted that, before the *Sumitomo Chemical and Sumika Fine Chemicals v Commission* case (see n 9 above), the CFI held that the concept of repeated infringement, as understood in certain legal systems, implies that a person has committed new infringements *after having been penalised* for similar infringements (emphasis added, Case T-141/94 *ThyssenStahl v Commission* [1999] ECR II-347 para 617, and Case T-203/01 *Michelin v Commission* [2003] ECR II-4071 para 284).

[58] Case C-3/06 P *Groupe Danone v Commission* [2007] ECR I-1331 para 41. See also T-38/02 *Groupe Danone v Commission* [2005] ECR II-4407.

of establishing recidivism would itself be subject to a limitation period or not. Here again, the approach of the EC was determined by the necessity to ensure a high deterrent effect for the Commission decision, such an objective being the very rationale of maintaining such a power for the Commission even though its sanctioning power is extinguished. In the absence of any explicit rule governing the matter, this approach also revealed a willingness to preserve the Commission's power of appraisal in exercising its power to impose fines, in compliance with constant case-law. Indeed, confirming the CFI position, the ECJ ruled in *Groupe Danone v Commission*[59] that the finding and the appraisal of the specific characteristics of a repeated infringement come within the Commission's discretion and that the Commission cannot be bound by any limitation when making such a finding. In order to come to this conclusion, the ECJ relied on the discretion conferred by the case-law to the Commission as regards the choice of factors to be taken into account for the purposes of determining the amount of fines and on the consideration that the purpose of taking repeated infringement into account is to induce undertakings which have demonstrated a tendency towards infringing competition rules to change their conduct. The objective of ensuring that a decision finding an infringement has a dissuasive effect thus superseded the 'right to oblivion' of the undertakings concerned.

The implications of the foregoing can prove significant as regards the calculation of the amount of a fine. According to paragraph 28 of the 2006 Commission Guidelines on the method of setting fines,[60] the basic amount of a fine can be increased by up to 100 % for each previous infringement established. Thus, in reality, through this mechanism, the Commission regains ex post the power to impose fines it has lost in respect of a time-barred infringement. Whilst this can be analysed as offering the Commission, together with the facilitation of private actions, another way to escape the application of limitation periods, it must however be noted that, contrary to the facilitation of private actions scenario mentioned above, in this case the resurrection of the Commission's power depends solely on the subsequent behaviour of the undertaking in question.

Nevertheless, if the passing of time were not to have any incidence on the extent to which the Commission may take account of recidivism, this might give rise to undesirable consequences. From a practical point of view, with the passing of time, undertakings often undergo multiple structural changes through transfers and acquisitions. This gives rise to the question of which undertaking(s) is liable to be considered responsible for recidivism. From a principled point of view, there is a risk of alienating the concept of recidivism from its underlying purpose, which is the idea that a person renewing a infringement for which it had previously been sentenced deserves a more severe sanction because it knew the consequences of its acts and showed a tendency not to take account of previous sanctions. Indeed, this idea relies on the assumption that this person

[59] *Ibid* para 38.
[60] See n 56 above.

is endowed with a memory, which, in the case of undertakings, can be held true during a certain period of time, but, arguably, not indefinitely, since their staff is constantly renewed and, contrary to natural persons, their life duration is, theoretically, unlimited.[61] The notion of recidivism, initially based on subjective and intent-oriented considerations, would thus undergo an objectivisation.

In this regard, some elements in the case-law indicate that recidivism may not be wholly preserved from the incidence of time. Thus, in *Groupe Danone v Commission*,[62] the ECJ indicated that the Commission *may*, in each individual case, take into consideration the time that has elapsed between the infringements in question. It is true that it did not compel the Commission to do so. However, the ECJ explicitly underlined that the CFI rightly established the history of the infringements of competition rules found against the applicant, and stated that '*on each occasion a relatively short time, namely less than ten years, had elapsed* between infringements' (emphasis added). The ECJ then agreed with the CFI's conclusion that the repetition of unlawful conduct by Groupe Danone demonstrated a tendency on its part not to draw the appropriate conclusions from a finding of infringement.[63] Moreover, interestingly, the ECJ expressly referred to point 30 of the Opinion of Advocate General Poiares Maduro in the same case, according to which 'the Commission and the Community Courts *must* consider the factors confirming such a tendency, including the time that has elapsed between infringements'.[64] This discrepancy (that is the use of 'may' in the ECJ judgment and 'must' in the Opinion of the Advocate General referred to in the judgment), together with the examination carried out by the ECJ at paragraph 40 of the *Groupe Danone v Commission* judgment, leave it unclear whether the ECJ intended to impose an obligation to take account of the duration of the period between the infringements, which would practically amount to imposing an indirect limitation period on recidivism.

In this regard, it is, in conclusion, worth noting that, in *BASF and UCB v Commission*,[65] the CFI, whilst confirming the finding of recidivism made by the Commission, expressed its unease in taking into account ancient infringements. In fact, the Commission had taken into consideration as elements of recidivism two separate infringements which had taken place between 1964 and 1967, and between 1980 and 1984. Significantly, after recalling the *Groupe Danone*

[61] In the same vein, Advocate General Poiares Maduro insisted, in his Opinion in Case C-3/06 P *Groupe Danone v* Commission, n 58 above, that '[t]he principle of legal certainty does not require a limitation period for repeated infringement. The Commission consequently has a certain discretion in determining the period over which it will take previous findings of infringements into account. However, particularly in view of the potentially extensive lifespan of undertakings, the Commission must exercise that discretion in a way that observes reasonable expectations about which past infringements are still of relevance and which infringements have to all intents and purposes been expunged' (point 29).

[62] See n 58 above, para 39.

[63] *Ibid* para 40.

[64] Among the other linguistic versions of the Opinion of Advocate General Poiares Maduro that have been examined (German, Portuguese, Spanish, Italian and French), only the French one refers to a possibility ('peuvent') and not to an obligation.

[65] See n 56 above, paras 64 *ff*.

*v Commission* judgment[66] on the absence of limitation periods applying to recidivism, the CFI ignored the older infringement and held that the latter of those two infringements can in itself justify the application of an increase of 50 % to the basic amount of the fine imposed on BASF. Furthermore, the CFI, in the exercise of its unlimited jurisdiction (by which it is entitled to take into consideration any additional information it deems appropriate), felt appropriate to underline, on its own initiative, that BASF had also been the object of Commission Decision 86/398/EEC of 23 April 1986 for participating in agreements and concerted practices between the end of 1978 or the beginning of 1979 and November 1983.

*

It results from the above that the cases where an undertaking is in a position to benefit from the operation of limitation periods on the Commission's powers will be few, especially if one takes into account the incentive given to undertakings, by the leniency notice,[67] to reveal as soon as possible their participation in an infringement of EC competition law. It does not mean, however, that the Community judge will not scrutinise potential negligence of the Commission, as exemplified by the requirement that its acts be necessary for the adoption of the decision in order to have an interruptive effect or that it demonstrates its legitimate interest in adopting a decision finding an infringement after extinguishment of its powers to impose penalties. This obligation imposed on the Commission to act in compliance with the principle of good administration is also the cornerstone of the principle of reasonable delay.

## THE PASSING OF TIME AND THE RIGHT NOT TO BE FORGOTTEN: THE PRINCIPLE OF REASONABLE DELAY

According to settled case-law, compliance with the reasonable time requirement in the conduct of administrative procedures relating to competition policy constitutes a general principle of Community law whose observance the Community judicature ensures.[68] Contrary to the mechanism of limitation periods, through the principle of reasonable delay, a defendant in administrative proceedings will not seek to escape a sanction due to the passing of time between the infringement and the action of the public authority, but it will request that the judge sanctions the excessive slowness of the Commission's action once it has been undertaken. Since both notions pertain to the effect of time passing and thus have been concomitantly relied upon by applicants, the EC judge has been confronted with the need to make a distinction between them. It will be seen that this distinction combined with the strict conditions to be fulfilled in order

[66] See n 58 above.

[67] Commission notice on immunity from fines and reduction of fines in cartel cases [2006] OJ C/298/17.

[68] Case C-105/04 P *Nederlandse Federatieve Vereniging voor de Groothandel op Elektrotechnisch Gebied v Commission* [2006] ECR I-8725 para 35.

to trigger the application of the principle of reasonable delay might diminish the effectiveness of this principle.

## The Distinction between Limitation Periods and the Principle of Reasonable Delay

The respective applicability of these two legal concepts was first defined in the *CMA CGM and Others v Commission* judgment,[69] and confirmed more recently in the *Hoechst v Commission*[70] and *Compagnie Maritime Belge v Commission*[71] judgments. In essence, the CFI recalled that the objective of the introduction of limitation periods was to ensure legal certainty. It further noted that, as far as the Commission's powers to fine and to enforce its decisions are concerned, Regulation No 2988/74 establishes a complete system of rules covering in detail the periods within which the Commission is entitled, without undermining the fundamental requirement of legal certainty, to impose fines on undertakings which are the subject of procedures under the Community competition rules. In particular, taking into account the overall ten-year limitation period, the CFI held that the Commission cannot put off a decision on fines indefinitely without incurring the risk of the limitation period expiring. It thus concluded that there is no room for consideration of the Commission's duty to exercise its power to impose fines within a reasonable period. According to the CFI, whilst the unreasonable length of a procedure, particularly where it infringes the rights of defence of the parties concerned, justifies the annulment of a decision establishing an infringement of the rules of competition, the same does not apply where what is disputed is the amount of the fines imposed by that decision, since limitation periods are set out for that purpose.

This formal reasoning seems to be based on the assumption that the principle of reasonable delay cannot, by its nature, be breached where the Commission acts within the limitation periods, and to grant to the principle of reasonable delay a merely subsidiary character. Another analysis would, however, be conceivable. As it has been set out above, limitation periods are a mechanism by which the Commission loses its powers because of its objective failure, due to negligence or ignorance, to act within a strictly defined time-frame, with a view, inter alia, to avoiding the risk of unreliable findings based upon old and uncertain facts. It is thus a rule related to the notion of competence, and deriving essentially from the principle of legal certainty. On its part, the principle of reasonable delay gives rise to a requirement that the Commission adopt its decisions within an acceptable timeframe, depending on the circumstances of each case, with a view to avoiding that the persons concerned by the decisions in question, that is, the

[69] See n 26 above, paras 317–326.

[70] Case T-410/03 *Hoechst v Commission*, judgment of 18 June 2008 nyr, paras 219–224.

[71] See n 18 above, paras 39–48. For a critical comment of this judgment, see L Idot, 'Reprise d'une décision annulée' (2008) 8 *Europe* 25.

undertakings subject to the enquiry but also third parties such as complainants potentially harmed by the infringement, do not suffer from an excessively long period of uncertainty due to the negligence of the administration. It is thus a rule flowing from the principle of good administration.[72]

Considering the effect of the limitation period, that is the impossibility for the Commission to adopt a decision imposing penalties, by hypothesis, the question whether action by the Commission will be compliant with the reasonable delay principle can only arise where this action is not time-barred. In that sense, the application of this principle can be analysed as an expression of the abuse of rights theory: although the Commission is, from a temporal point of view, on the basis of the applicable limitation period, entitled to adopt the decision at stake, it could still find itself in a situation where it exceeds its power if it does not act within the delay that one could reasonably expect, in the circumstances of the case, from a normally diligent administration.

In addition, it is worth noting that, as a consequence of the reasoning in the *CMA CGM and Others v Commission*, *Hoechst v Commission* and *Compagnie Maritime Belge v Commission* cases,[73] though an applicant is primarily conferred a guarantee – the right not to be fined for time-barred infringements – such applicant ends up being deprived of the possibility to rely on a higher ranked principle – the principle of reasonable delay. Indeed, in the *Sumitomo Chemical and Sumika Fine Chemicals v Commission* judgment,[74] the CFI stated clearly that 'limitation itself does not constitute a general principle of law', contrary to the principle of reasonable delay, which has been defined by the ECJ and the CFI itself since 1997[75] as a general principle of Community law.

A possible way to understand the solution retained by the CFI as to the respective applicability of these two principles is to consider that the rules on limitation set out in competition matters constitute a *lex specialis* of the principle of reasonable delay.

As it seems to result from the case-law that, as far EC competition law infringements are concerned,[76] the objective of limitation is essentially, if not exclusively, to ensure legal certainty, the principle of reasonable delay may

[72] As underlined by the CFI in Case T-67/01 *JCB Service v Commission* [2004] ECR II-49 para 36, where it held that the principle that the Commission must act within a reasonable time 'is incorporated, as an element of the right to good administration, in Article 41(1) of the Charter of fundamental rights of the European Union proclaimed in Nice on 7 December 2000 [2000] OJ C/364/1. Accordingly, while it is not necessary to rule on the applicability as such of Art 6(1) of the ECHR to administrative proceedings before the Commission relating to competition policy, it must be considered whether, in the present case, the Commission has breached the general principle of Community law that decisions must be adopted within a reasonable time in the procedure leading to the adoption of the contested decision'.

[73] See ns 26, 70 and 18 above.

[74] See n 9 above, para 98.

[75] Joined Cases T-213/95 and T-18/96 *SCK and FNK v Commission* [1997] ECR II-1739 para 56.

[76] See Case T-213/00 *CMA CGM and Others v Commission*, n 26 above, para 324; Case T-276/04 *Compagnie Maritime Belge v Commission*, n 18 above, para 223, and Case T-410/03 *Hoechst v Commission*, n 70 above, para 43. In particular, in the latter case, the CFI held that Reg 2988/74 expressly takes account of the need to ensure legal certainty, specifically by the introduction of the principle of a limitation period.

serve the same purpose, but in a general context. Such a statement, however, is quite difficult to reconcile with the *JCB Service v Commission* judgment,[77] where the principle of reasonable delay has been described as 'incorporated, as an element of the right to good administration, in Article 41(1) of the Charter of fundamental rights of the European Union'.

The reasoning adopted by the CFI in the *CMA CGM and Others v Commission, Hoechst v Commission* and *Compagnie Maritime Belge v Commission* judgments reveals another peculiarity. Indeed, following the approach taken by the CFI in those cases, the principle of reasonable delay is applicable only where no limitation periods are imposed on the powers of the Commission. Thus, since limitation periods do not apply to the Commission's power to find an infringement (as opposed to the powers to impose and execute fines), if an applicant cannot rely on the principle of reasonable delay in support of its claim for annulment or reduction of the fines imposed to it, it can invoke this principle in order to have the contested decision annulled as a whole.[78] One could argue that this can lead to artificial results, since, first, the examination of a plea drawn from a breach of the principle of reasonable delay will depend on the claim as formally expressed by the applicant[79] and, second, a claim for annulment of a decision, if successful, would ultimately, anyway, lead to the cancellation of the fine imposed.

However, one can only welcome the fact that, as such, the principle of reasonable delay may, at least, constitute a restriction on the statement made in the *Sumitomo Chemical and Sumika Fine Chemicals v Commission* judgment,[80] according to which the Commission's powers to find an infringement is not subject to any limitation period. The reasoning advanced in response to the plea based on the principle of legal certainty confirms this interpretation. Indeed, in that judgment, the CFI noted that, whilst it is not for the Community Courts to fix the time-limits, scope or detailed rules for the application of the limitation period in respect of an infringement, it is however clear from the case-law of the ECJ that the absence of legislative limitation does not preclude censure of the Commission's action, in a specific case, in the light of the principle of legal

[77] Case T-67/01 *JCB Service v Commission*, n 72 above.

[78] See Case T-213/00 *CMA CGM and Others v Commission*, n 26 above, para 321.

[79] Furthermore, in Case T-276/04 *Compagnie Maritime Belge v Commission*, n 18 above, although the applicant had formally raised a plea seeking the annulment of the contested decision, the CFI noted that, in reality, this plea sought the annulment of the fine imposed by that decision. Indeed, it considered that since the contested decision was aimed exclusively at imposing on the applicant, on the basis of infringements strictly identical to those established in a previous decision contested by the applicants and annulled by the ECJ, a new fine, the amount of which was lower than that of the initial fine annulled, and, second, at correcting the procedural flaws identified in that judgment, the contested decision was to be analysed exclusively as a decision imposing a fine, and not as a decision finding an infringement. In effect, the CFI took the view that the abuses had been definitively established by the Commission in the parts of the previous decision that were not annulled by the ECJ. Consequently, the CFI went even further than in previous case-law, and required that, for the principle of reasonable delay to be applicable, the applicant not only seek the annulment of the contested decision, but also be entitled to claim such an annulment.

[80] See n 9 above, paras 80–91.

certainty. In addition, the CFI recalled that, according to the ECJ, in the absence of any provision laying down a limitation period, the fundamental requirement of legal certainty has the effect of preventing the Commission from indefinitely delaying the exercise of its powers.

Accordingly, the Community judicature, when examining a complaint alleging that the Commission's action was carried out too late, must not merely find that no limitation period exists, but must satisfy itself that the Commission did not act excessively late.

Nevertheless, the CFI underlined that the Commission cannot be regarded as having acted excessively late if there is no delay or other negligent act imputable to it and that account should be taken in particular of the time when the institution became aware of the acts constituting the infringement and of the reasonableness of the duration of the administrative procedure. In the case at issue, it was considered that the delay in the Commission's action had not been caused by negligence on the part of the Commission in initiating or completing the administrative procedure, but by the mere and actual passing of time from the cessation of infringements, it not being alleged that the Commission was aware, or even could and should have been aware of them, at a time which would have enabled it to act sooner. In the CFI's view, there was nothing in the chronology of the facts to suggest that the procedure was unreasonably long, and, therefore, it concluded that the applicant had not proved any infringement of the principle of legal certainty.[81]

Notwithstanding the conclusions above, certain elements of the ruling may allow to consider that the position of the Community courts concerning the relationship between the principle of reasonable delay and limitation periods is not yet definitively settled. Indeed, firstly, the ECJ, in its ruling on appeal brought by the Commission against the *CMA CGM and Others v Commission* judgment, did not tackle this issue.[82] Secondly, in the *Hoechst v Commission* judgment,[83] whilst rejecting the applicant's argument based on the inapplicability of the principle of reasonable delay, the CFI nonetheless made the effort to underline that the conditions for the establishment of a breach of the reasonable delay principle were not fulfilled in the present case. Thirdly, in the *Compagnie Maritime Belge v Commission* judgment,[84] the CFI exceptionally took into account, in the part of its judgment relating to costs, the fact that the Commission delayed reopening the administrative procedure, and carried out an analysis almost suggesting a breach of the principle of reasonable delay. Thus, it noted that some 37 months had elapsed between the delivery of the judgment

[81] It is worth noting that this reasoning gives support to the interpretation proposed above, according to which, in the CFI's view, the principle of reasonable delay in competition proceedings tends to ensure legal certainty. Indeed, whilst obviously examining whether the applicants had shown that the duration of the proceedings had been unreasonable, thus referring to the principle of reasonable delay, the CFI concluded that there was no infringement of the principle of legal certainty.

[82] Order of 28 October 2004 in Case C-236/03 P *Commission v CMA CGM and Others* unreported. See n 26 above.

[83] See n 70 above, paras 227 and 228.

[84] See n 18 above, paras 142–145.

of ECJ annulling the first decision and the issue of the statement of objections. As the Commission did not reopen the procedure concerning the establishment of the infringements, the drafting of the statement of objections, a document of only 12 pages, was not a major task. The CFI also noted that that delay, for which no convincing explanation had been provided and which led the Commission to reduce of its own initiative the amount of the fine by 150,000 euros, was wholly attributable to the Commission. Therefore, although the action was dismissed, the Commission was condemned to bear one third of its costs and to pay one third of the costs incurred by the applicant.

Those last two elements could thus be interpreted as an expression of a certain discomfort of the CFI in relation to this issue, especially if one considers that the Commission itself, on its own initiative, has, on several occasions, granted a reduction of the fine imposed because of the length of the procedure. It remains however the case that, for the time being, the CFI's position on the respective applicability of the rules on limitation and the principle of reasonable delay results in a significant reduction of the scope of the latter principle as far as EC competition law administrative proceedings are concerned.

## The Conditions and Consequences of a Breach of the Principle of Reasonable Delay

The reasonable character of the duration of proceedings is, by its very nature, a subjective notion, depending on numerous factors particular to each case. The necessity to adopt a case-by-case approach was established by the CFI in its first case applying the principle of reasonable delay in competition law proceedings. Directly referring to the case-law of the European Court of Human Rights, the CFI stated, in the *SCK and FNK v Commission* judgment,[85] that the question whether the duration of an administrative proceeding is reasonable must be determined in relation to the particular circumstances of each case and, in particular, its context, the various procedural stages followed by the Commission, the conduct of the parties in the course of the procedure, the complexity of the case and its importance for the various parties involved.[86] Shortly after, the ECJ followed a similar approach, in dealing with a plea based on the alleged breach of the principle of reasonable delay in proceedings before the CFI, in its *Baustahlgewebe v Commission* judgment.[87]

[85] See n 75 above, para 57.

[86] See, by analogy, the judgments of the European Court of Human Rights *Erkner and Hofauer v Austria* Series A No 117 (1987) 62 EHRR 66, *Milasi v Italy* Series A No 119 (1986) 46 EHRR 15. Interestingly, this subjective approach is mitigated by the fact that, according to the ECJ, 'where appropriate, the duration of a procedural stage may be regarded as reasonable from the outset if it appears to be consistent with the average time taken in handling a case of its type', which introduces an objective criterion of general application (Joined Cases C-238/99 P, C-244/99 P, C-245/99 P, C-247/99 P, C-250/99 P to C-252/99 P and C-254/99 P *Limburgse Vinyl Maatschappij and Others v Commission* [2002] ECR I-8375 para 188).

[87] See n 14 above, para 29. See T-145/89 *Baustahlgewebe v Commission* [1995] ECR II-987.

As far as EC competition law proceedings are concerned, the preliminary question which had to be settled is that of the different procedural steps which must be taken into consideration and, consequently, are submitted to the requirement, for the Commission, to act within a reasonable delay. According to the case-law of the European Court of Human Rights relating to criminal matters, the relevant time runs from the time at which a person is charged, whereas, in administrative matters, it runs from the day of the final administrative decision or from the day the administrative action is brought against this decision if such an action is required before seizing the competent jurisdiction.[88]

In this regard, the CFI held, in its *Limburgse Vinyl Maatschappij and Others v Commission*[89] judgment (hereinafter *LVM v Commission* judgment), that, in order to determine whether the administrative procedure before the Commission was reasonable, a distinction must be made between the procedural stage opened with the investigations, based on Article 14 of Regulation No 17, and the procedural stage which starts on the date of receipt of notification of the statement of objections by the undertakings concerned. The CFI assessed these two steps in turn, the standard applicable to each of them not being the same. Indeed, the CFI underlined in this judgment that, as far as the procedural stage which started on the date of receipt of notification of the statement of objections is concerned, the criterion relating to what is at stake for the undertakings involved is of particular importance. Firstly, the notification of the statement of objections in a procedure for establishing an infringement presupposes the initiation of the procedure under Article 3 of Regulation No 17, by which the Commission evidences its intention to proceed to a decision finding an infringement. Secondly, it is only on receipt of the statement of objections that an undertaking may take cognisance of the subject-matter of the procedure which is initiated against it and of the conduct of which it is accused by the Commission. Undertakings thus have a specific interest in that second stage of the procedure being conducted with particular diligence by the Commission, without, however, affecting their rights of defence.

This reasoning was confirmed by the ECJ on appeal,[90] which considered that each of those two stages has its own internal logic. According to the ECJ, the first stage, covering the period up to notification of the statement of objections, begins on the date on which the Commission, exercising the powers conferred on it by Articles 11 and 14 of Regulation No 17 in the context of a preliminary investigation, takes measures involving a complaint that an infringement has been committed and having a significant impact on the situation of the suspected undertakings.[91] This stage must enable the Commission, after investigation, to

[88] Judgments of the European Court of Human Rights *König v Slovakia* Series A No 27 (1978) EHRR 98, and *Erkner and Hofauer v Austria*, n 86 above, 64.

[89] Joined Cases T-305/94 to T-307/94, T-313/94 to T-316/94, T-318/94, T-325/94, T-328/94, T-329/94 and T-335/94 *Limburgse Vinyl Maatschappij and Others v Commission* [1999] ECR II-931 para 124.

[90] Joined Cases C-238/99 P, C-244/99 P, C-245/99 P, C-247/99 P, C-250/99 P to C-252/99 P and C-254/99 P *Limburgse Vinyl Maatschappij and Others v Commission*, n 86 above.

[91] See, to that effect, with respect to a preliminary investigation in a criminal case, the judgments of the European Court of Human Rights of 16 July 1971 *Ringeisen v Austria* Series A No 13 (1974) 40 EHRR 110, and of 22 May 1998 *Hozee v Netherlands* No III (1998) 1091 EHRR 43.

adopt a position on the course which the procedure is to follow. The second stage covers the period from notification of the statement of objections to adoption of the final decision. It must enable the Commission to reach a final decision on the alleged infringement.

Surprisingly, the CFI followed a quite different approach in a later case, *Nederlandse Federatieve Vereniging voor de Groothandel op Elektrotechnisch Gebied and Technische Unie v Commission*[92] (hereinafter *FEG v Commission*), where it held that the excessive duration of the investigation phase of the administrative procedure is not in itself such as to detract from the rights of defence. Referring to the Opinion of Advocate General Mischo in the *LVM v Commission* appeal judgment,[93] and on the *Corigliano* judgment[94] of the European Court of Human Rights, the CFI considered that it is necessary, for the purposes of applying the principle of reasonable delay, to draw a distinction between the investigative phase prior to the statement of objections and the remainder of the administrative procedure. In that connection, the CFI observed, firstly, that, in criminal matters the reasonable time referred to in Article 6(1) of the European Convention for the Protection of Human Rights and Fundamental Freedoms (ECHR) signed at Rome on 4 November 1950 runs from the moment a person is charged and, second, that the fundamental rights guaranteed by the ECHR are protected as general principles of Community law. According to the CFI, in a procedure relating to Community competition policy, of the kind at issue, the persons concerned are not the subject of any formal accusation until they receive the statement of objections. Consequently, the CFI considered that the prolongation, even if excessive, of this stage of the procedure alone was not in itself capable of adversely affecting the rights of defence. Such an approach would have substantially reduced the scope of the principle of reasonable delay, confining its applicability to the sole period subsequent to the statement of objection.

The judgment of the CFI was quashed by the ECJ on this aspect in *Nederlandse Federatieve Vereniging voor de Groothandel op Elektrotechnisch Gebied v Commission* (hereinafter *FEG v Commission* appeal judgment).[95] In fact, the ECJ considered that the CFI wrongly ignored the fact that the excessive duration of the investigation stage might have an effect on the applicant's exercise of its rights of defence during the second phase of the administrative procedure. The ECJ underlined in this regard that the more time that elapses between measures of investigation, the more unlikely it becomes that exculpatory evidence relating to the infringements set out in the statement of objections can be obtained,

[92] Joined Cases T-5/00 and T-6/00 *Nederlandse Federatieve Vereniging voor de Groothandel op Elektrotechnisch Gebied und Technische Unie v Commission* [2003] ECR II-5761.

[93] See n 86 above.

[94] Judgment of the European Court of Human Rights *Corigliano v Italy* Series A No 57 (1982) EHRR 34.

[95] See n 68 above, paras 44 *ff*. See E Barbier de la Serre, 'Conséquences du délai excessif de la procédure administrative' [2007] 10 *Revue Lamy de la concurrence* 52; L Idot, 'Délai excessif de la procédure et droits de la défense' [2006 ]11 *Europe* 29, and F Zivy, 'Chronique Procédures' [2006] 4 *Concurrences* 115.

owing in particular to the changes that may have come about in the composition of the managing boards of the undertakings concerned and to the movements affecting their other staff.

The ECJ insisted that, since the respect of the rights of defence is of crucial importance in competition procedures, it is essential to prevent those rights from being irremediably compromised on account of the excessive duration of the investigation phase and to ensure that the duration of that phase does not impede the establishment of evidence designed to refute the existence of conduct susceptible of rendering the undertakings concerned liable. For that reason, examination of any interference with the exercise of the rights of the defence must not be confined to the actual phase in which those rights are fully effective, that is to say, the second phase of the administrative procedure. The assessment of the source of any undermining of the effectiveness of the rights of the defence must extend to the entire procedure and be carried out by reference to its total duration.[96]

In other words, although a reasonable delay can be assessed in respect of two separate periods corresponding to the two procedural stages defined by the CFI in the *LVM v Commission* judgment, the dividing point being the statement of objection, the question whether the excessive duration of one of the stages examined is liable to affect the rights of the defence of the applicant must be examined in respect of the whole period leading up to the final decision of the Commission. Thus, there is no presumption that the excessive duration of the first stage is incapable of breaching the rights of defence, even though such a breach can only manifest itself after the undertakings have been accused, that is, after they have received a statement of objections.

This is of particular importance since it determines the sanction applicable if the duration of administrative proceedings is found to be excessive. Indeed, it must be recalled that, according to constant case-law since the CFI *LVM v Commission* judgment,[97] infringement of the principle of reasonable delay, if established, would justify the annulment of the Commission decision only in so far as it also constituted an infringement of the rights of defence of the undertakings concerned. Where it has not been established that the undue delay has adversely affected the ability of the undertakings concerned to defend themselves effectively, failure to comply with the principle that the Commission must act within a reasonable time cannot affect the validity of the administrative procedure and can therefore be regarded only as a cause of damage capable of being relied on before the Community judicature in the context of an action based on Article 235 EC and the second paragraph of Article 288 EC.[98]

[96] *FEG v Commission* appeal judgment, n 68 above, paras 47–51.

[97] See n 89 above, para 122.

[98] This approach was confirmed by the ECJ in the *FEG v Commission* appeal judgment, n 68 above, para 43, where it held that '[i]t is perfectly lawful to make use of that criterion for the purpose of finding that there has been a breach of the 'reasonable time' principle. At paragraph 49 of the judgment in *Baustahlgewebe v Commission* the [ECJ] held, when evaluating the duration of the proceedings before the [CFI], that an indication that the length of the proceedings affected

*Cont.*

Whilst the necessity, for the undertaking concerned, to demonstrate a breach of its rights of defence due to the passing of time in order to obtain the annulment of the Commission decision seems legally unquestionable, it is a major obstacle to the effectiveness of the principle of reasonable delay in administrative proceedings. Indeed, the ECJ considered, in the *FEG v Commission* appeal judgment, referring to its *Baustahlgewebe v Commission* judgment,[99] that the excessive duration of the procedure before the Commission must entail the annulment of the contested decision if the undertaking's rights of defence have been compromised, in which case there is necessarily a possible effect on the outcome of the procedure. Thus, it seems that the undertaking is required to adduce evidence that, had the Commission acted within reasonable delay, the outcome of the decision would have been different.

One can anticipate that this is not an easy exercise. Particularly bearing in mind that the CFI considered, in the *FEG v Commission* judgment,[100] as regards the question of the loss of evidence because of the passage of time, that, by virtue of a general duty of care attaching to any undertaking or association of undertakings, the applicants are required to ensure the proper maintenance of records in their books or files of information enabling details of their activities to be retrieved, in order, in particular, to make the necessary evidence available in the event of legal or administrative proceedings. The CFI added that when the applicants received requests for information from the Commission under Article 11 of Regulation No 17, it was a fortiori incumbent on them to act with greater diligence and to take all appropriate measures in order to preserve such evidence as might reasonably be available to them.

This statement nearly amounts to a presumption that, where evidence disappears or deteriorates as a consequence of the passage of time, it is the responsibility of the undertaking concerned. In order to be able to validly claim the respect of the principle of reasonable delay by the Commission, an undertaking would consequently previously have to show that it has acted with care and diligence in so far as it has duly organised its defence.

Whilst not directly touching upon this issue on appeal, the ECJ implicitly rejected this approach, where it held, in its *FEG v Commission* appeal judgment,[101] that the more time elapses between a measure of investigation and the notification of the statement of objections, the more unlikely it becomes that exculpatory evidence relating to the infringements set out in the statement of objections can be obtained. The ECJ also gave indications as to the standard of proof required in this regard when, having set aside the CFI's judgment in so

their outcome may result in the judgment under appeal being set aside. The same approach is to be found in the reasoning followed by the [CFI] where it considered that the excessive duration of the procedure before the Commission must entail the annulment of the contested decision if the FEG's rights of defence have been compromised, in which case there is necessarily a possible effect on the outcome of the procedure'.

[99] See n 14 above, para 43.

[100] See n 92 above, para 87.

[101] See n 68 above, paras 49–58.

far as it determined that the prolongation of the first phase of the administrative procedure was not capable of adversely affecting the applicant's rights of defence, it gave final judgment in the matter. In particular, the ECJ, dealing with the applicant's arguments that, owing to the lapse of time, it found it increasingly difficult to obtain information from its management staff, noted that such arguments were theoretical and imprecise. It added that the applicant should have specified the persons who had worked at the company at the relevant time and whose departure prevented it from obtaining further information about the events to which the Commission's accusations related, the date on which they left, the nature and the scope of information or details which were necessary for its defence, or the circumstances which made it impossible to obtain testimony of those persons.

Admittedly, on the one hand, the standard of proof so established is demanding. It is nonetheless understandable, since there can be no assumption that any excessive duration of the Commission proceedings, even if regrettable in principle, might result in undermining a defendant's rights of defence. It is thus justified to require the claimant to bear the burden of proof in this respect, and to substantiate the specific circumstances of the case justifying the annulment of the contested decision. It is also legally coherent and in compliant with the necessity to take account of the general public interest and the interest of third parties (namely competitors, buyers, and end-users) to require that the undertaking concerned demonstrates, in order to escape a sanction, that this absence of due diligence is able to cast serious doubt on the very correctness of the conclusion reached by the Commission. On the other hand, the fact that the ECJ made the effort to provide concrete details as to the elements which should have been presented can be interpreted as showing willingness, in the future, where the circumstances allow, to sanction a breach of the principle of reasonable delay.

In the *FEG v Commission* appeal judgment,[102] the ECJ ultimately rejected the plea based upon a breach of the principle of reasonable delay, concluding that the applicant had not shown sufficient evidence of a breach of their right of defence resulting from the length of the proceedings. In order to obtain the annulment of a Commission decision, a mere breach of the principle of reasonable delay is thus not enough, for the reasons set out above. This could lead to the conclusion that, in fact, this principle is not an autonomous one, and needs to be combined with others, namely the rights of defence, in order to be applied. Given the high standard of proof required in order to obtain the annulment of a contested decision in such circumstances, and the fact that, as explained above, the CFI does not examine the issue of the excessive duration of the Commission's proceedings where a claimant merely requests reduction of the fines imposed, one could eventually question the real effectiveness of the principle of reasonable delay in EC competition law proceedings.

In addition to the interpretation given to the *FEG v Commission* appeal judgment and the ECJ's approach just mentioned, it is worth noting that in her

[102] *Ibid.*

Opinion in the same case, Advocate General Kokott[103] proposed as an alternative, should the ECJ not annul the CFI judgment and refer the case back to it, that the ECJ reduce the amount of the fine imposed to the appellant in consideration of the excessive duration of the Commission's proceedings. Interestingly, on this occasion, Advocate General Kokott did not examine a possible breach of the rights of defence, but simply referred to the fact that, when exercising its unlimited jurisdiction to review fines, the ECJ may also consider questions of expediency, appropriateness and fairness. She further noted that consideration must be given particularly to procedural defects, such as a breach of the principle that action must be taken within a reasonable period, which constitute an infringement of a fundamental right even if they have not affected the content of the Commission's decision and therefore do not lead to its annulment. Such a position is coherent both with paragraph 122 of the CFI *LVM v Commission* judgment[104] and with the solution adopted by the ECJ in the *Baustahlgewebe v Commission* judgment[105] where it held that in order to ensure an immediate and effective remedy regarding a procedural irregularity of that kind, it must be held that the plea alleging excessive duration of the proceedings before the CFI is well founded for the purposes of setting aside the contested judgment in so far as it set the amount of the fine imposed on the appellant.[106] In the latter judgment, the ECJ concluded however that in the absence of any indication that the length of the proceedings affected their outcome in any way, that plea cannot result in the contested judgment being set aside in its entirety.

The ECJ, in its *FEG v Commission* appeal judgment, did not provide an explicit echo, either negative or positive, to the proposal of Advocate General Kokott, confining itself, in four paragraphs, to noting that the Commission already took into consideration the excessive duration of the proceedings in reducing the amount of the fines, and that the applicants have produced no evidence to show why the ECJ should consider granting a further reduction. However, it is worth underlining that the ECJ did not simply content itself with ascertaining that the

[103] *Ibid* Opinion of Advocate General Kokott point 138.

[104] 'Where it has not been established that the undue delay has adversely affected the ability of the undertakings concerned to defend themselves effectively, failure to comply with the principle that the Commission must act within a reasonable time cannot affect the validity of the administrative procedure and can therefore be regarded only as a cause of damage capable of being relied on before the Community judicature in the context of an action based on Article 235 and the second paragraph of Article 288 of the Treaty'. See n 89 above.

[105] See n 14 above, paras 47 and 48.

[106] It could be argued that the *Baustahlgewebe v Commission* case, *ibid*, pertained to the question of the excessive duration of the judicial proceedings, as opposed to the administrative proceedings, and that the issues at stake might not be identical in both stages. In particular, the criterion of the undermining of the rights of defence might not be very relevant in the context of lengthy judicial proceedings, given the fact that, in the vast majority of cases, the CFI bases its judgment on elements which have been collected and argued preceding the action brought before it. As such, it is difficult to imagine circumstances other than very exceptional where a breach of the rights of defence may result from excessive duration of the judicial proceedings. Despite this apparent inadequacy, it remains that the ECJ seems to approach identically both types of proceedings. Thus, in the *FEG v Commission* appeal judgment, n 68 above, the ECJ confirmed the CFI's reasoning as to the conditions for obtaining annulment of the Commission decision by referring to its *Baustahlgewebe v Commission* judgment (para 49).

applicants failed to demonstrate a breach of their rights of defence so that, for the same reason, their claim for a reduction of the fine had to be rejected. Implicitly, this can be seen as leaving open the possibility for sanctioning a breach, during the administrative proceedings, of the principle of reasonable delay in an autonomous manner, that is, without resorting to the appraisal of a breach of the rights of defence. It is submitted that such a possibility would significantly reinforce the effectiveness of the principle of reasonable delay and therefore give a strong incentive to the Commission to act more rapidly. It could also be a way of clarifying the respective fields of application of the rules on limitation and the principle of reasonable delay, since, as exposed above, for the time-being, recent case-law of the CFI seems to exclude that a breach of the principle of reasonable delay might be invoked by an applicant to have its fine cancelled or reduced.

If such a possibility were eventually to be admitted, the question arises, as it has already arisen in relation to the excessive duration of judicial proceedings,[107] as to the appropriate way to compensate an undertaking for such a breach of the principle of the reasonable delay in cases in which this did not undermine its rights of defence. Two options can be envisaged in this respect. The first one consists, as proposed by Advocate General Kokott in *FEG v Commission*, in granting compensation through a reduction of the fine imposed by the Commission. Pursuant to Article 31 of Regulation No 1/2003, the ECJ and the CFI have unlimited jurisdiction to review decisions whereby the Commission has fixed a fine or periodic penalty payment, and may cancel, reduce or increase the fine or periodic penalty payment imposed. The reduction of the fine could thus simply be operated by resorting to the above-mentioned unlimited jurisdiction, similarly to what the ECJ decided in the *Baustahlgewebe v Commission* judgment. Whilst this solution would doubtlessly be in the interest of procedural economy, it is submitted that it would lead to a conceptual confusion.[108] Indeed, it is worth recalling that the notion of unlimited jurisdiction is aimed at providing the Community Courts with the powers to adjust the level of a fine imposed on undertakings, so as to ensure that it corresponds to the appropriate amount, without having to refer the case back to the Commission. The criteria defining this amount are laid down in Article 23(3) of Regulation No 1/2003, which provides that 'in fixing the amount of the fine, regard shall be had both to the gravity and to the duration of the infringement'. The possible excessive duration of the administrative proceedings and the damage it can cause to the undertakings concerned have little, if any, connection with the gravity of the infringement, nor with its duration, so that it is not certain that, in principle, the unlimited jurisdiction endowed to the EC judge could allow him to reduce the fine on the basis of a breach of the principle

[107] See Opinion of Advocate General Léger in Case C-185/95 P *Baustahlgewebe v Commission*, n 14 above, and the recent Opinion of Advocate General Bot of 31 March 2009 in Case C-385/07 P *Der Grüne Punkt – Duales System Deutschland v Commission* pending. The judgment will be given on 10 September 2009.

[108] See Opinion of Advocate General Léger in Case C-185/95 P *Baustahlgewebe v Commission*, n 14 above.

of reasonable delay during the proceedings before the Commission. In addition, this option would only be effective where the applicant has been imposed a fine, and not, for instance, in the case of a behavioural remedy.

The second option could be to ensure redress through actions for damages under Article 288(2) EC to be brought by the undertaking concerned. As set out above, this possibility was explicitly mentioned by the CFI in the *LVM v Commission* judgment.[109] It is also the method recommended, in the context of a breach of the principle of reasonable delay at the stage of judicial proceedings, in both the Opinion of Advocate General Léger in Case *Baustahlgewebe v Commission* and the recent Opinion of Advocate General Bot in the *Der Grüne Punkt - Duales System Deutschland v Commission* case.[110] The effectiveness of this option would greatly depend on the way the conditions for obtaining a right to compensation will be applied in those circumstances. Indeed, it must be recalled that, according to settled case-law, Community law confers a right to reparation where three conditions are met: the rule of law infringed must be intended to confer rights on individuals; the breach must be sufficiently serious; and there must be a direct causal link between the breach of the obligation resting on the author of the act and the damage sustained by the injured parties. As to the second condition, the decisive test for finding that a breach of Community law is sufficiently serious is whether the Community institution concerned manifestly and gravely disregarded the limits on its discretion. Where that institution has only considerably reduced, or even no, discretion, the mere infringement of Community law may be sufficient to establish the existence of a sufficiently serious breach.[111] Thus, in the context of an action for damages based on a breach of the principle of reasonable delay, a number of issues would have to be settled. In particular, the nature and the quantum of the damage would have to be defined, which could prove a difficult exercise since, at least at first sight, the damage can be nothing but a non-material one, which raises the question of the very possibility of such a damage being caused to legal persons.[112] Furthermore, it would be necessary to determine the conditions under which such a breach constitutes a manifest and grave disregard of the limits imposed on the Commission's discretion. Since, by hypothesis, no breach of the rights of defence was caused to the applicant and no limitation period or legally determined time-limit has elapsed, it could be considered that the Commission has acted, albeit at the edge, within the limits of the wide discretion it enjoys in conducting its proceedings

[109] See n 89 above, para 122.
[110] See ns 14 and 107 above.
[111] See, namely, Case C-312/00 P *Commission v Camar and Tico* [2002] ECR I-11355 paras 53 and 54.

## CONCLUDING REMARKS

Drawing clear-cut conclusions from the various elements presented above is not an easy task. Indeed, whilst the effects of the passing of time on both the powers of the Commission and the rights of undertakings is consistently described as deriving from higher ranked principles, such as legal certainty and good administration, the case-law reveals at the same time a certain degree of reluctance to fully draw the consequences of this recognition. One can suggest a certain number of legitimate reasons explaining this situation. Firstly, the specificity of EC competition law needs to be taken into consideration when applying general legal concepts. As mentioned above, EC competition law is aimed at sanctioning most often concealed business behaviours, highly detrimental to the objective of the internal market and to economic welfare, and will involve the responsibility of companies or associations of companies rather than natural persons. Secondly, if the EC judge can apply and interpret the law, it cannot take the place of the legislator by setting out, on its own initiative, new limitations on the powers on the Commission, an issue which is exemplified by the inapplicability of limitation periods to decisions finding an infringement and to recidivism. Thirdly, a sufficient margin of manoeuvre needs to be left to the Commission, acting as the EC competition policy-maker, in the way it conducts its proceedings and it determines its priorities. Fourthly, one cannot overlook the material constrains imposed on the Commission, and in particular on the Directorate General Competition, and the situation needs to be considered from a realistic point of view. It is submitted that the cases where the excessive duration of the administrative proceedings is due to the negligence of the Commission's officials are quite exceptional, and that this situation is rather due to the need to fix priorities in case management.[113] Despite these elements, it cannot be excluded, considering recent case-law,[114] that the principle of reasonable delay will receive a more effective implementation by the ECJ in relation to administrative proceedings. Such a new trend might be objectively justified by the effects of the entry into force of Regulation No 1/2003, applicable since 1st May 2004, on the workload of the Commission. In replacing the system of notification with a directly applicable exception system

[112] See V Wester-Ouisse, 'Le préjudice moral des personnes morales' (2003) *Jurisclasseur Périodique édition Générale* I 145.

[113] It is worth noting, in this regard, that the Commission explained in Case T-213/00 *CMA CGM and Others v Commission*, n 26 above, para 320, that the delay in adopting the contested decision was due to a shortage of staff. In the same vein, in its Opinion in Joined Cases C-403/04 P and C-405/04 P *Sumitomo Metal Industries and Nippon Steel v Commission* [2007] I-729 point 167, Advocate General Geelhoed underlined, in relation to the alleged excessive duration of the proceedings before the CFI, that 'if the demand for decisions by a Community judicial body structurally exceeds that body's capacity and internal measures to increase productivity are no longer possible without affecting the quality requirements with which that body's decisions must continue to comply, it is the responsibility of the framers of the Treaty to maintain the conditions under which the Court of Justice as a Community institution can continue to fulfil the task assigned to it in Article 220 EC'.

[114] In particular the *FEG v Commission* appeal judgment, n 68 above, and the Opinion of Advocate General Kokott in the same case.

in which competition authorities and courts of the Member States have the power to apply both Articles 81(1) and (3) EC, that Regulation was indeed designed to decentralise and simplify procedures to the greatest possible extent and to enable the Commission to concentrate its resources on curbing the most serious infringements.[115] Time will tell...

[115] See recitals 1 to 4 of Reg No 1/2003. In this regard, the Commission underlined at point 8 of the Communication from the Commission to the European Parliament and the Council, Report on the functioning of Reg 1/2003 [SEC(2009)574], that 'the system change has supported a shift in priorities of the Commission, enabling it to focus its resources on areas where it can make a significant contribution to the enforcement of Articles 81 [EC] and 82 EC. This proactive approach is clearly illustrated by the launch of large scale inquiries in key sectors of the EU economy which directly impact consumers... The more pro-active stance of the Commission is further illustrated by an increase in the number of enforcement decisions adopted, compared with earlier periods'.

# 14

# *Confidentiality Issues in Competition Law The Impact of Confidentiality Issues on Proceedings before the CFI*

SAVVAS S. PAPASAVVAS*

## INTRODUCTION

Competition cases often raise confidentiality issues at various stages of the .proceedings most often before the European Commission, but also before the Court of First Instance of the European Communities (hereinafter CFI). For instance, the Commission may receive information intimating the existence of a cartel from a source that needs protection, lest it suffer reprisals.[1] When the Commission carries out surprise inspections at companies' premises to investigate potential violations of Articles 81 EC and 82 EC, these companies may claim attorney-client privilege with respect to some of the documents seized by the Commission.[2] In cartel, abuse of dominance or merger cases, information obtained by the Commission may contain business secrets – both of the parties to the proceedings and of third parties – that require protection. Finally, confidentiality issues may arise when access to documents, either during or after the proceedings, is requested by the parties to the proceedings or by third parties.

Confidentiality issues arising during competition proceedings before the Commission, in particular issues relating to access to the file, have given rise to

* The views expressed here are strictly personal.

[1] See, eg Case 145/83 *Adams v Commission* [1985] ECR 3539 where the whistleblower in the Vitamins cartel was identified by its former employer, Hoffman La Roche, based on documents made available by the Commission during the proceedings. As a consequence, Hoffman La Roche filed a complaint for economic espionage under Swiss criminal law which led to the arrest, detention and conviction of the whistleblower.

[2] See, eg Joined Cases T-125/03 and T-253/03 *Akzo Nobel Chemicals and Akcros Chemicals v Commission* [2007] ECR II-3523. This judgment is currently under appeal, see Case C-550/07 P *Akzo Nobel Chemicals and Akcros Chemicals v Commission* pending.

extensive case-law from the Community courts. According to this case-law, the Commission has an obligation to

> make available to the undertakings involved in competition proceedings all documents, whether in their favour or otherwise, which it has obtained during the course of the investigation, save where the business secrets of other undertakings, the internal documents of the Commission or other confidential information are involved.[3]

Business secrets consist of information about an undertaking's activity the disclosure of which could cause serious harm (for example, technical and/or financial information relating to an undertaking's know-how, methods of assessing costs, production secrets or processes, supply sources, quantities sold or produced, market shares, customer and distributor lists, marketing plans, cost and price structure, and sales strategy).[4] In this context, 'other confidential information' includes information other than business secrets which may be considered confidential because its disclosure would significantly harm a person or an undertaking (for example, information that would enable the parties to identify the complainant).[5]

Rules on access to the file have been gradually clarified by the Community Courts' case-law, competition law regulations and the Commission's notice on access to the file.[6] Failure to grant access to documents in the Commission's file or, on the contrary, disclosure of documents which some party believed to be confidential, give rise to a number of actions before the Community courts and are examined at length in various publications.[7] They will therefore not be discussed further in this chapter.

[3] See, eg Case T-7/89 *Hercules Chemicals v Commission* [1991] ECR II-1711 para 54. See also Commission Notice on the rules for access to the Commission file in cases pursuant to Articles 81 and 82 of the EC Treaty, Articles 53, 54 and 57 of the EEA Agreement and Council Regulation (EC) No 139/2004 [2005] OJ C325/7, section II.

[4] Commission Notice on the rules for access to the Commission file, para 18.

[5] *Ibid* para 19.

[6] See Council Regulation (EC) No 1/2003 of 16 December 2002 on the implementation of the rules on competition laid down in Articles 81 and 82 of the Treaty [2003] OJ L/1/1; Council Regulation (EC) No 773/2004 of 7 April 2004 relating to the conduct of proceedings by the Commission pursuant to Articles 81 and 82 of the EC Treaty [2004] OJ L/123/18; Council Regulation (EC) No 139/2004 of 20 January 2004 on the control of concentrations between undertakings [2004] OJ L/24/1; Commission Regulation (EC) No 802/2004 of 7 April 2004 implementing Council Regulation (EC) No 139/2004 on the control of concentrations between undertakings [2004] OJ L/133/1, and Commission Notice on the rules for access to the Commission file, n 3 above, ch 3.

[7] See, eg BJ Drijber, 'Access to file and Confidentiality in EEC Competition Proceedings' (1994) 158 *Schwerpunkte des Kartellrechts* 1992/93: *FIW-Schriftenreihe* 113; J Pheasant, 'Confidentiality: business secrets', (1994) *Droits de la défense et droits de la Commission dans le droit communautaire de la concurrence = Rights of defence and rights of the European Commission in EC competition law* 227; JM Joshua, 'Balancing the public interests: confidentiality, trade secret and disclosure of evidence in EC competition procedures' (1994) 2 *European competition law review* 78; N Coutrelis and V Giacobbo, 'La pratique de l'accès au dossier en droit communautaire de la concurrence: entre droits de la défense et confidentialité' (2006) 2 *Concurrences: revue des droits de la concurrence* 30, and PO de Broux, 'La confidentialité des secrets d'affaires et les droits de la défense dans le contentieux administratif économique' (2007) 6 *Revue de droit commercial belge = Tijdschrift voor Belgisch handelsrecht* 563.

However, there has been far less discussion of the impact of confidentiality issues on proceedings before the CFI. This chapter intends to analyse the effect of such claims and to underline the specificity of the CFI's situation when confronted with confidentiality issues.

Unlike the Commission, which is required to engage in fact-finding to reach a decision on a specific matter, the CFI's role is limited to a legal review of the decision at issue and a full review of any fine imposed. Whenever the applicable provisions confer a margin of assessment on the Commission, for instance in merger cases, the CFI verifies compliance with the rules governing the procedure and the statement of reasons, the substantive accuracy of the facts, and the absence of manifest errors of assessment or misuse of powers.[8] Based on these reviews, the CFI must decide whether it is justified to annul the Commission decision, in whole or in part, or whether the amount of any fine imposed must be reduced, increased or cancelled.[9]

Nonetheless, much like the Commission, the CFI is required to strike a balance between protecting confidential information and safeguarding the parties' rights of defence. And like the Commission,[10] the CFI has to reach a decision based on the information submitted to the parties and on which they had an opportunity to state their views.[11]

This chapter will focus first on the impact of confidentiality issues both during the proceedings and through the organisation of proceedings before the CFI and secondly on the drafting of the final judgment. This analysis will focus on actions for annulment lodged in cartel, abuse of dominance, and merger cases, which, in 2008, gave rise to 36 confidentiality requests.[12]

## BALANCING THE PARTIES' RIGHTS

According to well-established case-law, it would

> infringe a fundamental principle of law to base a judicial decision on facts or documents of which the parties themselves, or one of them, have not been able to take cognisance and in relation to which they have not therefore been able to formulate an opinion.[13]

[8] See, eg Case T-282/06 *Sun Chemical Group and Others v Commission* [2007] ECR II-2149 para 60.

[9] Art 31 of Reg No 1/2003.

[10] See Art 27 of Reg No 1/2003; Art 18 of Reg No 139/2004, and Art 17 of Reg No 802/2004.

[11] Art 67(3) of the Rules of Procedure of the CFI.

[12] Out of a total of 100. This represents 15 cases out of a total of 55. These 36 confidentiality requests made in 15 cases can be broken down as follows: 18 requests were made in abuse of dominance cases (5 cases), 15 requests were made in cartel/anticompetitive agreements cases (8 cases), and 3 requests were made in merger cases (2 cases). The vast majority of the confidentiality requests were made in the context of interventions (34 requests in 13 cases). The remaining 2 requests were made in the context of joinders (2 requests in 2 cases).

[13] See Joined Cases 42/59 and 49/59 *Snupat v High Authority* [1961] ECR 101 para 84; Case C-480/99 P *Plant and Others v Commission and South Wales Small Mines* [2002] ECR I-265 para 24, and Case C-199/99 P *Corus UK v Commission* [2003] ECR I-11177 para 19.

This principle is also mentioned in Article 67(3) of the Rules of Procedure of the CFI, which provides that the CFI

> shall take into consideration only those documents which have been made available to the lawyers and agents of the parties and on which they have been given an opportunity of expressing their views.

In some instances, however, this principle has to be balanced against the general Community law principle of the right of undertakings to protect their business secrets.[14] A general obligation to respect business secrecy is imposed on the Community institutions by Article 287 EC and is reinforced by a number of legislative provisions in the field of competition.[15]

In competition cases, the CFI has adopted a pragmatic approach to reconcile, to the extent possible, these often-conflicting principles. Solutions vary depending on whether confidentiality is requested vis-à-vis interveners or vis-à-vis another party to the proceedings.

## Confidentiality and Disclosure vis-à-vis Interveners

In practice, confidentiality requests are quite common when companies are granted leave to intervene in competition cases. As explained above, in 2008, 34 confidentiality requests out of 36 were made in the context of an intervention (that is in 13 cases out of 15).[16]

During the administrative proceedings before the Commission, some specific third parties (for example, complainants in cartel or abuse of dominance cases, or a party to the proposed merger other than the notifying party(ies), such as the seller) are closely associated to the proceedings and may be granted access to documents but not necessarily to the entirety of the Commission's file.[17] For example, in merger cases, the Commission will grant access to its file to other involved parties who have been informed of the objections to the merger, but only in circumstances where access is necessary to enable the parties to prepare their comments.[18] In cartel cases, when complainants have been informed that the Commission intends to reject their complaint, they are only permitted access to the documents on which the Commission has based its provisional assessment.[19]

[14] See Case C-36/92 P *SEP v Commission* [1994] ECR I-1911 paras 36–38. See also Art 41 of the Charter of Fundamental Rights of the European Union, proclaimed in Nice on 7 December 2000 ([2000] OJ C/364/1) according to which the right to good administration includes 'the right of every person to have access to his or her file, while respecting the legitimate interests of confidentiality and of professional and business secrecy'.

[15] See Art 28 of Reg No 1/2003; Arts 17 and 18 of Reg No 139/2004, and Arts 17 and 18 of Reg No 802/2004.

[16] See n 12 above.

[17] Art 27(1) Reg No 1/2003, and Art 17(2) of Reg No 802/2004.

[18] Art 17(2) of Reg No 802/2004.

[19] Art 7 of Reg No 773/2004.

The situation of an intervener before the CFI is slightly different. Article 116(2) of the Rules of Procedure of the CFI lays down the principle that a copy of every document served on the parties must also be served on the interveners. It is only by way of derogation that Article 116(2) permits certain documents to be treated as confidential, thereby exempting them from the requirement that copies be served on the interveners. Accordingly, interveners are in a weaker position in proceedings than either an applicant or a defendant to proceedings before the CFI but they enjoy a stronger position than third parties during administrative proceedings before the Commission.

According to the Instructions to the Registrar of the CFI and the Practice Directions of the CFI, a confidentiality request must specify the confidential matters or passages and briefly state the reasons for which the matter or passage is considered confidential.[20] Consequently, a confidentiality request which is insufficiently detailed as to its subject-matter will be dismissed.[21]

For the purpose of determining the conditions under which confidential treatment may be given to certain matters, the CFI will, in respect of each document on the file or passage in a procedural document for which confidential treatment is sought, balance the applicant's legitimate concern to prevent substantial damage to its business interests and the interveners' equally legitimate concern to access the necessary information to enable them to fully assert their rights and state their case before the Community Courts.[22] This requires a case-by-case assessment whereby the CFI takes into account a wide range of relevant factors in order to determine whether the information is indeed secret or confidential (for example, whether the subject-matter of the information is susceptible to it being deemed confidential by nature, whether the information is already available to the public at large or to a circle of specialists, whether it is not sufficiently specific or precise, whether the information is old enough to be treated as historic etc.).[23] The CFI is not bound by the fact that certain documents and information were accorded confidential treatment by the Commission during the administrative procedure which has led to the adoption of the contested act.[24] In any event, an applicant for confidential treatment must, given the adversarial and public nature of the judicial proceedings, envisage the possibility that some of the secret or confidential documents or information that he has elected to place on the file may be deemed necessary for the exercise of the interveners' procedural rights and, consequently, the CFI may be required to disclose this information to the interveners.[25]

In order to lighten the burden resulting from this assessment and to expedite the proceedings, the CFI considers that, if interveners do not lodge any objection

[20] See Art 6 of the Instructions to the Registrar of the CFI [2007] OJ L/232/1; Practice Directions to Parties [2007] OJ L/232/7, points 72 to 79.

[21] See, eg order in Case T-336/04 *SBS TV and SBS Danish Television v Commission* [2007] ECR II-491 para 43.

[22] *Ibid* para 41.

[23] See, eg order in Case T-383/03 *Hynix Semiconductor v Council* [2005] ECR II-621 paras 54–79.

[24] *Ibid* para 40.

[25] *Ibid* paras 46 and 70.

to the confidentiality request, the application for confidential treatment will be upheld.[26] If the request for confidential treatment is not granted, the party that requested the confidentiality may ask for certain documents to be removed from the case-file but the CFI will not necessarily accede to the request.[27] If the request for confidential treatment is granted, the file will be divided into a confidential and a non-confidential section. Access to the confidential section of the file shall be confined to the parties in respect of whom no confidential treatment has been ordered.[28]

Though it is not expressly provided for by the Rules of Procedure of the CFI, in some cases, interveners may also request that some of the documents they submit remain confidential vis-à-vis principal parties or other interveners. For example, parties to a merger, which was authorised by the Commission and is subsequently challenged by a competitor before the CFI, may intervene in support of the Commission and submit documents that were not accessible to third parties during the administrative proceedings. In such cases, the interveners may request that these documents remain – wholly or partially – confidential.

Balancing the principal parties' rights and the interveners' rights is a frequent exercise for the CFI. The exercise is less frequent, and proves more problematic, when the CFI is faced with confidentiality requests as between the principal parties.

## Confidentiality and Disclosure among the Principal Parties to the Proceedings

It is well-established that when reaching a decision the CFI will only take into consideration evidence that was communicated to other parties and on which they have been able to formulate an opinion.[29] Therefore, a party wishing to withhold evidence from its opponent on confidentiality grounds takes the risk that this evidence will not be considered by the CFI and that, as a consequence, its plea will be rejected.

In actions for annulment in competition cases, there are a few occasions in which disclosure of evidence to the other parties will be limited for confidentiality reasons. This is mostly due to the fact that the principal parties before the CFI are not always the same as the principal parties before the

[26] See, eg order of 29 April 2008 in Case T-275/06 *Omya v Commission* unreported; order of 19 June 2007 in Case T-279/04 *Editions Odile Jacob v Commission* unreported, and Case T-336/04 *SBS TV and SBS Danish Television v Commission*, n 21 above, para 45. See also K Lenaerts, D Arts and I Maselis, *Procedural Law of the European Union* (London, Thomson Sweet & Maxwell, 2006) 576.

[27] See order in Case 236/81 *Celanese Chemical Company v Council and Commission* [1982] ECR 1183 para 11 (dumping case). See also Lenaerts, Arts and Maselis, n 26 above, at 576.

[28] See Art 5 of the Instructions to the Registrar of the CFI.

[29] In this regard, Art 6 of the Instructions to the Registrar of the CFI provides that 'Without prejudice to Article 67(3) of the Rules of Procedure, no consideration may be given to an application by the applicant for any information or documents on the case-file to be treated as confidential in relation to the defendant. Likewise, no such application may be made by the defendant in relation to the applicant.'

Commission. As a result, the Commission, in order to defend its decision, may have to rely on confidential material which was not made accessible to the applicant during the administrative proceedings. For instance, in a concentration case where the applicant before the CFI is a client of the merged entity, it is likely that confidential information transmitted by the parties to the transaction will be material to decide the case. Therefore, the question of whether it is necessary to grant full disclosure of this information to the applicant will be crucial.

There are typically three situations in which a party to competition proceedings before the CFI will request confidentiality vis-à-vis one or several other parties.

The first situation, which is the only one expressly provided for by the Rules of Procedure, arises when actions for annulment against the same Commission decision are joined. This usually occurs in cartel cases. According to Article 50(2) of the Rules of Procedure of the CFI, when cases are joined

> the agents, advisers or lawyers of all the parties to the joined cases, including interveners, may examine at the Registry the pleadings served on the parties in the other cases concerned. The President may, however, on application by a party, without prejudice to Article 67(3), exclude secret or confidential documents from that consultation.

The structure of Article 50(2) of the Rules of Procedure of the CFI results from the balancing act between the rights of defence and the need to protect confidential information. The general rule is that the parties to the joined cases should enjoy unlimited access to the other parties' pleadings. However, the Rules of Procedure acknowledge the fact that, in their pleadings, the parties may have used confidential information, which they would not have disclosed had they known that the cases would be joined. They can therefore request that other parties only be granted access to non-confidential versions of these documents.[30]

The second situation arises when parties request the CFI to order the production of documents in the possession of the Commission, which are relevant to the proceedings.[31] The Commission may object on grounds of confidentiality, especially in cases where it is asked to produce documents or to provide information that was transmitted to it by third parties on a confidential basis.

The Rules of Procedure of the CFI do not provide for formal sanctions for refusal to comply with the CFI's order to produce documents but this refusal may have an impact on the outcome of the case. In practice, it appears that the party will rather submit the information with a request to maintain its confidentiality. The relevant provisions of the Rules of Procedure[32] and the case-law suggest that, in such situations, the CFI will itself screen the evidence itself at a preliminary stage without disclosing it to the parties, and decide whether

[30] See, eg order in Joined Cases T-1/89 to T-4/89 and T-6/89 to T-15/89 *Rhône-Poulenc v Commission* [1990] ECR II-637, and order of 18 October 2007 in Joined Cases T-185/00, T-216/00, T-299/00 and T-300/00 *M6 v Commission* unreported.

[31] See Art 65 b) of the Rules of Procedure of the CFI.

[32] See 2nd subpara of Art 67(3) of the Rules of Procedure of the CFI.

it is necessary to make this evidence accessible, in whole or in part. The CFI will assess, with respect to each individual piece of information, whether the information is truly confidential and consider how to balance the need for the protection of confidential information and the need to have the document or the information disclosed in order for a party to exercise its rights.[33]

The case-by-case approach of the CFI will sometimes lead to full disclosure of the allegedly confidential information (for example, when the information is not specific enough and is therefore not truly confidential). In most cases, the circulation of a non-confidential version of a document where the sensitive data are redacted will be sufficient to reconcile confidentiality and the rights of defence. Non-confidential summaries of documents may also be used. Another means to enable parties to fully grasp an argument without disclosing confidential information is to prepare tables where the data are presented in aggregate form, which may work especially well regarding data such as market shares, production capacity of competitors, providers and customers, as well as costs and prices of competitors.

In some instances, confidentiality needs may require entire documents to be withheld from other parties. In the *Tetra Laval v Commission* case, the applicant was granted access to some non-confidential versions of the responses to the Commission's market investigation. The CFI found that four responses did not contain answers to the questions asked by the Commission and one response was clearly of an entirely confidential nature. Consequently, these five responses were not made accessible to the applicant.[34] The judgment suggests, however, that the confidential documents were not indispensable to support a plea or a line of defence.

The third situation in which a party may request confidentiality vis-à-vis other parties arises where the Commission is required to disclose confidential third party material in support of its line of defence.[35] This arose in the *Impala v Commission* and *Sun Chemical Group and Others v Commission* merger cases where the Commission admitted that, in order to explain the grounds of its decision, it would have to rely on confidential information submitted by the merging parties and by third parties.[36] In both cases, the parties requested that the CFI adjudicate on the case under an expedited procedure (often referred to as the 'fast-track' procedure).

This is probably the situation where the rights of defence and the principle of protection of business secrets are the most difficult to reconcile. In *Impala v Commission*, the applicant (a competitor of the merged entity), the interveners (the merging parties), and the Commission agreed that the Commission would disclose certain documents and information which had been transmitted to it

[33] See at n 21–25 above.

[34] See Case T-5/02 *Tetra Laval v Commission* [2002] ECR II-4381 para 78.

[35] Note that there is no provision of Community law requiring the automatic disclosure of the Commission's entire file to the CFI in competition cases.

[36] See Case T-464/04 *Impala v Commission* [2006] ECR II-2289 para 15, and Case T-282/06 *Sun Chemical Group and Others v Commission* [2007] ECR II-2149 para 33.

on a confidential basis by communicating them solely to the applicant's counsel, to the exclusion of the applicant itself.[37] This was made possible by a written confidentiality agreement between the applicant and the interveners, which specified the duties imposed on the applicant's counsel and the sanctions in case of disclosure of confidential information to the applicant itself. This agreement was formally endorsed by the CFI.[38]

Assuming that the parties can voluntarily limit their rights of the defence,[39] the *Impala* solution does not seem to contradict Article 67(3) of the Rules of Procedure of the CFI. Moreover, this solution solved confidentiality problems which would have significantly slowed down the proceedings. Had the parties and the interveners not reached an agreement, the Commission would have been obliged to engage in negotiations to obtain non-confidential versions of the documents, which would have been incompatible with the fast-track procedure in *Impala*.

It is not certain whether this solution, which has since been applied in one other merger case, may be generally used in cases raising similar issues. A 'Chinese wall' between the lawyer and its lay client might not seem practical in competition law cases, where the input of the client is essential to understand the facts of the case and to raise coherent pleas. Moreover, it entails a risk that the lawyer may inadvertently disclose confidential information to his or her client while discussing the case.

In any case, it appears that the solution in *Impala v Commission* should be regarded as a last resort, when there is no doubt that the information is both confidential by nature (for example, recent individualised pricing data) and absolutely necessary to ground a plea in law, and when it is not possible to summarise it or to provide it in an aggregate or non-confidential form. The fact that an agreement on confidentiality facilitates a 'fast-track' procedure, especially when all parties want to benefit from such a procedure, may encourage the parties to accept an alteration to their rights to access information themselves and to use the *Impala* solution.

## THE CFI'S 'NEED' TO DECIDE THE CASE

In the first part of this chapter, confidentiality in competition law cases has mostly been analysed as a general principle protecting one of the parties and which must be weighed against the rights of defence of other parties or

[37] See Case T-464/04 *Impala v Commission*, n 36 above, paras 17 and 18.

[38] *Ibid* para 19.

[39] See, eg Case T-299/05 *Shanghai Excell M&E Enterprise and Shanghai Adeptech Precision v Commission*, judgment of 18 March 2009 nyr, para 29, where the applicants, in a dumping case, agreed at the hearing that the CFI might, if necessary, use the information contained in the documents regarded as confidential by the Commission, which had not been communicated to them. The CFI, however, did not consider it necessary, for the purposes of the judgment, to use information which had not been made available to the applicants.

interveners. However, confidentiality issues also have a significant impact on the CFI's work as it may influence both the way decisions are reached and the way they are published.

## Confidentiality and the Contents of the CFI Judgment

As already mentioned above, Article 67(3) of the Rules of Procedure require that the CFI

> take into consideration only those documents which have been made available to the lawyers and agents of the parties and on which they have been given an opportunity of expressing their views.

This Article does not only safeguard the parties' rights of defence, it also imposes constraints on the CFI: should the CFI wish to take into account a document or piece of information in its decision, it must ensure that the information has been disclosed to the parties' lawyers or agents and that they have had the opportunity to comment on it.

Therefore, the need for the CFI to decide on a case may, in some rare instances, conflict with the confidentiality requests made by the parties.[40] The CFI may indeed consider that its understanding of the case and its final decision depends on information that has not already been produced or requested by the opposing parties. In order to remedy this deficiency, the CFI can adopt, of its own motion, measures of organisation of procedure or measures of inquiry.[41] In particular, the CFI may ask questions or order documents to be produced.[42] As in the case where measures of organisation of the procedure or measures of inquiry are adopted at the parties' request, the party providing the information or producing the document may request confidentiality vis-à-vis the other parties. Issues will most likely arise in cases where a merger was authorised and is challenged by third parties. In such cases, the CFI may, for instance, order the Commission to provide confidential replies to its market investigation in order to determine whether it correctly assessed the facts of the case. The rationale behind such measures is not to enable the Commission to justify the legality of its decision based on confidential elements that were not disclosed to the notifying parties. The rationale is rather to enable the CFI to examine all the relevant evidence and, possibly, to assess whether the Commission has not excluded, or assessed in a manifestly wrong way, some essential information.

In this situation, the circulation to the parties of non-confidential versions of documents, of summaries or, subject to the parties' agreement and to the practical conditions mentioned above, the implementation of the *Impala* solution (that is disclosure of the information to the CFI and to the opposing party's counsel only,

[40] This was discussed in particular in M Waelbroeck *et al*, 'La Cour de Justice' in *Commentaire Mégret* 10 (Brussels, Éditions de l'Université de Bruxelles, 1993) 436–438.

[41] See Ch 3 of the Rules of Procedure of the CFI.

[42] See Art 64(3) and Art 65 of the Rules of Procedure of the CFI.

to the exclusion of the party itself) would probably be sufficient for the CFI to decide the case and duly state the reasons.

It should be noted that the Court of Justice of the European Communities'(hereinafter ECJ) ruling in the *Impala* case on appeal did not address the confidentiality agreement between the parties.[43] It made clear, however, that confidentiality issues before the Commission have, in certain circumstances, an impact on the content of the judgment. In order to annul the Commission decision authorising the merger between Sony Music Entertainment's and Bertelsmann's global recorded music businesses, the CFI relied on evidence provided by Impala during the administrative proceedings on a confidential basis and that information was not submitted to the merging parties.[44]

Since, according to Article 18 of Regulation No 139/2004, the Commission could not have relied upon such undisclosed evidence without infringing the merging parties' right of defence, the ECJ held that the CFI

> committed an error of law in relying, as a basis for the annulment of the contested decision, on documents submitted by Impala on a confidential basis.[45]

Confidentiality may therefore have an impact both on the organisation of the proceedings but also on the substance of the judgment. The last instance in which confidentiality plays a role is at the stage of the publication of the judgment.

## Confidentiality and the Publication of the Judgment

According to Article 86 of the Rules of Procedure of the CFI, the Registrar shall arrange for the publication of the CFI's decisions. This duty is, of course, essential for all legal or natural persons who may be subject to Community law. Because it is enough for the public at large to understand the general reasoning of the CFI, confidential material can be redacted from the public version of the judgment without giving rise to any significant concerns. Article 18(4) of the Instructions to the Registrar provides that, upon request of a party or of its own motion, the CFI can decide that the names of parties or third parties or other information be omitted from the publications relating to a case if there is a legitimate interest in keeping the identity of a person or other information confidential.[46]

Drafting two versions of the judgment, one for the public and one for the parties, is therefore not exceptional[47] but requires special care on the part of the

[43] See Case C-413/06 P *Bertelsmann and Sony Corporation of America v Impala*, judgment of 10 July 2008 nyr.

[44] See Case T-464/04 *Impala v Commission*, n 36 above, paras 390 and 475. The evidence used by the CFI was not relied on by the Commission in its decision. The relevant test here is not whether the Commission relied on the evidence but whether it could have relied on it without infringing the notifying parties' rights of defence.

[45] See Case C-413-06 P *Bertelsmann and Sony Corporation of America v Impala*, n 43 above, paras 101 and 102.

[46] See Art 18(4) of the Instructions to the Registrar of the CFI.

[47] See, eg Case T-112/05 *Akzo Nobel and Others v Commission* [2007] ECR II-5049 para 74.

CFI in order to reconcile the protection of confidential information and the need to understand the reasoning on which the judgment is based.

This duty to exercise special care when drafting the judgment is particularly important in cases like Impala where the report for the hearing and the final version of the judgment cannot be fully disclosed to the applicant but only to its lawyer. Despite the confidentiality agreement, the applicant should indeed be able to understand the CFI's reasoning in detail in order to determine, with full knowledge of the circumstances, whether an appeal before the Court is possible and necessary.

## CONCLUDING REMARKS

As illustrated throughout this chapter, confidentiality issues impact both on the CFI's management of a case and on its decision-making. The solution explored in *Impala*, which has been implemented in a subsequent merger case, demonstrates the willingness of the CFI to adapt itself to the necessities and specificities of competition cases, especially where the principal parties before the CFI were not the principal parties during the administrative proceedings. Provided that the parties are in favour of the fast-track procedure and accept limitations to their access to information, the *Impala* solution should be a means to significantly speed up the proceedings, in a field where time is of essence. It might also be the only way to reconcile the confidential nature of the information with the rights of the adversaries when that information is truly necessary to decide the case.

# 15

# *Parallel Trade in the Pharmaceutical Industry from a Competition Point of View*

AITOR MONTESA LLOREDA*

## INTRODUCTION

Parallel trade takes place where products put into circulation in one well defined market are then imported by an intermediary into a second market without the authorisation of the person who put them in the market for the first time. It mainly takes place in relation to products protected by intellectual property rights (hereinafter IPRs) and subject to significant price differences along national borders.

Parallel trade is not just an interesting economic phenomenon, but has a special meaning within the European Union. The creation of the European Community was boosted by a widespread desire to achieve a single market, which was indeed one of the few common goals of the six founder Member States, economically exhausted after two world wars. Over the time, the EU has embraced other political, social or environmental objectives, but the idea of a single market remains both a leitmotiv and the cornerstone of the European construction. For that reason, EU competition rules, in theory bound to serve all the Community objectives, are particularly aimed at two of them: the establishment and protection of a competitive market economy and the achievement of market integration. The first of these purposes is common to any antitrust system. The second, by contrast, is a distinctive European feature. The underlying idea is that achieving a single market not only needs the removal of all barriers between States, but all obstacles imposed by the operators which could reconstruct such barriers,[1] including obstacles to trade. Accordingly,

* The author would like to thank Ángel Givaja Sanz and Javier Ruiz Calzado for their valuable comments. The views expressed are personal to the author.

[1] Joined Cases 56/64 and 58/64 *Consten and Grundig v Commission* [1966] ECR 429.

parallel trade has been traditionally protected by the European Commission, whose decisions were largely confirmed by the Court of Justice of the European Communities (hereinafter ECJ),[2] specially in the early years of the Community.[3] But the legal difficulties surrounding this kind of trade, far from diminishing, have increased over the time.

## THE PHARMACEUTICAL INDUSTRY FIGHTS BACK

Parallel trade is a major issue within the pharmaceutical industry, where drugs are usually protected under IPRs and often subject to large price differences based on national boundaries. It is difficult to quantify how much money pharmaceutical manufacturers lose every year because of the existence of such trade in Europe. Some experts hold that it amounts up to 5 % of European pharmaceutical sales.[4] A study revealed that, in 2004, parallel trade involved a £770 million loss for manufacturers in the United Kingdom only.[5] The enormity of these figures suffices to explain why pharmaceutical companies have fiercely, albeit not always successfully, fought this trend.

Many economists and lawyers argue that pharmaceutical companies are in a special position regarding parallel trade. The reasons why this could happen have been exposed by Advocate General Jacobs in his Opinion in *Syfait and Others*.[6] One can agree or not with the conclusions reached in this Opinion, but it seems fair to say that it sets a sound analytical framework within which the debate could take placed.

The elements which in Advocate General Jacob's view should be taken into account are first, the strong regulation of price and distribution of drugs; secondly, the impact of parallel trade upon the economics of the sector and thirdly, its effect upon consumers.[7]

[2] The ECJ has consistently held agreements aimed at partitioning national markets according to national borders or making the interpenetration of national markets more difficult, in particular those aimed at preventing or restricting parallel exports, to be agreements whose object is to restrict competition within the meaning of Art 81 EC. See, eg Joined Cases 96/82 to 102/82, 104/82, 105/82, 108/82 and 110/82 *IAZ International Belgium and Others v Commission* [1983] ECR 3369 paras 23–27; Case C-306/96 *Javico* [1998] ECR I-1983 paras 13 and 14, and Case C-551/03 P *General Motors v Commission* [2006] ECR I-3173 paras 67–69.

[3] Commission decisions protecting parallel trade have also been upheld consistently by the Court of First Instance of the European Communities. An example of this is Case T-62/98 *Volkswagen v Commission* [2000] ECR II-2707 paras 241 and 242, where Judge *Tiili* was the reporting judge.

[4] The 5 % figure appears consistently in papers produced by the European Federation of Pharmaceutical Industries and Associations. As for the size of the European market, it should be noted that in January 2008 the European Commission launched a sector inquiry into EU pharmaceuticals markets under the EC competition rules. A Preliminary Report, published on 28 November 2008, estimated the value of the market for prescription and non-prescription medicines at € 138 billion ex factory and € 214 billion at retail prices in 2007.

[5] S Szymanski and S Hall, 'Intellectual Property Rights: Trading in Pharmaceuticals', Economic and Social Research Council, ESRC award no. R022250213, available at: http://www.esrcsocietytoday.ac.uk/ESRCInfoCentre/ViewAwardPage.aspx?awardnumber=r022250213.

[6] Opinion of Advocate General Jacobs in Case C-53/03 *Syfait and Others* [2005] ECR I-4609.

[7] *Ibid* point 76.

Concerning price regulation and distribution, Advocate General Jacobs observed that Member States intervene to limit the prices payable for drugs within their territories. In his view, such intervention aims to protect the budgets of their social health insurance funds, which support most of the associated costs. The result of the diverse degrees and methods of intervention, which are subject only to limited EC harmonisation,[8] is that drugs are typically much more expensive in some Member States than in others.[9] Advocate General Jacobs also found that wholesalers must fulfil several requirements to be authorised to act in the medicinal market.[10] Besides, both wholesalers and producers are often subject to various duties. In particular, wholesalers are in practice bound to maintain a full and diversified stock of pharmaceutical products[11] and producers must ensure appropriate and continued supplies of drugs in a given Member State so that patients' needs are covered.[12] As a result, wholesalers are prevented from exporting all their stocks and pharmaceutical companies are not free to withdraw a product from a low price market.[13]

Concerning the impact of parallel trade upon the economics of the pharmaceutical industry, Advocate General Jacobs took the view that innovation is a key element of competition in that sector. Substantial investments in the research and development (hereinafter R&D) of new drugs are required.[14] Accordingly, the sector is characterised by high fixed costs (R&D) and low variable costs (manufacture). It would therefore seem rational for a producer to supply any market where the price is above variable cost, even if average costs are not covered at that price level.[15]

Finally, concerning the effect which parallel trade has upon consumers, Advocate General Jacobs held that they draw some benefits in the form of price cuts. However, he pointed out that such benefit is less important in Member States where the costs of drugs fall to the social health insurance. He also observed that, even in these cases, insurances might not benefit from parallel trade if pharmacists are entitled to payment at the rate applicable for products first supplied within the State in question, which is sometimes the case, unless those States have established claw-back schemes in order to recover a portion

[8] Art 152 EC states that 'Community action in the field of public health shall fully respect the responsibilities of the Member States for the organisation and delivery of health services and medical care'.

[9] Opinion of Advocate General Jacobs in Case C-53/03 *Syfait and Others*, n 6 above, points 78 and 79.

[10] The relevant provisions are contained in Title VII of Directive 2001/83/EC of the European Parliament and of the Council of 6 November 2001 on the Community code relating to medicinal products for human use [2001] OJ L/311/67, as amended by Directive 2004/27/EC of the European Parliament and of the Council of 31 March 2004 [2004] OJ L/136/34.

[11] 2nd para of Art 81 of Dir 2001/83. Opinion of Advocate General Jacobs in Case C-53/03 *Syfait and Others*, n 6 above, points 80–82.

[12] Art 81 of Dir 2001/83.

[13] Opinion of Advocate General Jacobs in Case C-53/03 *Syfait and Others*, n 6 above, point 86.

[14] Advocate General Jacobs points out that a Report prepared for the Enterprise Directorate-General of the European Commission states that an R&D project for a new drug is likely to last 8–12 years, with a cost in the range of US$ 350-650 millions.

[15] Opinion of Advocate General Jacobs in Case C-53/03 *Syfait and Others*, n 6 above, point 89.

of the profit from pharmacists.[16] Not surprisingly, Advocate General Jacobs did not take a clear view on whether the overall consumer benefit is significant or not, for there has been a long controversy in the economic literature as to the extent that consumers and public budgets draw benefits from parallel trade in the pharmaceutical sector. Some studies show that such trade involves no significant benefit for any party other than pharmacists and parallel traders.[17] Other studies show, on the contrary, that consumers and health insurance schemes do indeed enjoy clear advantages.[18] Most of those studies are financed either by pharmaceutical producers or by associations of parallel traders. The interests at stake are so high and so many experts have already taken a (paid) position on this issue that it may well remain for years more a passionate than a truly scientific controversy. It would be arguably difficult for a court wishing to have an independent advice on this matter to find a suitable fresh pair of expert eyes.

What seems to be a scientific truth is that pharmaceutical companies will continue trying to limit by all possible means the prejudice that parallel trade causes to their balance sheets and that parallel traders will still intend to sell outside their national markets as much as possible. These two opposing objectives face each other in a complex strategy game in which manufacturers have put in place a number of strategies. Four of them have been used particularly often. These are the use of IPRs to divide national markets, the imposition of more or less subtle modalities of export bans on wholesalers, the creation of double price lists and refusals and limitations of supply.

Strategies against parallel trade based on the use of IPRs, albeit certainly interesting from a legal point of view, do not concern primarily competition rules. Therefore, they shall not be examined in this chapter, which will only deal with the three other strategies identified. Some concrete applications of the three of them have been recently examined by the European Courts. The result of their judgments set the current limits in which parallel trade of pharmaceutical products in Europe can take place against the will of their manufacturers.

[16] *Ibid* points 96–98.

[17] A study of the London School of Economics, partially funded by Johnson & Johnson, showed that the British National Health System only saved €55.9 million from parallel imports in 2002, whereas parallel traders made profits of €469 million in the UK. P Kanavos, J Costa-i-Font, S Merkur and M Gemmill, *The Economic Impact of Pharmaceutical Parallel Trade in European Union Member States: a stakeholder Analysis* (London, LSE Health and Social Care, 2004, Special Research Paper).

[18] In 2003, the European Association of Euro-Pharmaceutical Companies commissioned the York Health Economics Consortium to produce a report highlighting the benefits from parallel-distribution of pharmaceuticals and to whom these benefits accrue. The report concluded that parallel trade produced benefits to consumers of €342 million only in the UK in 2002. P West and J Mahon, 'Benefits to payers and patients from parallel trade', *Health Economics Consortium* (York, 2003, www.yhec.co.uk). Another study by the University of Southern Denmark found the saving to be €237 million in the UK in 2004. U Enemark, K Møller and J Sørensen, *The economic impact of parallel import of pharmaceuticals* (University of Southern Denmark, 2006, http://www.sdu.dk/~/media/94800F7C939644E38319207A9E1F9CDE.ashx).

## EXPORT BANS

A manufacturer can obviously try to impede parallel trade from its wholesalers by imposing a direct contractual prohibition on them to engage in such practices. But clear export bans are too similar to restrictions on exports which, if instigated by a Member State, would violate the prohibition in Article 29 EC and the Commission and the Community Courts have always been ready to prevent private operators from dividing the single market in the same way that would be forbidden to a State. Export bans have therefore been soon considered 'hard core' restrictions of competition, contrary to Article 81 EC.[19]

Accordingly, manufacturers understood at a very early stage that contractual export bans could not be legally used to restrict parallel trade. Instead, some manufacturers turned subtle and tried to achieve the same result by exerting different sorts of pressure over their dealers whereas, at face value, the distribution contracts they had entered into with them would respect their freedom to engage in parallel trade. Many of these strategies were nonetheless condemned by the Commission and examined by the ECJ in the 1980s. Most judgments do not concern the pharmaceutical sector, but need to be briefly commented in order to understand the evolution that has taken place.

One of the main problems in approaching some of the measures put in place by manufacturers was the legal basis of the Commission decisions prohibiting them. The conducts at stake were apparently unilateral, mainly based on instructions and orders from the manufacturer to its dealers or on the exclusion of the dealers which did not respect those instructions from the distribution network. Article 81 EC prohibits collusive agreements and concerted practices and, therefore, cannot apply to one-sided conduct. Article 82 EC, prohibiting abusive practices, seemed a more suitable candidate. However, this is a complex provision in itself and it was not always easy to argue that the producers involved held a dominant position. As far as the pharmaceutical sector is concerned, the traditional market definition made by the Commission, based on all products with the same therapeutic properties, makes it certainly difficult to argue that a manufacturer is dominant in a given market.[20] Therefore, the Commission favoured the use of Article 81 EC.

[19] Joined Cases 56/64 and 58/64 *Consten and Grundig v Commission*, n 1 above.

[20] The Commission has established its practise concerning product market definition in medicines particularly in merger decisions such as those of 10 June 1991, Sanofi/Sterling Drug (Case IV/M.072), 29 April 1993, Procordia/Erbamont (Case IV/M.323), 18 April 1994, Rhône-Poulenc/Cooper (Case IV/M.426), 20 June 1994, La Roche/Syntex (Case IV/M.457), 19 September 1994, AHP/Cynamid (Case IV/M.500), 28 February 1995, Glaxo/Wellcome (Case IV/M.555), 3 April 1995, Behringwerke AG/Armour Pharmaceutical Co. (Case IV/M.495), 22 June 1995, Hoechst/Marion Merrell Dow (Case IV/M.587), 28 September 1995, Upjohn/Pharmacia (Case IV/M.631) or February 1998, Hoffmann La Roche/Boehringer Mannheim (Case IV/M.950). In those decisions the Commission has consistently stated that medicines may be subdivided into therapeutic classes by reference to the Anatomical therapeutic classification (ATC), which is recognised and used by the World Health Organisation. This classification allows medicines to be grouped together by reference to their composition and their therapeutic properties. The Commission has traditionally held that the third level of the ATC classification allows medicines to be grouped in terms of their therapeutic indications, ie their

*Cont.*

One of these cases was *BMW Belgium and Others v Commission*.[21] The Commission had exempted BMW's standard form distribution agreement, which contained no general export prohibition. BMW dealers agreed not to sell to non-approved dealers, but were allowed to sell to consumers anywhere in the Common Market. A temporary price-freezing measure imposed by the Belgian Government suddenly made BMW cars much cheaper in Belgium than in other Member States, which gave rise to an important parallel trade. BMW took preventing measures immediately. In particular, it required its Belgian subsidiary to propose to its dealers in writing that they should not sell cars, directly or indirectly, outside Belgium. Many dealers signed the proposal, which was applied until the Belgian subsidiary informed the dealers some months later that exports were permitted if made to approved dealers or consumers. The Commission took a decision that BMW Belgium and its dealers had infringed Article 81 EC by agreeing on a general export prohibition. This view was confirmed by the ECJ.[22] The ECJ stated that the consenting dealers were responsible even if the bonds of economic dependence existing between them and BMW could affect their freedom of decision.[23]

The most important conclusion that can be drawn from *BMW Belgium and Others v Commission* is not one deriving from the expectable, almost obvious, finding by the ECJ that the proposal made by BMW, once accepted by its dealers, constituted an agreement contrary to Article 81 EC. The most interesting part of this judgment for the legal analysis of parallel trade in the pharmaceutical sector is rather that the reasons that made parallel trade interesting for BMW dealers were somehow similar to those existing in the pharmaceutical industry, to the extent that State intervention was a major source of artificial price differences between Member States. The ECJ, though, did not hesitate to protect parallel trade in a clear manner and reminded the legal and business community that all vertical agreements aimed at preventing it would be regarded as prohibited under Article 81 EC.

The facts at the origin of *AEG-Telefunken v Commission*[24] were more subtle. In this case there was not a written confirmation of a will to restrict parallel trade, but a diffuse pressure on the part of the manufacturer, whose intention did not appear clearly. AEG, a manufacturer of consumer electronic products, notified to the Commission a system of selective distribution based on standard agreements concluded with qualified re-sellers and obtained an informal clearance. However, the Commission carried out an investigation and adopted a decision in which it found that AEG had infringed Article 81 EC by discriminating against certain distributors and by influencing directly or indirectly dealers' resale prices with a view to excluding certain forms of distribution and maintaining price levels.

intended use, and can therefore be used as an operational market definition. However, it has also recognised that it may be appropriate to carry out analyses at other levels of the ATC classification.

[21] Joined Cases 32/78, 36/78 to 82/78 *BMW Belgium and Others* [1979] ECR 2435.

[22] *Ibid* para 29.

[23] *Ibid* paras 30–36.

[24] Case 107/82 *AEG-Telefunken v Commission* [1983] ECR 3151.

AEG contended that the acts complained of in the contested decision, namely the failure to admit certain traders, were unilateral and could not fall within Article 81 EC. The ECJ however, whilst accepting selective distribution systems as a matter of principle,[25] stated that the refusal to approve a distributor which satisfied the relevant qualitative criteria with a view to maintaining a high level of prices or to excluding certain channels of distribution was unlawful and was not a unilateral conduct. It formed part of the contractual relations between the manufacturer and the resellers. According to the ECJ, the distributor's approval was based on its tacit or express acceptance of the policy pursued by AEG which required the exclusion from the network of all distributors which were not prepared to adhere to its policy.[26]

This rather imaginative approach was confirmed in *Ford-Werke and Ford of Europe v Commission*,[27] another case concerning selective distribution and showed the Commission an easy way to tackle future situations in which export bans were tacitly imposed. In *Tipp-Ex v Commission*,[28] the ECJ confirmed again a Commission decision penalising measures adopted in the framework of an exclusive distribution agreement which intended to prevent exports in the absence of any form of written ban. Tipp-Ex asked its French distributor, orally, to raise prices charged to a customer as to eliminate its economic interest in parallel imports.[29] The ECJ accepted that such a request had given rise to an agreement because the distributor implemented it, even though rather than examining its actual market conduct it took into account that the manufacturer carried out subsequent checks so as to give the exclusive distributor an incentive to adopt the suggested conduct.

The Commission's approach concerning pressures exerted by manufacturers on their dealers was first tested in the pharmaceutical sector in *Sandoz Prodotti Farmaceutini v Commission*.[30] The Commission had adopted an infringement decision against a subsidiary of this pharmaceutical company and imposed a fine on it based on the fact that Sandoz had systematically dispatched its customers invoices bearing the words 'export prohibited'. Sandoz did not contest this fact, but appealed the Commission's decision on the grounds that its course of action could not be regarded as an agreement. It should be noted that the specificities of the pharmaceutical industry vis-à-vis parallel trade were not really an issue before the ECJ and, accordingly, this debate reached the EU courts in the context of competition law only at a latter stage. The ECJ held that Sandoz's conduct was not unilateral, to the extent that it formed part of a set of continuous business relations governed by a general agreement drawn up in advance, based on the consent of Sandoz to the establishment of relations with each customer and the tacit acceptance by the customers of the conduct adopted by Sandoz in their

[25] But only to the extent that their aim is an improvement in qualitative competition, see *ibid* para 34.
[26] *Ibid* paras 37 and 38.
[27] Joined Cases 25/84 and 26/84 *Ford-Werke and Ford of Europe* [1985] ECR 2725.
[28] Case C-279/87 *Tipp-Ex v Commission* [1990] ECR I-261.
[29] *Ibid* para 21.
[30] Case C-277/87 *Sandoz Prodotti Farmaceutici v Commission* [1990] ECR I-45.

regard. This acceptance was attested, in the ECJ's view, by renewed orders placed without protest on the same conditions.[31] The ECJ held that the fact that Sandoz did not take steps to ensure the observance by its customers of the behaviour it intended to impose, was not sufficient to remove the ban on exports that, in practice, it had put in place, from the prohibition of Article 81 EC.

After the ECJ judgment in *Sandoz Prodotti Farmaceutini v Commission*, one could arguably conclude that export bans were prohibited under Article 81 EC, no matter whether they were agreed between manufacturers and dealers, more or less clearly imposed on such dealers or even proposed to them in the framework of a set of continuous business relations governed by a general agreement drawn up in advance. The Commission had apparently found a suitable way to prevent companies, among which manufacturers of pharmaceutical products, from achieving that their dealers could not sell in countries other than theirs. Encouraged by that, it tackled cases which were more and more distant of the concept of bilateralism which seems inherent in Article 81 EC. It was in that context that in *Bayer v Commission*[32] the Court of First Instance of the European Communities (hereinafter CFI) made a key contribution in this field.

## A CASE OF LIMITATION OF SUPPLY WHICH THE COMMISSION TRIED TO TREAT AS ANOTHER EXPORT BAN

The facts at the origin of *Bayer v Commission* were a paramount example of a parallel trade conflict in the pharmaceutical sector. However, although the specificities of this sector were discussed to some extent, they did not play a relevant role in the CFI's reasoning. The price of Adalat, a drug produced by Bayer and prescribed for certain cardiovascular diseases, was 40% lower in France and Spain than in the United Kingdom. A number of Spanish and French wholesalers began to buy large quantities of Adalat in their countries and sold them in the UK at a slightly lower price. The UK sales of Bayer were soon halved and Bayer decided to refuse to supply orders requested by Spanish and French wholesalers beyond the real needs of these two markets. It took care not to reproduce, though, the strategies of Sandoz. No export ban was ever written in any invoice nor notified to its customers.

The Commission, however, thought that a case against this conduct could travel in the rails of *Sandoz Prodotti Farmaceutini v Commission* and adopted a decision finding, in substance, that Bayer's French and Spanish subsidiaries had breached Article 81 EC by imposing on their regular clients a ban on parallel trade. The Commission found that Bayer would supply its clients depending on whether they respected the ban or not, a situation which was in fact not very different from that found in the *Sandoz Prodotti Farmaceutini v Commission* or even in *AEG-Telefunken v Commission*. Accordingly, the Commission assumed

[31] *Ibid* para 10.
[32] Case T-41/96 *Bayer v Commission* [2000] ECR II-3383.

that the wholesalers which continued to buy Adalat had given a tacit consent to Bayer's practice. However, it was only Bayer which was fined. It was also ordered to notify its wholesalers that parallel trade was permitted. Bayer brought an action against this decision, the outcome of which was a serious blow to the Commission's approach.

The CFI stressed that unilateral conduct escapes the prohibition set out in Article 81 EC,[33] but held that a distinction should be drawn between cases in which an undertaking has adopted a genuinely unilateral measure and those in which the unilateral character of the measure is merely apparent and may therefore fall within the scope of that provision. The latter would be the case, in particular, with practices which, though apparently adopted unilaterally by the manufacturer in the context of its contractual relations with its dealers, nevertheless receive a tacit acquiescence of those dealers.[34] The CFI held that the Commission had not proved that Bayer imposed an export ban on their wholesalers, monitored systematically the final destination of Adalat, applied a policy of threats and penalties or made supplies conditional on compliance with the alleged export ban.[35] Nor, in the CFI's view, did the documents reproduced in the contested decision show that Bayer sought to obtain any form of agreement from the wholesalers concerning the implementation of its policy or made its supply policy for each wholesaler conditional upon the actual conduct of the latter.[36] But, above all, the CFI examined the actual conduct of the wholesalers and found that it was not consistent with their supposed acquiescence.[37] Finally, in a reasoning that seemed to depart from that of the ECJ in *AEG-Telefunken v Commission*, the CFI ruled that the Commission could not infer the existence of an agreement within the scope of Article 81 EC from the fact that wholesalers did not interrupt their relationship with Bayer after the introduction of its new policy.[38] Proving such an agreement required evidence of a common will. Needless to say, pharmaceutical companies and parallel traders are normally far from having a common will.

The CFI judgment was appealed, giving the ECJ the opportunity to clarify the concept of agreement under Article 81 EC. To the surprise of many commentators, the ECJ confirmed entirely the CFI judgment.[39]

[33] *Ibid* para 66.

[34] *Ibid* para 71.

[35] It is not clear, though, how these measures, if they had been put in place by Bayer, would have played a role.

[36] Case T-41/96 *Bayer v Commission*, n 32 above, para 109.

[37] *Ibid* paras 111–157. The CFI found, in particular, that the wholesalers continued to try to obtain Adalat for export and persisted in that line of activity, even if, for that purpose, they considered it more productive to use different systems to obtain supplies, namely the system of distributing orders intended for export among the various agencies on the one hand, and that of placing orders indirectly through small wholesalers on the other. In those circumstances, the fact that the wholesalers changed their policy on orders and established various systems for breaking them down or diversifying them, should not be construed as evidence of their intention to satisfy Bayer. On the contrary, it could be regarded as demonstrating their firm intention to continue carrying on parallel exports.

[38] *Ibid* paras 173–181.

[39] Joined Cases C-2/01 P and C-3/01 P *BAI and Commission v Bayer* [2004] ECR I-23.

It is worth noting that the ECJ made an uncommon, obscure and extremely significant preliminary remark. In paragraph 42 of its judgment it noted that, in the contested decision, the Commission had confined itself strictly to the examination of the existence of an agreement within the meaning of Article 81 EC and that it did so in the context of a market defined by reference to the main therapeutic indications for Adalat. The ECJ made it clear that neither the possible application of other aspects of Article 81 EC, nor Article 82 EC, nor any other possible definitions of the relevant market, were at issue.

This reference seems to suggest that the concept of agreement under Article 81 EC is not the right path to address policies such as the one Bayer implemented and, more generally, measures by which dealers are only supplied quantities that they can sell in their national market. Arguably, the ECJ was suggesting other ways of action for the Commission. By referring to 'other elements of Article 81 EC' it can only mean the notion of concerted practice. However, it is not obvious whether caselaw on concerted practices, used primarily in the framework of horizontal restraints, could be useful in this context. What it is clear is that the explicit mention of Article 82 EC and 'other possible definitions of the relevant market' is a message that this provision may be the right instrument and that the ECJ is ready to explore different methods to define market dominance in the pharmaceutical sector.

The core of the ECJ's judgment came right after. The ECJ stated, in the most general possible terms, that for an agreement within the meaning of Article 81 EC to be capable of being regarded as having been concluded by tacit acceptance, it is necessary that the manifestation of the will of one of the contracting parties to achieve an anti-competitive goal constitute an invitation to the other party, whether express or implied, to fulfil that goal jointly, and that applies all the more where such an agreement is not at first sight in the interests of the other party.[40] Accordingly, the CFI was right to examine whether Bayer's conduct supported the conclusion that the latter had required that the wholesalers, as a condition for their future contractual relations, should comply with its new commercial policy.[41] Moreover, the ECJ made it clear that the mere fact that a measure adopted by a manufacturer, which has the object or effect of restricting competition, falls within the context of continuous business relations between the manufacturer and its wholesalers is not sufficient for a finding that an agreement contrary to Article 81 EC exists.[42] The ECJ reminded that the Commission bears the burden of proof,[43] and gave it some guidelines in this increasingly difficult task. The ECJ stressed that such an agreement cannot be based on what is only the expression of a unilateral policy of one of the contracting parties, which can be put into effect without the assistance of others, since any other interpretation would provoke a confusion of the scope of Article 81 EC with that of Article

[40] *Ibid* para 102.
[41] *Ibid* para 103.
[42] *Ibid* para 142.
[43] *Ibid* para 62.

82 EC.[44] This implies that measures adopted by manufacturers that do not require the cooperation of their wholesalers, such as refusals to supply or supply limitations, cannot be caught by Article 81 EC. Besides, although the existence of an agreement does not necessarily follow from the fact that there is a system of subsequent monitoring and penalties, the establishment of such a system may constitute an indicator of the existence of an agreement.[45] Finally, as mentioned above, the behaviour of the wholesalers is essential.

The statements made by the ECJ in the Bayer case do not seem restricted to the individual circumstances of the case or the specificity of the pharmaceutical sector. They are constructed in such a wide way that they can only be considered as the interpretation of the notion of agreement within the meaning of Article 81 EC. But it cannot be denied that they are not easily reconciled with previous ECJ judgments which, nonetheless, were not expressly ruled out. Paragraph 38 of *AEG-Telefunken v Commission* and paragraph 21 of *Ford-Werke and Ford of Europe v Commission* seemed to entail that a distributor's admission into a selective distribution network implies its explicit or tacit adherence to the policy pursued by the manufacturer. That case-law could also be interpreted in the sense that a call by a manufacturer to its authorised dealers, when it forms part of a set of continuous business relations governed by a general agreement drawn up in advance, does not constitute a unilateral act which falls outside the scope of Article 81 EC, but an agreement within the meaning of that provision.[46]

The ECJ, however, held that the facts at the origin of *Bayer v Commission* and *BAI and Commission v Bayer* were different from those in *AEG-Telefunken v Commission* and *Ford-Werke and Ford of Europe v Commission*, on the one hand, and *Sandoz Prodotti Farmaceutini v Commission*, on the other hand. Concerning *Sandoz Prodotti Farmaceutini v Commission*, the ECJ found that the manufacturer had sought the cooperation of wholesalers in order to reduce parallel imports, the insertion by the manufacturer of the words 'export prohibited' on its invoices amounting to a demand for a particular line of conduct on the part of the wholesalers.[47] As for *AEG-Telefunken v Commission* and *Ford-Werke and Ford of Europe v Commission*, the ECJ admitted that in those cases it had accepted the existence of an agreement within the meaning of Article 81 EC without enquiring as to the existence of a demand on the part of the manufacturer, but held that such a need did not arise then because the measures adopted by the manufacturers formed part of selective distribution agreements previously concluded.[48] This explanation does not appear to be very satisfactory. It might even be interpreted as recognition that measures adopted within a selective distribution system are more easily regarded as having been taken bilaterally, given the strong contractual links that are usually present in such systems, or even that the ECJ findings were not applicable to selective distribution systems.

[44] *Ibid* para 101.
[45] *Ibid* para 83.
[46] See Joined Cases 25/84 and 26/84 *Ford-Werke and Ford of Europe*, n 27 above, para 21.
[47] Joined Cases C-2/01 P and C-3/01 P *BAI and Commission v Bayer*, n 39 above, para 104.
[48] *Ibid* paras 105–109.

This question was solved soon after, when the ECJ confirmed a judgment of the CFI,[49] which reproduced almost literally the conclusions reached in *Bayer v Commission*. That judgment concerned some measures of an apparent unilateral nature adopted by Volkswagen within the framework of its selective distribution network. Volkswagen's dealership agreement stipulated that the dealer would comply with all instructions issued by Volkswagen regarding the distribution of new cars and that Volkswagen would issue non-binding price recommendations. But when Volkswagen discovered that some of its dealers were selling a given model below its recommended price, it asked its dealers to observe 'strict price discipline'. The Commission adopted a decision finding that such conduct infringed Article 81 EC. However, the CFI annulled the decision on the grounds that the Commission had failed to establish the existence of an agreement.

The ECJ annulled part of the CFI's reasoning, but rejected the Commission's view that, in signing a dealership agreement, dealers gave their prior consent to all measures adopted by the manufacturer in the context of that contractual relationship. The ECJ held that its previous case-law did not imply that any call by a manufacturer constitutes an agreement within the meaning of Article 81 EC. On the contrary, a concurrence of wills would still be needed.[50] That concurrence of wills could result from the clauses of the dealership agreement, this being probably the case, in the ECJ's view, of *Ford-Werke and Ford of Europe v Commission*, *AEG-Telefunken v Commission* and *BMW Belgium and Others v Commission*; or from the conduct of the parties, which would be the case of *Sandoz Prodotti Farmaceutini v Commission*.

*Bayer v Commission* and *BAI and Commission v Bayer* were probably perceived by the Commission as a serious defeat for its policy concerning companies which try to prevent parallel trade.[51] The pharmaceutical industry considered these judgments as a great and maybe just first victory[52] and parallel traders almost certainly saw them as an extremely dangerous precedent. However, the two judgments were most likely only a clarification of the notion of agreement between undertakings within the meaning of Article 81 EC and, even more than that, a restoration of the concept of bilateralism as the core of that notion. That was a restoration which, implicitly, though perhaps not fully satisfactorily from

[49] Case T-208/01 *Volkswagen v Commission* [2003] ECR II-5141, and Case C-74/04 P *Commission v Volkswagen* [2006] ECR I-6585.

[50] Joined Cases C-2/01 P and C-3/01 P *BAI and Commission v Bayer*, n 39 above, paras 36–39.

[51] According to the New York Times (January 7, 2004, s W, p 1, New York edition) a spokeswoman for the Commission said the ECJ ruling was a disappointment. However she announced that the ruling would not deter the Commission from pursuing other suspected antitrust behaviour by drug companies, and insisted the ruling only reflected a lack of proof. In spite of these words the Commission has not taken since then any other decision based on competition law against drug manufacturers which limited their supplies to their wholesalers or exerted pressure on them to eliminate parallel trade, except for a decision concerning a dual pricing system, which will be examined hereinafter, and which differs quite dramatically from the system put in place by Bayer.

[52] According to the New York Times (January 7, 2004, s W, p 1, New York edition) Bayer said that the ECJ judgment meant that 'pharmaceutical manufacturers are under no obligation to supply the entire European market from the Member State with the lowest state-regulated prices for the product in question.'

an intellectual point of view, corrected a previous interpretation which perhaps appeared too flexible and as departing from the rationale of the interdiction of collusion.

A practical conclusion which can be drawn from *Bayer v Commission* and *BAI and Commission v Bayer* is that manufacturers intending to prevent parallel trade from its dealers must take unilateral measures and avoid all indications, written or oral, contractual or extra contractual, which could be interpreted as an invitation to collude. Limitations of supplies seem to be on the safe side, as long as the manufacturer in question does not enjoy a dominant position in the market for the drug at stake. Creating a system of monitoring and punishments might, on the contrary, entail a higher risk from a competition point of view, although it is not completely sure whether its sole presence would suffice to build a case on Article 81 EC. The answer could be in the negative if the clear intention of the dealers is to continue trading in parallel.

The existence of such uncertainties might have pushed manufacturers to opt for another strategy, known as dual pricing, which might have all the elements to reduce parallel trade efficiently and also to avoid, on the one hand, the use of export bans and similar measures based on pressure on the part of the manufacturer and, on the other hand, the risk that a limitation of supply could be examined under Article 82 EC, as suggested by the ECJ in *BAI and Commission v Bayer*.

## DUAL PRICING

Dual pricing is a practice by means of which a manufacturer charges different prices to its wholesalers depending on the final destination of the product. A lower price is charged for products to be sold on the domestic market and a higher price for products to be exported. A clear advantage of such a practice is that the higher price can be imposed as a default price, in other words, the price applied unless evidence is provided that a given medicine has been sold within the domestic market. This possibility makes monitoring simple and very efficient and eliminates all incentives for parallel traders to export quantities originally destined to their home markets.

The first decision adopted by the Commission in this field concerned the Spanish subsidiary of Glaxo Wellcome, a British pharmaceutical company (now and hereinafter GlaxoSmithkline, or GSK).[53] The Spanish subsidiary of GSK adopted a creative pricing system whereby drugs which were publicly financed in Spain were charged a given price, provided that they were sold within the Spanish market. If they were sold in other Member States, such as the UK, a

[53] Commission Decision of 8 May 2001 relating to a proceeding pursuant to Article 81 of the EC Treaty Cases: IV/36.957/F3 Glaxo Wellcome (notification), IV/36.997/F3 Aseprofar and Fedifar (complaint), IV/37.121/F3 Spain Pharma (complaint), IV/37.138/F3 BAI (complaint), IV/37.380/F3 EAEPC (complaint) (notified under document number C (2001) 1202) [2001] OJ L/302/43.

substantially higher price would apply. That system was accepted by many dealers and notified to the Commission. GSK asked for a negative clearance or alternatively, an individual exemption.

The Commission held that the system had both the object and the effect of restricting competition and prohibited it. The Commission, acting in a predictable and, arguably, orthodox manner,[54] stated that it was intended to have the effect of a complete ban on parallel trade and was capable of achieving that goal. GSK brought an action against the decision and in *GlaxoSmithkline Services v Commission*,[55] the CFI examined the case and provoked a legal revolution.

The CFI rejected, first, GSK's argument that the pharmaceutical sector was so specific that it could not be subject to competition rules in the same way as other sectors. The CFI reminded that Article 81 EC is inapplicable only in sectors in which regulation precludes all competition, and underlined that this was not the case in the pharmaceutical industry. It admitted that State price regulations may distort competition and favour a certain market partition, but held that interbrand competition still takes place, mainly on the basis of innovation, and that parallel trade creates some intrabrand competition.[56]

The CFI pointed out that, in order to decide whether the agreements entered into between GSK and its dealers had the object or the effect of restricting competition within the meaning of Article 81 EC, account should be taken of their legal and economic context.[57] It reminded that if, in that context, the clauses of the agreement revealed the existence of an alteration of competition, it would be regarded as having such an object, there being no need to examine its effect.[58]

The CFI observed that the dual pricing system at stake had the obvious intention of limiting parallel trade between Spain and other Member States and admitted that agreements which ultimately seek to prohibit or treat clearly unfavourably parallel trade are in principle regarded as having as their object the prevention of competition.[59] However, it stated that, having regard to the legal and economic context of the agreement at stake, that could not be the case. That was the beginning of an innovative but sometimes complex line of reasoning, which might well not have been used before by the EU courts.

In a statement which could have been directly copied from a Chicago school text book, the CFI declared that the objective of Article 81 EC is to prevent

[54] Traditionally agreements aimed at prohibiting parallel trade have been clearly considered as having an object contrary to competition by their very nature, eg Case 19/77 *Miller International Schallplatten v Commission* [1978] ECR 131.

[55] Case T-168/01 *GlaxoSmithKline Services v Commission* [2006] ECR II-2969.

[56] *Ibid* paras 104–107.

[57] The CFI referred to Case 56/65 *LTM* [1966] ECR 337, and Joined Cases 56/64 and 58/64 *Consten and Grundig v Commission*, n 1 above, among other precedents in this sense.

[58] Case T-168/01 *GlaxoSmithKline Services v Commission*, n 55 above, paras 110–113.

[59] The CFI referred in this sense to Joined Cases 56/64 and 58/64 *Consten and Grundig v Commission*, n 1 above; Case 19/77 *Miller International Schallplatten v Commission*, n 54 above, paras 7 and 18; Joined Cases 32/78, 36/78 to 82/78 *BMW Belgium and Others*, n 21 above, paras 20–28 and 31; Case C-277/87 *Sandoz Prodotti Farmaceutici v Commission*, n 30 above, para 16; Joined Cases 96/82 to 102/82, 104/82, 105/82, 108/82 and 110/82 *IAZ International Belgium and Others v Commission*, n 2 above, paras 23–25, and Case C-551/03 P *General Motors v Commission*, n 2 above, paras 67 and 68.

undertakings from reducing the welfare of the final consumer[60] and held, in substance, that competition law protects parallel trade only if it benefits consumers, something which, seemly, had to be assessed on a case per case basis.[61] The CFI, by a five judge chamber, was thus introducing in a clear and novel manner the theory of the rule of reason as the very cornerstone of EC competition law. The enormity of this step has probably been underestimated as most commentators place the judgment in the context of the particular nature of the pharmaceutical sector,[62] although the finding of the CFI contains no such reference. One can legitimately wonder whether the CFI proposes that the existence of per se violations of competition law should no longer be admitted, although some commentators, criticizing the judgment's reasoning, point out that the case-law cited in support of this view[63] does not appear to confirm such a conclusion.[64]

In any case, the CFI stated that the agreement at stake did not have the object to restrict consumer's welfare, since the particularities of the case showed that wholesalers might not pass on to the final consumers the advantage in terms of price which parallel trade may entail. Those particularities were, in the CFI's view, admitted by the contested decision itself. They were, namely, the fact that parallel trade was due to price differences originating in State intervention and, sometimes, variations of exchange rates[65] and that consumers typically bear a minimal percentage of the final costs. The CFI also held that certain Member States have adopted provisions which may encourage parallel trade. For instance, the UK's insurance fund pays pharmacists a sum equal to the manufacturer's

[60] It is worth noting that as authority to support this statement the CFI cited Joined Cases T-213/01 and T-214/01 *Österreichische Postsparkasse v Commission* [2006] ECR II-3963 para 115. It is true that in that judgment the CFI had stated that the ultimate purpose of EC competition rules is to increase the well-being of consumers. But it is not obvious that 'ultimate goal' should mean 'only goal'. Besides, the CFI had made that finding only in order to recognise customers who show that they have suffered economic damage as a result of an agreement or conduct liable to restrict or distort competition a legitimate interest in seeking from the Commission a declaration that Arts 81 EC and 82 EC have been infringed, and not to exclude an agreement from the scope of Art 81 EC. The CFI had concluded that such recognition contributed to the attainment of the objectives of competition law. As a more indirect authority to its statement, the CFI also cited Joined Cases 56/64 and 58/64 *Consten and Grundig v Commission*, n 1 above, and Case 28/77 *Tepea v Commission* [1978] ECR 1391 para 56. None of these cases seem, however, to contain an express or implied confirmation of such a plain statement. Indeed, whereas most commentators would agree that the ultimate goal of competition law is to protect consumer welfare, as it was said in Joined Cases T-213/01 and T-214/01 *Österreichische Postsparkasse v Commission*, cited above, it is more difficult to argue that that is its only goal, as the CFI seems to suggest here, and that competition law cannot promote other objectives such as market integration. The discussion might however be more byzantine than useful if one considers that market integration is, in the philosophy of the EC Treaty, beneficial to consumers.

[61] Case T-168/01 *GlaxoSmithKline Services v Commission*, n 55 above, paras 114–121.

[62] Even those criticising strongly the judgment seem to do so. See, for instance, V Junod, 'An end to parallel imports of medicines? Comments on the judgment of the Court of First Instance in Glaxo Wellcome' (2007) 2 *World Competition* 291, at 296.

[63] Case 56/65 *LTM*, n 57 above; Joined Cases 56/64 and 58/64 *Consten and Grundig v Commission*, n 1 above; Case C-7/95 *Deere v Commission* [1998] ECR I-3111, and Case C-399/93 *Oude Luttikhuis and Others* [1995] ECR I-4515.

[64] See Junod, n 62 above, 297.

[65] Case T-168/01 *GlaxoSmithKline Services v Commission*, n 55 above, paras 122–130.

British price minus a standard discount of 4 to 5 %, which is supposed to correspond to the savings made by pharmacists where they obtain their supplies elsewhere. The CFI concluded that it could not be presumed that parallel trade has an impact on the prices charged to the final consumers of medicines reimbursed by the national sickness insurance scheme and thus confers on them an appreciable advantage analogous to that which it would confer if those prices were determined by the play of supply and demand.[66]

It is worth noting that the CFI excluded that a parallel could be drawn between the case at stake and *BMW Belgium and Others v Commission*, as the Commission argued. The reason given by the CFI is that the price of medicines falls structurally outside the play of supply and demand.[67] However it is not entirely clear why this would not apply to *BMW Belgium and Others v Commission*, where price differences were a direct result of State intervention.

As a result of the above, the CFI annulled the contested decision in so far as it had concluded that the agreement at stake had as its object the restriction of competition. It therefore examined the agreement against the Commission's finding that it also had a restrictive effect.

The CFI observed in this regard that the fact that an agreement has the effect of limiting parallel trade and wholesalers freedom does not necessarily restrict competition, and held that it is the repercussions which that agreement may have on the parameters of competition, such as the quantity in which a product is supplied or the price at which it is sold, that provides evidence of a restriction.[68] In that regard, the CFI pointed out that, in substance, the Commission had concluded in the contested decision that GSK's agreement resulted in applying dissimilar conditions to equivalent transactions within the meaning of Article 81(1)(d) EC and held that, given that each Member States constitutes a distinct market, a difference in price according to the destination of the products was not sufficient to show a discrimination and could reflect differences in the ability to pay in different Member States.[69] However, the CFI pointed out that the Commission had also concluded in the contested decision that the agreement at stake had the effect of reducing consumer welfare by preventing patients and national insurance schemes from taking advantage, in the form of a reduction in prices, of the participation of the Spanish wholesalers in intrabrand competition.

The CFI accepted that view. This is surprising, given that it had rejected a similar, if not identical, argument when holding that the agreement was not restrictive by its object.[70] Now, even finding that benefits could be minimal, since parallel traders could apply resale prices which are lower than national prices only to the extent strictly necessary to make them attractive, the CFI held that

[66] *Ibid* paras 131–134.

[67] *Ibid* para 141.

[68] *Ibid* paras 167–173.

[69] *Ibid* paras 177–180.

[70] As it has just been exposed, the CFI had concluded in substance that, as the prices of medicines are to a large extent shielded from the free play of supply and demand, it cannot be taken for granted that parallel trade tends to reduce those prices and thus to increase the welfare of final consumers.

the benefit was still there, as proved, for instance, by the fact that, for some drugs, the UK insurance system paid pharmacists an average price 4 % lower than the British price.[71] The decision was consequently confirmed as far as it had found that the agreement at stake had the effect of restricting competition.

The CFI then focused on whether the dual pricing system met the conditions for an exemption to be granted under Article 81(3) EC. The contested decision had reached a negative view on this. The CFI reminded that any agreement which restricts competition, whether by its effects or by its object, may in principle benefit from an exemption, provided that the person who relies on Article 81(3) EC demonstrates that the conditions contained therein are satisfied, by means of convincing arguments and evidence which the Commission must adequately examine. The CFI observed that, in certain cases, those arguments and that evidence may be of such a kind as to require the Commission to provide an explanation or justification, failing which it is permissible to conclude that the burden of proof borne by the person who relies on Article 81(3) EC has been discharged.[72] The CFI considered that in the case in question, the Commission had focused its examination on the first condition for the application of Article 81(3) EC, the other conditions been examined only summarily.[73] According to that condition, agreements which can be exempted must contribute to improving the production or distribution of goods or to promoting technical or economic progress.

GSK had claimed that its dual pricing system, by encouraging innovation, would create efficiencies in both interbrand and intrabrand competition. That argument had been supported, in particular, by five economic studies concerning the sector for patented medicines reimbursed by a national sickness insurance scheme. Those studies showed, in substance, that interbrand competition depends on very expensive, high-risk, long-term and worldwide R&D. That R&D, again, depends on current and anticipated returns, which varies from one Member State to another, according to the income which the applicable price makes available. Such returns are reduced by parallel trade. Finally, the studies showed that competitive pressure from other manufacturers obliges companies such as GSK to invest extra profits in new R&D. Less parallel trade thus equals more R&D, which entails stronger interbrand competition in the long run. The Commission had found, on the contrary, that it was not proved that parallel trade had a negative impact on GSK's R&D activities.

The CFI stated that, having regard to the relevance of the factual arguments and the evidence submitted by GSK, the Commission's examination of the loss in efficiency associated with parallel trade could not be accepted as sufficient to support its conclusions.[74] The CFI found that the arguments and the supporting evidence submitted by GSK appeared to be relevant, reliable and credible,[75]

[71] Case T-168/01 *GlaxoSmithKline Services v Commission*, n 55 above, paras 185–191.
[72] *Ibid* paras 233–237.
[73] *Ibid* paras 237–247.
[74] *Ibid* paras 262–269.
[75] In particular *ibid* paras 264–268.

since they were in some way confirmed in a Commission communication.[76] That communication had stated, inter alia, that, although the European pharmaceutical industry is a powerful sector where investments in R&D tripled in 1997 by reference to the ten previous years, it shows a decline in competitiveness as the financial profitability ratio is lower than in the United States. The CFI added that there were indicia in the file that the fact that extra profit is retained by the producer will in all likelihood give rise to a gain in efficiency by comparison with the situation in which the profit is shared with the intermediary, because a rational producer which is able to ensure the profitability of its innovations and which operates in a sector characterised by healthy competition on innovation has every interest in reinvesting at least a part of its surplus profit in innovation.[77] The CFI held that, in those circumstances, the Commission should have carried out a more thorough and serious examination, in the light of the supporting evidence submitted, instead of merely stating, for instance, that GSK could have responded to the alleged loss of efficiency caused by parallel trade by reducing other budgetary items or using a part of its substantial profits.[78] As a result, the CFI found that the Commission could not lawfully conclude that GSK had not demonstrated that the first condition for the application of Article 81(3) EC was satisfied.[79] Besides, since it had found that the summary conclusions which the Commission reached concerning the existence of a passing-on to consumers, the indispensability of the dual pricing system and the absence of elimination of competition rested on the conclusion relating to the existence of a gain in efficiency, the CFI held that those conclusions were themselves invalid.[80] Accordingly, it annulled the decision in so far as the Commission had concluded that the agreement at stake could not be exempted and that the infringement should be brought to an end immediately. Finally, the CFI reminded that, although the notification procedure provided for in Regulation No 17 no longer exists under Regulation No 1/2003,[81] it falls upon the Commission, in the light of the partial annulment of the decision and the retroactive effect thereof, to rule on the request for exemption presented by GSK by reference to the date of that request, in so far as that request remains before it.[82]

The judgment of the CFI was appealed by the Commission.[83] The outcome of the ECJ judgment is much awaited. It is not difficult to imagine that many sectors which require intensive R&D investments might intend to use the possibility

[76] Communication COM(1998) 588 final of 25 November 1999 on the single market in pharmaceuticals.

[77] Case T-168/01 *GlaxoSmithKline Services v Commission*, n 55 above, paras 273 and 274.

[78] *Ibid* paras 277–279 and 294.

[79] *Ibid* paras 308.

[80] *Ibid* paras 310.

[81] Council Regulation (EC) No 1/2003 of 16 December 2002 on the implementation of the rules on competition laid down in Articles 81 and 82 of the Treaty [2003] OJ L/1/1. Regulation No 17: First Regulation implementing Articles 85 and 86 of the Treaty [1962] OJ L/13/204.

[82] Case T-168/01 *GlaxoSmithKline Services v Commission*, n 55 above, paras 316–320.

[83] Joined Cases C-501/06 P, C-513/06 P, C-515/06 P and C-519/06 P, *GlaxoSmithKline Services v Commission* pending.

offered by the CFI to justify restrictions of competition on the basis that extra profits will be reinvested in R&D. The software sector or that of bio technologies are good candidates. Besides, it would be interesting to have a concrete view of the ECJ on the application of the rule of reason in EU competition law and the proposed test of consumer harm as an exclusive benchmark of anticompetitive behaviour. Finally, a confirmation of the judgment of the CFI would entail, in practice, the elimination of parallel trade in pharmaceuticals and, possibly, in other products. A clear confirmation of the judgment might well imply a revolution concerning many of the basic principles on which EC competition law has been constructed.

## LIMITATIONS OF SUPPLY

The Commission did not take the tacit invitation of the ECJ in *BAI and Commission v Bayer* to analyse unilateral refusals or limitations of supply from pharmaceutical companies to wholesalers under Article 82 EC. One possible reason for this might be that the Commission hesitated to find pharmaceutical companies dominant for the products which they marketed. The course of things, however, confronted the ECJ with such an analysis in a case which, again, met all the ingredients of a classic situation of parallel trade in pharmaceuticals and, once again, involved GSK.

GSK distributed three drugs called Imigran, for migraine, Lamictal, for epilepsy, and Serevent, for asthma, in Greece, from where some of its wholesalers were supplying other EU markets, particularly Germany and the UK. During a shortage of the three products, GSK stopped meeting its wholesalers' orders and supplied hospitals and pharmacies through the company Farmacenter AE. Soon after, it reinstated normal supplies to the wholesalers, albeit to a limited extent. The wholesalers, in practice unable to export to the same extent as before, brought two types of action against GSK. First, they started administrative proceedings before the Epitropi Antagonismou (Greek Competition Commission), seeking to establish that GSK had committed an abuse of a dominant position within the meaning of a Greek provision which mirrors Article 82 EC. A decision of the Epitropi Antagonismou ordering interim measures required GSK to meet the orders of the three products in question. However, national law being interpreted in the light of Community law, it stayed the proceedings and referred certain questions relating to the interpretation of Article 82 EC to the ECJ for a preliminary ruling.[84]

The ECJ did not address the substance of the dispute because it found that it was not competent to answer questions referred by a body which is not a court within the meaning of Article 234 EC. However, Advocate General Jacobs issued an Opinion full of interesting remarks[85] and reaching a final conclusion that,

[84] Case C-53/03 *Syfait and Others*, n 6 above.

[85] *Ibid* Opinion of Advocate General Jacobs, which has been already commented in part.

albeit in most cases the benefits of parallel trade are clear, a closer examination of the particular context of the pharmaceutical sector justifies a restriction of supply by a dominant manufacturer in order to limit parallel trade.[86]

The Greek wholesalers had also filed four lawsuits against GSK before a Greek court, where they argued that GSK had abused its dominant position on the market for the three products in question and sought an order that it continue to supply them in the quantities corresponding to the monthly average supplied during a given period plus 20 %. The Greek court dismissed the actions and the wholesalers appealed to a Greek court of appeal. This court stayed the proceedings and referred to the ECJ for a preliminary ruling the same questions that the latter had found inadmissible when made by the Greek Competition Commission and which go into the core of the debate concerning parallel trade in the pharmaceutical sector.[87]

The Greek Court of Appeal asked in substance, whether a refusal of a firm in a dominant position to meet fully the orders sent by its dealers in order to reduce parallel trade is, per se, an abuse within the meaning of Article 82 EC, in particular if such trade is profitable because of different prices resulting from State intervention. The Court of Appeal also asked the ECJ to clarify when such refusal would amount to an abuse, if the answer to the first question were negative. The Court of Appeal was looking for guidance on the following questions: the percentage by which normal domestic consumption could be exceeded, the tolerable loss suffered by the dominant firm, or the benefits that consumers and social insurance bodies must eventually draw from parallel trade.

In its observations lodged before the ECJ, GSK contended that its refusal to supply the requested quantities did not constitute an abuse for a number of reasons. In particular, it did not put the wholesalers at risk of being eliminated from the market, since its supplies enabled them to cover requirements going even beyond the Greek market. GSK did not deny that it aimed to limit parallel exports by its wholesalers to the markets of the Member States in which the selling prices of its drugs were higher. However, it contended that such intention had to be read in the light of the particularities of the pharmaceuticals sector. By contrast, the wholesalers, as well as the Italian and Polish Governments and the Commission, maintained that GSK's declared intention to restrict parallel trade was an abuse of a dominant position.

The ECJ, by its Grand Chamber, stated that in the light of the objective of the Treaty to achieve the integration of national markets through the establishment of a single market, as well as that of ensuring that competition in the internal market is not distorted,[88] there can be no escape from the prohibition laid down

[86] *Ibid* points 74, 75 and 100–102. As for the outcome of the case before the Greek Competition Commission, that authority issued a decision finding that GSK was dominant only in respect of Lamictal and that it had abused its position only during the time when it had refused to supply companies other than Farmacenter AE.

[87] Joined Cases C-468/06 to C-478/06 *Sot. Lélos kai Sia and Others*, judgment of 16 September 2008 nyr.

[88] It is worth noting that market integration clearly appears, unlike in the CFI's reasoning in Case T-168/01 *GlaxoSmithKline Services v Commission*, n 55 above, as one of the objectives of EC competition law.

in Article 82 EC for the practices of an undertaking in a dominant position which are aimed at avoiding all parallel exports from a Member State to other Member States, practices which, by partitioning the national markets, neutralise the benefits of effective competition in terms of the supply and the prices that those exports would obtain for final consumers in the other Member States.[89]

The ECJ also reviewed its established case-law on refusal by firms on a dominant position to meet the orders of existing customers.[90] It found that a refusal by an undertaking to deliver its products in one Member State to wholesalers which export those products to other Member States may restrict competition not only if it impedes the wholesalers' activities in that first Member State, but equally if it prevents their effective competition in the other Member States.[91] This was in itself a sort of general defence of parallel trade. But the ECJ made an even more complete, militant and concrete defence of such trade. It stated that a firm abuses its dominant position by restricting parallel trade, particularly when it neutralises the more favourable prices which may apply in other areas[92] or when it creates barriers to re-importations which come into competition with its distribution network.[93] It concluded that parallel imports enjoy protection in EC law because they encourage trade and help reinforce competition.[94]

It is not obvious whether the ECJ believes that these final conclusions are entirely applicable to the pharmaceutical sector, for it made clear that they were drawn from caselaw which did not concern that sector. One could however assume that they are applicable, since they were made after a general remark concerning the defence of parallel trade[95] and they were followed by a plain condemnation of practices aimed at eliminating parallel trade completely which did not contain such reference either.[96]

In any case, the ECJ observed that there are objective considerations based on which a refusal to supply by a dominant company cannot be regarded as abusive.[97] It is worth noting that this statement was not linked either to the specificities of the pharmaceutical sector, which reinforces the impression that those made before were of a general nature. The ECJ reminded in substance that, according to its caselaw, a dominant undertaking is entitled to take reasonable steps to protect its commercial interests if they are attacked, provided that those steps are not specifically aimed to strengthen its dominant position and abuse it.[98]

[89] Joined Cases C-468/06 to C-478/06 *Sot. Lélos kai Sia and Others*, n 87 above, para 66. The portioning of the markets seems to involve per se a damage for the consumer.

[90] Joined Cases 6/73 and 7/73 *Commercial Solvents v Commission* [1974] ECR 223 para 25, and Case 27/76 *United Brands and United Brands Continentaal v Commission* [1978] ECR 207 para 183.

[91] Joined Cases C-468/06 to C-478/06 *Sot. Lélos kai Sia and Others*, n 87 above, para 35.

[92] Case 26/75 *General Motors Continental v Commission* [1975] ECR 1367 para 12.

[93] Case 226/84 *British Leyland v Commission* [1986] ECR 3263 para 24.

[94] Joined Cases C-468/06 to C-478/06 *Sot. Lélos kai Sia and Others*, n 87 above, paras 37 and 65.

[95] *Ibid* para 35.

[96] *Ibid* para 65.

[97] See, to that effect, Case 27/76 *United Brands and United Brands Continentaal v Commission*, n 89 above, para 184, and Case C-95/04 P *British Airways v Commission* [2007] ECR I-2331 para 69. See Joined Cases C-468/06 to C-478/06 *Sot. Lélos kai Sia and Others*, n 87 above, para 39.

[98] Case 27/76 *United Brands and United Brands Continentaal v Commission*, n 90 above, para 189, and Joined Cases C-468/06 to C-478/06 *Sot. Lélos kai Sia and Others*, n 87 above, para 50.

It was only in this context that the ECJ examined whether particular circumstances are present in the pharmaceutical sector by reason of which the refusal by an undertaking in a dominant position to supply clients in a given Member State who engage in parallel exports to other Member States where prices for medicines are higher does not, generally speaking, constitute an abuse. The result was not, at first sight, a positive one for GSK and might well run contrary to some of the CFI findings in *GlaxoSmithKline Services v Commission*.

In fact, the ECJ rejected GSK's argument that parallel trade brings only minimal benefits to consumers and even seemed to question whether such a factor should be taken into account at all.[99] The ECJ was probably relying more on its own convictions and common sense than on specific market studies when it held that such trade (i) opens up an alternative and cheaper source of supply to buyers in the higher price countries, even where the prices of medicines are subject to State regulation and (ii) might bring down prices in Member States which obtain their supplies by means of a public procurement procedure.[100]

The ECJ examined next whether State price regulations should have an impact on the assessment. It admitted that price differences between Member States for certain medicines are the result of State intervention on resale prices or reimbursement scales. However, it underlined that prices are not entirely removed from the law of supply and demand. Even in very interventionist Member States, manufacturers initiate negotiations where their price proposals constitute the starting point and retain some influence upon the level at which prices and reimbursement levels are set.[101] The ECJ noted that the task of the authorities when setting prices of medicines is not only to control expenditure connected with public health systems and to ensure the availability of adequate supplies of medicinal products at a reasonable cost, but also to promote efficiency in the production of medicinal products and to encourage research and development into new medicinal products.[102] Thus, the ECJ agreed with Advocate General RuizJarabo Colomer that final prices or reimbursement levels reflect the relative strength of both the relevant authorities and the industry,[103] rather than with Advocate General Jacobs, who suggested in its Opinion in *Syfait and Others* that prices were imposed on pharmaceutical companies at State level.[104] The ECJ also stressed, in favour of the protection of parallel trade in relation to the pharmaceutical industry, that, during the period of patent protection, such

[99] In Joined Cases C-468/06 to C-478/06 *Sot. Lélos kai Sia and Others*, n 87 above, para 57, the ECJ seems to cast some doubt on whether it is for an undertaking in a dominant position to assess its conduct vis-à-vis a trading party in the light of the degree to which that party's activities offer advantages to the final consumers.

[100] *Ibid* paras 53–57.

[101] *Ibid* paras 59–63.

[102] According to the 2nd and 3rd recitals of Council Directive 89/105/EEC of 21 December 1988 relating to the transparency of measures regulating the prices of medicinal products for human use and their inclusion in the scope of national health insurance systems [1989] OJ L/40/8.

[103] Opinion of Advocate General Ruiz-Jarabo Colomer in Joined Cases C-468/06 to C-478/06 *Sot. Lélos kai Sia and Others*, n 87 above, points 90–93.

[104] The reasoning of the ECJ also seems to contradict that of the CFI in Case T-168/01 *GlaxoSmithKline Services v Commission*, n 55 above, on this point.

trade is the only possible form of competition.[105] Accordingly, the ECJ held that the degree of price regulation in the sector cannot preclude EC competition rules from applying.

However, the ECJ did not stop its reasoning here, but considerably modified the scope of its conclusions by what seems to be a compromise solution. The compromise was based on acceptance of the principle that parallel trade is protected in the pharmaceutical sector as in any other sector, but adding an important exception to that principle. The ECJ pointed out that competition rules must not be interpreted in such a way that, in order to defend its own commercial interests, the only choice left for a pharmaceuticals company in a dominant position is not to sell its medicines in the lower price Member States.[106]

The above conclusion was probably, for the ECJ, a concretisation of its previous finding that a dominant undertaking can take reasonable steps to protect its own commercial interests if attacked.[107] But it was still a vague concretisation. The ECJ made it more precise by giving a rule of thumb to judge whether these steps are reasonable. This rule might well be the most important concrete contribution of the judgment. In substance, the ECJ held that a refusal to meet orders sent by existing wholesalers involved in parallel exports could be abusive, regardless the degree of price regulation.[108] However, it would be justified not to meet those orders when they are out of the ordinary.[109] Such could be the case, in a given Member State, if certain wholesalers ordered quantities which are out of all proportion to those previously sold by them to meet the needs of the market in that Member State.[110]

The ECJ noted that in the cases of referral the wholesalers had not demanded that GSK should fulfil their orders in their entirety, but that it should deliver them quantities of medicines corresponding to their monthly average increased at a maximum percentage of 20 % and said that it was for the referring court to ascertain whether those orders were ordinary in the light of both the previous business relations between GSK and the wholesalers and the size of the orders in relation to the requirements of the Greek market.[111]

The judgment of the ECJ clarifies a number of issues and leaves some substantial questions open. What became clear was that refusals to supply or limitations of supply to wholesalers are, if made by a dominant company, prohibited under Article 82 EC if they completely eliminate parallel trade. That is in itself an important ruling which might give some comfort to parallel traders. But it can also be deduced from the judgment that wholesalers can be denied orders which go beyond normality. It therefore seems that the ECJ's approach to

[105] Joined Cases C-468/06 to C-478/06 *Sot. Lélos kai Sia and Others*, n 87 above, paras 64 and 65.

[106] *Ibid* paras 67 and 68.

[107] *Ibid* para 69.

[108] *Ibid* para 69.

[109] *Ibid* paras 69 and 70. It is worth noting that, in doing so, the ECJ referred to the most traditional caselaw on refusal to supply ie, Case 27/76 *United Brands and United Brands Continentaal v Commission*, n 89 above, para 182.

[110] Joined Cases C-468/06 to C-478/06 *Sot. Lélos kai Sia and Others*, n 87 above, paras 71 and 76.

[111] *Ibid* paras 72 and 73.

the protection of parallel trade under Article 82 EC in the pharmaceutical sector (and probably in all sectors) can be resumed under the axiom that dominant undertakings must tolerate *some* parallel trade but not *too much* parallel trade. It is also more or less clear what *too much* parallel trade means. Dominant manufacturers can refuse to meet orders made by their wholesalers which are out of all proportion to those previously sold by them to meet the needs of the market in their Member State. But that raises some further questions. First, it is not evident what *out of all proportion* means. One possible interpretation is that this notion excludes orders which go beyond what a wholesaler ordered traditionally to cover domestic demand. However that interpretation is not plausible. It would appear inconsistent with the finding that preventing all parallel trade is abusive. The correct interpretation thus seems to be that wholesalers are entitled to buy from a dominant manufacturer a quantity which exceeds its domestic sales by a moderated amount. What should be understood by moderated amount remains an unresolved matter which, most probably, will raise future cases at national level as well as further preliminary rulings.

A second open question is whether new wholesalers are also entitled to order quantities of medicines covering an exportable amount. The ruling of the ECJ cannot answer this question because it was given in a factual context in which all the wholesalers involved were existing wholesalers. However, nothing seems to justify that newcomers can be simply excluded from the activity of parallel trade. That would freeze the market at the distribution level and might create inefficiencies for no clear reason. The situation might be clarified in future cases at national level.

## A BALLOON FLIGHT OVER THE BATTLEFIELD

Since the American Civil War and for a number of years, balloon flights were used for reconnaissance purposes during battles on the assumption that some elevation was needed in order to understand correctly the armies' strengths, positions and movements and to predict imminent manoeuvres and the future evolution on the ground. The merits of this practice are a matter for military studies and not for a paper on competition issues. However the principle that some distance and cold reflection are needed for a proper observation of a fight might well apply to the analysis of the arm-wrestling that pharmaceutical companies are having with parallel traders.

Seen from a balloon, the landscape of the battle for parallel trade in medicines seems quite entangled. Both armies have reasons to fear and reasons to hope and an end to the battle does not clearly appear to be forthcoming.

One of the first conclusions is that pharmaceutical companies cannot rely on their specificity in order to obtain an exclusion from the general application of competition rules. This argument has been openly dismissed by the ECJ in *Sot. Lélos kai Sia and Others* and even by the CFI in *GlaxoSmithKline Services v Commission.*

In spite of the above, a second visible element is that the Community courts seem to have, to some extent, mixed views and feelings on this issue. This is apparent in *GlaxoSmithKline Services v Commission* where some of the industry's arguments were first upheld by accepting that practices which normally would have been considered as a per se violation of competition rules did not have an anticompetitive object, but where later rejected when finding that the same practices had an anticompetitive effect. Such mixed views and feelings can also be perceived in *Sot. Lélos kai Sia and Others*, where the ECJ, after making a passionate defence of the concept of parallel trade, accepted to impose some limitations based on a not entirely clear concept of proportionality. One reason for this might be that the European courts believe that both the interests of pharmaceutical companies in limiting parallel trade and those of the companies trying to make use of what has been one of the basic freedoms of trade which EC competition rules have ensured for years, merit some protection. Arguably, the case-law and, especially, *Sot. Lélos kai Sia and Others,* has strived for a balance where parallel trade in medicines is permitted but only to an extent which does not dramatically reduce the return that pharmaceutical companies obtain for their R&D investments. The concrete result of that balance is a matter which needs to be further clarified in the years to come. However, it might well vary depending on the evolving perception of judges about the real impact that parallel trade has on European medical R&D.

A third visible element is that the battlefronts opened by the manufacturers have produced different results.

Concerning direct or indirect contractual bans, manufacturers have lost any hope of success. It is a battlefront in which they do not have any interest to be engaged. But there are some features of the systems which they might intend to put in place in order to reduce parallel trade which could attract them to that battlefront, such as mechanisms to monitor the behaviour of their wholesalers or threats and punishments imposed on them.

Concerning refusals to supply, *Bayer v Commission* and *BAI and Commission v Bayer* has provided for a safe harbour to all manufacturers which are not in a dominant position. There is nowadays a minimal risk for those non dominant pharmaceutical companies which decide to supply their wholesalers with the quantities which are strictly needed for their national markets. However, companies which are held to be in a dominant position would be arguably required to supply wholesalers with quantities which exceed their domestic sales in a reasonable way, according to the ECJ's reasoning in *Sot. Lélos kai Sia and Others.*

Finally, in the battlefront of dual pricing, the outcome of the appeal against *GlaxoSmithKline Services v Commission* will be decisive. A confirmation of that judgment could provide pharmaceutical companies with real kryptonite against parallel traders. If that is the case, the next predictable battle will be about the conditions for a dual pricing system to get an exemption under Article 81(3) EC. If those conditions are easy to fulfil, as suggested by *GlaxoSmithKline Services v*

*Commission*, the parallel trade in pharmaceuticals could well cease in practice. But if the ECJ imposes stricter conditions, then a new debate would be opened in which manufacturers would have an incentive to test the limits of Article 81(3) EC. Of course, another possible scenario would be the annulment of the CFI judgment in *GlaxoSmithKline Services v Commission*. In such a scenario dual pricing would probably be excluded and this would refocus the debate on the quantities that dominant companies can be obliged to supply to their dealers beyond the needs of their national markets.

Both manufacturers and parallel traders face challenges which need to be further explored.

For manufacturers, without prejudice to the outcome of the appeal against *GlaxoSmithKline Services v Commission*, the most urgent matter to explore might well be the minimum amount of parallel trade that they are obliged to tolerate if they are dominant. Most likely those manufacturers will supply parallel traders with quantities which exceed their national needs only marginally and wait for those dealers to take them to court for an abuse of their dominant position. Those proceedings will probably involve referrals to the ECJ for a preliminary ruling. Accordingly, their outcome might be known years later and many wholesalers might have disappeared or lost critical size and commercial contacts in the meanwhile. Testing the limits of the amount of parallel trade that they are obliged to tolerate may therefore seem to be a profitable option for manufacturers no matter what the outcome of this test is. Besides, it might discourage parallel traders from placing excessive orders with manufacturers.

The most urgent question to explore for parallel traders might be the possibility of using new market definitions for medicines or new concepts of dominance in order to tackle those situations in which manufacturers are not dominant according to the traditional Commission's test and are therefore covered by *Bayer v Commission* and *BAI and Commission v Bayer*. Wholesalers might for instance find it helpful to assert – and prove –, that they would be excluded from the market if they could not provide pharmacists with a full set of a number of products, which would possibly entail that the manufacturers of those particular products are in a dominant position in relation to them even if they are not dominant according to the Commission's traditional market definition. Wholesalers might also have an interest in exploring whether a series of manufacturers acting in a similar way could be considered as abusing their collective dominant position.

Given the nature of the open questions raised by the current caselaw and the relative passivity of the Commission in this matter, one could expect that the focus in the near future will be on actions entered at national level by parallel traders against manufacturers. These actions would also permit wholesalers to claim damages based on violations of competition law. Without such claims being made, wholesalers may find themselves defenceless against a never ending series of strategies put in place by producers, even if the latter, some years later, would lose in court the cases brought by the wholesalers.

In view of the current state of the law and the existing uncertainties involving parallel trade in medicines, it is very likely that there will be more and more complex legal battles. There is a need for more clarity to be provided by the Community Courts, following the example set in *Bayer v Commission* and *BAI and Commission v Bayer*, to reduce uncertainty and expensive litigation. In any case, whether seen from the centre of the battlefield or from some hundred metres above, it is not difficult to predict that interesting times are ahead.

# 16

# *Administrative Law under the Pressure of Competition Law – Some Reflections on Their Interplay*

HEIKKI KANNINEN

## TRANSFORMATION OF PUBLIC ADMINISTRATION AND DIFFICULTIES OF A STRICT DICHOTOMY BETWEEN PRIVATE LAW AND PUBLIC LAW

Administrative law and competition law may at first sight seem two distinctly separate fields of law. Competition law affects relations between undertakings in their business activity, whereas administrative law concerns internal questions of public administration as well as relations between administration and individuals. This point of departure reflects the dichotomy between public law and private law. When looking at competition law more closely, however, we can see that it extends to both public and private law, creating thereby a sort of cross-disciplinary field of law.

The dichotomy between public and private law has long been one of the general features of Roman-Germanic law – however, the question became significant no earlier than the 19th century, that of the era of economic liberalism.[1] The relation between these two fields of law has also been characterised by the classification of private law as primary in relation to public law. Since the latter was supposed to have a 'special' character compared to the former, its scope was meant to remain restricted.[2] This is also in conformity with the idea that economic activity should, as far as possible, be based on private autonomy.

The restricted and secondary position of public law reflects the fact that until the end of the 19th century, the main task of administrative law was to create foundations of civil service administration. As a concrete branch of constitutional law, administrative law gained an important role in building up

[1] See L Björne, *Oikeusjärjestelmän kehityksestä* (Vammala, Suomalainen Lakimiesyhdistys, 1979) 135 and 136.

[2] See J Chevallier, 'Le droit administratif, droit de privilège ?' (1988) 46 *Pouvoirs* 57.

a state governed by law from the end of the 19th century. At the same time, the interest of administrative law evolved more and more into analysing relations between public administration and individuals. An individual's position changed from that of an object of administration to a person whose rights against public administration were secured by administrative law. After the First World War and later after the Second World War, developed countries were faced with the need to build up a Welfare State in the aftermath of a long upswing in the economy. At the same time, this signified an expansion of public administration and changed its role to a provider of benefits and services. Securing public services became a central task of administrative law. The activity of public administration was not limited to ordinary administrative services (such as health care, education and social services), but public administration also got engaged in industrial and commercial activity for example in the form of undertakings owned by the State. In its latter role public administration operated in the same area with private undertakings.

Public administration, *sensu largo*, covered on the one hand functions relating to the maintenance of public order and control as well as measures to safeguard fundamental rights, and providing public services on the other, which could accordingly be divided into administrative and industrial-commercial services.[3]

Especially since the beginning of the 1980s, the extent and effectiveness of the Welfare State financed by public administration has been questioned, which has led to a re-evaluation of the division between the public and the private sector. This evaluation has been characterised by tendencies towards privatisation or at least implementation of principles of the private sector in public administration. Privatisation of the public sector can include many kinds of changes, from working methods to a total transfer of a certain activity.[4] Privatisation in its classic form consists of the total or partial transfer of ownership or control of a public undertaking from the public to the private sector. But it may also consist of the transfer of an activity which has included use of public authority.

Privatisation in its different forms involves many difficult legal questions. Of course, it could be argued that if an activity carried out by the public sector is transferred to the private sector, it is sufficient to operate with principles and legal remedies governed by private law. However, the privatisation and liberalisation of private markets have given rise to a need to create and improve public control.[5]

From the point of view of administrative law, the retreat of the State as an entrepreneur (producer of goods or provider of services which do not normally

[3] See P-L Frier and J Petit, *Précis de droit administratif*, 5th edn (Paris, Montchrestien, 2008) 214–217.

[4] See Recommendation of the Council of Europe on Privatisation of Public Undertakings and Activities, Rec(93)7E, 18 October 1993 (available on the web site of the Council of Europe, www.coe.int).

[5] H Kanninen, 'Privatisation and the Guarantees of Good Administration' in M Niemivuo and T Majuri (eds), *Outlooks on Democratic Institutions in the Baltic Sea Region* (Helsinki, Ministry of Justice in collaboration with Council of the Baltic Sea States, 1999) 92.

belong to public administrative activity) has little significance, especially as regards the guarantees of good administration. The situation is different when the activity transferred is of a public nature. Administrative law has developed a sophisticated system of principles and regulations to protect individuals with regard to the exercise of public power. The question is therefore to what extent these principles and regulations have to be taken into account when deciding on privatisation.[6] What can be privatised, in particular in view of the continuity of public service? Which elements of administrative law safeguarding the legal protection of individuals should be maintained (for example access to documents, protection of minorities, access to justice, penal responsibility and liability in damages)?

Following the period of privatisation, the latest development is to re-strengthen the role of public administration in order to supervise the effective enforcement of rules governing economic activity, which is a reaction to the problems caused by economic liberalisation.

The dichotomy between private law and public law is not only imprecise but also in constant motion due to transformation in society. These changes are primarily a consequence of the evolving character of public law, whereas private law has remained more stable. Thus, administrative law is under permanent pressure, aiming to follow the speed of social change. Administrative law has only seldom been able to fit the requirements of predictability or responsiveness.

The prognosis of the decadence of administrative law and disappearance of the borderline between private and public law, due to the State stepping back to take care only of its narrow basic tasks, has not become reality.[7] Public and private do still exist, but the question is not about their juxtaposition but about their interplay, in which the borderline is easy to cross. Rules deriving from both public law and private law are progressively applying hand-in-hand to the same legal phenomenon. This may be the case, for example, in situations where a state or municipality pursues a certain activity in collaboration with the private sector. For a lawyer, the situation is certainly complex. It is no longer sufficient to ask as a preliminary question whether to apply norms of private or public law, since one may need to apply both of them simultaneously.

Some modern fields of law are, indeed, difficult to classify outright under private law or public law, in particular environmental law and social law. However, certain older branches of law, such as labour law or economic law (as understood in a wider sense) also have a multiple character.

In terms of legal development, the usage of terms deriving from private law and public law is problematic without further definition. An illustrative example thereof is Article 6 of the European Convention for the Protection of Human Rights and Fundamental Freedoms (ECHR) signed at Rome on 4 November

[6] See, eg S 124 of the Finnish Constitution: 'A public administrative task may be delegated to others than public authorities only by an Act or by virtue of an Act, if this is necessary for the appropriate performance of the task and if basic rights and liberties, legal remedies and other requirements of good governance are not endangered. However, a task involving significant exercise of public powers can only be delegated to public authorities' (www.finlex.fi/fi/laki/kaannokset/1999/en19990731.pdf).

1950. It contains provisions on the right of access to justice and standards on court proceedings. Even though the text of the said article has been written solely for civil and criminal matters ('civil rights and obligations' and 'criminal charge'), its practical scope of application has extended too many administrative matters. If the matter falls under public law according to national law, it is sometimes difficult to determine whether Article 6 applies or not.

As it is, we can ask why the legal protection of an individual should not form part of uniform and same-level requirements, irrespective of the subject matter. On the one hand, when the abovementioned provision was drafted, its scope of application was meant to be restricted – this is clearly reflected by the French wording 'droits et obligations de caractère civil' in the article. On the other hand, the case-law of the European Court of Human Rights depicts how difficult it has been to follow this dichotomy in front of practical needs of judicial relief.[8]

Economic law is maybe one of the clearest examples of the relativity in drawing the line between private law and public law, if economic law is not considered a closed branch of law but rather a glossary of norms belonging partly to private law and partly to public law. Economic law, *sensu largo*, covers all norms governing economic activity – firstly, it includes norms of private law, for instance, on how to set up an undertaking or conclude an agreement; secondly, it includes norms of labour law and consumer protection law and thirdly, it includes norms of public law that affect the general preconditions for business, starting from the freedom of trade.[9]

Public economic law and economic administrative law in particular concern primarily macro-economic structures. When analysing the interplay between economic life and public administration, it is necessary to underline the positive impact good governance has on economic prerequisites. In an ideal situation these prerequisites are created by the public administration for undertakings, and such prerequisites should remain neutral in relation to competition amongst the latter. In such a passive but significant role of public administration, the interplay between administrative law and competition law remains minor. The situation changes when public administration takes an active role as a supervisor of the rules on competition law, since such an activity makes administrative law and competition law meet. In this case competition law is largely influenced

[7] See, eg C Harlow, 'European Administrative Law and the Global Challenge' in P Graig and G de Burga (eds), *The Evolution of EU Law* (Oxford, Oxford University Press, 1999) 261.

[8] The case-law of the European Court of Human Rights on civil servants belonging to the scope of Art 6 of the ECHR (judgments *Eskelinen and Others v Finland*, 19 April 2007, and *Pellegrin v France* (1998) VIII) reflects on the one hand the difficulty of drawing a line between matters of private law and matters of public law, and on the other hand it depicts the viewpoints that are changing. It is interesting to note that the European Court of Human Rights referred in the *Pellegrin v France* case to Art 48(4) of the EEC Treaty [now Art 39(4) EC], which provides for a derogation from the principle of freedom of movement for workers within the Community in respect of 'employment in the public service'. The Court of Justice of the European Communities (hereinafter ECJ) has developed a restrictive interpretation of this derogation, see, eg Case C-47/02 *Anker and Others* [2003] ECR I-10447 para 60.

[9] About economic law and terms relating thereto, see D Linotte and R Romi, *Services publics et droit public économique*, 4th edn (Paris, Litec, 2001) 11 and 12.

by administrative law, at least as regards its enforcement. On the other hand, if administrative action includes economic activity subordinated to obligations in competition law, the significance of competition law increases in relation to administrative law. This type of interplay results in the close coexistence of administrative law and competition law, which speaks in favour of a rejection of the idea that the relations between these fields of law are fundamentally tense.

## EUROPEAN COMMUNITY LAW – PUBLIC ECONOMIC LAW

The economy is nowadays strongly based on international trade regulated by international agreements. International economic law has become an important branch of public international law.

The main purpose of European Community law is to govern economic activity. The three Founding Treaties of the European Communities (Treaty establishing the European Economic Community, Treaty establishing the European Coal and Steel Community and Treaty establishing the European Atomic Energy Community) reflected such a purpose. The aim of the Economic Community was to create an internal market between the Member States. This implies on the one hand the free movement of goods and a common customs tariff towards third countries, and on the other hand the free movement of productive resources, that is, persons, services, capital and enterprises. The common policies in areas such as agriculture, transport and external trade relations are not goals or activities distinct from the common market but support it.

The provisions of the Treaty establishing the European Community (hereinafter the EC Treaty) on the four basic freedoms are primarily addressed to the Member States, by prohibiting them certain measures that would limit the functioning of the common market or by imposing on them certain obligations to act. The obstacles on the free movement of goods, workers, services and capital have been primarily caused by legislative and administrative measures taken by the governments, which have had a discriminatory effect on cross-border economic activity. Due to the principles of primacy and direct effect of Community law, an individual can rely on the provisions of the EC Treaty in a national court and get a national norm or administrative action that is in conflict with Community law repealed or set aside. Conflicts or other tensions between norms of Community law and national provisions or measures appear most often in the course of a single national administrative procedure.

The provisions of the EC Treaty on the free movement of goods, workers, services and capital have had, on the other hand, only relatively little significance in direct horizontal relations between individuals, so that an individual could rely on them against another individual.[10]

[10] The question is more about the practical implications for individuals than whether the provisions of the EC Treaty can also have a direct effect on the relations between them. It appears eg from Case 36/74 *Walrave and Koch* [1974] ECR 1405 paras 17 and 18; Case 43/75 *Defrenne* [1976] ECR 455

*Cont.*

The public-law character of the European Community is also underlined by the fact that directives are still an important legislative instrument of secondary Community law. Even if directives have been granted direct effect in the case-law, their primary addressees are Member States as legislators – directives can only secondarily create rights for individuals, and even then only against bodies governed by public law.[11] European Community law does not in principle take a stand on the form in which a directive should be implemented in the Member States – whether the provision would fall under private law or public law. However, such a choice may follow directly from the material content of a directive.[12]

Free competition can be distorted not only by measures taken by bodies governed by public law when they restrict the free movement of goods, workers, services and capital, but also by certain behaviour of undertakings. In order to avoid these problems, Title VI of the EC Treaty (Common rules on competition, taxation and approximation of laws) contains a separate chapter (Chapter 1) on competition rules (Articles 81 EC to 89 EC), a part of which is expressly directed to undertakings and not to Member States (Articles 81 EC to 86 EC). In addition, the same chapter contains provisions on State aid (Articles 87 EC to 89 EC), which are primarily addressed to Member States. Finally, Article 90 EC prohibits internal taxation that discriminates against products from other Member States.

As a result of the foregoing considerations, the competition rules set out in the EC Treaty make an exception to the general structure of the said Treaty, since they impose direct obligations on undertakings. Those rules can be regarded as the most central provisions of material Community law falling under private law.[13]

paras 31 and 39; Case C-415/93 *Bosman* [1995] ECR I-4921 paras 82 and 83; Case C-309/99 *Wouters and Others* [2002] ECR I-1577 para 120, and Case C-438/05 *International Transport Workers' Federation and Finnish Seamen's Union* [2007] ECR I-10779 paras 58–66, that many provisions of the EC Treaty can extend to situations where an obstacle or restraint is caused by a measure of a non-public body. However the general question of the extent to which the provisions on fundamental freedoms of the EC Treaty may be invoked against private acts of individuals is not yet fully clear (see, eg Case C-281/98 *Angonese* [2000] ECR I-4139 para 70 concerning Art 28 EC).

[11] See, eg Case 152/84 *Marshall* [1986] ECR 723 para 48, and Joined Cases C-397/01 to C-403/01 *Pfeiffer and Others* [2004] ECR I-8835 para 108.

[12] Unlike Art 6 of the ECHR, Art 47 of the Charter of Fundamental Rights of the European Union [2007] OJ C/303/1, does not make a classification based on different fields of law, but speaks generally about rights and freedoms guaranteed in the law of the European Union.

[13] In Joined Cases C-430/93 and C-431/93 *van Schijndel and van Veen* [1995] ECR I-4705 para 13, the ECJ stated that 'the competition rules mentioned by the national court are binding rules, directly applicable in the national legal order. Where, by virtue of domestic law, courts or tribunals must raise of their own motion points of law based on binding domestic rules which have not been raised by the parties, such an obligation also exists where binding Community rules are concerned'. The Court of First Instance of the European Communities has, on the other hand, stated eg in Joined Cases T-228/99 and T-233/99 *Westdeutsche Landesbank Girozentrale and Land Nordrhein-Westfalen v Commission* [2003] ECR II-435 para 193, that the competition rules are fundamental rules.

**Enforcement of Competition Law According to Private Law or Public Law**

Undertakings have to take into account the provisions of Articles 81 EC and 82 EC in their business activity and in their relations with other undertakings (in addition to the corresponding national norms).[14] The system based on the prohibition of restrictive practices includes undertakings' opportunity to rely on competition norms in a national court against other individuals. Depending on the case, that may be either the plaintiff or the defendant, that is, in an action concerning nullity of contractual terms or in an action for damages.[15] The question is about private-law-related enforcement of competition norms (private enforcement).

On the other hand, the public-law supervision of competition law is carried out by national competition authorities. Administrative complaints can be made to the competition authority, or the authority may on its own initiative undertake investigations (public enforcement). The competition authority may take its own decisions or take the action to court in order to impose a penalty, where applicable. The European Commission's competencies as a competition authority correspond to those of national competition authorities.

Even if Articles 81 EC and 82 EC are subject to private law and therefore addressed to undertakings, competition law is largely applied in administrative procedures through the supervision by the Commission and national competition authorities.[16] According to case-law, competition law proceedings in the Commission are expressly administrative and are thus not considered to constitute court proceedings.[17] The same ought to apply to national competition authorities.

Instead of taking legal action against another undertaking in a national court, undertakings often tend to turn to competition authorities, which then initiate an administrative procedure to find out whether competition rules have been infringed or not.[18]

This system of competition law where private law and public law are intermingled seems, at first sight, an exceptional arrangement, which, in fact, it is not. On the whole we can see that in the area of business, a sort of triangular relation

[14] See Case 127/73 *BRT and Société belge des auteurs, compositeurs et éditeurs* [1974] ECR 51 para 16: 'As the prohibitions of Articles [82(1) EC] and [82 EC] tend by their very nature to produce direct effect in relations between individuals, these articles create direct rights in respect of the individuals concerned which national courts must safeguard'.

[15] See, eg R Nazzini, *Concurrent Proceedings in Competition Law* (Oxford, Oxford University Press, 2004) 79.

[16] Council Regulation (EC) No 1/2003 of 16 December 2002 on the implementation of the rules on competition laid down in Articles 81 and 82 of the Treaty [2003] OJ L/1/1 mainly concerns public enforcement of competition rules.

[17] See Joined Cases 209/78 to 215/78 and 218/78 *Van Landewyck and Others v Commission* [1980] ECR 3125 para 81, and Case T-348/94 *Enso Española v Commission* [1998] ECR II-1875 paras 56–64.

[18] See R Wish, *Competition Law*, 6th edn (Oxford, Oxford University Press, 2009) 290 and 291, and DG Goyder, *EC Competition Law*, 4th edn (Oxford, Oxford University Press, 2003) 460.

prevails. Parties thereto are firstly, in a horizontal relation, two undertakings or an undertaking and a consumer, and secondly, in a vertical relation, a body governed by public law as a macro-level regulator and supervisor. Private law and public law meet in such a pyramid-like construction. The administrative supervision system operates as a means for control of respect of private law. As a consequence, the legal character of the material provisions becomes less clear – are Articles 81 EC and 82 EC related to private law or public law? The question may arise whether Articles 81 EC and 82 EC primarily serve the purpose of protecting undertakings against other undertakings that follow inappropriate competition methods or if the goal is to safeguard consumers' interests and, ultimately, the proper functioning of the whole economy in the name of public interest.[19]

## Bodies Governed by Public Law as Addressees of Norms of Competition Law

### *Bodies Governed by Public Law in their Business Activity*

Public administration is not only the supervisor of competition rules but is also in many ways itself obliged to follow them. Indeed, Article 4(1) EC obliges the Member States (and the European Community) to adopt an economic policy that is conducted in accordance with the principle of an open market economy with free competition.

The starting point of Community law is that undertakings owned by States, municipalities or other public entities running a business (including services) fall under the rule on prohibition of restrictive practices in the same way as private companies do. Competition law is neutral in this sense, and an undertaking owned by a body governed by public law does not have a special status.[20] The criterion is not organic but functional. According to case-law, an undertaking referred to in Articles 81 EC and 82 EC, 'encompasses every entity engaged in an economic activity, regardless of the legal status of the entity and the way in which it is financed'.[21] On the other hand, activity which is connected by its nature, its aim and the rules to which it is subject with the exercise of public authority is not of an economic nature justifying the application of the EC Treaty rules on competition.[22] This means that a business run by an administrative authority can qualify the latter as an undertaking within the meaning of competition rules, whereas if an undertaking with an ordinary company form performs duties of an authority, it does not qualify it as an undertaking subject

[19] On the functions of competition law, see Wish, n 18 above, 19–25.

[20] This rule is completed by the prohibition of any State aid which distorts or threatens to distort competition by favouring certain undertakings (Art 87 EC).

[21] Eg Case C-41/90 *Höfner and Elser* [1991] ECR I-1979 para 21, and Case C-280/06 *ETI and Others* [2007] ECR I-10893 para 38.

[22] See, eg Case C-364/92 *SAT Fluggesellschaft* [1994] ECR I-43 para 30 (Eurocontrol, international organisation to coordinate air navigation control), and Case C-343/95 *Diego Calì & Figli* [1997] ECR I-1547 para 23 (public law body entrusted by the public authorities with anti-pollution surveillance in an oil port).

to competition rules.[23] Such a definition of the concept of an undertaking is supported by Article 86(1) EC, which specifies, inter alia, that competition rules concern public undertakings or undertakings to which Member States grant special or exclusive rights. Article 295 EC (according to which the EC Treaty shall in no way prejudice the rules in Member States governing the system of property ownership) means that a Member State does not have to shut down business-running undertakings owned by the State or other public entity, but the general rule set out in Article 86 EC confirms the fact that the activity of these undertakings has to be in accordance with the general rules on free competition.

From the point of view of administrative law, the submission to competition law of business activity exercised by public bodies is normally not problematic since administrative law has little impact on this kind of activity which falls outside the normal functions of the public sector. However, one important consequence may be the necessity to differentiate the business activity from the administrative activity if they have been exercised in the same organisation.

### *Business Activity of Public Administration in the Name of Public Interest*

The relationship between administrative law and competition law becomes complex if a body governed by public law runs economic activity or other activity that is of public interest and affects the market, with the purpose of providing public services and therefore following the traditional role of public administration.

Administrative law is (or at least has been) to a great extent the law of public services and administrative law is needed as long as public services are considered necessary.

On the basis of the aforesaid, it could be argued that administrative law should by all possible means defend the immunity of public services against the effects of competition law or economic law as a whole. However, such juxtaposition would be needless and outdated. It would be more correct to state that competition law touches the field of administrative law, which therefore has a branch of competition law. The essential question is therefore to what extent the principle and the scope of public services are maintained while competition law is about to touch several fields of law horizontally as a sort of all-crossing super norm. This observation is, however, not only legal but also socio-political.

State monopolies with a commercial character as well as special and exclusive rights granted to undertakings are not easily compatible with the idea of free competition. However, EC competition law does not entirely condemn them. This is important since monopolies and special and exclusive rights are usually maintained in the name of public interest as important elements of public administration.

[23] Eg in Case C-207/01 *Altair Chimica* [2003] ECR I-8875, the activity of an electricity company as a tax collector was no economic activity.

Article 31 EC obliges Member States to adjust state monopolies with a commercial character so as to prevent discrimination against undertakings of other Member States.[24] It does not require the total abolition of monopolies. Article 31 EC is in the chapter on the free movement of goods in the EC Treaty and it only concerns monopolies dealing with procuring and marketing goods (not services).[25] Even if a monopoly is contrary to Article 31 EC, its existence can be justified by Article 86(2) EC.[26]

Article 86(1) EC restricts opportunities to establish or maintain public undertakings or undertakings that are or have been granted special or exclusive rights by public authorities, since maintaining such undertakings or arrangements may infringe competition rules in particular. For example, if the activity of an undertaking entrusted with special or exclusive rights automatically leads to abuse of a dominant position, the State can be condemned on the basis of Article 86(1) EC.[27]

Still, that restriction is not absolute, which is confirmed by Article 86(2) EC. The question is whether bodies subject to public law can maintain public services that have an economic character, or to what extent obligations of service in certain areas of economic activity (such as energy and telecommunication, postal services and transport) can be imposed on private operators. EC law does not remain fully silent on public services. In EC law, the importance of services of general economic interest and their significance for the promotion of social and territorial cohesion are recognised amongst the shared values of the Union (Article 16 EC).[28]

EC law has contributed to the partial deregulation of public administration. However, it is not only in national law but also in EC law that the principle of public services has emerged as a counterbalance to the supremacy of competition law. The principle of public services can even be seen as a general principle of administrative law – as a right to ongoing public services. On the other hand, it is true that this principle still seems to have a subordinate nature in Community Law since it is an exception to a general rule and it emphasises only the economic and not the social character.[29]

According to Article 86(2) EC, 'undertakings entrusted with the operation of services of general economic interest or having the character of a revenue-producing monopoly shall be subject to the rules contained in this Treaty, in particular to the rules on competition, in so far as the application of such rules

[24] See Case 59/75 *Manghera and Others* [1976] ECR 91.

[25] See, eg Case C-6/01 *Anomar and Others* [2003] ECR I-8621.

[26] See Wish, n 18 above, 243.

[27] Case C-260/89 *ERT* [1991] ECR 2925.

[28] Furthermore, Art 36 of the Charter of Fundamental Rights of the European Union contains the provision on access to services of general economic interest: 'The Union recognises and respects access to services of general economic interest as provided for in national laws and practices, in accordance with the Treaties, in order to promote the social and territorial cohesion of the Union'. In the Lisbon Treaty, [2007] OJ C/306/1, if entered into force, Art 16 would get a new, more precise wording; see also Protocol on Services of General Interest, annexed to the Lisbon Treaty.

[29] J-P Colson and P Idoux, *Droit public économique*, 4th edn (Paris, LGDJ, 2008) 83.

does not obstruct the performance, in law or in fact, of the particular tasks assigned to them. The development of trade must not be affected to such an extent as would be contrary to the interests of the Community'.

This provision enables derogating from the obligations set out in Articles 81 EC and 82 EC (and also from Articles 31 EC and 87 EC).[30] Nevertheless, the provision has been formulated in such a way that the main rule is that undertakings referred to therein have to comply fully with the norms of the EC Treaty. Thus, derogations enabled by Article 86(2) EC have to be interpreted strictly.

The provision set out in Article 86(2) EC is addressed to all undertakings, without making a difference between public and private undertakings. The derogation set out in the provision requires that the 'services of general economic interest' have been assigned to the undertaking by a public measure (a law or a corresponding measure).[31] As a result, it has to be a conscious intention of the body governed by public law that an undertaking takes care of an economic task of public interest. In case-law, in particular, many tasks relating to transport, power supply and communication services have been covered by this rule. These matters are therefore often related to the infrastructure of society.[32]

The provisions of Article 86 EC do not as such touch upon the question of provision of public services. If public services are provided in the exercise of public duties or otherwise without any business characteristics, it cannot be argued that Community law would require the closing down of the Welfare State.

Finally, the difficulties in reconciling Article 87 EC on State aid with financial support to the providers of public services for compensation for costs incurred in the discharge of public service obligations may be recalled. The present case-law of the Court of Justice of the European Communities (hereinafter ECJ) admits that this kind of compensation can fall outside the prohibition set out in Article 87 EC, but only under strict conditions.[33]

## COMPETITION LAW AS A GENERAL PRINCIPLE OF ADMINISTRATIVE LAW

Articles 81 EC and 82 EC apply to undertakings only. Public administrative activity of a classical nature (such as unilateral administrative acts and administrative regulation) falls outside the scope of these provisions. On the other hand, the worst distortions to competition are often caused by state intervention. As we have seen, Articles 31 EC, 86 EC to 89 EC and 90 EC in particular are addressed to Member States in order to prevent them from distorting free

[30] C Bellamy and G Child, *European Community Law of Competition*, 6th edn (Oxford, Oxford University Press, 2008) 1062.

[31] See, eg Case C-393/92 *Almelo* [1994] ECR I-1477.

[32] 'Fiscal monopolies' are also included in the scope of application of the provision set out in Art 86(2) EC.

[33] See especially Case C-280/00 *Altmark Trans and Regierungspräsidium Magdeburg* [2003] ECR I-7747. On the relationship with Arts 87 EC and 86(2) EC, see C-172/03 *Heiser* [2005] ECR I-1627 para 51.

competition but, at the same time, these provisions take into account, to some extent, the public interest even in their business activity.

The case-law of the ECJ shows that Articles 81 EC and 82 EC have gained through the loyalty obligation based on Article 10 EC a wider dimension in relation to measures of bodies governed by public law than could be deduced from the provisions themselves.[34] The ECJ has stated that even though Articles 81 EC and 82 EC are expressly addressed to undertakings only, it follows from Article 10 EC that Member States have an obligation to abstain from any measure which could jeopardise the attainment of the objectives set out in Articles 81 EC and 82 EC.

The conformity of legislative and other measures of a Member State with Articles 81 EC and 82 EC is therefore admissible, even though these articles do not concern such measures directly. In Case *Van Eycke*, the ECJ stated the following:[35]

> It must be pointed out in that regard that Articles [81 EC and 82 EC] per se are concerned only with the conduct of undertakings and not with national legislation. The Court has consistently held, however, that Articles [81 EC and 82 EC], in conjunction with Article [10 EC], require the Member States not to introduce or maintain in force measures, even of a legislative nature, which may render ineffective the competition rules applicable to undertakings. Such would be the case, the Court has held, if a Member State were to require or favour the adoption of agreements, decisions or concerted practices contrary to Article [81 EC] or to reinforce their effects, or to deprive its own legislation of its official character by delegating to private traders responsibility for taking decisions affecting the economic sphere.

When analysing the tension between competition law and public services, one can ask a broader question: whether competition neutrality or, generally speaking, competition law should also be a general principle of administrative law. It would then cover public administration not only in its business activity but also in the exercise of its traditional powers and more generally in all activities that public authorities are engaged in, which affect economic life as well.

The idea that competition law could be ignored where economic or administrative activity is based on public law or administrative decisions is outdated. On a national level, such reasoning could be taken so far that the legality of administrative action could always be reviewed on the basis of the extent to which it fulfils the requirements of competition law.

For instance, authorisation issued or refused, prohibition decided or a planning decision made by an administrative authority may affect the market situation of economic operators, even if material legislation governing the administrative decision-making does not mention this consequence as a matter to be taken into account. As a general principle, the requirements of competition law could be observed already in the administrative decision and not first later when the

[34] Art 3(1)(g) EC can also be mentioned in this context. This provision provides for the Community 'a system ensuring that competition in the internal market is not distorted'.

[35] Case 267/86 *Van Eycke* [1988] ECR 4769 para 16.

activity of an undertaking is reviewed from the point of view of competition law.[36]

## CONCLUDING REMARKS

The interplay between administrative law and competition law and their changing roles depict transformation in society. The core areas of administrative law and competition law are relatively far from each other: administrative law concerns basic functions of public administration, whereas competition law is at work in relations between undertakings. In systems based on economic liberalism such a dichotomy is clear. However, a closer analysis shows many interfaces. Firstly, compliance with competition rules and their supervision has a strong public interest, for the purpose of which administrative law is engaged in public supervision and enforcement of competition law. Secondly, certain norms of competition law are directly addressed to public administration, which is to prevent an indirect negative influence by public administration on the proper functioning of competition norms addressed to undertakings. Thirdly, the tendency towards privatisation in public administration has not led to a full privatisation of public services. The aim is to provide and secure these services in a more efficient and company-like way, without fully forfeiting their public character. To attain such reconciliation, administrative law and competition law must look for common solutions where partly controversial objectives are accommodated.

[36] French administrative law is an interesting example of a legal order where competition law has gained a wide orbit; see, eg D Chauvaux and T-X Girardot, 'Application des règles de concurrence aux actes administratifs' (1997) 2 *Actualité juridique – Droit administratif* 142; S Nicinski, 'Les évolutions du droit administratif de la concurrence' (2004) 14 *Actualité juridique – Droit administratif* 751; J Michel, 'Police administrative et droit de la concurrence' (2005) 2 *Actualité juridique – Droit administratif* 77, and D Linotte, 'Existe-t-il un principe général du droit de la libre concurrence ?' (2005) 28 *Actualité juridique – Droit administratif* 1549.

# 17

# *Value Added Tax and Distortion of Competition*

ALLAN ROSAS

## INTRODUCTION

According to Article 3(1)(g) EC, the activities of the Community shall include 'a system ensuring that competition in the internal market is not distorted'. Article 4(1) of the EC Treaty instructs the Member States and the Community to adopt an economic policy which, inter alia, is conducted 'in accordance with the principle of an open market economy with free competition'. The principle of free competition applies within the framework of an internal market which, to quote Article 14(2) EC, 'shall comprise an area without internal frontiers in which the free movement of goods, persons, services and capital is ensured in accordance with the provisions of this Treaty'.[1]

These objectives and principles are to be advanced not only through competition and State aid law in the strict sense but also in the context of many other common policies and activities. For instance, in the context of the provisions of the EC Treaty on the approximation of laws, Article 96 EC instructs the European Commission to take action if it finds that a difference between the national legal provisions of Member States 'is distorting the conditions of competition in the common market'.

Such distortion of the conditions of competition may, of course, also be caused by national tax regimes. While the tax provisions of the EC Treaty (Articles 90 EC to 93 EC, Article 94 EC as compared to Article 95(2) EC) do not contain any explicit reference to the notion of distortion of competition, it is clear, for instance, that the prohibition of Article 90 EC to impose on the products of

[1] See also Art 98 EC, according to which the Member States and the Community 'shall act in accordance with the principle of an open market economy with free competition, favouring an efficient allocation of resources, and in compliance with the principles set out in Article 4'. On such substantive or material provisions of the EC Treaty in general see A Rosas, 'EU Primary Law as Substantive Law' in A Fischer-Lescano *et al* (eds), *Frieden in Freiheit: Festschrift für Michael Bothe zum 70. Geburtstag* (Baden-Baden, Nomos Verlagsgesellschaft, 2008) 957.

other Member States any taxation in excess of that imposed on similar domestic products serves to guarantee a level playing field between undertakings of different Member States.

The harmonisation of the Value Added Tax (hereinafter VAT) regime goes further in so far as it purports to minimise distortions of competition also, and in particular, between undertakings operating in the same Member State. Some of the national indirect tax regimes predating the Community VAT system provided for cumulative turnover taxes ('cascade systems'), implying that the tax levied was added at different stages of production and distribution so that the tax burden increased along the chain. Particularly when the tax rate is high, cumulative taxes easily result in a distortion of competition even within the same country and concerning the same goods or services, especially between long and short production and distribution chains (the longer the chain, the higher the tax burden).[2]

In order to limit the negative effects of such cumulative systems, Article 97 of the original EC Treaty enabled Member States which levied a turnover tax 'calculated on a cumulative multistage tax system' to fix average rates for imported and exported products or groups of products so as to compensate for the fact that part of the production or distribution chain was situated in another country. While such compensation was required to be in conformity with Articles 95 and 96 of the original EC Treaty, in other words not to provide an advantage to national production, this non-harmonised system could not guarantee tax neutrality between domestically produced and distributed goods and imported or exported goods.[3]

A Community VAT system was considered the only possible solution. It was launched in 1967 by adopting two directives, one providing a statement of principles and the second containing more detailed provisions on the structure and modalities of the future system.[4] According to the recitals of the First Directive, the objective of a common market whose characteristics are similar to those of a domestic market presupposes a harmonised turnover tax 'such as will not distort conditions of competition or hinder the free movement of goods and services'. It had therefore become necessary to achieve a harmonised system which would 'eliminate, as far as possible, factors which may distort conditions of competition, whether at national or Community level'.

To achieve this goal, cumulative multi-stage taxes had to be replaced by a common system of value added tax. Even if rates and exemptions were not yet to be harmonised and the distinction between trade within and trade between

[2] See, eg B Terra and J Kajus, *A Guide to European VAT Directives, Vol I: Introduction to European VAT* (Amsterdam, IBFD, 2008) 301 and 302.

[3] J-J Philippe, *La TVA à l'heure européenne* (Paris, Litec, 1993) 26 and 27.

[4] First Council Directive 67/227/EEC of 11 April 1967 on the harmonisation of legislation of Member States concerning turnover taxes [1967] OJ/71/1301 (English special edition: Series I Ch 1967 14); Second Council Directive 67/228/EEC of 11 April 1967 on the harmonisation of legislation of Member States concerning turnover taxes – Structure and procedures for application of the common system of value added tax [1967] OJ/71/1303 (English special edition: Series I Ch 1967, 16).

Member States was not yet to be abolished, the new system would result in 'neutrality in competition, in that within each country similar goods bear the same tax burden [...] and that in international trade the amount of the tax burden borne by goods is known so that an exact equalisation of that amount may be ensured'.[5]

Article 2 of the First Directive, often referred to in the VAT case-law of the Court of Justice of the European Communities (hereinafter ECJ),[6] sets out the basic principle of the common system of VAT: it involves 'the application to goods and services of a general tax on consumption exactly proportional to the price of the goods and services, whatever the number of transactions which take place in the production and distribution process before the stage at which tax is charged'. Moreover, the tax shall be chargeable on each transaction 'after deduction of the amount of value added tax borne directly by the various cost components'. These basic features of the VAT, introduced by the First and Second Directives, have not been changed by subsequent directives, notably the Sixth Directive of 1977 and its recasted version of 2006.[7] The recitals of these directives contain ample references to the principle of neutrality and the need to avoid distortions of competition.

## THE PRINCIPLE OF FISCAL NEUTRALITY

The 'neutrality in competition' announced by one of the recitals of the First Directive has been repeatedly referred to by the ECJ as 'the *principle of fiscal neutrality*' inherent in the common system of VAT. This implies, inter alia, that within each country similar goods and services should bear the same tax burden whatever the length of the production and distribution chain and that the taxable person (a person who independently carries out an economic activity) is not charged an amount exceeding the tax paid by the final consumer.[8] The deduction system 'is meant to relieve the trader entirely of the burden of the VAT payable or paid in the course of all his economic activities'.[9] The tax is thus meant to be passed over to the consumer; this 'shifting' concerns an amount that is certain as it is expressed as a percentage of the retail price.[10]

The principle of fiscal neutrality, 'inherent' in the common system of VAT, and also characterised by the ECJ as a 'fundamental principle of the common system

[5] For one of the early VAT judgments of the Court of Justice of the European Communities recalling the basic objectives of the 1st Dir see Case 126/78 *Nederlandse Spoorwegen* [1979] ECR 2041.

[6] See, eg Case 15/81 *Schul Douane Expediteur* [1982] ECR 1409 para 10, and Case C-475/03 *Banca popolare di Cremona* [2006] ECR I-9373 para 21.

[7] Sixth Council Directive 77/388/EEC of 17 May 1977 on the harmonization of the laws of the Member States relating to turnover taxes – Common system of value added tax: uniform basis of assessment [1977] OJ L/145/1; Council Directive 2006/112/EC of 28 November 2006 on the common system of value added tax [2006] OJ L/347/1.

[8] See, eg Case C-317/94 *Elida Gibbs* [1996] ECR I-5339 paras 20–24.

[9] Case 268/83 *Rompelman* [1985] ECR 655 para 19.

[10] See Terra and Kajus, n 2 above, 292–294, who speak of 'legal neutrality' which will prevent a distortion of competition and thus enable also 'competition neutrality'.

of VAT',[11] has been used by the ECJ in different contexts to back up a certain interpretation of Community secondary law, notably the Sixth Directive. Some instances concern what could be described as the essence of the principle, the elimination of cumulative tax or 'cascades' and the legal certainty concerning the amount of tax which is 'passed forward' to the final consumer. In this respect, the unconditional nature of the right to deduct all the taxes charged on transactions relating to inputs is an important guarantee for this basic aspect of the principle of neutrality and the need to avoid double taxation.[12]

But this 'internal' neutrality relating to the chain of production and distribution of a product also – and this is the ultimate objective of the system – serves to put businesses dealing with same or similar goods or services on an equal footing so as not to distort competition between them. The ECJ has indeed had occasion to refer to the principle of neutrality also in situations specifically involving a comparison between transactions and traders, holding that the principle requires that 'economic operators carrying out the same transactions may not be treated differently in the relation to the levying of VAT'.[13] In this context, the Court has stated that the principle 'includes the principle of elimination of distortion in competition as a result of differing treatment for VAT purposes' and that 'distortion is established once it is found that supplies of services are in competition and are treated unequally for the purposes of VAT'.[14] The ECJ has further specified that the principle of neutrality does not require the transactions to be identical but that the principle precludes, in particular, treating 'similar' goods and supplies of services differently.[15]

With regard to the relations between traders, the ECJ has observed that 'the principle of fiscal neutrality is the reflection, in matters relating to value added tax, of the principle of equal treatment'.[16] But the Court has added that while the principle of neutrality may be envisaged only as between competing traders,

[11] Case C-454/98 *Schmeink & Cofreth and Strobel* [2000] ECR I-6973 para 59; Case C-255/02 *Halifax and Others* [2006] ECR I-1609 para 92, and Case C-288/07 *Isle of Wight Council and Others*, judgment of 16 September 2008 nyr, para 42.

[12] See, eg Case 50/87 *Commission v France* [1988] ECR 4797 paras 15–24; Case C-110/94 *INZO* [1996] ECR I-857 paras 19–23; Case C-45/95 *Commission v Italy* [1997] ECR I-3605 para 15; Case C-155/01 *Cookies World* [2003] ECR I-8785 para 60, and Case C-280/04 *Jyske Finans* [2005] ECR I-10683 paras 36–39. See also Terra and Kajus, n 2 above, 80.

[13] The quotation is from Case C-280/04 *Jyske Finans*, n 12 above, para 39. See also points 56–58 of the Opinion of Advocate General Kokott in Case C-309/06 *Marks & Spencer* [2008] I-2283. Sometimes the ECJ simply refers to the risk of distortion of competition, without mentioning explicitly the principle of fiscal neutrality, Case C-260/95 *DFDS* [1997] ECR I-1005 para 23.

[14] The quotation is from Case C-363/05 *JP Morgan Fleming Claverhouse Investment Trust and The Association of Investment Trust Companies* [2007] ECR I-5517 para 47. For other similar observations see, eg Case C-498/03 *Kingscrest Associates and Montecello* [2005] ECR I-4427 para 54, and Joined Cases C-443/04 and C-444/04 *Solleveld and van den Hout-van Eijnsbergen* [2006] ECR I-3617 para 39.

[15] Case C-363/05 *JP Morgan Fleming Claverhouse Investment Trust and The Association of Investment Trust Companies*, n 14 above, para 46.

[16] Joined Cases C-443/04 and C-444/04 *Solleveld and van den Hout-van Eijnsbergen*, n 14 above, para 35; Case C-106/05 *L.u.P.* [2006] ECR I-5123 para 48; Case C-309/06 *Marks & Spencer*, n 13 above, para 49; Case C-484/06 *Koninklijke Ahold*, judgment of 10 July 2008 nyr, para 36, and Case C-302/07 *J D Wetherspoon*, judgment of 5 March 2009 nyr, para 57.

infringement of the more general principle of equal treatment may be established also by other kinds of discrimination which affect traders who are not necessarily in competition with each other but who are nevertheless in a similar situation in other respects.[17]

Leaving aside the principle of equal treatment in this more general sense, and coming back to its application in the context of the principle of fiscal neutrality, the ECJ has held, for instance, that the principle precludes a generalised differentiation between lawful and unlawful transactions, except where all competition between a lawful and an unlawful sector can be ruled out (competition can be ruled out if, for instance, there is a total prohibition to put a certain product into circulation in all Member States).[18] The ECJ has also requested national courts to examine whether a Member State, in imposing in its national VAT law specific conditions, inter alia, on exemptions, has observed the limits of its discretion in applying Community law principles, notably the principles of fiscal neutrality and equal treatment.[19]

On the other hand, as traders who calculate the price of their sales inclusive of VAT have been held to be in a different situation to those effecting the same type of transactions at prices exclusive of VAT, the former cannot according to the ECJ invoke the principle of fiscal neutrality in order to claim the same right to round down the amounts of VAT due.[20] And in a recent case concerning universal postal services, the Court held that the universal service provider (the Royal Mail in the United Kingdom) supplied services 'under a legal regime which is substantially different' to that under which another operator which was not a designated universal service provider supplied postal services.[21] The assessment of the comparability of the services in question, according to the ECJ, did not hinge on a comparison of individual services, but on the legal context in which the services were supplied. As the legal regimes were substantially different, there was no violation of the principle of neutrality.

The principle of neutrality has further been referred to in the context of the taxable amount as well as the rate of VAT. To give an example, France was found not to have violated VAT law in maintaining different rates for reimbursable and non-reimbursable medicinal products. The ECJ observed that these products are not similar products in competition with each other and added the following:[22]

[17] Case C-309/06 *Marks & Spencer*, n 13 above, paras 49–54.

[18] Case 269/86 *Mol* [1988] ECR 3627 para 18; Case 289/86 *Vereniging Happy Family Rustenburgerstraat* [1988] ECR 3655 para 20; Case C-111/92 *Lange* [1993] ECR I-4677 paras 16–19; Case C-283/95 *Fischer* [1998] ECR I-3369 paras 21–31, and Case C-349/96 *CPP* [1998] ECR I-973 paras 33–36.

[19] See, eg Case C-216/97 *Gregg* [1999] ECR I-4947 paras 19 and 20; Case C-45/01 *Dornier* [2003] ECR I-12911 paras 69 and 74; Joined Cases C-443/04 and C-444/04 *Solleveld and van den Hout-van Eijnsbergen*, n 14 above, para 36, and Case C-106/05 *L.u.P.*, n 16 above, para 48.

[20] Case C-302/07 *J D Wetherspoon*, n 16 above, paras 58–64.

[21] Case C-357/07 *TNT Post UK*, judgment of 23 April 2009 nyr, paras 37-39.

[22] Case C-481/98 *Commission v France* [2001] ECR I-3369 para 29. See also Case C-384/01 *Commission v France* [2003] ECR I-4395; Case C-109/02 *Commission v Germany* [2003] ECR I-12691 paras 20–23, and Case C-442/05 *Zweckverband zur Trinkwasserversorgung und Abwasserbeseitigung Torgau-Westelbien* [2008] ECR I-1817.

> It should be added that this conclusion also accords with Community law on competition. In this connection, the French Government rightly refers to Commission Decision 95/C 65/04 of 28 February 1995 declaring a concentration to be compatible with the common market (Case No IV/M.555 – Glaxo/Wellcome) (OJ 1995 C 65, p. 3), in which the Commission accepted that the market in reimbursable medicinal products can be distinguished from that of non-reimbursable medicinal products.

This case thus offers an interesting example of the ECJ accepting as an additional argument a conclusion drawn in the context of competition law *stricto sensu*. While in that case, the Commission's action against France was dismissed, a French practice to accept that establishments such as restaurants and hairdressers could exclude under certain conditions service charges from the taxable amount was in violation of the Sixth VAT Directive. The ECJ noted that operators offering the same service, for the same total price, could find themselves having to pay different sums in respect of VAT depending on whether or not they indicated the service charge on their bills. Such a practice 'violates the principle of fiscal neutrality and gives rise to a distortion of competition'.[23]

The tax rate has not been fully harmonised in the EU and can thus, provided that the minimum rates fixed at EU level are observed, vary from Member State to Member State without this being considered a violation of the principle of neutrality.[24] Intra-Community acquisitions of goods (acquisitions from another Member State) are taxed in the Member State of destination, in which case the supplier is exempt with a right of deduction.

Also a number of more specific exceptions and exemptions have been authorised. Up till 1994, an example was offered by the trade in second-hand goods. Article 32 of the original Sixth Directive requested the Council to adopt common rules, while authorising, in the meantime, to continue to apply a special national system to second-hand goods. The ECJ observed that the result was a difference in treatment distorting competition between second-hand goods which passed directly from one consumer to another and such goods which were supplied by a consumer to a taxable trader who then resold the goods. In the latter case, there was double taxation as the trader was not able to deduct the VAT which the goods had already born at an earlier stage.[25] Despite this fact, and the lack of Council action pursuant to Article 32 of the Sixth Directive, the ECJ, in 1989, declined to rule that Member States were under an obligation to introduce national schemes to avoid double taxation of second-hand goods:[26]

> On the whole the Community system of VAT is the result of a gradual harmonisation of national legislation pursuant to Article 99 and 100 of the Treaty. The Court has consistently held that this harmonisation, as brought about by successive directives and in particular by the Sixth Directive, is still only partial.

[23] Case C-404/99 *Commission v France* [2001] ECR I-2667 paras 46 and 47.

[24] See Title VIII (Arts 93–129) of Dir 2006/112.

[25] Case 16/84 *Commission v Netherlands* [1985] ECR 2355 paras 15–19. See also Case 17/84 *Commission v Ireland* [1985] ECR 2375.

[26] Case C-165/88 *ORO Amsterdam Beheer and Concerto* [1989] ECR 4081 paras 21–24.

> The harmonisation is designed in particular to preclude double taxation, so that the deduction of input tax at each stage of taxation is an integral part of the system of VAT.
>
> That objective has not yet been achieved, however, as is clear from Article 32 of the Sixth Directive, and nowhere in the common system of value-added tax, as it stands at present, are to be found the necessary bases for determining and laying down detailed rules for applying a common system of taxation enabling double taxation to be avoided in trade in second-hand goods.
>
> Until the Community legislature has taken action, it is therefore necessary to continue to apply Article 32 of the Sixth Directive, which merely authorises Member States that apply a special system of VAT to second-hand goods to retain that system but does not impose on them any obligation to introduce such a system if none exists.

This conclusion is no doubt explained by the fact that there is no rule of primary EU law prohibiting double taxation as such.[27] But primary law (Article 90 EC) prohibits discrimination between imported and national products. The ECJ accordingly found that there was a violation of Article 90 EC when VAT was levied on second-hand goods imported from another Member State and supplied by private persons where no such tax was levied on the supply of similar products by private persons within the Member State of importation, to the extent that the VAT still contained in the value of the imported good was not reduced when calculating the amount of VAT payable on importation.[28]

While the ECJ thus did not rule out any possibility of double taxation of second-hand goods, the reference in its judgments to the need for harmonisation was expressly noted by the Community legislator when it, in 1994, adopted Community rules applicable to VAT treatment of second-hand goods 'with the purpose of avoiding double taxation and distortion of competition between taxable persons'.[29]

Many other exceptions and exemptions still exist today in Community VAT secondary law which may distort conditions of competition within the internal market. The most tangible diversion from the idea of an internal market without internal frontiers is the above-mentioned latitude Member States are granted in fixing the tax rate, combined with the system of intra-Community trade which is based on the general rule that acquisitions by taxable persons and non-taxable legal persons are taxed in the country of destination, while the supply of the goods from the country of origin is exempt with the right of deduction, thus implying a

[27] See Art 293 EC and, with respect to direct taxation, Case C-513/04 *Kerckhaert and Morres* [2006] ECR I-10967; Case C-298/05 *Columbus Container Services* [2007] ECR I-10451, and Case C-67/08 *Block*, judgment of 12 February 2009 nyr.

[28] Case 15/81 *Schul Douane Expediteur*, n 6 above, paras 23–40. See also Case 47/84 *Schul Douane-Expediteur* [1985] ECR 1491; Case C-165/88 *ORO Amsterdam Beheer and Concerto*, n 26 above, para 18, and E Rother, *Eurooppaoikeus ja arvonlisäverotus* (Helsinki, Werner Söderström Lakitieto, 2003) 150–153.

[29] See 3rd and 5th recitals of Council Directive 94/5/EC of 14 February 1994 supplementing the common system of value added tax and amending Directive 77/388/EEC – Special arrangements applicable to second-hand goods, works of art, collectors' items and antiques [1994] OJ L/60/16.

zero rate in the latter country.[30] The possible distortions of competition following from the differences in tax rate and the rules on intra-Community trade are thus not considered illegal despite the principle of fiscal neutrality, which is allowed to operate fully only within the confines of the VAT Directive and is not provided for in EU primary law. Hence the ECJ, in an infringement case initiated by the Commission against a Member State, held that national rules extending a restriction of the right to deduct were in violation of Articles 17(5) and 19 of the Sixth Directive and, in that context, dismissed the Member State's defence that the national rules enabled balance in terms of competition, and hence the principle that VAT should be neutral, to be observed:[31]

> The Spanish Government's argument that its interpretation of Article 19 of the Sixth Directive enables balance in terms of competition, and hence the principle that VAT should be neutral, to be observed must be rejected. The Member States are required to apply the Sixth Directive even if they consider it to be less than perfect. As indicated in Case C-388/98 *Commission v Netherlands* [...], paragraphs 55 and 56, even if the interpretation put forward by certain Member States better served certain aims of the Sixth Directive, such as fiscal neutrality, the Member States may not disregard the provisions expressly laid down in that directive by introducing, in this case, limitations of the right to deduct other than those laid down in Articles 17 and 19 of that directive.

The Directive, on the other hand, not only should be interpreted and applied in the light of the principle of neutrality but also contains some express references to the prevention of distortion of competition. It is to such explicit provisions in the Directive that we shall now turn.

## PROVISIONS IN THE VAT DIRECTIVE ON NON-DISTORTION OF COMPETITION

Among the provisions of the Sixth Directive and its recast of 2006 which refer expressly to the avoidance of distortion of competition, at least Article 5(8) of the Sixth Directive and in the recast, at least Articles 19, 27 and 34(2), authorise Member States to adopt national measures with a view to preventing distortion of competition. It is thus a question of an encouragement to adopt positive measures rather than of a negative condition for national measures which may pose a risk for competition.

Other provisions are drafted in terms of an outright obligation to prevent distortions of competition or a prohibition to take certain measures if such measures would distort competition. In the Sixth Directive, the main provisions in this regard are Article 4(5), relating to the economic activities of public bodies,

[30] The supply of services will, as from 1 January 2010, follow a similar pattern in that the place of supply, if the recipient is a taxable person, is the place where the latter has established a business and not, as has been the general rule so far, the place where the supplier has established a business. See Title V, Ch 3, of Dir 2006/112, and Council Directive 2008/8/EC of 12 February 2008 amending Directive 2006/112/EC as regards the place of supply of services [2008] OJ L/44/11.

[31] Case C-204/03 *Commission v Spain* [2005] ECR I-8389 para 28. See also Case C-338/98 *Commission v Netherlands* [2001] ECR I-8265 paras 55 and 56.

and Article 13 A(1) (f) (l) and (o) and Article 13 A(2) (a), relating to exemptions for certain activities in the public interest.[32] In the recast, these provisions correspond to Articles 13, 132 and 133, respectively. Other similar provisions in the latter Directive include Article 26(2), providing for a right to derogate from rules assimilating certain activities to a supply of services, Article 102, which allows a reduced rate for the supply of natural gas, electricity or district heating, Article 107(c), relating to the possibility of authorising reduced rates for restaurant and other similar services and Article 191 concerning derogations from certain provisions relating to the adjustment of reductions.

These provisions are not drafted in strictly identical terms. For instance, Article 13 of the recast provides that public authorities shall be regarded as taxable persons where their treatment as non-taxable persons 'would lead to significant distortions of competition', while according to Article 102 Member States may apply a reduced rate to the supply of natural gas, electricity or district heating 'provided that no risk of distortion of competition thereby arises' and Article 107 requires that reduced rates for restaurant and similar services be limited to services which are mainly local 'and not likely to cause distortion of competition'. In the following I shall limit myself principally to Article 13 of the recast, corresponding to Article 4(5) of the Sixth Directive, as it is this provision which has been most often examined in ECJ case-law.

At the outset, the general scheme of the provision should be briefly outlined. The point of departure is as follows: According to Article 9(1) of the recast, a 'taxable person' shall mean any person who, independently, carries out in any place 'any economic activity, whatever the purpose or results of that activity'. Article 13(1) of the recast, corresponding to Article 4(5) of the Sixth Directive, provides for a derogation, stating that states, regional and local government authorities and other bodies 'governed by public law' shall not be regarded as taxable persons in respect of the activities or transactions 'in which they engage as public authorities', even where they collect dues, fees, contributions or payments in connection with those activities or transactions.[33]

The ECJ has confirmed that two conditions must be fulfilled in order for the derogation to apply: 1) the activities must be carried out by a body governed by public law and 2) they must be carried out by that body acting as a public authority.[34] It has also confirmed that the treatment of public bodies acting as public authorities as non-taxable persons constitutes a 'derogation' from the

[32] See also Art 20(5) of the 6th Dir.

[33] See, eg Case 235/85 *Commission v Netherlands* [1987] ECR 1471, holding that notaries and bailiffs carry out an economic activity and that they may not rely on the exemption contained in Art 4(5) of the 6th Dir since they pursue their activities, not in the form of bodies governed by public law and forming part of the public administration, but in the form of an independent economic activity carried out in the exercise of a liberal profession. See also Joined Cases 231/87 and 129/88 *Comune di Carpaneto Piacentino and Others* [1989] ECR 3233 paras 11–19, and Case C-4/89 *Comune di Carpaneto Piacentino and Others* [1990] ECR I-1869 paras 7–12.

[34] Case 235/85 *Commission v Netherlands*, n 33 above, para 21; Joined Cases 231/87 and 129/88 *Comune di Carpaneto Piacentino and Others*, n 33 above, para 12, and Case C-202/90 *Ayuntamiento de Sevilla* [1991] ECR I-4247 para 18.

general rule that activities of an economic nature are subject to VAT.[35] But it is not a facultative derogation. The ECJ has held that Member States are not entitled to regard public bodies falling under the first subparagraph of Article 4(5) of the Sixth Directive as taxable persons, unless they are also covered by the second or third subparagraphs considered below.[36]

As to the second condition (a body acting as a public authority) in particular, the ECJ has held that it concerns activities engaged in by public bodies 'under the special legal regime applicable to them and do not include activities pursued by them under the same legal conditions as those that apply to private traders'.[37] While the Court has not always insisted on a particularly strict interpretation of the notion of public authority,[38] more recent case-law suggests a somewhat stricter approach. It remains somewhat unclear, however, to what extent activities carried out in the public interest and governed by public law but not implying the use of public powers in the strict sense are covered by the derogation contained in the first subparagraph of Article 4(5).[39]

Be that as it may, Article 13(2) of the recast (Article 4(5), fourth subparagraph, of the Sixth Directive) provides that Member States may consider activities carried out by public bodies and which are exempt under certain other provisions of the Directive as activities in which those bodies engage as public authorities. The ECJ has held that this may lead to the inclusion in the category of non-taxable persons public bodies which carry out exempted activities 'even if they are performed in a similar manner to those of a private trader' and thus are *not* engaged in as public authorities.[40]

While especially the latter possibility could give rise to distortions of competition, the second subparagraph of Article 13(1) of the recast provides an 'exception to the exception' in requiring that public bodies, *even when*

[35] Case C-288/07 *Isle of Wight Council and Others*, n 11 above, para 30. In Joined Cases 231/87 and 129/88 *Comune di Carpaneto Piacentino and Others*, n 33 above, para 11, the rule in question is characterised as an 'exception' to the general rule that persons who independently carry out economic activities are taxable persons.

[36] Case C-276/98 *Commission v Portugal* [2001] ECR I-1699 para 27.

[37] Joined Cases 231/87 and 129/88 *Comune di Carpaneto Piacentino and Others*, n 33 above, para 16; Case C-4/89 *Comune di Carpaneto and Others*, n 33 above, para 8; Case C-247/95 *Marktgemeinde Welden* [1997] ECR I-779 para 17, and Case C-276/97 *Commission v France* [2000] ECR I-6251 para 40.

[38] See especially Case C-276/97 *Commission v France*, n 37 above, paras 41–43: Case C-358/97 *Commission v Ireland* [2000] ECR I-6301 paras 39–41; Case C-408/97 *Commission v Netherlands* [2000] ECR I-6417 paras 36–38, and Case C-260/98 *Commission v Greece* [2000] ECR I-6537 paras 36–38.

[39] In Case C-446/98 *Fazenda Pública* [2000] ECR I-11435 paras 22 and 24, the ECJ held that the use of public powers showed that it was a situation of engaging in an activity as a public authority (in French: 'prérogatives de puissance publique'), but the cited passages do not seem to rule out that other situations could be covered by subparagraph 1 as well. In Case C-288/07 *Isle of Wight Council and Others*, n 11 above, paras 31 and 60, respectively, the ECJ observed that the derogation covers principally activities 'engaged in by bodies governed by public law acting as public authorities which, while fully economic in nature, are *closely linked* to the exercise of *rights and powers of public authority*' (emphasis added) and, more generally, that the first subparagraph must be interpreted 'strictly'. Compare points 97–114 of the Opinion of Advocate General Kokott in Case C-369/04 *Hutchison 3G and Others* [2007] ECR I-5247.

[40] Case C-247/95 *Marktgemeinde Welden*, n 37 above, paras 20 and 22. See also Case 107/84 *Commission v Germany* [1985] ECR 2655 paras 14 and 15.

they engage in activities or transactions as public authorities, shall be treated as taxable persons if doing otherwise would lead to significant distortions of competition. The third subparagraph supplements this rule by providing that 'in any event' public bodies shall normally (that is, when not carried out on such a small scale as to be negligible) be regarded as taxable persons in respect of activities listed in an annex (this list includes telecommunication services, supply of water, gas electricity and thermal energy, transport of goods and passengers, port and airport services and activities of travel agencies).[41] For these listed activities of a clearly economic nature, the risk of a distortion of competition has been considered sufficiently serious to merit express exclusion of the possibility for a public body to claim non-taxable status under the first subparagraph.[42]

The ECJ has confirmed that the reservation made in the second subparagraph of Article 4 (5) of the Sixth Directive for activities or transactions which would lead to significant distortions of competition applies also to activities which, while not fulfilling the criteria of non-taxable persons of the first subparagraph, have been included by a Member State in that category in application of the fourth subparagraph of the same provision.[43] The reservation included in the second subparagraph thus serves to mitigate the possible anti-competitive effects of a Member State's decision to use the fourth subparagraph in order to broaden the category of non-taxable public bodies as compared to the more strict definition given in the first subparagraph.

To sum up, if the concept of public authority in the first subparagraph of Article 13(1) (Article 4(5) of the Sixth Directive) is not interpreted narrowly, or if a Member State has made use of its right, under Article 13, paragraph 2, to broaden the scope of non-taxable persons by including activities which would otherwise be taxable, there is a risk that activities of public bodies are not subject to VAT even if private traders carrying out similar activities were taxable persons. If the activities in question are not listed in Annex I referred to in the third subparagraph of Article 13(1), the only possibility to bring them under the VAT regime is to invoke the second subparagraph relating to 'significant distortions of competition'. The purpose of the subparagraph, as the ECJ has noted, is to 'ensure compliance with the principle of fiscal neutrality'.[44]

How should this provision be interpreted and applied? First of all, the ECJ has held that, in view of Article 249 EC relating to the legal effects of directives, Member States are required to ensure that public bodies are treated as taxable persons where the contrary would lead to significant distortions of competition but that they are, on the other hand, 'not obliged to transpose that criterion

[41] Annex I to Dir 2006/112.

[42] See Case C-442/05 *Zweckverband zur Trinkwasserversorgung und Abwasserbeseitigung Torgau-Westelbien*, n 22 above, para 31, and Case C-288/07 *Isle of Wight Council and Others*, n 11 above, paras 35–39.

[43] Case C-247/95 *Marktgemeinde Welden*, n 37 above, para 21, and Case C-446/98 *Fazenda Pública*, n 39 above, para 43.

[44] Case C-288/07 *Isle of Wight Council and Others*, n 11 above, para 43. See also Joined Cases 231/87 and 129/88 *Comune di Carpaneto Piacentino and Others*, n 33 above, para 22, and Case C-430/04 *Feuerbestattungsverein Halle* [2006] ECR I-4999 para 24.

literally into national law or to lay down precise quantitative limits for treatment as non-taxable persons'.[45] The ECJ has further held that if the criterion is transposed into national law, the Member State concerned may entrust an administrative body with the task of specifying the situations in which an activity may be regarded as bringing about significant distortions of competition, provided that the decisions of the administrative authority may be reviewed by the national courts.[46]

If, again, sufficient national measures of transposition are lacking, the question arises as to whether private traders who are in competition with a public body may rely on the second subparagraph of Article 13(1) (Article 4(5) of the Sixth Directive) in order to assert that their rights have been infringed by the treatment of that body as a non-taxable person. The ECJ has answered this question in the affirmative, thus accepting that the provision has direct effect.[47]

Concerning the interpretation of the expression 'where treatment as non-taxable persons would lead to significant distortions of competition', the ECJ has had occasion to provide some further guidance in two fairly recent cases. In *Götz*, which concerned the transfer of reference quantities to German milk producers by a so-called milk-quota sales point ('*Milchquoten-Verkaufsstelle*'), the issue was whether a sales point which was operated by a regional public body ('*Landesanstalt*') was a taxable or non-taxable person.[48]

The national court, basing itself on the assumption that the activities of the sales point fell under the first subparagraph of Article 4(5) of the Sixth Directive, wanted to know, inter alia, what was the relevant geographic market if one was to assess whether there would be significant distortions of competition. The ECJ answered that as the transfer of reference quantities could take place only within a defined transfer area (which in the case in question was a German *Land*) and as, under national law, the transfer, within that area, could not be carried out by private operators liable to VAT, there was no competition situation within the area and it was thus the transfer area that constituted the relevant geographic market for the purpose of establishing whether there were significant distortions of competition.

Whereas this case concerned a public monopoly within a given area, *Isle of Wight Council* concerned so-called off-street car-parking facilities provided by both local public authorities and the private sector.[49] The national court, apparently assuming as in *Götz* that the activity was covered by the first subparagraph of Article 4(5) of the Sixth Directive, asked, inter alia, whether the expression 'distortions of competition' was to be ascertained by reference to each area where the public body in question (a local Council) provided off-street parking or by reference to the totality of the national territory of a Member State.

[45] Joined Cases 231/87 and 129/88 *Comune di Carpaneto Piacentino and Others*, n 33 above, para 23, and Case C-4/89 *Comune di Carpaneto and Others*, n 33 above, para 13.
[46] Case C-446/98 *Fazenda Pública*, n 39 above, paras 32–35.
[47] Case C-430/04 *Feuerbestattungsverein Halle*, n 44 above, paras 28–32.
[48] Case C-408/06 *Götz* [2007] ECR I-11295.
[49] Case C-288/07 *Isle of Wight Council and Others*, n 11 above.

The local authorities concerned advocated the first alternative, and the Italian Government expressly suggested that competition law principles concerning the definition of the relevant geographic market be applied.[50]

The ECJ did not agree with this thesis, however. It considered first of all that the second and third subparagraphs of Article 4(5) of the Sixth Directive 'are to be interpreted as a whole'.[51] As the third subparagraph dealt with activities as such (such as telecommunication services), it was natural to take the same approach with respect to the second subparagraph. Moreover, a 'local' approach would lead to different treatment even among bodies governed by public law and was thus not in line with the principle of fiscal neutrality. Finally, such an approach would be likely to jeopardise not only the principle of neutrality but also the principle of legal certainty, as some local authorities would be taxable persons and others would not, and as further uncertainty could be caused by changes affecting the conditions of competition prevailing on a given local market.

It should be underlined that the ECJ in its answer to this question did not speak of a national market but referred to the activity in question (off-street car-parking), as such. As *Götz* indicates, a regulatory framework relevant for assessing the application of Article 13 of the recast (Article 4(5) of the Sixth Directive) may be a sub-federal state or region smaller than the national territory.

In general, the Court in *Isle of Wight Council* stressed the derogatory nature of the first subparagraph of this provision. While it should be interpreted strictly, that should not be the case for the second subparagraph. This led the ECJ to hold, in answer to other questions put by the national judge, that the expression 'would lead to' [significant distortions of competition] encompasses not only actual competition, but also potential competition.[52] In the same vein, the ECJ held that for there to be 'significant' distortions of competition, it is enough if the actual or potential distortions are 'more than negligible'.[53]

This judgment clarifies some important aspects of the status of public bodies under VAT law and in particular the notion of distortion of competition in this context. Some questions certainly remain. Without being exhaustive, it a worth noting that in a recent case, the ECJ was asked whether public bodies which engage in economic activities can invoke the second subparagraph of Article 4(5) of the Sixth Directive if they assert that competition is being distorted by the activities of private persons with which they are in competition, or whether the provision is designed to benefit private traders only.[54] The Court's answer is in

[50] *Ibid* paras 13 and 16.

[51] *Ibid* para 39.

[52] *Ibid* para 63. The ECJ added, on the other hand, that the 'purely theoretical possibility of a private operator entering the relevant market, which is not borne out by any matter of fact, or by any objective evidence or by any analysis of the market, cannot be assimilated to the existence of potential competition. To make such an assimilation, that possibility must be real, and not purely hypothetical' (para 64). See also points 123–139 of the Opinion of Advocate General Kokott in Case C-369/04 *Hutchison 3G and Others*, n 39 above.

[53] *Ibid* para 79.

[54] Case C-102/08 *SALIX Grundstücks-Vermietungsgesellschaft*, judgment of 4 June 2009 nyr.

the affirmative. A pending infringement case raises more generally issues relating to the correct transposition of Article 4(5) of the Sixth Directive, including the scope of the first subparagraph and the relation between it and the other subparagraphs considered above.[55]

Of the other provisions of the Directive which refer expressly to the prevention of distortion of competition, it seems that it is only those contained in Article 6(2) and Article 13 of the Sixth Directive (corresponding to Article 26(2) and Articles 132 and 133 of the recast), which have been examined by the ECJ. According to Article 6(2) of the Sixth Directive, a Member State may derogate from the definition of the supply of services in paragraph 1 provided that such derogation does not lead to distortion of competition. The ECJ has made a cursory reference to the latter condition in holding that the right of derogation must be interpreted strictly.[56]

According to Article 13 A(1)(f) of the Sixth Directive, the services rendered by a group of persons to its members should be exempt from VAT if the activities of the members are exempt, provided, inter alia, that such exemption 'is not likely to produce distortion of competition'. The ECJ has held that this expression covers not only immediate but also future distortions of competition if the risk of such distortion is 'real' and that a Member State may provide a temporary exemption from tax if it is renewed only for as long as the conditions of the provision continue to be satisfied.[57]

In this context, it should be recalled that, apart from the judgments addressing the provisions of Article 13 of the Sixth Directive which refer explicitly to the prevention of distortions of competition and thus implicitly the principle of neutrality, the ECJ has on numerous occasions referred to the principle of fiscal neutrality in the interpretation of the exemption provisions of Article 13 of the Sixth Directive or in examining the legality of Member States national solutions in this regard.[58]

[55] Case C-554/07 *Commission v Ireland* pending. The oral hearing was held on 22 March 2009. The judgment will be given on 16 July 2009.

[56] Case C-155/01 *Cookies World*, n 12 above, paras 58 and 59.

[57] Case C-8/01 *Taksatorringen* [2003] ECR I-13711 paras 63, 64 and 68. Case C-407/07 *Stichting Centraal Begeleidingsorgaan voor de Intercollegiale Toetsing*, judgment of 11 December 2008 nyr, also concerned Art 13A(1)(f) of the 6th Dir, but in this case the parties before the national court had agreed that there was no distortion of competition so the ECJ did not go into this question.

[58] See, eg Case C-349/96 *CPP*, n 18 above, para 4; Case C-216/97 *Gregg*, n 19 above, paras 19 and 20; Case C-246/00 *Commission v Netherlands* [2003] ECR I-7485 paras 32–34 and 44–46; Case C-45/01 *Dornier*, n 19 above, paras 42, 49, 69 and 74; Joined Cases C-453/02 and C-462/02 *Linnewebert and Akritidis* [2005] ECR I-1131 paras 24–26; Case C-498/03 *Kingscrest Associates and Montecello*, n 14 above, paras 29, 41–47 and 52–54; Joined Cases C-443/04 and C-444/04 *Solleveld and van den Hout-van Eijnsbergen*, n 14 above, paras 35–40, and Case C-363/05 *JP Morgan Fleming Claverhouse Investment Trust and The Association of Investment Trust Companies*, n 14 above, paras 22, 29 and 46–49.

## CONCLUDING REMARKS

The principle of fiscal neutrality, according to the ECJ, is not only inherent in the Community VAT system but constitutes its 'fundamental principle'. The *ratio* of the principle is to prevent measures which distort competition. In its narrow sense the principle is the antidote of a system of cumulative turnover taxes ('cascade taxes') and thus serves to guarantee that the imposition of tax in each stage of the production or distribution chain is neutralised by the right of deduction so that the taxable amount is borne not by the traders but by the final consumer.

But as the *ratio* is to prevent distortions of competition, the principle is also directly relevant for the comparison of activities and traders. If they are in competition, carrying out 'similar' transactions, the tax should ideally be the same. The ECJ has held that the principle of neutrality is, in the context of VAT matters, the reflection of the principle of equal treatment. If traders or activities are not in competition, the principle of neutrality ceases to be directly relevant but in this case the ECJ can apply the general principle of equal treatment inherent in Community law.

As the common VAT system does not imply complete harmonisation, the principle of neutrality is not absolute. The most serious departure consists in the variety of tax rates applicable in the different Member States. Also the existence of other national derogations and exemptions may, according to the ECJ, 'interfere to some extent with the application of fiscal neutrality'.[59] This is possible because the principle is not rooted in primary Community law, which prohibits discrimination between national and imported goods but does not rule out different tax rates in different Member States. The principle of fiscal neutrality thus has the following three main functions:

- it serves as a tool of interpretation of the provisions of the VAT Directives
- it provides a limit to the margin of appreciation of Member States when they take national derogatory measures
- some of the provisions of the VAT Directive make an explicit reference to the need to prevent distortions of competition, often as a condition for derogations or exemptions.

As the main purpose of the principle of fiscal neutrality is to prevent distortions of competition, the question arises as to the relevance of Community competition law for the application and interpretation of the principle. It seems obvious that competition law may be a useful point of reference and comparison in VAT contexts as well. In at least one case, the ECJ even mentioned that a certain interpretation of what constitutes similar products in competition with each other accords with a conclusion reached in the context of Community competition law.[60] In another case, the ECJ answered a question relating to the definition of the relevant geographic market, holding that it coincided with the

[59] Case C-288/07 *Isle of Wight Council and Others*, n 11 above, para 44.
[60] Case C-481/98 *Commission v France*, n 22 above, para 29.

area in which a public body had a monopoly, thus excluding the possibility of competing traders.[61]

On the other hand, the ECJ has held that it is not the situation prevailing on the local market (at city or similar level) which determines if the non-taxation of off-street car-parking facilities provided by a local public body would lead to significant distortions of competition in view of the presence on the market of private providers.[62] The Court instead based itself on the activity as such (off-street car-parking) and thus implicitly on a certain regulatory framework accepting private car parks and thus the possibility of competition. It is submitted that the result could have been different if such a regulatory framework (whether at national, regional or local level) made car-parking facilities a public monopoly (assuming that such a monopoly would not be ruled out by other Community law principles such as freedom of establishment).

These examples show, on the one hand, that competition law may be relevant as a point of reference or at least comparison but, on the other hand, that one cannot take for granted that competition law concepts or conclusions reached in that context are as such applicable in VAT contexts as well. VAT law is fiscal law whereas competition law in the strict sense concerns the relations between undertakings. And the VAT principle of fiscal neutrality and prevention of distortion of competition is expressed at the level of secondary law whereas the prohibition of agreements and concerted practices between undertakings which distort competition appears in primary law, that is, Article 81 EC.

[61] Case C-408/06 *Götz*, n 48 above.

[62] Case C-288/07, *Isle of Wight Council and Others*, n 11 above. See also at n 49–53 above.

# 18

# *State Aid and Direct Taxation*

KOEN LENAERTS*

## INTRODUCTION

Having had the honour of sitting next to the recipient of this contribution at the Court of First Instance of the European Communities (hereinafter CFI), I ideally could have, in order to pay her the homage she is due, dealt with questions in the field of competition as fundamental as those of the legality of the European Commission's guidelines on the method of setting fines for the violation of competition rules,[1] the legality of which was recognised by the CFI in the case of pre-insulated pipes[2] and confirmed by the Court of Justice of the European Communities (hereinafter ECJ) on appeal,[3] or of the concept of agreement within the meaning of Article 81(1) EC.[4]

Considering her scientific background and her conceptions of EU law, however, it appeared to me more appropriate to deal with EU competition law by addressing it in a specific context (*law in context*). This is why I have chosen to present, in light of the jurisprudence of the Community Courts, the question of State aid and direct taxation.

It is interesting, on the one hand, to analyse how the EC Treaty provisions on State aid (Articles 87 EC and 88 EC) apply to national measures on direct taxation, certain authors having seen here relationships of 'tension'.[5] And it is

* The views expressed in this article are personal to the author.

[1] Guidelines on the method of setting fines imposed pursuant to Article 15(2) of Regulation No 17 and of Article 65(5) of the ECSC Treaty [1998] OJ C/9/3; these guidelines were replaced by Guidelines on the method of setting fines imposed pursuant to Article 23(2)(a) of Regulation No 1/2003 [2006] OJ C/210/2.

[2] See Case T-21/99 *Dansk Rørindustri v Commission* [2002] ECR II-1681; Case T-9/99 *HFB and Others v Commission* [2002] ECR II-1487; Case T-17/99 *KE KELIT v Commission* [2002] ECR II-1647; Case T-23/99 *LR AF 1998 v Commission* [2002] ECR II-1705; Case T-15/99 *Brugg Rohrsysteme v Commission* [2002] ECR II-1613; Case T-16/99 *Lögstör Rör v Commission* [2002] ECR II-1633, and Case T-31/99 *ABB Asea Brown Boveri v Commission* [2002] ECR II-1881.

[3] See Joined Cases C-189/02 P, C-202/02 P, C-205/02 P to C-208/02 P and C-213/02 P *Dansk Rørindustri and Others v Commission* [2005] ECR I-5425 paras 169 *ff*.

[4] See Case T-208/01 *Volkswagen v Commission* [2003] ECR II-5141.

[5] J Wouters and B Van Hees, 'Les règles communautaires en matière d'aides d'État et la fiscalité directe: quelques observations critiques' (2001) 5–6 *Cahiers de droit européen* 647.

appropriate in this respect to analyse the judicial control in this matter after the Commission officially announced that it was taking a hold of the question of direct business taxation with regard to the Treaty rules on State aid.[6]

It is, on the other hand, also fascinating to verify if and, if need be, how EU law on State aid frames direct taxation of Member States just as the free movement principle does. Member States are indeed required, in the exercise of their competences in the field of direct taxation, to respect the free movement of workers (Article 39 EC) and self-employed persons (Article 43 EC), the freedom of establishment of companies or firms (Articles 43 EC and 48 EC), the freedom to provide services (Article 49 EC), the free movement of capital (Article 56 EC) and the general freedom of movement granted to citizens of the Union (Article 18 EC).

As I have previously attempted to demonstrate,[7] this obligation is expressed by a requirement of equality in tax treatment of Community situations and internal situations, insofar as these situations are objectively comparable. This requirement implies, unless justified, the prohibition of discrimination – direct or indirect – and of barriers to entry (in the host State) and to exit (in the State of origin).

Can we find the same model of interpretation in the matter of State aid, a matter in which incompatibility with Community law does not result in a denied tax advantage – a national restriction – but in an allowed advantage – State aid?

The application to direct taxation of Member States of the Community law on State aid stems from the functional, or extensive, interpretation of the concept of aid developed by the Courts since the early 1960s.[8] In light of this interpretation, the concept of aid obviously contains positive benefits, such as subsidies, loans or equity investments in undertakings. It is, nevertheless, more general than the concept of a subsidy, because it embraces not only positive benefits, such as subsidies themselves, but also interventions dependent on public resources, which, in various forms, mitigate the charges which are normally included in the budget of an undertaking and which, without therefore being subsidies in the strict meaning of the word, are similar in character and have the same effect.[9] The tax advantage granted to a firm therefore potentially constitutes State aid within the meaning of Article 87(1) EC.

[6] Commission Notice on the application of the State aid rules to measures relating to direct business taxation [1998] OJ C/384/3, hereinafter 'Communication of 1998'; see also the Report on the implementation of the Commission notice on the application of the State aid rules to measures relating to direct business taxation, COM (2004) 434 final (hereinafter 'Communication of 2004').

[7] On the framing of direct taxation by free movement see K Lenaerts, *Die Gemeinschaftsrechtliche Umrahmung der direkten Besteuerung*, 66th Deutscher Juristentag (Münich, Beck, 2007).

[8] See Case 30/59 *De Gezamenlijke Steenkolenmijnen in Limburg v Haute Autorité* [1961] ECR-1 paras 20 and 21.

[9] See Case C-387/92 *Banco Exterior de España* [1994] ECR I-877; Case C-39/94 *SFEI and Others* [1996] ECR I-3547; Case C-241/94 *France v Commission* [1996] ECR I-4551; Case C-200/97 *Ecotrade* [1998] ECR I-7907; Case C-75/97 *Belgium v Commission* [1999] ECR I-3671; Case C-6/97 *Italy v Commission* [1999] ECR I-2981; Case C-156/98 *Germany v Commission* [2000] ECR I-6857; Case C-126/01 *GEMO* [2003] ECR I-13769 para 28, and Joined Cases C-182/03 and C-217/03 *Belgium and Forum 187 v Commission* [2006] ECR I-5479 para 86.

This analysis cannot be challenged by the competence retained by Member States in the area of direct taxation, since the taxation nature of a measure is not enough to prevent the application of Article 87 EC. In fact, the objective of this provision is to prevent trade between Member states from being affected by the advantages granted by public authorities, dependent on public resources, which in diverse forms distort competition by favouring certain firms or certain products. Thus, Article 87 EC does not distinguish between measures of State intervention by reference to their causes or aims but defines them in relation to their effects, such that the alleged fiscal nature of the measure in issue will not suffice to shield it from the application of Article 87 EC.[10] In other words, Article 87 EC does not exclude tax rules from its scope[11] any more than do Articles 39 EC, 43 EC, 48 EC, 49 EC, 56 EC and 18 EC.

Indeed, even if direct taxation falls under the competence of Member States, such competence must nevertheless be exercised while respecting Community law. This principle, set out numerous times by the ECJ when it has been faced with measures of direct taxation affecting free movement,[12] can also be found in matters of State aid. In this matter as well, Community law frames direct taxation such that a taxation measure may turn out to be against Article 87 EC.[13]

Even though these principles were established relatively early on, it was not until the end of the 1990s that the Commission took its first significant decisions regarding State aid and direct taxation,[14] something legal scholars have not failed to note.[15]

[10] See Case 173/73 *Commission v Italy* [1974] ECR 709 para 13. See also Case C-241/94 *France v Commission* [1996] ECR I-4551 para 20, and Case C-480/98 *Spain v Commission* [2000] ECR I-8717 para 16.

[11] See Joined Cases C-182/03 and C-217/03 *Belgium and Forum 187 v Commission*, n 9 above, para 81.

[12] On this question, see K Lenaerts and L Bernardeau, 'L'encadrement communautaire de la fiscalité directe' (2007) 1–2 *Cahiers de droit européen* 19.

[13] Case T-67/94 *Ladbroke Racing v Commission* [1998] ECR II-1 para 14. This judgment was the subject of an appeal which was rejected by the ECJ in Case C-83/98 P *France v Ladbroke Racing and Commission* [2000] ECR I-3271. See also Case C-156/98 *Germany v Commission* [2000] ECR I-6857 para 79.

[14] See in particular, State Aid C45/2001 (ex NN39/2000) – Coordination centres ('quartiers généraux') and logistics centres [2001] OJ C/302/2; State Aid C46/2001 (ex NN41/2000) – Central corporate treasuries [2001] OJ C/302/7; State Aid C47/2001 (ex NN42/2000) – Control and coordination centres of foreign companies [2001] OJ C/304/2; State Aid C 48/2001 (ex NN43/2000) – Vizcaya coordination centres [2001] OJ C/304/6; State Aid C49/2001 (ex NN46/2000) – Coordination centres [2001] OJ C/304/10; State Aid C50/2001 (ex NN47/2000) – Finance companies [2001] OJ C/306/2; State Aid C51/2001 (ex NN48/2000) – International financing activities [2001] OJ C/306/6; State Aid C54/2201 (ex NN 55/2000) – Foreign income [2001] OJ C/308/2; State Aid C55/2001 (ex NN98/2000) – Åland Islands captive insurance [2001] OJ C/309/4.

[15] See in particular, JM Communier, *Droit fiscal communautaire* (Bruxelles, Bruylant, 2001) 161–167; AJ Easson, 'State aid and the Primarolo list' (2001) 2 *EC Tax Journal* 109; J Blumenberg and M Lausterer, 'Staatliche Beihilfen im Bereich der direkten Unternehmensbesteuerung' in *Steuerrecht und europäische Integration: Festschrift für Albert J. Rädler zum 65. Geburtstag* (München, Beck, 1999) 1; J Flynn, 'Anti-competitive tax breaks: how to attack them under the State aid rules' (2001) 2 *EC Tax Journal* 101; V Götz, 'Steuervergünstigungen als Gegenstand der europäischen Beihilfenaufsicht' in *Staaten und Steuern: Festschrift für Klaus Vogel zum 70. Geburtstag* (Heidelberg, Müller, 2000) 579; JP Keppenne, 'Politiques fiscales nationales et contrôle communautaire des aides d'État' (2000) 66 *Journal des tribunaux – Droit européen* 25; K Lenaerts, 'Tax law and the Court of First Instance of

*Cont.*

In its Communication of 1998, the Commission announced its intention 'to examine or re-examine case by case, on the basis of this notice, the tax arrangements in force in the Member States'.[16] The Commission above all highlighted its undertaking 'to draw up guidelines on the application of Articles [87 EC] and [88 EC] to measures relating to direct business taxation and committed itself' to the strict application of the aid rules concerned.[17]

This undertaking regarding State aid in the form of tax measures forms part of 'the wider objective of clarifying and reinforcing the application of the State aid rules in order to reduce distortions of competition in the single market'. The Commission considered that 'the principle of incompatibility with the common market and the derogations from that principle apply to aid "in any form whatsoever", including certain tax measures'. The question whether a tax measure can be qualified as aid under Article 87(1) EC, however, 'calls for clarification' which the Communication proposed to provide.[18]

The encompassing of tax measures by the law of State aid raises the central question in what way State aid in the form of tax measures can be distinguished from general tax policy measures. This presents the question of the specificity of the aid, that is, the central question with regard to the concept of aid within the meaning of Article 87(1) EC. But this understanding also particularly highlights the extent of the control by the Community of the exercise by Member States of their competences in the area of direct taxation, that is, the Community law framing of the exercise of national sovereignty in this area.

Going beyond this question, the case-law of the ECJ requires that four conditions be cumulatively met in order for State aid within the meaning of Article 87(1) EC to exist: the existence of an advantage to the benefit of certain firms, the selectivity of this advantage, the requirement according to which the aid must be funded by State resources and be attributable to the State, and the requirement according to which the aid scheme must affect trade between Member States and distort or threaten to distort competition. In relation to direct taxation, some of these elements appear to be somehow problematic.

the European Communities' (2001) 1 *EC Tax Review* 2; R Luja, 'Tax Treaties and State Aid, some thoughts' (2004) 5 *European Taxation* 234; P Nicolaides, 'Fiscal Aid in the EC; A Critical Review of Current Practice' (2001) 3 *World Competition* 319; P Nicolaides, 'Fiscal State Aid in the EU, The Limits of Tax Autonomy' (2004) 3 *World Competition* 365; C Panayi, 'State Aid and Tax, the Third Way?' (2004) 6/7 *Intertax* 283; C Panayi, 'European Union, Limitation on benefits and State aid' (2004) 2–3 *European Taxation* 83; C Pinto, 'European Union, EC State aid rules and tax incentives, a U-turn in Commission policy? (Part I)' (1999) 39 *European Taxation*; C Pinto, 'European Union, EC State aid rules and tax incentives, a U-turn in Commission policy? (Part II)' (1999) 9 *European Taxation* 343; W Schön, 'Taxation and State aid in the European Union' (1999) 5 *Common Market Law Review* 911; see also FC de Hosson, 'Tax Facilities for State-Induced Costs under the EC State Aid Rules' (2007) 12 *Intertax* 719; P Rossi-Maccanico, 'The specificity criterion in fiscal aid review, proposals for State aid control of direct business tax measures' (2007) 2 *EC Tax Review* 90.

[16] Communication of 1998, recital 4; this communication extended the code of conduct in the domain of business taxation, adopted in 1997 and having as objective the invitation of the Member States to a greater discipline in the matter of direct taxation in order to reduce harmful tax competition between Member States in this domain ([1998] OJ C/2/1).

[17] Communication of 1998, recital 1.

[18] Communication of 1998, recital 2.

## ADVANTAGE

For there to be State aid within the meaning of Article 87(1) EC, the taxation measure must, first, procure a taxation advantage to its beneficiaries that reduces the burdens that normally encumber their budget.[19]

Such an advantage may be obtained by a reduction in the tax burden of the firm in various ways, including by a reduction in the tax base (such as special deductions, accelerated or special depreciation), by a total or partial reduction in the amount of tax (such as tax exemption on profits, tax credit, exemption of reserves), by a deferment or cancellation, or even by a special rescheduling of tax debt.[20]

Thus, in the case that gave rise to the judgment *Banco Exterior de España*, the ECJ held that a 'measure by which the public authorities grant to certain undertakings a tax exemption which, although not involving a transfer of State resources, places the persons to whom the tax exemption applies in a more favourable financial situation than other taxpayers constitutes State aid within the meaning of Article [87(1) EC]'.[21] In this particular case, the question related to Spanish legislation in which public institutions were exempted from all types of tax.

Similarly, in the case giving rise to the judgment *Belgium and Forum 187 v Commission*, the ECJ recognised that the Commission rightfully found that the Belgian tax regime at issue allocated advantages to the benefit of certain firms.[22] In comparing that regime with the ordinary tax system, based on the difference between profits and outgoings of an undertaking carrying on its activities in conditions of free competition, the ECJ held that the advantages resulted from rules relating to the assessment of taxable income,[23] exemption from property tax,[24] exemption from capital duty[25] and exemption from withholding tax.[26]

[19] In his Opinion in Case C-308/01 *GIL Insurance and Others* [2004] ECR I-4777, Advocate General Geelhoed considered that the notion that a distortion created by an exceptional burden may be viewed as the grant of aid in favour of the economic operators who continue to come within the general rule is in principle incorrect on both legal and economic grounds and on policy grounds. This leads to the conclusion that a specific distortion created by an exceptional burden can never be regarded as the grant of aid in favour of the market participants coming under the general measure, and that, consequently, if the relevant distortion must be eliminated in the interest of the common market the Community will have to eliminate the source of that distortion, namely the exceptional burden; in that connection it must make use of its competences under Arts 96 EC and 97 EC and not those under Arts 87 EC and 88 EC (points 73–77 of the Opinion).

[20] See Communication of 1998, recital 9, and of 2004, recitals 9–17.

[21] See Case C-387/92 *Banco Exterior de España*, n 9 above, para 14.

[22] Joined Cases C-182/03 and C-217/03 *Belgium and Forum 187 v Commission*, n 9 above.

[23] *Ibid* paras 90–102.

[24] *Ibid* paras 103–105.

[25] *Ibid* paras 106–108.

[26] *Ibid* paras 109–112.

STATE RESOURCES

Secondly, in order for the advantages to qualify as aid within the meaning of Article 87(1) EC, they must, on the one hand, be granted directly or indirectly by means of State resources, and on the other hand, be attributable to the State.[27]

State support may be provided just as well by means of legislative, regulatory or administrative tax provisions as through the practices of tax authorities.[28]

According to the Commission, the loss of tax revenue is equivalent to consumption of State resources in the form of fiscal expenditure.[29] This reasoning, which is equally applicable concerning regional or local public bodies below central state level,[30] has been criticised. It has been particularly pointed out that the loss of tax revenue or the improvement in the financial situation of beneficiaries of a tax measure is indeed inherent in all measures involving an effective reduction of tax burdens, even if the measure is of general application.[31]

According to the ECJ, however, what matters is the existence of a connection between the tax concession and the advantage given to the undertakings in question since, in economic terms, the alteration of market conditions which gives rise to the advantage is the consequence of the public authorities' loss of tax revenue.[32]

It should be added in this context that, according to the Commission, the fact that an aid scheme in the area of direct taxation has a positive overall effect on public revenue cannot, by itself, rule out its classification as State aid. Indeed, the Commission considers that the concept of State resources, within the meaning of Article 87(1) EC, must be assessed at the level of the individual recipient and without taking into account the indirect effects of the tax measure at issue in economic or budgetary terms.[33]

This approach appears to have been endorsed by the ECJ in *Belgium and Forum 187 v Commission*. In that case, it was undisputed that the condition of imputability of the measure to the State had been satisfied, since the tax scheme in question had been drawn up by the Belgian Government. Forum 187, however, argued that the Belgian State had received 500 million euros per year in tax revenues and social security contributions from the coordination centres, such that the condition of State resources was not satisfied.[34] On this point, the ECJ limited itself to finding that the shortfall of tax and social security revenue on that State's part resulting from the exemptions at issue meant that the advantages which they gave rise to were granted through State resources.[35]

[27] Case C-126/01 *GEMO*, n 9 above, para 24, and Joined Cases C-182/03 and C-217/03 *Belgium and Forum 187 v Commission*, n 9 above, para 128.

[28] See Communication of 1998, recital 10.

[29] *Ibid.*

[30] See Communication of 2004, recitals 18 and 20.

[31] See, mainly, Wouters and Van Hees, n 5 above, at 655.

[32] Case C-156/98 *Germany v Commission*, n 9 above, para 27.

[33] See Communication of 2004, recitals 19 and 20.

[34] Joined Cases C-182/03 and C-217/03 *Belgium and Forum 187 v Commission*, n 9 above, para 128.

[35] *Ibid* para 129.

Thus, just as the loss of tax revenue cannot justify a fiscal restriction to free movement,[36] the earning of tax revenue also cannot justify a measure which in principle constitutes State aid.

## AFFECTING TRADE BETWEEN MEMBER STATES AND DISTORTION OF COMPETITION

Thirdly, for there to be State aid within the meaning of Article 87(1) EC, the benefiting tax measure must affect trade between Member states and distort or threaten to distort competition.

In this respect, it emerges from the ECJ's jurisprudence that competition is threatened as soon as a measure reduces the burdens of the beneficiary undertaking and thus strengthens its position compared to other competing undertakings.[37]

This criterion presupposes that the beneficiary of the measure exercises an economic activity, independent of the beneficiary's legal status or means of financing. Under settled case-law, for the purposes of this provision, the condition of trade being affected is met if the recipient firm carries on an economic activity involving trade between Member States. Neither the fact that aid is relatively small in amount,[38] nor the fact that the recipient is moderate in size or its share of the Community market very small,[39] nor indeed the fact that the recipient does not carry out exports[40] or exports virtually all of its production outside the Community[41] do anything to alter this condition.[42]

In *Belgium and Forum 187 v Commission*, the ECJ determined that the advantages granted to coordination centres had the effect of distorting competition between them and service providers in the financial, taxation, trust, information technology and recruitment sectors by encouraging group companies to make use of the services provided by those centres. Furthermore, the wide-ranging nature of the activities carried on by the multinational groups which have established a coordination centre meant that the tax scheme in

[36] In the litigation of direct taxation and free movement, certain States have emphasised the objective of preventing the erosion of the tax base so as to prevent taxpayers from gaining an advantage from the differences that exist between the tax regimes of Member States. This objective is always excluded, since it does not appear in the Treaty and does not constitute a mandatory requirement of the general interest. It thus cannot be invoked in order to justify a measure in principle contrary to free movement: Case C-264/96 *ICI* [1998] ECR I-4695 para 28; Case C-9/02 *de Lasteyrie du Saillant* [2004] ECR I-2409 paras 51 and 60; Case C-319/02 *Manninen* [2004] ECR I-7477 para 49; Case C-196/04 *Cadbury Schweppes and Cadbury Schweppes Overseas* [2006] ECR I-7995 para 49, and Case C-194/06 *Orange European Smallcap Fund* [2008] ECR I-3747.

[37] See Case 730/79 *Philip Morris Holland v Commission* [1980] ECR 2671 para 11; Case 259/85 *France v Commission* [1987] ECR 4393 para 24, and Joined Cases C-182/03 and C-217/03, *Belgium and Forum 187 v Commission*, n 9 above, para 131.

[38] See, however, the Communication of the Commission on the *de minimis* rule [1996] OJ C/68/9.

[39] See Joined Cases C-278/92 to C-280/92 *Spain v Commission* [1994] ECR I-4103.

[40] See Case 102/87 *France v Commission* [1988] ECR 4067.

[41] See Case C-142/87 *Belgium v Commission* [1990] ECR I-959.

[42] Communication of 1998, recital 11.

question inevitably had an impact on competition. Lastly, the scheme necessarily affected trade between Member States, since the coordination centres were set up by multinational companies which were established in at least four States.[43]

## SELECTIVITY

According to settled case-law, Article 87(1) EC requires a determination whether, under a particular statutory scheme, a State measure is such as to favour 'certain undertakings or the production of certain goods' over others which are in a legal and factual situation that is comparable in the light of the objective pursued by the measure in question. If so, the measure satisfies the condition of selectivity which defines State aid as laid down by that provision.[44]

Thus, fourthly and lastly, for there to be State aid, within the meaning of Article 87(1) EC, the taxation measure in question must be specific or selective in the sense that it favours certain firms or products. The observance of this condition is crucial when the national measure in question concerns direct taxation. Indeed, the rules of direct taxation are normally of general application.

According to the Commission, tax measures open to all economic actors operating in the territory of a Member State are in principle general measures. They must effectively be open to all firms on the basis of equality of access, and their scope cannot be de facto reduced, for instance by the retention of discretionary power for the tax authorities or by other means which restrain their practical effect. This condition, however, does not limit the power of Member States to choose the economic policy which they judge the most appropriate and, in particular, to distribute the tax charge to different factors of production as they see fit.[45]

Nevertheless, certain direct taxation measures can define their scope *ratione personae* (the tax measure is only applicable to certain types of companies), *ratione temporis* (the tax measure is only applicable to companies established before or after a certain date), *ratione materiae* (the tax measure is only applicable to certain activities), or *ratione loci* (the tax measure is only applicable to certain geographic zones).

In this respect, the Commission considers that the fact that certain firms or sectors benefit more than others from certain of these tax measures does not necessarily result in them entering in the scope of competition rules concerning matters of State aid.[46]

[43] Joined Cases C-182/03 and C-217/03 *Belgium and Forum 187 v Commission*, n 9 above, paras 132–134.

[44] Case C-143/99 *Adria-Wien Pipeline and Wietersdorfer & Peggauer Zementwerke* [2001] ECR I-8365 [hereinafter *Adria-Wien Pipeline*] para 41; Case C-409/00 *Spain v Commission* [2003] ECR I-1487 para 47; Case C-308/01 *GIL Insurance and Others*, n 19 above, para 68; Case C-172/03 *Heiser* [2005] ECR I-1627 para 40; Joined Cases C-182/03 and C-217/03 *Belgium and Forum 187 v Commission*, n 9 above, para 119, and Case C-487/06 *British Aggregates v Commission*, judgment of 22 December 2008 nyr, para 82.

[45] See Communication of 1998, recital 13, and of 2004, recitals 26–29.

[46] Communication of 1998, recital 14. The Commission notes in this respect that the measures designed to reduce taxation of labour for all firms have a relatively greater effect on labour-intensive

*Cont.*

In spite of the delicate character of its assessment, the selectivity of the tax measures involved remains the cardinal condition for them to qualify as State aid within the meaning of Article 87(1) EC, just as the objective comparability of internal and Community situations constitutes the cardinal condition for the framing of national direct taxation measures by the free movement principle.[47]

As one can see, it is the granting of an advantage to certain taxpayers that makes it possible for a measure to fall under Article 87(1) EC, whereas the framing of national direct taxation measures by the free movement principle requires that taxpayers covered by a Community situation to whom the grant of a tax advantage is often refused be treated like taxpayers covered by a similar internal situation. In both cases, the Treaty generates an obligation of equality of tax treatment of objectively comparable situations.[48] In the first case, it is the non-application of the (more burdensome) general tax law which relates the measure to the notion of State aid and makes it in principle forbidden. In the second case, it is the non-application of the (less burdensome) tax regime applicable to internal situations which results in the measure constituting a restriction forbidden in principle by the free movement provisions.

Let us recall at this juncture that in his Opinion in *Tiercé Ladbroke v Commission*, Advocate General Cosmas saw an application of the principle of equality of treatment in the assessment of the condition of selectivity of State aid.[49]

It is of course in the classical cases that the question of selectivity does not raise any particular difficulties. Thus, in *Belgium and Forum 187 v Commission*, the ECJ found that the exemptions from property tax, withholding tax and capital duty constituted derogations from the ordinary Belgian tax regime and that the selective character of those exemptions was accordingly established. Also, as regards the method of determining taxable income, the ECJ found that the regime applied only to international groups having subsidiaries which were established in at least four different countries, which had capital and reserves of

industries than on capital-intensive industries, without necessarily constituting State aid, and that tax incentives for environmental, R&D or training investment favour only the firms which undertake such investment, but again do not necessarily constitute State aid.

[47] See, in particular, Case C-418/07 *Papillon*, judgment of 27 November 2008 nyr, paras 27–32.

[48] See also below.

[49] Thus, in point 30 of his Opinion in Case C-353/95 P *Tiercé Ladbroke v Commission* [1997] ECR I-7007, Advocate General Cosmas pointed out that 'the wording of Article [87(1) EC] is imprecise' and that 'the idea of treatment "favouring" an undertaking, that is, which gives it an advantage measurable in monetary terms, implies a preliminary comparison between the treatment applied to the undertaking supposedly benefiting from aid and that reserved to other undertakings. In other words, it is essential to determine the point of reference for the comparison in order to determine whether or not it grants an advantage. There are two possible definitions of the concept of "advantage" and, most of the time, it turns out that in the final analysis, the two are synonyms. In general terms, the advantage may consist of a profit other than that which can be obtained in conditions of open competition. Following another method, perhaps more certain, the favourable treatment must be defined with regards to that applied to firms (competitors) who find themselves in the same factual and legal situation as the undertaking supposedly favoured, and which practice an activity of the same nature as that of the latter. Seen from this perspective, the prohibition on State aid arises as an emanation of the general principle of equality and of the rule which follows from it according to which identical situations are always subject to the same regulatory instrument.'

at least BEF 1 000 million, and had an annual consolidated turnover of at least BEF 10 000 million, such that the regime in question was also selective in that regard.[50]

There are, however, numerous cases in which the condition of selectivity raises difficulties. This is the case, for instance, where the aid is granted by a region or where the Member State or the Commission consider that the measure does not constitute aid, since it is justified by the nature or general scheme of the tax system.

## REGIONAL AID

The fact that an aid programme was adopted by a state in a federation or by a regional authority and not by the federal or central power does not prevent the application of Article 87(1) EC if the relevant conditions are satisfied. In referring to 'any aid granted by a Member State or through State resources in any form whatsoever', Article 87(1) EC is directed at all aid financed from public resources. It follows that aid granted by regional and local bodies of the Member States, whatever their status and description, must be scrutinised to determine whether it complies with Article 87 EC.[51]

In this respect, the Commission considers that only measures whose impact applies to the whole of the State's territory escape the criteria of specificity established by Article 87(1) EC.[52] Certainly, measures of regional or local territorial impact may indeed favour certain firms. And it is true that the Treaty itself qualifies measures destined to favour the economic development of a region as aid. It explicitly provides under Article 87(3)(a) and (c) EC for derogations from the general principal of incompatibility set forth by Article 87(1) EC for this type of aid.

Does that mean that all measures of direct taxation whose application is geographically limited are necessarily selective and susceptible to constituting State aid in the sense of the Treaty rules on this subject?

In its decision regarding the taxation system of the Azores, the Commission gave its opinion on the question of regional selectivity by analysing a tax measure which consisted of a reduction of the tax rate on the revenue taken by the regional authorities in the Azores as part of their tax autonomy recognised by the Portuguese constitution.[53] The Commission found that the selectivity of the measure was based on a comparison between the advantageous tax system granted to certain undertakings and the treatment that applied to other

[50] Joined Cases C-182/03 and C-217/03 *Belgium and Forum 187 v Commission*, n 9 above, paras 120–123. See also Case T-55/99 *CETM v Commission* [2000] ECR II-3207 paras 47–49.

[51] Case 248/84 *Germany v Commission* [1987] ECR 4013 para 17.

[52] See Communication of 1998, recital 17.

[53] Commission Decision 2003/442/EC of 11 December 2002 on the part of the scheme adapting the national tax system to the specific characteristics of the Autonomous Region of the Azores which concerns reductions in the rates of income and corporation tax [2003] OJ L/150/52.

undertakings within the same reference framework, which it defined as being the territory of the Member State.

Since, in this case, the reductions granted by the regional authorities in the Azores could not be regarded as a mechanism that would allow all local authorities of a particular level to introduce and levy local taxes with no reference at all to national taxation, the Commission decided that the measure involved a reduction applicable solely in the Azores in the rate of tax established by national legislation and applicable in the rest of the Portuguese territory, and as a result had to be regarded as selective.[54]

Faced with an action for annulment of this decision by Portugal, the ECJ had a chance to provide the necessary interpretation of the condition of selectivity for regional tax measures to be regarded as State aid.[55]

First, the ECJ recalled that, in order to determine whether the measure at issue was selective it was appropriate to examine whether, within the context of a particular legal system, that measure constituted an advantage for certain undertakings in comparison with others which were in a comparable legal and factual situation, the determination of the reference framework having a particular importance in the case of tax measures, since the very existence of an advantage may be established only when compared with 'normal' taxation. The 'normal' tax rate is the rate in force in the geographical area constituting the reference framework.[56]

In this respect, the ECJ specified that the reference framework need not necessarily be defined within the limits of the Member State concerned, so that a measure conferring an advantage in only one part of the national territory is not selective on that ground alone for the purposes of Article 87(1) EC. Indeed, according to the ECJ, it is possible that an infra-State body enjoys a legal and factual status which makes it sufficiently autonomous in relation to the central government of a Member State, with the result that, by the measures it adopts, it is that body and not the central government which plays a fundamental role in the definition of the political and economic environment in which undertakings operate. In such a case it is the area in which the infra-State body responsible for the measure exercises its powers, and not the country as a whole, that constitutes the relevant context for the assessment of whether a measure adopted by such a body favours certain undertakings in comparison with others in a comparable legal and factual situation, having regard to the objective pursued by the measure or the legal system concerned.[57]

The ECJ thus clearly established the rule that a measure cannot be selective within the meaning of Article 87(1) EC solely for the reason that it is only

[54] See Communication of 2004, recitals 30–33.

[55] Case C-88/03 *Portugal v Commission* [2006] ECR I-7115. The ECJ was also faced with this question concerning a decision of the same import in the cases Juntas Generales de Guipúzcoa and Diputación Foral de Guipúzcoa (C-400/97), Juntas Generales d'Alava and Diputación Foral d'Alava (C-401/97) and Juntas Generales de Vizcaya (C-402/97), in which the Advocate General presented his Opinion, but which were removed from the register of the ECJ by order [2000] ECR I-1073.

[56] Case C-88/03 *Portugal v Commission,* n 55 above, paras 53–56.

[57] *Ibid* paras 57 and 58.

applicable in a limited geographic zone of a Member State. It is appropriate, in order to determine the selectivity of a measure adopted by an infra-State body which, like the measure at issue, seeks to establish in one part of the territory of a Member State a tax rate which is lower than the rate in force in the rest of that State, to examine whether that measure was adopted by that body in the exercise of powers sufficiently autonomous vis-à-vis the central power.[58]

In this respect, the ECJ specified that in order that a decision taken in such circumstances can be regarded as having been adopted in the exercise of sufficiently autonomous powers, that decision must, first of all, have been taken by a regional or local authority which has, from a constitutional point of view, a political and administrative status separate from that of the central government. Next, the decision must have been adopted without the central government being able to directly intervene as regards its content. Finally, the financial consequences of a reduction of the national tax rate for undertakings in the region must not be offset by aid or subsidies from other regions or the central government.[59] Those three conditions, commonly considered to be the criteria of institutional, procedural, economic and financial autonomy, were very recently confirmed by the ECJ in a case concerning tax measures adopted by the Territorios Históricos and the Autonomous Community of the Basque Country.[60]

In the case which gave rise to the judgment *Portugal v Commission*, the ECJ considered that, failing to satisfy the three-fold condition of autonomy, the relevant legal framework for determining the selectivity of the tax measures at issue could not be defined exclusively within the geographical limits of the Azores region, and that those measures had to be assessed in relation to the whole of the Portuguese territory, in the context of which they appeared to be selective.[61] The ECJ consequently examined whether the tax measures at issue could be justified by the nature or general scheme of the Portuguese tax system.[62]

## NATURE OR GENERAL SCHEME OF THE TAX SYSTEM

Just as the ECJ recognises that tax restrictions to free movement may be justified as mandatory requirements of general interest, it recognises equally that a tax measure forbidden in principle by Article 87(1) EC may be justified – and this beyond the exemptions provided for in Article 87(2) and (3) EC – by the nature or overall structure of the tax system.

It is interesting to recall that the Commission clarified in its Communication of 1998 that for Article 87(1) EC to apply to a tax measure, that measure must

[58] *Ibid* para 62.

[59] *Ibid* para 67.

[60] Joined Cases C-428/06 to C-434/06 *Unión General de Trabajadores de La Rioja*, judgment of 11 September 2008 nyr, para 51. In this judgment, the ECJ especially clarified the criteria for economic and financial autonomy (see paras 123–129).

[61] Case C-88/03 *Portugal v Commission*, n 55 above, paras 69–79.

[62] *Ibid* para 80.

provide an exception to the application of the common tax system in favour of certain undertakings in the Member State, but that this exception may be justified by the nature or general scheme of the tax system, that is to say, if it derives directly from the basic or guiding principles of the tax system in the Member State concerned. If this is not the case, then State aid is involved.[63] According to the Commission, the differential nature of some measures does not necessarily mean that they must be considered to be State aid, that being the case with measures whose economic rationale makes them necessary to the functioning and effectiveness of the tax system.[64]

The Commission relied for its finding on a judgment of 1974 in which the ECJ judged that a partial reduction of social charges pertaining to family allowances devolving upon employers in the textile sector was a measure intended partly to exempt undertakings of a particular industrial sector from the financial charges arising from the normal application of the general social security system 'without there being any justification for this exemption on the basis of the nature or general scheme of the system'.[65]

It is now settled case-law that a measure which, although conferring an advantage on its recipient, is justified by the nature or general scheme of the system of which it is a part does not fulfil that condition of selectivity.[66]

Thus, in the case which gave rise to the judgment *Adria-Wien Pipeline*, the ECJ was charged in particular with the question of determining if national measures which provided for a rebate of energy taxes on natural gas and electricity in the case of undertakings whose activity was shown to consist primarily in the manufacture of goods must be regarded as State aid within the meaning of Article 87(1) EC. After having considered that the supply of energy on preferential terms to undertakings manufacturing goods was capable of constituting State aid, the ECJ recalled its case-law from 1974 according to which a measure which, although conferring an advantage on its recipient, is justified by the nature or general scheme of the system of which it is part does not fulfil that condition of selectivity.[67]

In this regard, the ECJ considered that the grant of advantages to undertakings whose principal activity was the manufacture of goods did not find justification in the nature or general scheme of the tax system in question. Indeed, the ECJ held, for one thing, that undertakings supplying services may, just like undertakings manufacturing goods, be major consumers of energy and incur

[63] Communication of 1998, para 16.

[64] Communication of 1998, para 23.

[65] See Case 173/73 *Commission v Italy*, n 10 above, para 28. The approach taken by the Commission was criticised. It was pointed out in particular that this justification resulted from an *obiter dictum*, and that its implementation was a source of legal uncertainty, as compared to the systematic nature of Art 87 EC: Wouters and Van Hees, n 5 above, at 660–670.

[66] Case C-75/97 *Belgium v Commission*, n 9 above, para 33; Case C-143/99 *Adria-Wien Pipeline*, n 44 above, para 42; Case C-308/01 *GIL Insurance and Others*, n 19 above, para 72; Case C-148/04 *Unicredito Italiano* [2005] ECR I-11137, para 51; Case C-88/03 *Portugal v Commission*, n 55 above, para 52, and Case C-487/06 *British Aggregates v Commission*, n 44 above, para 83.

[67] Case C-143/99 *Adria-Wien Pipeline*, n 44 above, paras 38–42.

energy taxes beyond the threshold above which undertakings manufacturing principally goods are eligible for the energy tax rebate. According to the ECJ, for another thing, the ecological considerations underlying the national legislation at issue did not justify treating the consumption of natural gas or electricity by undertakings supplying services differently than the consumption of such energy by undertakings manufacturing goods, energy consumption by each of those sectors being equally damaging to the environment. In conclusion, although objective, the criterion applied by the national legislation at issue was justified neither by the nature nor by the general scheme of that legislation, so that it could not save the measure at issue from being in the nature of State aid.[68]

More recently, in the case giving rise to the aforementioned judgment *Portugal v Commission*,[69] the ECJ, after having established that the measures reducing the tax rates in question had a selective character, examined whether, as argued by the Portuguese Government, these measures were justified by the nature or general scheme of the Portuguese tax system.

In this respect, the ECJ specified that a measure which creates an exception to the application of the general tax system may be justified by the nature or general scheme of the tax system if the Member State concerned can show that that measure results directly from the basic or guiding principles of its tax system, a distinction being required to be made between, on the one hand, the objectives attributed to a particular tax scheme which are extrinsic to it and, on the other, the mechanisms inherent in the tax system itself which are necessary for the achievement of such objectives.[70]

The ECJ then considered that the tax measures in question, which applied to all economic operators without any distinction as to their financial circumstances, could not be regarded as ensuring that for the purpose of redistribution the criterion of ability to pay was observed, and that the fact of acting on the basis of a regional development or social cohesion policy was not sufficient in itself to justify a measure adopted within the framework of that policy. The Portuguese Government did not show that the adoption of the measures at issue by the Autonomous Region of the Azores was necessary for the functioning and effectiveness of the general tax system. Having simply made a general statement to that effect without providing specific evidence in support of it, it had not, therefore, demonstrated that the measures at issue were justified by the nature or general scheme of the Portuguese tax system.[71] It is indeed for the Member State to provide proof of such a justification.[72]

In an equally recent case, the CFI rejected an action directed against a decision of the Commission which found that a tax, supplied with certain exemptions, did not contain elements of State aid within the meaning of Article 87(1) EC insofar as, in substance, its field of application was justified by the logic and nature of

[68] *Ibid* paras 50–53.
[69] Case C-88/03 *Portugal v Commission*, n 55 above.
[70] *Ibid* para 81.
[71] *Ibid* paras 82 and 83.
[72] *Ibid* para 80. See also Case T-55/99 *CETM v Commission*, n 50 above, paras 51–54.

the tax regime. Briefly, the CFI held that the protection of the environment constituted a legitimate objective, relating to the competence of Member States, allowing them to freely define the scope of the field of application of environmental taxes.[73]

On appeal, this decision was overturned. The ECJ recalled that it had held on numerous occasions that the objective pursued by State measures was not sufficient to exclude those measures outright from classification as 'aid' for the purposes of Article 87 EC, as this provision does not distinguish between the causes or the objectives of State aid, but defines them in relation to their effects.[74] Finally, the ECJ concluded that the CFI disregarded Article 87(1) EC by holding that Member States are free, in balancing the various interests involved, to set their priorities regarding the protection of the environment and, as a result, to determine which goods or services they decide to subject to an environmental levy, with the result that the fact that such a levy does not apply to all similar activities which have a comparable impact on the environment does not mean that similar activities, which are not subject to the levy, benefit from a selective advantage.[75]

The question could of course be asked when the ECJ will recognise, on the merits, an advantageous and selective tax measure as justified by the nature or general scheme of the tax system. To date, one cannot but notice that this justification has always been rejected by the ECJ:[76] once the regime in question distances itself from the ordinary tax system, whatever the objective pursued, the measure is considered as being selective and consequently falls under Article 87(1) EC, all the more if it turns out that it is aimed at reinforcing the international competitiveness of the beneficiary undertakings.

* *
*

It is clear that a direct taxation measure cannot be easily justified with respect to the rules of the EC Treaty concerning State aid in view of the nature or general scheme of the tax system, just as the justification for a tax restriction to free movement derived from the cohesion of the tax system is not often accepted.

The ECJ indeed considers that the necessity of preserving the cohesion of a tax system may justify the regulatory instruments that by nature restrict the free movement guaranteed by the Treaty.[77] But since the first two judgments

[73] Case T-210/02 *British Aggregates v Commission* [2006] ECR II-2789 paras 115–117.

[74] *Ibid* paras 84 and 85 and the case-law cited.

[75] *Ibid* para 86.

[76] In addition to the cited cases, n 66 above, see also Case C-159/01 *Netherlands v Commission* [2004] ECR I-4461 paras 42–47; Case C-66/02 *Italy v Commission* [2005] ECR I-10901 paras 94–102; Case C-148/04 *Unicredito Italiano*, n 66 above, paras 46–51, and Case C-222/04 *Cassa di Risparmio di Firenze and Others* [2006] ECR I-289 para 137.

[77] See Case C-204/90 *Bachmann* [1992] ECR I-249 paras 21–28; Case C-300/90 *Commission v Belgium* [1992] ECR I-305 paras 14–21; Case C-436/00 *X and Y* [2002] ECR I-10829 para 51, and Case C-386/04 *Centro di Musicologia Walter Stauffer* [2006] ECR I-8203 para 52. On this justification, see Lenaerts and Bernardeau, n 12 above, at 155–161, and F Vanistendael, 'Cohesion: the Phoenix rises from his ashes' (2005) 4 *EC Tax Review* 208.

which established and embraced this justification, the ECJ until very recently systematically rejected it.

Thus, in the case which gave rise to the judgment *Papillon*, the ECJ considered that the refusal to grant a tax advantage – in this situation to a group scheme once the resident sub-subsidiaries who wanted to integrate the resident parent company were held through a non-resident subsidiary – was appropriate to ensure the cohesion of the tax system.[78] Certainly, in the judgment *Papillon*, the ECJ rejected this justification on the grounds of proportionality.[79] In the case giving rise to the judgment *Krankenheim Ruhesitz am Wannsee-Seniorenheimstatt*, however, the ECJ completely accepted this justification.[80]

It is undeniable that by maintaining the possibility of justification on the ground of the economy or the cohesion of the tax system pursuant to the framing of direct taxation by the law of State aid and free movement, the ECJ remains careful not to affect Member State sovereignty in the matter of direct taxation. Indeed, the Community law framing national rules on direct taxation cannot affect the sovereign choices of Member States, provided that these choices conform to the demands of the Union in terms of equality of treatment.

[78] See Case C-418/07 *Papillon*, n 47 above, paras 41–51.

[79] *Ibid* paras 52–61.

[80] See Case C-157/07 *Krankenheim Ruhesitz am Wannsee-Seniorenheimstatt*, judgment of 23 October 2008 nyr, paras 40–45. In this judgment, the ECJ ruled that the freedom of establishment does not preclude a national tax system which, after having allowed the taking into account of losses incurred by a permanent establishment situated in a State other than the one in which its principal company is situated, for the purposes of calculating the tax on that company's income, provides for a tax reintegration of those losses at the time when that permanent establishment makes profits, where the State where that same permanent establishment is situated does not confer any right to carry forward losses incurred by a permanent establishment belonging to a company established in another State, and where, under a convention for the prevention of double taxation between the two States concerned, the income of such an entity is exonerated from taxation in the State in which the principal company has its seat.

# 19

# *The Tension between Member States' Autonomy and Commission Control in State Aid Matters: Selected Aspects*

JOSEF AZIZI*

## PROLOGUE

In a ceremony which took place in Luxembourg on 18 January 1995, *Virpi Tiili* and myself were sworn in as judges at the Court of First Instance of the European Communities (hereinafter CFI). Ever since that moment, *Virpi* and myself have lived our common commitment to the European idea, or, more precisely, to the consolidation of the European Rule of Law. This contribution is written to honour *Virpi* on the occasion of her retirement from the Court. This undoubtedly sad event at least gives me the opportunity to tell her sincerely not only my personal affection but also my professional esteem and above all to thank her for all her kindness.

## INTRODUCTORY REMARKS

From a policy point of view, EC State aid law can be seen as creating a field of tension between, on the one hand, the European Commission's mission and privilege to define and pursue a Community-wide competition policy and to monitor the observance of EC competition rules in order to preserve unaltered competition within the single market and, on the other hand, the Member States' willingness to use State aid as a tool to put into effect their own economic and societal policy objectives.[1]

* All views expressed in this contribution are strictly personal and do not engage anybody but the author. The author would like to thank Hanns Peter Nehl for critically reading through the manuscript as well as for his valuable remarks.

[1] It is well known that, as things stand today in State aid proceedings, interested third parties, like the beneficiary of the aid or his competitors, have, in principle, only a marginal role to play. *Cont.*

From this perspective, judgments rendered by the Community Courts in State aid matters might often be perceived by outsiders as yet another (mostly final) step in a political conflict and even sometimes be criticised as being essentially political in nature.

Yet, it would certainly be naïve and even nonsense to suggest that the Court's decisions are the product of mere mathematical operations in a legal sphere that would be unaffected by any political considerations, so to say aseptically clean from the germs of political impacts. Nonetheless, it seems worth recalling that the proceedings before the Community Courts are aimed at resolving legal conflicts (whatever their possible political background might be) by clarifying the underlying legal questions in a way that settles a pending case and possibly avoiding similar conflicts in the future.

Indeed, as it has been recognised by the Court of Justice of the European Communities, the European Community is a community based on the rule of law, inasmuch as – within the scope of EC law – neither its Member States nor its institutions can avoid judicial review of the question as to whether the measures adopted by them are in conformity with the EC's basic constitutional charter, the EC Treaty. That Treaty established a complete system of legal remedies and procedures designed to permit the Community Courts to review the legality of measures adopted by the institutions.[2]

Thus, within the scope of application of the EC Treaty,[3] Member States and Community institutions are bound by the same overall system of law. Therefore, it would seem appropriate, before having a closer look at some aspects of the legal dimension of the relationship between the Commission and Member States in State aid matters, to recall – on a more theoretical level – some basic structural premises.

See, eg A Rosas, 'Judicial Protection in EU State Aid Law' in Mario Monti *et al* (eds), *Economic Law and Justice in Times of Globalisation: Festschrift for Carl Baudenbacher* (Baden-Baden, Nomos Verlagsgesellschaft, 2007) 579, at 582 *ff*; J Azizi, 'Judicial Review of EC State Aid Procedure – Current Problems in the Community Courts' Case Law and their Impact on Possible Reform' in Andreas Bartosch (ed), *New Developments in European State Aid Law 2007* (Berlin, Lexxion Verlagsgesellschaft, 2008) 21 *ff*, and J Azizi, 'Droits de la défense en matière d'aides d'Etat: le point de vue judiciaire' in Association Européenne des Avocats (AEA) (ed), *Un rôle pour la défense dans les procédures communautaires de concurrence* (Bruxelles, Bruylant, 1997) 87, at 93 *ff*. Nonetheless, the legal protection of complaints, which, for some time, had been paid little consideration by the Court of Justice of the European Communities (hereinafter ECJ) (see Case C-367/95 P *Commission v Sytraval and Brink's France* [1998] ECR I-1719 paras 58–62) has recently been to some extent revalued in the ECJ (Case C-521/06 P *Athenaïki Techniki v Commission*, judgment of 17 July 2008 nyr, paras 51–62).

[2] Case 294/83 *Les Verts v Parliament* [1986] ECR 1339 para 23.

[3] Outside the scope of application of the EC Treaty (1), as well as to the extent to which the EC law refrains from fully determining the Member States' activities (2), the Member States act in genuine (1) or conceded (2) autonomy.

GENERAL THEORETICAL PREMISES

**Basic Structural Parameters**

Any legal act bears (if not subjectively, at least objectively) the characteristics of an expression of a (at least fictitious) will[4] of its author aimed at regulating human behaviour and possibly delegating parts of its decision making powers for further precision and concretisation to others.

If, on the basis of such an empowerment, a new legal act is adopted, which specifies more precisely the content of the more general one, two kinds of will-making components predetermine its content: on the one hand, the legal predetermination by the earlier legal act(s) which constitute(s) its legal basis and point of departure (heteronomous determinant) and, on the other hand, the autonomous will-component added by the author of the new legal act within the margin of discretion left by the previous legal act(s) (autonomous determinant).[5]

In this sense, any legal system is based on a complex hierarchy of legal acts.[6] The structure of this hierarchy is characterised by a (sometimes huge) number and variety of chains of legal acts,[7] each legal act being preconditioned by 'higher ranking' legal acts and possibly preconditioning itself some 'lower ranking' legal acts.

On top of the hierarchy, one could normally find legal norms whose enactment or modification is subject to formal conditions which are more difficult to be met. In Community law, it is obvious that the Treaties constitute the legal acts whose modification is most difficult in procedural terms.

[4] It would seem appropriate to comprehend a legal norm as the sense of a volitive act, it being understood that this 'sense' would not be the actual will of the legislator, but would have to be ascribed to him in accordance with the rules of communication. See, eg M Potacs, *Auslegung im öffentlichen Recht: Eine vergleichende Untersuchung der Auslegungspraxis des Europäischen Gerichtshofs und der österreichischen Gerichtshöfe des öffentlichen Rechts* (Baden-Baden, Nomos Verlagsgesellschaft, 1994) 24, and the literature cited. As to the arguments speaking in favour of such an 'objective' will rather than of a psychological 'subjective' will, see, eg O Pfersmann, 'Le sophisme onomastique. À propos de l'interprétation de la constitution' in FM Soucramamien (ed), *L'interprétation constitutionnelle* (Paris, Dalloz, 2005) 33–60.

[5] See AJ Merkl, 'Das doppelte Rechtsantlitz, Eine Betrachtung aus der Erkenntnistheorie des Rechtes' (1918) 47 *Juristische Blätter* 425–427, 444–447 and 463–465.

[6] This statement should not be seen as having any impact on the distinction between monist and dualist legal systems: the internal structure of a system based on predetermining and predetermined legal acts is present in any legal order independently of the general recognition and full inclusion, eg by a national Constitution, of external sources of law in the system. As for the principle of the hierarchy of norms within the scope of the EC Treaty, see eg Joined Cases C-393/07 and C-9/08 *Italian Republic and Beniamino Donnici v Parliament*, judgment of 30 April 2009 nyr, paras 47 and 48, and Case T-113/96 *Dubois et Fils v Council and Commission* [1998] ECR II-125 para 41.

[7] These chains of legal acts may also be possibly crossing each others once or more often.

### The 'Measurement of Legality'

#### *Generalities*

Roughly speaking, the legality, that is to say the legal correctness, of a legal act is to be measured against the yardstick of the higher ranking legal acts which form the legal frame for the act in question. On the whole, if a comparison of the act in question with its legal frame shows that its author has added autonomous components transcending the limits set by the previous heteronomous determinants, this constitutes an infringement of the aforesaid legal frame and can – depending on the applicable rules – lead to legal consequences of various kinds in order to restore the consistency of the legal system in conformity with the higher ranking rules.

In order to ensure the functioning of the legal system by correcting or eliminating illegalities (and thus also to strengthen its legitimacy and credibility) specific mechanisms of monitoring and review can be foreseen. It is obvious that the revision of the legality of an act may not exceed what has been defined by the legal rules governing the specific procedural role of the body in charge of this revision. In particular, that body may not consider an act as being illegal as long as that act does not, in itself, transcend the limits set up by the heteronomous determinants of its legal frame.

#### *Legality of Volitive Elements*

Thus, so far as the legal frame allows it, the inclusion by its author, in the act examined, of an autonomous will-component of whatever kind, including various policy considerations, may not be put into question from an exclusively legal point of view.

The larger the margin of manoeuvre left by the heteronomous determinants to the possible author of an act is, the more leeway he has to bring in his own and autonomous components when creating this act.

Mostly, the margin of manoeuvre left by the relevant legal frame would relate to *decisional elements* of a purely *volitive* character: such a margin of discretion can concern, firstly, the freedom to act or not to act at all, and, secondly, in the case of acting, the freedom to choose between different alternative contents for the act to be taken. As the case may be, this might also cover a certain degree of creativity for bringing about new normative situations.

#### *Legality of Fact Findings*

In the case of evaluation of *facts* when applying a given legal frame, prima facie a similar logic would seem to apply: Facts circumscribed in a rather precise and unambiguous way or defined in the legal frame through objectively verifiable elements would leave to the author of the act only a little margin for autonomous appreciation of the relevant factual circumstances. Where, on the contrary, the legal frame does not define with high precision the relevant facts and especially where, due to their very complex nature, their ascertainment requires a high degree of expertise, the legality of the assessment of the facts in the examined act may depend on the degree of diligence, seriousness and reliability with which these facts have been established by the author. Thus, where a certain level of complexity is an inherent characteristic of factual circumstances described in the legal framework, a specific feature of verification of the legality of an act comes into play.

As to the establishment of facts, the findings concerning the presence or absence of factual elements are *merely cognitive and descriptive* and cannot, as such, be volitive in nature. Therefore, there cannot, in principle, be any autonomous component left to the decision-maker's free will as to whether or not certain facts exist or do not exist. But given the high degree of complexity of certain factual circumstances described by the legal frame, the existence of such facts has often to be proven by means of likelihood and probability[8] rather than full evidence. Thus, in the absence of totally reliable means of perception, the establishment of such complex facts boils down to a question of probability, amenable to review in terms of *plausibility*: in this sense, one might say that the decision-maker would have the freedom to stop investigating if he finds that there is sufficient probability[9] for the existence of certain facts on the basis of the best scientific and technological standards available.

In such a situation, the burden of proof may become of a decisive importance: indeed, the correctness of the decision may be challenged via more sophisticated proof showing a different result with a higher degree of likelihood or probability.[10] In this sense, the higher the degree of sophistication and scientific accuracy of the proof retained for the ascertainment of a complex factual situation is, the more likely is it to be considered as sufficient in terms of probability[11] and, consequently, to be found to provide the legal act based on such a proof with sufficient plausibility in order to withstand legal review.

Wherever the finding of such complex facts is involved, the *respect of procedural rules* aiming at ensuring an optimal level of correctness for the establishment of the facts, including the rights of the defence in the light of the possible switching of the burden of proof may take decisive importance for the assessment of the legality of an act based on those facts.[12]

[8] As to the limitation of evidence to the standard of 'a sufficient degree of probability' to assess complex economic effects, see eg Joined Cases C-68/94 and C-30/95 *France and Others v Commission (Kali & Salz)* [1998] ECR I-1375 para 246.

[9] In particular, as to the evaluation of economic facts and circumstances, the ground relied on must be supported by 'appropriate evidence' (see, in this respect, already Case 6/54, *Netherlands v High Authority* [1954] ECR 201).

[10] This amounts to a standard of proof equivalent to a balance of probabilities; see, in this sense, Case C-12/03 P *Commission v Tetra Laval* [2005] ECR I-987 para 43.

[11] A practical difficulty with this probability approach may be the problem of quantification of probabilities (see, in this respect, A-L Sibony and E Barbier de la Serre, 'Charge de la preuve et théorie du contrôle en droit communautaire de la concurrence: pour un changement de perspective' (2007) 2 *Revue Trimestrielle de Droit Européen* 205, at 230 *ff*).

[12] See more generally Case C-269/90 *Technische Universität München* [1991] ECR I-5469 para 14; as regards EC State aid law specifically, see Case C-525/04 P *Spain v Lenzing* [2007] ECR I-9947 para 58.

*Interim Conclusion*

Seen from this perspective, two basic features have to be distinguished in the relationship between the legal frame and the act adopted on its basis: On the one hand, there is the freedom to model the contents of an act by including autonomous volitive elements within the margin of discretion left by the legal frame. On the other hand, in the necessary absence from the outset of full and 'watertight' evidence for establishing highly complex facts, the legal act adopted may rely on a probability assessment of those facts. In such a case, the plausibility of the exercise by the decision-makers of his margin of appreciation is to be judged by taking into account the imperfection or even impossibility of an exact definition of the relevant facts referred to by the legal frame *rather than* from a delegation of volitive elements. In the second case, the margin of manoeuvre therefore appears to be the result of the limits inherent to cognitive capacities rather than of the freedom of introducing volitive elements. This may for example be the case, when the facts at stake include the assessment of the risk of an undesired future development.

Nonetheless, even when it comes to finding and ascertaining complex economic facts, it may well be that the legal determinants do not give any precision as to which specific economic theory should provide the conceptual frame for doing so. Since the underlying economic theory may be of importance for the assessment of complex economic facts, the choice of the basic economic theory may after all include to this extent also a (supplementary autonomous) volitive element. But even so, it would seem possible that essential guiding principles for this choice could be found in the relevant legal rules.[13]

## QUESTIONS RELATING TO THE MARGIN OF ACTION AND CONTROL IN STATE AID MATTERS

### General Remarks

In the field of EC State aid law, different actors have to be distinguished in what seems to be an allocation of gradual roles:

First, the *Member States*, as the main addressees of EC State aid law: regulating restrictively their activities is the central function of EC State aid law. Second, the *Commission*, whose principal role is to supervise the legality of the Member States' activities and who is invested with the power to authorise or prohibit, in the light of the relevant provisions of EC law, any measures proposed or taken by them. Third, the *Community judicature*, mainly the CFI, which, on its part, is competent for reviewing the legality of the aforementioned exercise by the Commission of its supervisory task.

[13] One of the legal parameters for the choice of an economic theory may be the *principle of effectiveness* in its application: in this sense, it would seem likely that much of the problem of qualification of probabilities (see n 11 above) is linked to the choice of the basic economic theory and the corresponding tools thereto.

Therefore, the freedom of and the limits to the *Member States' activity* in this field are to be measured, first of all, against the backdrop of the relevant provisions of EC State aid law.

Next, the extent and depth of the *Commission control* as to the legality of such Member States' activities depends on the degree of freedom to act left to the Member States by the relevant legal frame. Where there is – exceptionally – a large degree of freedom left for the input of the Member States' autonomous will,[14] the scope and depth of control by the Commission in that respect might be reduced to one of manifest error. Where, on the contrary, the Commission enjoys itself, by virtue of the EC Treaty, a wide discretion, it has large powers to accept or refuse a measure intended or taken by a Member State. Moreover, inasmuch as the relevant provisions of EC law do not leave any room for interpretation,[15] the Member States and the Commission are equally bound by these heteronomous determinants without any possibility to substitute or alter them by their autonomous will.

Finally, the breadth and depth of the *Community Courts' judicial review* of the legality of the Commission's decisions in State aid matters is necessarily limited in parallel to the legal predetermination of the Commission's own supervisory powers. Where, with regard to the relevant legal framework, the Commission enjoys a high degree of autonomy in its monitoring of the Member States' activities in State aid matters, the Courts' review is limited to the ascertainment of a manifest error. On the contrary, where no margin of discretion is left to the Commission, the Courts will have to exercise full control as to the correct application of the relevant legal provisions by the Commission.

Yet, let us think of a situation which – at least at first sight – may seem to be paradoxical: What if, under specific legal and factual circumstances determining certain Member State activities, there were, from the outset, good reasons for assuming that both the Member State as well as the Commission enjoy a large margin of decisional discretion and/or of assessment of certain complex facts? In this respect, the definite answer will certainly depend on the concrete circumstances of the case, in particular on the context and character of these powers.[16] However, generally speaking, it seems logical to say that in a system

[14] The latitude of the Member States will vary following different parameters. When making use of competences falling *outside* the scope of the EC Treaty, the Member State has a genuine autonomy of its own, which is not predetermined by EC law. When acting *within* the scope of the EC Treaty, the freedom of action of the Member States depends on whether, and to what extent, the Community legislator refrained from (heteronomously) predetermining the Member State (acting possibilities) (see n 3 above). In this sense, EC State aid law itself might overlap with (specific) other fields of Community legislation, where the frame of legal predetermination depends, inter alia, on the form of the relevant legal basis within the meaning of Art 249 EC. See, in that respect, eg Case T-374/04 *Germany v Commission* [2007] ECR II-4431 paras 77–82, as well as annotation to that judgment ChW Backes, 'AB 2008, 133' (2008) *AB Rechtspraak Bestuursrecht* 617, at 633, and NML Dhondt and WW Geursen, 'Overgedeelde bevoegdheden en hiërarchie in interpretatiemethoden' (2008) 10 *Nederlands Tijdschrift voor Europees Recht* 276, at 278 *ff*.

[15] The derogations from the principle of Art 87(1) EC have anyway to be interpreted strictly; see Case T-200/04 *Regione autonoma della Sardegna v Commission*, judgment of 14 December 2005 unreported, para 71.

[16] See, eg, in this respect the control regarding the fulfilment of the *Altmark* criteria (see Case C-280/00 *Altmark Trans and Regierungspräsidium Magdeburg* [2003] ECR I-7747 paras 87–93)

*Cont.*

of limited control of the *legality* of an act, the reviewing body may not substitute its own appreciation for that of the author of the act reviewed. In this logic, the Commission would have to limit its control of the Member State's decision to detecting a manifest error. Nonetheless, there are good reasons to assume that the Court, in turn, when reviewing in the same context the Commission's decision, would have to exercise full review as to its legality. Otherwise, if subsequent to such 'light' control by the Commission the Court were to limit additionally its own review to sanctioning manifest errors on the part of the Commission only, the effectiveness of the whole two-stage control and thus the useful effect of the applicable substantive Community rules would be endangered. Indeed, in such a situation, the review procedure would not even be capable of guaranteeing that the Commission at least takes seriously its though limited role by sanctioning in any case all serious breaches of Community law. Thus, generally speaking, one should assume that, the more the breadth and depth of a legal control at the first stage is limited, the more accurately the exercise of this control will have to be reviewed at the second stage.

## Ascertaining the Presence of State Aid

Much of the freedom to act left to the Member States depends on whether the measure they intend to take or have taken constitutes prohibited State aid. Article 87(1) EC sets out the general prohibition of State aid which is, in principle, incompatible with the common market. A measure constitutes State aid within the meaning of that prohibition if it shows the following four cumulative characteristics: The measure must (1) consist of aid (economic advantage) granted by a Member State or through State resources, (2) favour certain undertakings or the production of certain goods (selectivity), (3) distort or threaten to distort competition and (4) affect trade between Member States.[17]

The Community Courts' case-law has made it clear that the elements defining State aid in the sense of Article 87(1) EC are objectively determined concepts of law,[18] which are to be interpreted strictly. Therefore, there is, in principle, no room for introducing volitive elements in the interpretation and application of this provision. Nonetheless, some of the four elements of that abstract definition

and, in particular, of the proportionality of a Member State's decision in a field of mostly national competence: due to its genuine autonomous competences falling still at least partly outside the scope of the EC Treaty - the Member State might dispose of a genuine large margin of discretion as to determining its action in a certain policy field and hence to shape its decision following its own will. On the other hand, the Community judicature traditionally recognises a large margin of discretion of the Commission for ascertaining complex economic aspects in that regard.

[17] See in this respect, eg W Mederer, 'V. 2 Artikel 87 EG-Vertrag - vereinbare und unvereinbare Beihilfen' in H Schröter, T Jakob and W Mederer (eds), *Kommentar zum Europäischen Wettbewerbsrecht* (Baden-Baden, Nomos Verlagsgesellschaft, 2003) 1989, at 1994 *ff*; see also J Zeitz, *Der Begriff der Beihilfe im Sinne des Artikels 87 Abs. 1 EGV* (Baden-Baden, Nomos Verlagsgesellschaft, 2005), and M Dony, F Renard and C Smits, *Contrôle des aides d'État*, 3rd edn (Brussels, Éditions de l'Université de Bruxelles, 2007) 15–189.

[18] Case C-487/06 P *British Aggregates v Commission*, judgment of 22 December 2008 nyr, para 111.

of State aid describe in a rather general manner highly complex economic situations.[19]

Yet, the correct application of this provision depends on the amount and quality of the information available including the degree and level of expertise to comprehend that complex information. These undeniable limits as to a full perception of the relevant facts are likely to be present not only at the level of the Commission's monitoring but also at the level of judicial control. Thus, the scope of control of the assessment of complex economic facts in the light of the definition of Article 87(1) EC will depend, successively, on the Commission's and the Community judiciary's capacity to perceive and apprehend the relevant information. More particularly, the Court's infrastructure is not designed to gather, verify and process complex facts, it is even much more limited than the infrastructural possibilities of the Commission administration. So, even if the Court had, in principle, the investigatory powers to complement on its own the Commission's fact-findings or to reassess those findings in depth, for instance, by making use of measures of inquiry,[20] such as the commissioning of an additional expert's report,[21] the use of this remains highly theoretical.

Moreover, there are two principles of Community law in particular that would prevent the CFI from systematically exercising an in depth review of such complex Commission decisions: On the one hand, the Community Courts' procedures have to respect, inter alia, the principle of procedural economy (*'économie de procédure'*) and, on the other hand, the Court has to be careful not to endanger the (inter)institutional balance[22] by systematically redoing the Commission's appreciation and thus affecting the principle of separation of powers between the executive and the judiciary. Hence, a restrained judicial control[23] of the Commission's assessment of complex economic facts in the light of the definition of Article 87(1) EC is sufficient.[24] In this sense, if there is

[19] See, eg, regarding the *Altmark* criteria, Case T-289/03 *BUPA and Others v Commission* [2008] ECR II-81 paras 152 *ff*; regarding the 'private investor test' Case T-196/04, *Ryanair v Commission*, judgment of 17 December 2008 nyr, para 104, and eg W Frenz, *Handbuch Europarecht*, Band 3 Beihilfe- und Vergaberecht (Berlin, Springer Verlag, 2007) 56 *ff* (recital 183).

[20] See Art 65(2) of the Rules of Procedure of the CFI. Unlike the ordinary situation before the CFI, which is limited to the review of legality of Commission decisions, it is likely that in proceedings before *national courts*, measures of enquiry may be indispensable in order to ensure the compliance with the *principle of effectiveness* in State aid matters: see Case C-526/04 *Laboratoires Boiron* [2006] ECR I-7529 para 55.

[21] Or by measures of organisation of procedure, see Art 64(3) of the Rules of Procedure of the CFI.

[22] As to the (inter)institutional balance between the administration and the judiciary, see, eg Case T-374/04 *Germany v Commission*, n 14 above, para 146.

[23] As to the notion of 'restrained judicial control', see, eg D Ritleng, 'Le juge communautaire de la légalité et le pouvoir discrétionnaire des institutions communautaires' (1999) *Actualités juridiques – Droit administratif* 645, at 655.

[24] As for this restrained judicial control of the appraisal of complex economic matters in the context of Art 81(1) EC (ex Art 85(1) of the EC Treaty) see already Case 42/84 *Remia and Others v Commission* [1985] ECR 2545 para 34. The importance of the ECJ's *Remia and Others v Commission* judgment has already been underlined in 1999 by V Tiili and J Vanhamme, 'The "Power of appraisal" (Pouvoir d'appréciation) of the Commission of the European Communities vis-à-vis the powers of judicial review of the Communities' Court of Justice and Court of First instance' (1999) 3 *Fordham International Law Journal* 885, at 889.

enough evidence to support the high likelihood and probability of the existence and correctness of the facts underlying this assessment, so as to give serious *plausibility* of the conclusions reached in a Commission decision based on it, that decision would have to be confirmed by the CFI. Thus, with regard to judicial review, the Commission as well as the Member States have – in this respect – to show in terms of likelihood and probability the plausibility of the application or non application of this definition to the facts of the case. As explained above, this circumstance as well as, subsequently, the ensuing Community Courts' own limitation to such a review of plausibility or lack of manifest error are mainly – directly or indirectly – the result of *difficulties of a cognitive and descriptive nature* as to the imperfection of possible evidence (not only at the Commission level, but even more so at the level of the Community Courts), and not primarily of some increased autonomous decision-making power of the Commission. It is mainly due to these difficulties that, in such cases involving complex economic facts, the Community judge refrains from substituting his or her own assessment of such facts for that made by the Commission and limits his or her review to ascertaining that the Commission complied with the rules of procedure and the rules relating to the duty to give reasons and also that the facts relied on were accurate and that there has been no error of law, manifest error of assessment or misuse of powers.[25]

When it comes to ascertaining State aid elements under Article 87(1) EC whose definition would at least partly depend on the internal law of the Member State, the establishment of the relevant rules of the Member State's legal order and their interpretation are factual and not legal questions. But inasmuch as these facts depend on an autonomous national competence, the monitoring by the Commission will have to be limited in that respect.[26]

## Assessing the Compatibility of State Aid with the Common Market

### *Introductory Remark*

Although State aid falling under the definition of Article 87(1) EC is in principle prohibited as being incompatible with the common market, it nonetheless

[25] See, eg Case C-525/04 P *Spain v Lenzing*, n 12 above, para 58, and Case T-196/04 *Ryanair v Commission*, n 19 above, para 41.

[26] Such questions of national competence not governed by the EC Treaty could be, with regard to the selectivity criterion, eg the devolution of sovereign taxation powers to regional bodies; see Case C-88/03 *Portugal v Commission* [2006] ECR I-7115, where the ECJ has actually acknowledged, *within* the Member State's genuine and sovereign overall constitutional autonomy to create or maintain independent legal bodies, three specific aspects of the *'internal autonomy'* of such regional bodies. Yet, in spite of their origin in the Member State's own constitutional system, these three types and characteristics of internal autonomy, *as seen from an EC State aid perspective under Art 87(1) EC*, would form three *cumulative* preconditions for the non selective character of an aid measure operated by a regional body: (i) the condition of institutional autonomy, (ii) the condition of procedural autonomy, (iii) the condition of economic autonomy (paras 66 and 67).

remains that (even) such a measure may be declared lawful if it is covered either by an explicit exception featuring in the EC Treaty or by an individual or general exemption granted by the Commission. Whereas in the first category the Commission' power is limited to finding as to whether or not the legal preconditions for an exception are present, the Commission has a large margin of volitive discretion in the second category as to whether or not it would grant an exemption.

### *Ex Lege Exceptions: Articles 87(2) EC and 86(2) EC*

As to *ex lege* exceptions, more recently the Commission's assessment of facts giving rise to the application of an exception[27] under Article 87(2) EC has been less important in practice[28] than the Member State's position under Article 86(2) EC. Indeed, in that latter respect, a number of specific difficulties are likely to overlap: First, as it has been recognised by the case-law, the Member States have a wide discretion to define what they regard as services of general economic interest (SGEI).[29] In this respect, the Commission's control is limited to the existence of a 'manifest error'. This would more particularly be the case where the Member State may use genuine autonomous competences falling at least partly outside the scope of the EC Treaty and for which it would have by definition a large margin of discretion as to determining its action in a certain field of policy and hence to shape an SGEI.[30] Second, as to the criteria for ascertaining the existence of an SGEI mission, as specified more recently in the *Altmark* case-law, especially as regards the necessity and the proportionality of the compensation foreseen for discharging an SGEI mission, this ascertainment may – in cases somewhat different from the facts in the *Altmark* case – be likely to involve the assessment of very complex economic facts which do not squarely fit into the actual wording of the *Altmark* criteria.[31] Thus, inasmuch as the Member State acts in the exercise of an autonomous competence to create an SGEI, there may arise a situation in which its authorities, when relying on the SGEI, would be deemed to have a wide margin of appreciation as to

[27] Like all derogations from general principles, the derogations under Art 87(2) EC must be narrowly construed; see, eg Case T-445/05 *Associazione italiana del risparmio gestito and Fineco Asset Management v Commission*, judgment of 4 March 2009 nyr, para 179, and Case C-156/98 *Germany v Commission* [2000] ECR I-6857 para 49; see also, more generally, eg KPE Lasok, T Millett and A Howard, *Judicial Control in the EU: procedures and principles* (Richmond, Richmond Law & Tax, 2004) 400, paras 690 *ff*.

[28] See, as to the little practical importance of the *ex lege* exceptions under Art 87(2) EC, T Jestaedt and M Schweda in M Heidenhain (ed), *Handbuch des europäischen Beihilfenrechts* (Munich, Beck, 2003) ch 14 n 2.

[29] See Case T-17/02 *Olsen v Commission* [2005] ECR II-2031 para 216, and the case-law cited, and Case T-289/03 *BUPA and Others v Commission*, n 19 above, paras 166 and 167.

[30] Like for what has been explained above under the title 'Ascertaining the Presence of State Aid', *in fine*, questions falling under the Member State's sovereign autonomy are in the present context – from the viewpoint of EC State aid law – questions of *facts*, which to a large extent rest on the Member State's autonomous definition. To that extent, the Commission's margin of appreciation of such facts is therefore limited.

[31] Case T-289/03 *BUPA and Others v Commission*, n 19 above, paras 220–222 and 266–270.

the assessment of those very complex economic facts. In such a situation, as described above, the Commission could not substitute its own appreciation for that of the Member State, but would have to limit itself to detecting a 'manifest error' and to a plausibility control, which, in turn, would be subject to full review by the Community Courts.

*Possible Exemption by the Commission: Article 87(3) EC*[32]

Where the Member State claims the legality of a State aid measure on the grounds of factual circumstances described in Article 87(3)(a) to (e) EC, the Commission enjoys – within its prerogative to define the Community competition policy – not only a wide margin of (cognitive) appreciation as to the establishment of complex economic facts, but also a wide margin of (volitive) discretion as to whether or not that measure should be exempted from the general prohibition of Article 87(1) EC.[33] Indeed, in this context, by contrast to the above-mentioned *ex lege* exceptions, the EC Treaty refrains from strictly imposing clearly predetermined consequences for the facts circumscribed in Article 87(3) EC.[34] Thus, judicial review by the Community Court would itself be confined to verifying that the measure in question is not vitiated by a manifest error or a misuse of powers, that the Commission did not clearly exceed the bounds of its discretion and that the procedural guarantees have been observed.[35]

## FINAL REMARKS

The relationship between the Commission and the Member States in State aid matters is characterised by many parameters, some of which have been briefly touched upon in the foregoing remarks. When it comes to discussing the relationship of gradual control between a Member State as first actor in State aid matters and the Commission exercising its function of a monitoring authority, one must bear in mind that, at a later stage, the Commission's own decision might be subject to review before the CFI.

Thus, in its confrontation with the Member State, the Commission undergoes a sequential change of roles between being at first controlling and then controlled.

[32] Also in the context of Art 87(3) EC, derogations from Art 87(1) EC must be interpreted strictly; see Case T-348/04 *SIDE v Commission* [2008] ECR II-625 para 62.

[33] As a matter of fact, the Community case-law often includes the economic assessment in the overall 'wide margin of discretion' for the Commission's exercise of its powers under Art 87(3) EC without drawing a clear dividing line; see, eg Case C-88/03 *Portugal v Commission*, n 26 above, para 99, and the case-law cited.

[34] As to the Commission's large margin of discretion for deciding whether and in what form it might make use of its powers under Art 87(3) EC, see, eg V Götz and J Martínez Soria, 'H. III. Subventionsrecht' in M Dauses (ed) *Handbuch des Wirtschaftsrechts* (Munich, Beck, 2008) EL 19 61–66, at paras 133 *ff*.

[35] See, eg Case T-374/04 *Germany v Commission*, n 14 above, para 81, and the case-law cited.

It flows from Article 87(1) EC read in conjunction with Article 88 EC, that there is, in principle, a presumption of illegality against State aid measures falling under the general definition of Article 87(1) EC and that the Commission has the task to monitor the observance of EC State aid rules by the Member States. In case a Member State intends to grant or has granted aid, it is likely to have an objective interest in convincing the Commission, firstly, that the measure does not fall under the prohibition of Article 87(1) EC and/or, secondly, that it either falls under one of the legal exceptions provided for by Articles 87(2) EC and/or 86(2) EC or that the Commission ought to exempt it on the basis of Article 87(3) EC.

In what appears to be a possible conflict of political interests between the Community, as represented by the Commission, on the one side, and the Member State on the other side, it may not always be easy to strike the right balance with regard to judicial review. Indeed, confusion is likely to arise between the *(volitive) freedom to decide, in principle, and to follow a certain policy,*[36] and the fact that the legality under the EC Treaty of certain measures often depends on *the (cognitive) ascertainment of very complex economic facts*, which requires in a great number of cases even a prospective analysis of future economic developments. Yet, this ascertainment may be decisive for the orientation and material content of a Commission decision in a specific case and hence for the legality of that decision when being reviewed by the Community judiciary.

From the perspective of the underlying conflict of interest, two kinds of parameters may be distinguished: the economic theory upon which the ascertainment is to be based on the one hand and the proof of the relevant facts on the other. The choice of the relevant economic theory – if it is not indicated by some legal provision – depends mainly on (often undisclosed or tacit) conventional assumptions.

The rules governing the proof of complex economic facts, however, could be determined in the light of the possible conflict of interests at stake between the Commission and the Member State as well as of their specific procedural role. In this sense, the initial burden of proof in the administrative proceedings would largely depend on the precise procedural context: normally, that is, subsequent to the notification of a State measure, it would be in the first place the Commission's role to put forward evidence as to its qualification as aid in the sense of Article 87(1) EC. It would then be up to the Member State to bring counterevidence or, in case that the existence of State aid is undisputed, bring evidence supporting the facts fulfilling the conditions of a legal exception (Articles 87(2) EC and 86(2) EC) or a possible exemption (Article 87(3) EC).[37]

[36] See, in this sense, also Case T-13/99 *Pfizer Animal Health v Council* [2002] ECR II-3305 para 166, which, in the context of agricultural policy, emphasises the Community institutions' broad discretion regarding definition of the objectives to be pursued and choice of the appropriate means of action. In that regard, 'review by the Community judicature of the substance of the relevant act must be confined to examining whether the exercise of such discretion is vitiated by a manifest error or a misuse of powers or whether the Community institutions clearly exceeded the bounds of their discretion'.

[37] Wherever there is a general legal presumption for the illegality of a measure (like by virtue of Art 87(1) EC), the burden of proof for the justification of an exemption lies with the person who

*Cont.*

As far as complex economic assessments are to be made, the balance of interests involved finds its expression in the shifting of the burden of proof along the following lines: from the outset, the Commission has the duty to examine carefully and impartially all relevant aspects of the individual case.[38] In this context, the Member State will have to offer the Commission its version of the facts by expert opinion providing a reasoned analysis of the relevant facts of the case in the light of the current knowledge about the specific subject matter. This opinion, in order to be followed, has to be full, consistent and relevant. To the extent to which the Commission is not convinced by this opinion, it must provide specific reasons for its own findings by comparison with those made in the opinion and *its statement of reasons must be of a scientific level at least commensurate with that of the opinion in question*. In that case, the Commission may take as its basis either the same analysis complemented by a supplementary analysis or any other evidence whose probative value is *at least commensurate with that of the opinion* which it would like to reject.[39]

So, in the end, the balance of interests, in State aid law, between the Member States' autonomy and the Commission control manifests itself, on a case-by-case basis, above all through the correct application of basic *procedural* principles governing in a specifically balanced way the burden and standard of proof between these main actors.[40] In this respect, it is the particular task of the Commission carefully to lay down its assessment in its statement of reasons, in order to enable the CFI to exercise its review.[41] Thus, on the whole, one could say that the delicate problem of tension between the autonomy of the Member States and the Commission control in State aid matters is being taken care of by Community law through what might be called 'legitimation through procedure'.[42]

applies for that exemption. See, in this sense, already Joined Cases 43/82 and 63/82, *VBVB and VBBB v Commission* [1984] ECR 19, and Case 42/84 *Remia and Others v Commission*, n 24 above, para 45. See also Art 2 of Council Regulation (EC) No 1/2003 of 16 December 2002 on the implementation of the rules on competition laid down in Articles 81 and 82 of the Treaty [2003] OJ L/1/1.

[38] Case C-269/90 *Technische Universität München*, n 12 above, para 14, and Case C-525/04 P *Spain v Lenzing*, n 12 above, para 58.

[39] Case T-13/99 *Pfizer Animal Health v Council*, n 36 above, paras 198 and 199.

[40] On the relevance of legal principles of procedure see, eg HP Nehl, 'Good Administration as Procedural Right and/or General Principle?' in HCH Hofmann and AH Türk (eds), *Legal Challenges in EU Administrative Law – Towards an Integrated Administration* (Cheltenham, Edward Elgar Publishing, 2009) 322, and HP Nehl, *Principles of Administrative Procedure in EC Law* (Oxford, Hart Publishing, 1999) 115 *ff*.

[41] As to the specific procedural role of the Community judge in such a context, see Sibony and Barbier de la Serre, n 11 above, at 252. See also, as to possible future judicial review of the appropriateness and robustness of *econometric* evidence Y Botteman, 'Mergers, standard of proof and expert economic evidence' (2006) 1 *Journal of Competition Law and Economics* 71, at 100, where he concludes, for the merger context, that the Court could review (i) whether the econometric analyses were conducted in a transparent manner, (ii) whether the analyses essentially fit well with key market conditions and support the other elements of evidence in the file and (iii) whether the Commission has adequately weighed the econometric evidence in support of its conclusions against competing models.

[42] See per analogy and in a sociological context, N Luhmann, *Legitimation durch Verfahren*, 7th edn (Frankfurt, Suhrkamp, 2008).

# 20

# *The Standing of the Competitors of the Aid Recipient in State Aid Cases*

MARC BARENNES

## INTRODUCTION

As recently pointed out, access to the Community judicature is 'an area in which, more than any other, the law must be clear and consistent'.[1]

Over the past five years, the Court of Justice of the European Communities (hereinafter ECJ) has consistently applied two distinct tests to determine whether the competitors of the aid recipient have standing in State aid cases.[2] Without taking part in the debate as to whether these tests should be reformed to provide the competitors of the aid recipient with larger and easier access to the Community judicature,[3] this article suggests that the applicable case-law of the ECJ provides these applicants with sufficient legal clarity and certainty to self-assess what conditions they must satisfy to challenge a State aid decision.

[1] Opinion of Advocate General Bot in Joined Cases C-75/05 P and C-80/05 P *Germany v Kronofrance*, judgment of 11 September 2008 nyr, point 105.

[2] The scope of this article is limited to the examination of the applicable case-law of the ECJ as it stands before 2 April 2009.

[3] See, eg U Soltéz and H Bielesz 'Judicial review of State aid decisions: recent developments' (2004) 3 *European Competition Law Review* 133; L Flynn, 'Remedies in European Courts' in A Biondi *et al* (eds), *The Law of State Aid in the European Union* (Oxford, Oxford University Press, 2004); G Schohe 'Le Statut du plaignant' in M Dony and C Smits (eds), *Aides d'état* (Brussels, Bruylant, 2005) 213; M Honoré, 'The Standing of Third Parties in State Aid Cases: the lessons to be drawn from the judgment in Case C-78/03 P, *Aktionsgemeinschaft Recht und Eigentum v Commission*' (2006) 2 *European State Aid Law Quarterly* 269; C Arhold, 'The Case Law of European Court of Justice and the Court of First Instance on State Aids in 2006/2007 (Part 2)' (2007) 3 *European State Aid Law Quarterly* 450; A Meij, 'Balancing Substance and Procedure in State Aid Practice – an Update on Recent Developments in EC Case Law' in A Bartosh (ed), *New developments in State European State Aid Law* (Berlin, Lexxion, 2007); E Fridensköld, 'Locus Standi in Article 88(2) cases: no cure for the Plaumann-blues I' (2008) 1 *European Law Reporter* 17; M Schmauch, 'Locus Standi in Article 88(3): no cure for the Plaumann-blues II' (2008) 2 *European Law Reporter* 21, and A Maitrepierre, 'Locus Standi: The ECJ confirms its case-law on locus standi *(Gluntz c/Commission)*' (2008) 4 *Concurrences* 127.

Firstly, I shall provide some relevant background information regarding the rights of the competitors of the aid recipient at the various stages of the European Commission's procedure for reviewing State aid. Secondly, I shall review the conditions that the competitors of the aid recipient must satisfy under each one of the two standing tests which are currently applied by the ECJ. Thirdly, I shall draw some general conclusions regarding these tests and expose the most recent criticisms put forward against them.

## THE COMMISSION'S PROCEDURE AND THE RIGHTS OF THE COMPETITORS OF THE AID RECIPIENT

The Commission's procedure for reviewing the grant of a State aid is, in essence, a bilateral dialogue between the Commission and the Member State against which a procedure is initiated.[4] For this reason, third parties such as the competitors of the aid recipient have 'no special role'[5] in the Commission's procedure but merely one of 'information sources'.[6] They are not therefore entitled to engage in an adversarial debate with the Commission.[7]

The procedural rules laid down in the EC Treaty concerning State aid vary according to whether the aid is existing or new, the former being governed by Article 88(1) and (2) EC, the latter being governed (in chronological order) by Article 88(3) and (2) EC.[8] Regulation No 659/1999 laying down detailed rules for the application of Article 88 EC[9] enumerates in its Articles 4 and 7 the decisions that the Commission must adopt to either close the preliminary phase of its procedure (hereinafter the 'preliminary investigation stage') or, alternatively, the formal stage of its procedure (hereinafter the 'formal investigation stage') of a new aid. These decisions must be adopted whether the investigation was triggered by a notification of a Member State or by a complaint.[10]

According to settled case-law, the preliminary investigation stage under Article 88(3) EC is governed by Articles 4 and 5 of Regulation No 659/1999 and is intended merely to allow the Commission to form a prima facie opinion on the partial or complete conformity of the aid in question. The preliminary investigation stage must be distinguished from the formal investigation stage envisaged by Article 88(2) EC which is governed by Articles 6 and 7 of that

[4] See, eg Joined Cases C-74/00 P and C-75/00 P *Falck and Acciaierie di Bolzano v Commission* [2002] ECR I-7869 para 81, and Case C-276/03 P *Scott v Commission* [2005] ECR I-8437 para 33.

[5] Joined Cases C-74/00 P and C-75/00 P *Falck and Acciaierie di Bolzano v Commission*, n 4 above, para 83.

[6] *Ibid* paras 80 and 82.

[7] *Ibid* para 82, and Case C-367/95 P *Commission v Sytraval and Brink's France* [1988] ECR I-1719 para 59.

[8] See, eg Case C-47/91 *Italy v Commission* [1992] ECR I-4145 para 22.

[9] Council Regulation (EC) No 659/1999 of 22 March 1999 laying down detailed rules for the application of Article 88 EC [1999] OJ L/83/1.

[10] Pursuant to Art 13(1) of Reg No 659/1999, the Commission's investigation regarding an aid which has not been notified must be terminated by a decision. See also in that regard Case C-521/06 P *Athinaïki Techniki v Commission*, judgment of 17 July 2008 nyr, para 40.

regulation and is designed to enable the Commission to be fully informed of all the facts of the case.[11]

It must be underlined that, but for the rights of third parties to lodge a complaint with the Commission that it must examine and take a position on by way of a decision based on Article 4 of Regulation No 659/1999,[12] no provision is made in the EC Treaty and in Regulation No 659/1999 for the participation of the competitors of the aid recipient in the Commission's procedure at the preliminary investigation stage. Where the investigation has been triggered by the notification of a Member State, the Commission does not have to inform third parties of that notification of the aid project.[13] Where a complaint is lodged with the Commission, it is under no obligation to conduct an exchange of views and arguments with the complainant in the context of the preliminary investigation stage.[14] However, the Commission is required, 'in the interests of sound administration of the fundamental rules of the Treaty relating to State aid, to conduct a diligent and impartial examination of the complaint, which may make it necessary for it to examine matters not expressly raised by the complainant'.[15]

At the end of the preliminary investigation stage, the Commission must adopt one of the following three decisions.[16] Firstly, the Commission may decide that the measure is not a State aid.[17] Secondly, it may find that there is no doubt that the measure is compatible with the common market. In such a case, it must decide not to raise objections to the grant of the aid in question. Thirdly, pursuant to Article 4(4) of Regulation No 659/19999, it must decide where 'doubts'[18] are raised as to the compatibility with the common market, to initiate the formal investigation procedure pursuant to Article 88(2) EC. The ECJ held that the publication of a notice in the *Official Journal of the European Union* is an appropriate means of informing all the parties concerned that a procedure has been initiated.[19] Under Article 6 of Regulation No 659/1999, the decision to initiate the formal investigation stage must summarise the relevant issues of fact and law. It must also include a preliminary assessment of the measure and set out the doubts that the Commission has as to its compatibility with the common market.

[11] See, eg Case C-225/91 *Matra v Commission* [1993] ECR I-3203 para 22; Case C-198/91 *Cook v Commission* [1993] ECR I-2487 para 22, and Case C-78/03 P *Commission v Aktionsgemeinschaft Recht und Eigentum* [2005] ECR I-10737 para 34.

[12] Art 10(1) of Reg No 659/1999. See also Case C-521/06 P *Athinaïki Techniki v Commission*, n 10 above, para 33.

[13] Joined Cases 91/83 and 127/83 *Heineken Brouwerijen* [1984] ECR 3435 para 15.

[14] Case C-367/95 P *Commission v Sytraval and Brink's France*, n 7 above, para 59.

[15] *Ibid* para 62.

[16] Art 4 of Reg No 659/1999.

[17] Art 4(2) of Reg No 659/1999.

[18] Pursuant to constant case-law, if the preliminary investigation stage does not enable the Commission to overcome all the 'difficulties' involved in determining whether the aid is compatible with the common market, the Commission is under a duty to carry out all the requisite consultations and for that purpose to initiate the procedure under Art 88(2) EC (see, eg Case C-198/91 *Cook v Commission*, n 11 above, para 29; Case C-225/91 *Matra v Commission*, n 11 above, para 33, and Case C-78/03 P *Commission v Aktionsgemeinschaft Recht und Eigentum*, n 11 above, para 34).

[19] Case 323/82 *Intermills v Commission* [1984] ECR 3809 para 17.

It must be stressed that it is only in the context of the formal investigation stage of its procedure that the Commission is required to gather all the opinions necessary in order to assess the compatibility of the aid with the common market and that it is required pursuant to Article 88(2) EC to obtain the observations of all the 'interested parties'. Under Article 20(1) of Regulation No 659/1999, any 'interested party' may submit comments following a Commission decision to initiate the formal investigation procedure. As defined in a long line of case-law[20] and as enshrined in Article 1(h) of Regulation No 659/1999, 'interested parties' are any Member State, person, undertaking or association of undertakings whose interests might be affected by the granting of aid, in particular the beneficiary of the aid, competing undertakings and trade associations. However, even at that stage of the Commission's investigation, the competitors of the aid recipient cannot pretend to be a party to the procedure and their procedural rights are not therefore as extensive as the ones conferred to Member States.

At the end of the formal investigation stage, the Commission must adopt one of the following three decisions. Firstly, it may decide eventually that the measure is not a State aid.[21] Secondly, it may adopt a decision whereby it finds the aid compatible with the common market unconditionally[22] or it may attach conditions to its compatibility.[23] Thirdly, the Commission may declare the aid incompatible with the common market[24] and order the Member State concerned to take all necessary measures to recover it from the beneficiary.[25] For all the decisions it adopts at the end of the preliminary or of the formal investigation stages, any 'interested party' may obtain a copy of that decision.[26] Furthermore, the Commission must send that decision to the 'interested party' that lodged a complaint.[27]

By way of conclusion, it is submitted that the procedural rights of the competitors of the aid recipient are almost inexistent during the preliminary investigation stage and very limited during the formal investigation stage.[28] In practice, the competitors of the aid recipient that are not satisfied with the Commission's appraisal at the end of its preliminary investigation stage may therefore seek to obtain the annulment of the Commission decisions that either do not raise objections or find that the measure is not a State aid. Alternatively, where the Commission initiated the formal investigation stage, the competitors of the aid recipient may seek the annulment of the Commission's decision finding that the aid is compatible with the common market, whether the Commission attached conditions to this finding or not.

[20] *Ibid* para 16.
[21] Art 7(2) of Reg No 659/1999.
[22] Art 7(3) of Reg No 659/1999.
[23] Art 7(4) of Reg No 659/1999.
[24] Art 7(5) of Reg No 659/1999.
[25] Art 14(1) of Reg No 659/1999.
[26] Art 20(3) of Reg No 659/1999.
[27] Art 20(2) of Reg No 659/1999.

THE APPLICABLE STANDING TESTS

Under Article 230(4) EC, an action may be brought before the Community judicature against a decision adopted by the Commission by any natural or legal person, to which that decision was addressed or to which it is of direct and individual concern.

The addressee of a decision adopted by the Commission in the context of its procedure for reviewing a State aid may only be the Member State which granted the aid.[29] For this reason, the competitors of the aid recipient must establish that they are directly and individually concerned by that decision.[30]

In practice, the admissibility of an action brought by a competitor of the aid recipient against a State aid decision will always depend on the question as to whether it may be considered 'individually concerned'.[31]

According to a long line of case-law following the landmark *Plaumann v Commission* judgment, applicants such as the competitors of the aid recipient 'may claim to be individually concerned only if the decision in question affects them by reason of certain attributes peculiar to them or by reason of circumstances which differentiate them from all other persons, and thus distinguishes them individually'.[32]

However, concerning the decisions that the Commission adopts in the context of its procedure for reviewing the grant of a new State aid, the ECJ has acknowledged that the 'individual concern' requirement should be applied in a particular way to the competitors of the aid recipient, having regard to the aim and the specific features of the procedure provided for in Article 88(2) EC and Article 88(3) EC respectively.[33]

Since the ECJ's Grand Chamber delivered its landmark judgment of 13 December 2005 in Case *Commission v Aktionsgemeinschaft Recht und Eigentum*[34] (hereinafter '*ARE*') and the subsequent ECJ rulings that are discussed hereinafter, two clearly distinct tests of standing are applied to the competitors of the aid recipient. These two tests which I will respectively refer to for the sake of clarity as the 'simple effects' test[35] as opposed to the 'substantial effects' test may be described as follows.

[28] See, eg A Bartosch, 'The Procedural Regulation in State Aid Matters – A case for profound reform' (2007) 3 *European State Aid Law Quarterly* 474–483, and Schohe, n 3 above, 213–216.

[29] Case C-367/95 P *Commission v Sytraval and Brink's France*, n 7 above, para 45. See also in that regard Case C-521/06 P, *Athinaïki Techniki v Commission,* n 10 above, para 30.

[30] It must be pointed out that the admissibility of such an action is a question of public policy that may and must be raised by the Community judicature of its own motion and, thus, that an inadmissibility plea may be raised by the defendant at any stage of the proceedings (Case C-298/00 P *Italy v Commission* [2004] ECR I-4087 para 35).

[31] It is sufficient to note that the 'directly concerned' requirement does not raise difficulties in practice because either the Member State will have already granted the aid or that there is no uncertainty as to the fact that it will grant the aid.

[32] Case 25/62 *Plaumann v Commission* [1963] ECR 197 para 107. See, eg Case C-198/91 *Cook v Commission*, n 11 above, para 20; Case C-225/91 *Matra v Commission*, n 11 above, para 14, and Case C-78/03 P *Commission v Aktionsgemeinschaft Recht und Eigentum*, n 11 above, para 33.

[33] Case C-225/91 *Matra v Commission*, n 11 above, para 15.

[34] See n 11 above.

[35] The 'simple effects' test is often referred to as the 'interested party' test or the 'party concerned' test as the first condition under that is that the applicant ought to be an 'interested party'. In my

*Cont.*

*The 'simple effects' test* – The initial version of that test was set out by the ECJ in 1993 in the cases that gave rise to the *Matra v Commission*[36] and *Cook v Commission*[37] rulings. In these judgments, the ECJ ruled in essence that, where without initiating the formal investigation procedure, the Commission adopts a decision finding that an aid is compatible with the common market, the 'interested parties' which are intended to benefit from the procedural guarantees provided for in Article 88(2) EC may secure compliance therewith only if they are able to challenge that decision before the Community judicature.[38] In both these cases, the ECJ admitted the applicants' actions after finding that they were competitors of the aid recipient, and thus that the grant of that aid could affect their interests.[39]

In its *ARE* judgment,[40] the ECJ confirmed that the *Matra v Commission* and *Cook v Commission* rulings remained applicable law, therefore rejecting implicitly Advocate General Jacobs's proposal to abandon the 'simple effects' test and apply uniformly 'the substantial effects' test to all the decisions of the Commission, regardless as to whether those decisions were adopted at the end of the preliminary or of the formal investigation stage.[41] The ECJ also clarified and refined the conditions under which an action is admissible. As it follows from the *ARE* judgment, and in particular the ECJ's reasoning exposed in paragraphs 35 to 37, two conditions must be satisfied by an applicant to fall under that test in cases where it brings an action against a decision adopted by the Commission at the end of the preliminary investigation stage. Firstly, the applicant must establish that it is an 'interested party': it must therefore demonstrate that its interests may be affected by the grant of the aid, the sole evidence of a competitive relationship between the plaintiff and the aid recipient being sufficient in that regard.[42] Secondly, and more notably, the ECJ limits the admissibility of the applicant's action to instances where it expressly seeks to safeguard its procedural rights: the applicant must therefore expressly raise pleas and arguments in relation to the fact that it considers that the Commission wrongly decided not to initiate the formal investigation stage of its procedure.[43] In the case at hand, the ECJ found that the Court of First Instance of the European Communities (hereinafter CFI) wrongfully reinterpreted the application lodged before it as the applicant had not raised expressly any specific pleas alleging that its procedural rights had been infringed.[44]

opinion, the reference to 'the simple effects' test allows to oppose it in a clearer way to the 'substantial effects' test.

[36] See n 11 above.

[37] See n 11 above.

[38] Case C-225/91 *Matra v Commission*, n 11 above, para 17, and Case C-198/91 *Cook v Commission*, n 11 above, para 26.

[39] Case C-225/91 *Matra v Commission*, n 11 above, para 19, and Case C-198/91 *Cook v Commission*, n 11 above, para 25.

[40] See n 11 above, para 36.

[41] *Ibid* Opinion of Advocate General Jacobs, points 142 and 143.

[42] Case C-78/03 P *Commission v Aktionsgemeinschaft Recht und Eigentum*, n 11 above, para 37.

[43] *Ibid* para 44.

[44] *Ibid* para 49. It is worth noting in this respect that the CFI had chosen to give more importance, for the admissibility of the action, to the very substance of the application rather than to the

*Cont.*

Finally, it should be underlined that the ECJ held that should the applicant call into question in its application the 'merits of the decision appraising the aid as such', the mere fact that it may considered as an 'interested party' is not sufficient to consider its action admissible. In that situation, the applicant must meet the conditions provided for by the 'substantial effects' test.[45]

The judgments subsequently delivered by the ECJ repeat the reasoning exposed in paragraphs 35 to 37 of the *ARE* judgment and make a strict application of the conditions set out therein.

In the case that gave rise to its *Stadtwerke Schwäbisch Hall and Others v Commission* judgment, the ECJ set aside the CFI's ruling finding that the applicants' action was admissible.[46] Firstly, the ECJ observed that, in its application lodged with the CFI, the applicants expressly and exclusively contested the merits of the Commission's decision finding that the measure was not a State aid. On that basis, the ECJ found that the CFI wrongly reinterpreted the application lodged before it and erred in finding that the applicants had sought to safeguard their procedural rights.[47] Against this background, the ECJ held that the applicants failed to satisfy the 'simple effects' test. It then went on to examine whether the conditions provided for by the 'substantial effects' test were fulfilled and found that the applicants had also failed to satisfy that test.[48] This ruling therefore confirms the ECJ's reasoning in the *ARE* judgment in particular with regard to the fact that an action is admissible under the 'simple effects' test only if the applicant expressly argues that its procedural rights were infringed by the Commission's decision not to initiate the formal investigation stage.

In the *Germany and Others v Kronofrance* judgment, the ECJ upheld the CFI's finding of admissibility of the action brought by the applicant.[49] Firstly, the ECJ observed that the applicant 'had sought annulment of the contested decision on the ground that the Commission had wrongly refused to initiate the formal investigation procedure provided for in Article 88(2) EC'.[50] Secondly, the ECJ observed that the applicant was an 'interested party' as it was undisputed that a competitive relationship existed between it and the aid recipient.[51] In the light of these elements, the ECJ expressly stated that 'there was no necessity for the [CFI] particularly in view of the judgments in *Cook v Commission* and *Matra v Commission*, to require in addition proof that the position of [the applicant] on the market concerned was substantially affected by the adoption of the contested decision',[52] and therefore to meet the conditions of the 'substantial effects' test.

express pleas raised by the applicant (see Case T-114/00 *Aktionsgemeinschaft Recht und Eigentum v Commission* [2002] ECR II-5121 para 22).

[45] Case C-78/03 P *Commission v Aktionsgemeinschaft Recht und Eigentum*, n 11 above, para 37.

[46] Case C-176/06 P *Stadtwerke Schwäbisch Hall and Others v Commission*, judgment of 29 November 2009 unreported, para 32.

[47] *Ibid* paras 25 and 28.

[48] *Ibid* para 31.

[49] Joined Cases C-75/05 P and C-80/05 P *Germany and Others v Kronofrance*, n 1 above, para 54.

[50] *Ibid* para 42.

[51] *Ibid* para 43.

[52] *Ibid* para 44.

this background, the situation of the applicant and found that 'it [was] apparent from [the judgment under appeal] that the [CFI] did not merely note in general terms that Lenzing and [the aid recipient] were in competition with other, but based its findings as to the adverse effect on Lenzing's position on the market on a number of factors adduced by the latter to show in essence the distinctiveness of the competitive situation on the (market concerned), which was characterised by a very small number of producers and by serious overcapacity, the significance of the distortion created by the grant of the aid to an undertaking operating in such a market, and the effect of that aid on the prices applied by [the aid recipient]'.[81] The ECJ then distinguished the situation of the applicant in that case from the situation of the applicant in the case that gave rise to the *ARE* judgment 'in which the [ECJ] held that there was no substantial adverse effect on the competitive position of the members of the applicant association in that case, owing to the fact that a very large number of operators, namely all the farmers in the European Union, could be regarded as competitors of the beneficiaries of the land acquisition scheme in question'.[82] Finally, as far the rules on allocation of the burden of proof in these circumstances are concerned, it is worth noting that the ECJ held that the CFI did not err in considering 'in accordance with the requirements laid down in [paragraph 28 of *Cofaz v Commission*] that it is for Lenzing alone to adduce pertinent reasons to show that the Commission's decision may adversely affect its legitimate interests by seriously jeopardising its position on the market in question'.[83] It may therefore be considered that applicants that challenge the merits of a State aid decision should provide the Court with as much information as possible regarding the actual adverse impact of the grant of the contested aid on their market position.

The *British Aggregates v Commission* judgment delivered a bit less than two years after the *Sniace v Commission* and *Spain v Lenzing* rulings reiterates the reasoning that the ECJ used in these two cases[84] and provides for two further elements of confirmation regarding the 'substantial effects' test. Firstly, in that case, the Court dismissed the Commission's argument that a stricter test than that of the 'substantial effects' test should be applied in cases where the contested decision relates to a general aid scheme. In that regard, the ECJ observed unambiguously that 'irrespective of whether the aid measure in question is individual or general in nature, an applicant must, when bringing into question the soundness of the decision assessing the aid as such, demonstrate that he has a "special status" within the meaning of the [*Plaumann v Commission* ruling], which will be the case, inter alia, where the position of the applicant on the market in question is substantially affected by the aid which is the subject of the decision in question'.[85] Secondly, while the ECJ expressly held after relying on previous case-law, that 'an action brought by an association acting in place of

[81] *Ibid* para 37.
[82] *Ibid* para 39.
[83] *Ibid* para 41.
[84] Case C-487/06 P *British Aggregates v Commission*, n 53 above.
[85] *Ibid* para 35.

one or more of its members who could themselves have brought an admissible action will be itself admissible'.[86]

To sum up, as Advocate General Mengozzi put it in his Opinion in Case *British Aggregates v Commission*,[87] 'the conditions governing the admissibility of actions against Commission decisions on State aid [since the *ARE* ruling] vary according to the procedural stage at which they are adopted and the objective sought by the person bringing the action, and the margin of variation essentially reflects the difference in the degree of damage to his own interests which that is required to prove'. The ECJ has confirmed this approach in all its judgments delivered so far.

On the one hand, the 'simple effects' test, which is clearly less stringent than the 'substantial effects' test, exclusively applies to actions brought against decisions adopted at the end of the preliminary investigation stage in which the Commission found that the contested measure was not a State aid or that no objections should be raised. In that context, an action brought by a competitor of the aid recipient is only admissible if, firstly, it establishes that its interests might be (simply) affected by the grant of the aid. Such condition is fulfilled if it shows that some competitive relationship exists between it and the aid recipient. Secondly, the applicant must expressly seek to safeguard its procedural rights without calling into question the merits of the case. Should it contest the merits of the Commission's appraisal of the aid as such, its action will not be admissible unless it meets the conditions set out in the 'substantial effects' test.

On the other hand, the 'substantial effects' test applies to actions brought against all State aid decisions, regardless as to whether the Commission adopted it at the end of the preliminary or of the formal investigation stage, and in which that the applicant calls into question the merits of that decision as such. In this context, its action is only admissible if it establishes that it is 'individually concerned'. Such a condition is undoubtedly met if the applicant shows that its position on the market is 'substantially affected' by the grant of the aid, whether or not it was significantly involved in the Commission's procedure. It is submitted that if that applicant provides reasons and evidence that show that given, inter alia, the market structure on which it operates with the aid recipient and its specific position on that market, the grant of the aid will substantially affect its market position in a negative way, then its action is admissible.

## SOME GENERAL CONCLUSIONS AND CRITICISMS REGARDING THE APPLICABLE CASE-LAW

In my view, three general conclusions may be drawn in light of the recent rulings of the ECJ. Firstly, legal certainty in the field may be considered achieved as the two standing tests set out by the ECJ have now been applied in a consistent manner since the *ARE* judgment. As to legal clarity, it is submitted that the

[86] *Ibid* para 39.
[87] *Ibid* Opinion of Advocate General Mengozzi, point 35.

applicable standing tests provide the competitors of the aid recipient with sufficient guidance to identify what conditions they need to satisfy for their actions to be admissible.

Secondly, by continuing to apply the less stringent 'simple effects' test to applicants which seek to challenge a Commission's decision not to initiate the formal investigation stage, the ECJ acknowledges the specificities of the preliminary investigation stage during which the competitors of the aid recipient are conferred almost no procedural rights. It must also be pointed out in that regard that the existing 'simple effects' test may offer an opportunity for a category of applicants that would otherwise fail to meet the more stringent 'substantial effects' test to have access to the Community judicature.

Thirdly, it may be noted that the ECJ has loosened up to some extent the 'substantial effects' test by abandoning the prerequisite condition that the applicant ought to have been significantly involved in the procedure. Even though the conditions under that test remain stringent and they much depend on the circumstances of each case, the fact that the 'significant involvement' prerequisite condition has been abandoned may increase the situations in which actions brought by the competitors of the aid recipient are admissible.

Notwithstanding these considerations, the applicable case-law of the ECJ regarding standing has not been immune from criticisms. In that respect, it must be underlined that three Advocate Generals in some of the most recent cases mentioned above[88] criticised the applicable 'simple effects' test in severe terms. In essence, they suggested that the scope of the 'simple effects' test should be extended to all the applicants that bring an action against a Commission decision not to open the formal investigation stage of the procedure, regardless as to whether these applicants raise pleas regarding their procedural rights or the merits as such of that decision.[89]

In the view of these Advocate Generals, such a reform would be needed for two main reasons. Firstly, they consider that the current case-law is 'artificial',[90] 'unnecessarily formalistic'[91] and 'not readily comprehensible'.[92] In this regard, these Advocate Generals criticise the fact that admissibility of an action depends on the pleas expressly raised by an applicant whereas the purpose of its action is, in any event, that the Commission be forced to initiate the formal investigation stage of the procedure.[93] Secondly, according to these Advocate

[88] See Opinion of Advocate General Bot in Joined Cases C-75/05 P and C-80/05 P *Germany v Kronofrance*, n 1 above; Opinion of Advocate General Mengozzi in Case C-487/06 P *British Aggregates v Commission*, n 53 above, points 69–76, and Opinion of Advocate General Sharpston in Case C-319/07 P *3F*, n 56 above, points 26–49.

[89] Opinion of Advocate General Bot in Joined Cases C-75/05 P and C-80/05 P *Germany v Kronofrance*, n 1 above, point 110.

[90] *Ibid* point 106.

[91] Opinion of Advocate General Sharpston in Case C-319/07 P *3F*, n 56 above, point 41.

[92] Opinion of Advocate General Bot in Joined Cases C-75/05 P and C-80/05 P *Germany v Kronofrance*, n 1 above, point 104.

[93] *Ibid* point 109, and Opinion of Advocate General Sharpston in Case C-319/07 P *3F*, n 56 above, point 43.

Generals, that distinction as it stands is 'complex'[94] and 'not necessarily easy'[95] to operate for the Community judicature. Moreover, it has also been submitted that it was particularly difficult for these applicants not to deal with the merits of the contested decision in their application while trying at the same time to demonstrate that 'there [are] still serious difficulties remaining in the Commission's initial assessment of the aid in issue'.[96]

According to Advocate General Mengozzi in particular, whereas the ECJ has sought, in an unsatisfying way, to make sure that 'the Community judicature's review of the contested decision does not go beyond what is needed to ensure the procedural rights conferred by [Article 88(2) EC]',[97] that goal might be more appropriately achieved if the Community judicature limited itself, regardless of the question as to whether the pleas raised formally by the applicant concern the merits of the decision or its procedural rights, 'to verifying whether the conditions justifying non-initiation of the formal investigation are satisfied, or to establishing that there are no serious doubts that the measure does not constitute aid or, is in any event, compatible with the common market'.[98] In Advocate General Mengozzi's opinion, such an approach 'would make it possible to avert the possibility that, in making a definitive ruling on matters regarding which the Commission has really made only a prima facie finding on conclusion of a preliminary examination, the Community exceeds the limits of the normal review of legality which it must carry out in the context of applications for annulment'.[99]

The ECJ has resisted so far to these criticisms and proposals to reform the conditions that the competitors of the aid recipient must satisfy to establish their standing.

However, in an area where the Commission is conferred exclusive and large powers of appraisal as to the compatibility with the common market of State aids, it cannot be excluded that the ECJ will decide at some stage to simplify the applicable tests for standing with a view to reinforce the effective judicial control of the Commission decisions in the field.

[94] Opinion of Advocate General Mengozzi in Case C-487/06 P *British Aggregates v Commission*, n 53 above, point 71.

[95] Opinion of Advocate General Bot in Joined Cases C-75/05 P and C-80/05 P *Germany v Kronofrance*, n 1 above, point 107.

[96] Opinion of Advocate General Sharpston in Case C-319/07 P *3F*, n 56 above, point 42.

[97] Opinion of Advocate General Mengozzi of in Case C-487/06 P *British Aggregates v Commission*, n 53 above, point 71.

[98] *Ibid* point 75.

[99] *Ibid* point 75.

This judgment therefore confirms that, provided that the applicant shows that it (potentially) has a competitive relationship with the aid recipient, its action will be held admissible under the 'simple effects' test as long as it expressly raises pleas seeking to safeguard its procedural rights and that it does not challenge the merits of the Commission's decision as such.

In the case that gave rise to *British Aggregates v Commission* judgment, the ECJ upheld the CFI's finding of admissibility of the action brought by an association against a Commission decision not to raise objections with regard to the grant of an aid scheme.[53] In that judgment, the Court observed that 'the [CFI] held, without being contradicted on this point by the Commission, that [the applicant] was not merely seeking to challenge the Commission's refusal to initiate the formal investigation procedure but [it] was also calling into question the merits of the contested decision'.[54] Under those circumstances, the ECJ ruled that the CFI acted correctly in law by examining whether the contested aid was liable to have a substantial effect on the position of at least one of the members of the association which was active on the market concerned by the aid scheme in question.[55] As Advocate General Sharpston recently opined in essence, it seems that it may be inferred from the *British Aggregates v Commission* judgment that, where the applicant not only seeks in its application to safeguard its procedural rights but that it also calls into question the merits of the Commission decision, the test for standing that must be applied in such a case is the 'substantial effects' test.[56]

*The 'substantial effects' test* – The initial version of that test was set out by the ECJ in 1986 in the case that gave rise to its *Cofaz v Commission* ruling.[57] In that case, the ECJ declared that the action brought by a competitor of the aid recipient against the Commission's decision finding, at the end of the formal investigation stage, the aid compatible with the common market was admissible.[58] To support this conclusion, firstly, the ECJ relied on its *Timex v Council and Commission*[59] judgment in the anti-dumping area that it found applicable to State aid procedures.[60] The ECJ therefore considered that it was 'necessary to examine in that regard the part played [by the applicant in the Commission's procedure]' and in particular 'if the [applicant] was at the origin of the complaint which led to the investigation procedure, the facts that its views were heard during that procedure and the fact the conduct of the procedure was largely determined by its observations'.[61] According to the ECJ, these conditions were met in that instance.[62] Secondly, the ECJ observed that while it

[53] Case C-487/06 P *British Aggregates v Commission*, judgment of 22 December 2008 nyr.
[54] *Ibid* para 37.
[55] *Ibid* para 38.
[56] Opinion of Advocate General Sharpston of 5 March 2009 in Case C-319/07 P *3F* pending, point 35.
[57] Case 169/84 *Cofaz and Others v Commission* [1986] ECR 391.
[58] *Ibid* para 32.
[59] Case 264/82 *Timex v Council and Commission* [1985] ECR 849.
[60] Case 169/84 *Cofaz and Others v Commission*, n 57 above, paras 24 and 25.
[61] *Ibid* para 24.
[62] *Ibid* para 26.

was not for the Community judicature where assessing whether an action was admissible 'to make a definitive finding on the competitive relationship between the applicant and the aid recipient', that applicant was nonetheless required to 'adduc[e] pertinent reasons to show that the Commission's decision may adversely affect their legitimate interests by seriously jeopardising their position on the market in question'.[63] The doctrine therefore considered[64] that, pursuant to the *Cofaz v Commission* ruling, an action against a decision adopted by the Commission at the end of the formal investigation stage was admissible under the dual condition that, firstly, the applicant had been substantially involved in the Commission's procedure and, secondly, that its position on the market was substantially affected by the grant of the aid.

After holding in its *ARE* judgment that the 'substantial effects' test was applicable where the applicant called into question the merits of a State aid decision, the ECJ brought substantial clarifications to the content of that test in its two leading *Spain v Commission*[65] and *Sniace v Commission*[66] judgments. These two judgments that were delivered on the same day and by the same chamber concerned the same aid scheme.

As to the first condition set out in the *Cofaz v Commission* ruling, namely that the applicant ought to have been significantly involved in the procedure,[67] the ECJ ruled in its *Sniace v Commission* judgment that it did not constitute a prerequisite condition.[68] In that regard, the ECJ expressly held that the CFI erred in law as 'contrary to what is asserted by the Commission [in its pleadings], it does not follow from the case-law of the [ECJ] that such participation in that procedure is a necessary condition for the finding that a decision is of individual concern to an undertaking within the meaning of the fourth paragraph of Article 230 EC, precluding the possibility of the undertaking putting forward other specific circumstances which distinguish it individually in a way that is similar to the case of the person addressed by that decision'.[69] Secondly, the ECJ noted that the CFI had correctly found that the applicant did not fulfil the 'substantial effects' test as it 'ought, on any view of the matter, to have demonstrated that the contested decision was likely to substantially affect its position on the market'.[70] To the extent that it found that the CFI's error in requiring that the fact that the applicant had not been significantly involved in the procedure had no effect on the outcome of its ruling, the ECJ upheld the CFI's finding of inadmissibility.[71] It therefore follows clearly from the *Sniace v Commission* judgment that an action brought against a Commission decision by

[63] *Ibid* para 28.

[64] See, eg Honoré, n 3 above, 279, and Opinion of Advocate General Kokott of 1 February 2007 in Case C-525/04 P *Spain v Lenzing* [2007] ECR I-9947 point 25.

[65] Case C-525/04 P *Spain v Lenzing* [2007] ECR I-9947.

[66] Case C-260/05 P *Sniace v Commission* [2007] ECR I-10005.

[67] Case 169/84 *Cofaz and Others v Commission*, n 57 above, paras 24 and 25.

[68] Case C-260/05 P *Sniace v Commission*, n 66 above, para 57.

[69] *Ibid* para 57.

[70] *Ibid* para 60.

[71] *Ibid* para 59.

a competitor of the aid recipient that challenges the merits of that decision is only admissible if that applicant demonstrates that its interests are substantially affected by the grant of the aid in question, the fact that it may have been significantly involved or not in the Commission's procedure merely being a circumstance that the Community judicature may take into consideration in the context of that assessment. Finally, it is worth mentioning that, in *Sniace v Commission*, the ECJ dismissed the applicant's plea that the CFI wrongly found that its action was not admissible with regard to its right to effective judicial protection. In that regard, the ECJ stated that such rights were not violated as the applicant had failed to demonstrate that it was individually concerned by the contested decision.[72]

As to the second condition set out in the *Cofaz v Commission* judgment, namely that the applicant's interests ought to have been significantly affected by the grant of the aid,[73] the *Spain v Lenzing* ruling[74] provides applicants with very useful guidance. Firstly, after recalling its line of case-law since its *Plaumann v Commission* judgment and, notably its *Cofaz v Commission* and *ARE* judgments,[75] the ECJ observed that it 'has had occasion to clarify that the mere fact that a measure such as the contested decision may exercise an influence on the competitive relationships existing on the relevant market and that the undertaking concerned was in a competitive relationship with the addressee of that measure cannot in any event suffice for that undertaking to be regarded as individually concerned by that measure'.[76] The ECJ went on by recalling that 'an undertaking cannot rely solely on its status as a competitor of the undertaking in receipt of aid but must additionally show that its circumstances distinguish it in a similar way to the undertaking in receipt of the aid'.[77] According to the ECJ, 'demonstrating a substantial adverse effect on a competitor's position in the market cannot therefore, simply be a matter of the existence of certain factors indicating a decline in its commercial or financial performance' such as a decline in turnover, appreciable financial losses or a significant reduction in market share following the grant of the aid as an undertaking may totally or partially limit these negative effects by, for example, making savings or expanding'.[78] In that regard, the ECJ expressly referred to Advocate General Kokott's Opinion in that case[79] and observed that 'the grant of State aid can have an adverse effect on the competitive situation of an operator in others ways too, in particular by causing the loss of an opportunity to make a profit or a less favourable development that would have been the case without such aid'.[80] Secondly, the ECJ examined, against

[72] *Ibid* paras 64–67.
[73] Case 169/84 *Cofaz and Others v Commission*, n 57 above, para 28.
[74] See n 65 above.
[75] *Ibid* para 31.
[76] *Ibid* para 32.
[77] *Ibid* para 33.
[78] *Ibid* para 34.
[79] *Ibid* Opinion of Advocate General Kokott, points 43–45.
[80] Case C-525/04 P *Spain v Lenzing*, n 65 above, para 35.

# INDEX

www.ingramcontent.com/pod-product-compliance
Ingram Content Group UK Ltd.
Pitfield, Milton Keynes, MK11 3LW, UK
UKHW020905190926
475560UK00010B/293

9 781849 460347